Essays in
CONTEMPORARY
ECONOMIC
PROBLEMS

Essays in
CONTEMPORARY
ECONOMIC
PROBLEMS

Disinflation

William Fellner, Project Director

American Enterprise Institute
Washington and London

Support from Alex C. Walker Educational and Charitable Foundation aided in the funding of this project.

ISBN 0-8447-1364-3 (paper)
ISBN 0-8447-1365-1 (cloth)

ISSN 0732-4308

Printed in the United States of America

CONTENTS

Foreword   *William J. Baroody, Jr.*

William Fellner In Memoriam   *Gottfried Haberler*   1

Introduction   *William Fellner*   5

The Cost of Disinflation, Credibility, and the Deceleration of Wages 1982–1983   *Phillip Cagan and William Fellner*   7

   Summary   7

   The Costs of Disinflation   7

   The Effect of Inflationary Full-Employment
     Policies on Credibility   8

   The Turn of Policy to Disinflation   9

   Statistical Analysis of the Recent
     Deceleration of Wages   10

   Conclusion   18

Monetary Policy and Subduing Inflation   *Phillip Cagan*   21

   Summary   21

   The Cycles in Inflation and Economic Activity   23

   Monetary Policy since 1979   32

   Postmortem on the First Stage of Disinflation,
     1979–1983, and the Problems to Be Faced
     in the Second   46

Monetary and Fiscal Policy in a Disinflationary Process: Justified and Unjustified Misgivings about Budget Deficits
William Fellner   55

Summary 55

The Relation of Money-Supply Target Ranges to
  Desirable Nominal Demand Objectives 57

The Dilemma Caused by the Behavior of
  Velocity in 1982 59

Summary of Two Propositions to Be Justified
  in the Subsequent Two Sections 61

The "Conventional" or "Normal" Assumptions
  Concerning the Demand Effects
  of Money Creation 62

The "Conventional" or "Normal" Assumptions
  Concerning the Expansionary
  Effect of Deficits 64

The Monetary-Fiscal Mix: Do Deficits Absorb
  Savings Despite Revaluations of
  Real Net Worth? 67

Tax Liabilities as Offsets: The Equivalence
  Theorem 70

The Effect on Saving Ratios of Real Revaluations
  of Net Worth: General Indications of an Effect 73

Some Specifics about Substitution Ratios
  of Inflationary and Other Real Revaluations
  for Savings 79

Substitution of Capital Inflows for Domestic
  Savings 82

A Consistency Requirement for Tax Policy 83

**The International Monetary System in the World
Recession** *Gottfried Haberler*   87

Summary 87
Part One: The State of the World Economy 92
  Scope and Causes of the World Recession 92
  The Role of the Oil Shocks 97
  The International Debt Problem 98
Part Two: The International Monetary System 99
  How Floating Originated—the Decline
  of the Dollar 99

The Rise of the Dollar since 1980 and
the Recent Criticism of Floating
Exchange Rates   102

The Problem of the "Overvalued" Dollar   113

The Recent Policy of "Coordinated
Interventions" in the Foreign
Exchange Market   117

Concluding Remarks on Floating: Summing Up   119

The External Effects of U.S. Disinflation   *Sven W. Arndt*   **131**

Summary   131
Introduction   132
A Review of Recent Developments   132
Analytical Aspects   136
Foreign Options   145
Conclusion   147
Appendix   147

Disinflation in the Housing Market   *John C. Weicher*   **155**

Summary   155
The Effect of Inflation on House Prices   157
Homeownership Costs   171
Homeownership   180
The Amount of Housing Investment   184
Rental Housing   190
The Housing Finance System   193
Conclusion   195

Corporate Liquidity under Stagflation and Disinflation
Murray F. Foss   **205**

Summary   205
Liquidity: Recent History, Concepts,
and Measures   208
The Overall Picture for Nonfinancial
Corporations: Trends and Cycles   213
Disinflation Thus Far   221
Analysis of Individual Firm Data   228
Near-Term Outlook   237
Conclusions   240
Appendix A. Description of Sample   241
Appendix B. Glossary of Terms Used
in Compustat Tabulations   243

Disinflation in the Labor Market   *Marvin H. Kosters*   **247**

  Summary   247
  Introduction   248
  Postwar Inflation and Labor Cost Trends   249
  Trends in Unionism and Collective Bargaining   251
  Collective Bargaining and Overall
     Wage Changes   254
  Wage Changes for Union and
     Nonunion Workers   258
  Sectoral Collective Bargaining Cycles   261
  Wage and Benefit Concessions   266
  Perspectives on Concessions   272
  Incomes Policies   275
  Recent Developments   277
  Conclusions   280

Collective Bargaining and Industrial Relations:
The Past, the Present, and the Future   *Mark Perlman*   **287**

  Summary   287
  Introduction   289
  Labor Relations Trends during World War II   296
  The Postwar Era   300
  The Questions of the Hour   305

Contributors   **323**

FOREWORD

This is the seventh volume of AEI's annual series on Contemporary Economic Problems. It is the last to be edited by William Fellner, the distinguished scholar who conceived the project for AEI and guided it until his death on September 15, 1983. This series of studies on current economic issues has, over the years, become an integral part of the American Enterprise Institute's research program. Under Dr. Fellner's leadership, the series has achieved a prominent place among the professional literature while fulfilling its primary objective—to contribute to the public discourse on economic policy.

Dr. Fellner's death saddened and touched all of us who were fortunate enough to know him and work with him. His absence will be deeply felt. We will miss his intellectual brilliance, which served as a guiding light for much of the economic research done at AEI.

He became a resident scholar at AEI in 1975 after leaving the President's Council of Economic Advisers. He was Sterling Professor of Economics Emeritus at Yale University and was a prolific writer throughout his illustrious career. His accomplishments are reviewed in this book in the memorial tribute by his colleague, Gottfried Haberler.

This volume addresses a problem that concerned Dr. Fellner greatly in his later years: the process of economic adjustment that takes place during a disinflationary period.

The steady increase in the rate of inflation in the United States and many other industrial countries over the past two decades seemed to have become chronic in the late 1970s. This prolonged experience with inflation, in many ways unique in our peacetime history, revealed that when inflationary expectations become embedded in the system the problem becomes self-perpetuating. This not only debilitates the economy, it creates significant social and political problems. It was the general recognition of this phenomenon in the late 1970s that led to a change in the official and public attitudes toward inflation. There was a national consensus that controlling inflation had become our most important economic priority.

The first step in establishing a disinflationary policy was taken by the Federal Reserve Board in October 1979 when it changed its operating procedure to take greater control of the growth of the money supply. The election in 1980 of a new president whose primary objectives were said to be reducing inflation and government spending helped to solidify the national commitment to price stability.

As a result of the economic policies of the past three years, the rate of inflation has been reduced dramatically. This accomplishment, however, has not been painless. It has been accompanied by financial strains and an extended period of economic slowdown. This was not totally unexpected by economists, but many aspects of the adjustment, such as the magnitude and duration of the recession, have given rise to new questions about the cost of achieving price stability following a prolonged period of inflation.

To analyze the current process of disinflation in the light of these concerns, a group of scholars met regularly at the American Enterprise Institute over the past twelve months under the direction of Dr. Fellner to monitor, discuss, study, and analyze many aspects of our disinflationary environment. Their research focused on a number of specific topics ranging from the unique qualities of current anti-inflationary policies to particular sectoral responses and adjustments to it.

The situation is viewed not only from the American point of view, but also in the context of how the disinflationary process affects the world economic order, particularly international trade and the international monetary system. The authors look at the impact of projected budget deficits, national patterns in household savings, U.S. monetary policy, and the recent performances of three vital sectors of the economy—housing, manufacturing, and labor.

This volume should clarify many of the uncertainties concerning the disinflationary process and its effects on short-term and long-term economic activity. We hope it will contribute to a better understanding of the need to retain the gains made so far in the battle against inflation. If it provides a better foundation for public policy decision making on this vital question, it will have fulfilled the mission of the American Enterprise Institute and will stand as a lasting tribute to one of its most valued scholars, William Fellner.

WILLIAM J. BAROODY, JR.
President
American Enterprise Institute

William Fellner
In Memoriam

Gottfried Haberler

This is the seventh volume in our annual series, which William Fellner conceived in 1976 and has directed ever since. Fellner died on September 15, 1983, shortly after he had put the finishing touches on the present volume, which contains his last major contribution to economics, as well as a joint paper written in collaboration with Phillip Cagan.

Fellner was born May 31, 1905, in Budapest, Hungary. Willy, as he was called all his life by his relatives and friends, received his first schooling, including one year at the university, in Budapest. From 1926 to 1927 he attended the famous Federal Institute of Engineering in Zürich, Switzerland, where he acquired a diploma in chemical engineering. Then he switched to economics and took a Ph.D. at the University of Berlin (1929). In Zürich and Berlin he enjoyed the company of his lifelong close friend, the great mathematician John von Neuman; their friendship dated back to their high school years in Budapest.

Coming from a leading industrial family, he spent the next nine years (1929–1938) as a partner in family enterprises in Hungary. In 1938 he emigrated to the United States, and in 1944 he became a U.S. citizen.

Fellner received his first university appointment in 1939, from the Department of Economics, Univerity of California (Berkeley), where he taught until 1952. From 1952 to 1973 he was professor of economics (from 1959 to 1973 Sterling Professor) in the Department of Economics, Yale University. In 1973 he retired from Yale and became resident scholar at the American Enterprise Institute.

Fellner's first economic publications were two articles written jointly with Howard S. Ellis ("Hicks and the Time-Period Controversy," *Journal of Political Economy,* 1940) and with Harold M. Somers ("Alternative Monetary Approaches to Interest Theory," *Review of Economic Statistics,* 1941); they were followed by two books, *A Treatise on War Inflation* (University of California Press, 1942) and *Monetary Policies and Full Employment* (University of California Press, 1946). Thus

1

started a most remarkable career. His bibliography lists seven books and over fifty articles, in addition to newspaper articles and other short pieces. His major field of interest was what we now call macroeconomics, including the theory of money, inflation, and the business cycle, as well as international monetary economics, the theory of balance-of-payments adjustment, and exchange rates. But his writings cover a much larger area, encompassing pure theory, the theory of "oligopoly and similar market structures" (the subtitle of a book, *Competition among the Few;* first edition, 1949; second edition, with an interesting new introduction, 1960), *Probability and Profit* (Homewood, Illinois, Richard D. Irving, 1965), and the history of economic thought *(Emergence and Content of Modern Economic Analysis,* New York, McGraw-Hill, 1960).

It was characteristic of Fellner to bring all branches of economic theory to bear on each particular problem. I take his second book, *Monetary Policies and Full Employment* (1946), as an example. The book appeared during the heyday of the Keynesian revolution when money had taken a back seat. What was required was the "rediscovery of money," in Howard Ellis's felicitous phrase. Fellner was one of the first to restore money to its pivotal place, long before monetarism came into full bloom.

The same is true of his attention to the role of expectations. He frequently mentioned expectations of market participants as influencing, favorably or unfavorably, the outcome of policy measures, foreshadowing the modern theory of rational expectations.

What are now called the micro foundations of macroeconomics are explicitly developed in Fellner's book cited above. The effects of wage and price rigidities and of oligopolies and other forms of noncompetitive market structures on macro processes, inflation or deflation, are explored. All these themes recur in Fellner's later writings in refined and more sophisticated form, in modern terminology and with full credit to later writers. He gave members of the monetarist and rational expectations schools their just due, while rejecting extreme claims of both. For example, he did not share the view that large budget deficits pose no danger to price stability. (On this last point, see his contributions to the present volume.) But he was much too modest to let his readers know that he had already discussed these problems many years ago.

Fellner was not a pure theorist. While he had a healthy skepticism about the usefulness of elaborate econometric models, he used facts and figures effectively to flesh out theoretical skeletons, and he could handle sophisticated statistical methods to support his generalizations.

In the 1960s Fellner was very active in the international monetary area. In 1963 Secretary of the Treasury Douglas Dillon announced that a thorough investigation of the international monetary system was planned, but without the help of academic economists who, Dillon thought, could never agree on anything. Fellner joined Fritz Machlup and Robert Triffin to organize what later became known as the Bellagio Group—a committee of academics—to demonstrate that theoreticians were well able to agree on certain principles. A few years later senior officials of central banks and international institutions joined the group. The annual meetings of the enlarged group had a considerable impact on the development of the international system by helping to persuade reluctant policy makers that a shift from fixed to flexible exchange rates was necessary. Fellner had been an early advocate of floating. Unlike many others, however, he recommended floating not as an escape from financial discipline but rather as an alternative to controls. He argued that under floating a declining exchange rate would provide a strong inducement for policy makers to curb inflation by monetary and fiscal restraints.

In the last few years most of Fellner's work was concerned with the problem of inflation and disinflation. He was one of the first to argue that there is no long-term trade-off between inflation and unemployment. If inflation is not brought down to near zero, we shall be condemned to continue the vicious pattern of stop and go, with the stops—recessions—getting increasingly more severe. The consequences would be increasing government expenditures and more and more controls of wages and prices. As a convinced liberal in the classical nineteenth-century tradition, he rejected controls on the grounds not only that they reduce efficiency but also that they are incompatible with a free society.

He criticized Keynesian policies of expansion, but he distinguished between Keynesian economics and the economics of Keynes himself. Actually, his views came much closer to those of D. H. Robertson than to those of Keynes, as his article "The Robertsonian Revolution" (*American Economic Review,* June 1952) shows. Among modern economists he admired most D. H. Robertson and Joseph A. Schumpeter. An ardent champion of economic and political freedom, Fellner was greatly concerned with the Schumpeterian vision of the decline of capitalism.

Fellner was a lucid and elegant speaker and very effective in classrooms. In curious contrast, his written style was complex and often involved. The reason was not that he lacked clarity in thinking but rather that he was fully aware of the great complexity of most economic problems and tried hard to avoid oversimplification.

Fellner was also active in public service. For years he was a regular consultant of the Department of the Treasury, the Board of Governors of the Federal Reserve System, and the Congressional Budget Office and a member of the Brookings Panel on Economic Activity. From October 1973 to February 1975 he was a member of the Council of Economic Advisers under Presidents Nixon and Ford.

Fellner received many honors. He was president of the American Economic Association in 1969; he was awarded the Commander's Cross of the Order of Merit by the German Federal Republic in 1979 and the Bernhard-Harms Prize of the Institute of World Economics at the University of Kiel in 1982.

Fellner was one of the great economists of our times. Like all great economists, he was more than an economist. He had a keen sense of history and put problems of the day in historical perspective. He was a man of great culture, fluent in several languages, well versed in Hungarian, English, and German literature, a lover and connoisseur of the visual arts and music, a man of impeccable manners and old-world courtliness. He held strong convictions on many issues and was a shrewd, often stern, judge of people, but Willy was at the same time one of the most generous, kind, and considerate persons I have ever met. He had many friends, even among those with whose views he strongly disagreed. His death leaves a great void. His memory will always be cherished. His scientific work will endure and inspire future generations of economists.

Introduction

William Fellner

Since 1980 the U.S. economy and that of other countries as well have embarked upon a process of disinflation. Prices and wages have decelerated considerably, though by the standards of the 1950s and 1960s and those of many earlier periods, inflation in 1983 is far from over. The process of disinflation has been far-reaching in its economic consequences; it has begun to reverse the attempts of firms, households, and governments to adjust to an escalating inflation. Financial, commodity, and foreign exchange markets, saving, and capital formation—all became exposed to the difficulties of disinflationary adjustment.

The essays in this volume describe and analyze various consequences of the process of disinflation as it has recently unfolded. Many of these consequences were to be expected from experience with disinflation at the end of World War II and the 1950s, and earlier in history, but other developments were not expected either because these were significantly influenced by unique events or because there was still much to learn about the disinflationary process. The volume starts with an essay on the problem usually described as the cost of disinflation in terms of the temporary underutilization of resources, and the volume includes essays on the effects of disinflation on money and financial markets, the federal deficit, international financial flows and exchange rates, the housing market, business liquidity, labor markets, and industrial relations.

During the year we had several discussions at AEI of each others' papers, but each author is responsible for his own analysis and conclusions. The last paper in the volume is that by Sven Arndt on the external effects of U.S. disinflation. The author of the paper was appointed to direct an international trade project at AEI and the paper containing his thoughts on the subject described by its title is included in the present series.

Eduardo Somensatto's collaboration in organizing the project and his helpful comments on the papers are greatly appreciated.

The Cost of Disinflation, Credibility, and the Deceleration of Wages 1982–1983

Phillip Cagan and William Fellner

Summary

In our appraisal, the data suggest an improved "trade-off" for the past two years. By this we mean that during this period we obtained more disinflation per unit of economic slack (unemployment) than would be suggested by the same type of trade-off for the 1970s. The choice of the functions used in the quantitative analysis leading to this result, however, inevitably involves personal judgment, as we point out.

The Costs of Disinflation

Over the past decade the unsuccessful attempts to contain the escalating inflation elicited much discussion of appropriate policies for subduing inflation and the "costs" to the economy of returning to reasonably stable prices. The word "costs" is placed in quotation marks because the costs of chronic inflation would be even greater than those of disinflation: before long, a regime of steepening inflation in a market economy would be highly destructive. Hence, the costs of disinflation are acceptable in order to avoid the greater costs of allowing inflation to become chronic. One could say at best that a very high degree of time preference may justify avoiding the near-future costs of disinflation in lieu of the somewhat postponed very large costs of chronic major inflation. But such a degree of time preference would in reality express an inclination to choose, through the route of inflation and the subsequent introduction of a system of wage and price controls, a political system of a very different kind.

Yet the fact remains that disinflation after an extended period of inflationary demand policy entails costs in the particular sense of

In addition to our having benefited, as has the project as a whole, from Eduardo Somensatto's collaboration, we appreciate the help and collaboration of Maryam Homayouni in carrying out our research for this study.

7

inevitably leading a country through a period—say, through several years covering a full business cycle or more—during which the performance of the economy in real terms is weaker than it normally is, that is, than it can be expected to be in corresponding phases of cycles after disinflation is completed. This cost arises partly because payment commitments implying continued steep inflation had been accepted before the disinflationary process started. An important second reason is that, even if the authorities do have the determination to carry the disinflationary program through, it takes time to establish their credibility. At the end of the European postwar hyperinflations of this century, the first of these factors—the carry-over effect of previous commitments—played a minor role because longer-run cost commitments in domestic currency had become very rare. In those countries even the second factor—the need to establish credibility— may have played a somewhat smaller role than it does in the present Western environment because those countries had arrived at a point at which a major proportion of the population was convinced that the government had no choice but to put an immediate end to the inflationary process. But in the present Western circumstances both the need to establish credibility and the carry-over effect of past cost commitments suggest the inevitability of an adjustment period with some distinctly uncomfortable properties.

The Effect of Inflationary Full-Employment Policies on Credibility

The observation that the credibility of policies could influence the disinflationary process attracted attention in the postwar inflationary era. As demand-management policies took on more ambitious "real" objectives, it soon became clear that they could be accomplished only if the public believes that with rising prices the rising money incomes correspond to higher real incomes than turns out to be the case in fact. In effect, inflation can provide stimulus only so long as those benefiting from sales and work at inflated prices and wages are not fully aware of the real values they will receive in exchange when they subsequently make purchases at higher prices. This is another way of saying that an inflationary trend is helpful in achieving "real" objectives only so long as the typical member of the public underestimates the effect of the inflation on his real income for any given money income. In view of the ability of the public to learn from experience, the allegedly helpful policy of generating inflation at a steeper rate than had been assumed by the buyers of goods cannot be kept up in the longer run. The public learns to see through the essentials of this mechanism, and the longer-run outcome will show a steepening inflation along with increasingly poor results in real terms, including poor productivity trends, in an environment of significant uncertainty. It was disappointment with such a policy that led to disinflationary efforts.

The Turn of Policy to Disinflation

In the United States a disinflationary policy, long proposed and intermittently attempted, was seriously adopted at the end of the inflationary decade of the 1970s. The basic idea behind such an effort is to abandon the false hope that the accommodation of inflationary cost trends will continue to lead to desirable output and employment results, and instead to condition market expectations to a desired rate of creation of nominal (current-dollar) demand. The desired rate of nominal demand creation is presumably the rate compatible with normal real growth at a reasonably stable and predictable price level over periods in which cyclical fluctuations are regarded as inevitable.

Once a policy of this sort has been adopted consistently and has acquired credibility, market participants can confidently take steps to keep their cost- and price-setting practices in line with actual developments. The more complete are the adjustments of the market's cost- and price-setting practices to a nominal demand constraint enforced by the authorities, the better will be the results over each cycle in real terms.

The authorities in charge of demand policy must, of course, have means of taking actions in which they are guided for intervals much shorter than business cycles, and these actions should relate to policy variables over which the authorities have more control in the short-run than they do over nominal demand (say, over nominal GNP). Money-growth target ranges belong among the devices the authorities can use for guiding their shorter-run operations, and money-growth ranges of moderate width can enable them to take account to some extent of presumptive variations of velocity. In exceptional circumstances very unusual velocity movements can even justify moving outside the money-growth target ranges, but this should be done only in rare cases that have exceptional characteristics, because, to some extent at least, such actions are apt to be taken at the expense of the monetary authority's credibility and thus at the expense of the desired effect of expectations on cost and price trends.

At any rate, given our highly imperfect knowledge of the degree of inertia in economic behavior and of policy lags, anything like full compensation of velocity variations by adjusting the money-growth rates would be overly ambitious and would run the risk of becoming significantly counterproductive. Moderate compensatory moves within the money-target ranges may, however, often serve a useful compensatory purpose without creating the risk of loss of credibility and of the desired effects of expectations.

Statistical Analysis of the Recent Deceleration of Wages

Various estimates have been published implying appreciable costs of lost output for a given amount of disinflation.[1] These estimates were derived from past periods in which inflation was generally rising. There has been much skeptical discussion of the general applicability of these estimates. There has been discussion also of the role that the consistency and credibility of a disinflationary policy can play in leading the market participants to adjust their practices more rapidly and thereby to reduce the costs of the disinflationary policy.[2] In 1980–1982 the economy underwent two recessions and appreciable disinflation. It is too soon yet to separate the transitory from the lasting effects on prices and wages, but that the speed of deceleration was more rapid, given the degree of the business recession costs, than had generally been predicted is already a widely held casual impression. To provide some evidence to quantify this impression, we present a statistical analysis of wage behavior. We compare the recent deceleration of wages with its past behavior as described by a conventional wage equation.

It would be gratifying to be able to make definitive statements about the comparative cost of recent disinflationary policy because of the major importance of the issue. Although the desire to avoid sensational or irresponsible statements prevents us from trying to be "decisive" in an appraisal of the evidence, we believe that our preliminary investigation has substantial content.

We proceed within the framework of conventional wage equations. Wage increases are described mainly by three variables: unemployment, the change in unemployment, and the past rate of inflation.[3] At certain times over the past three decades, wages have stepped to a permanently higher rate of increase than these variables account for. These steps have been attributed to increased expectations of long-run inflation, which the inflation variable fails to capture, presumably because past inflation does not fully predict changes in the public's perception of the extent and persistence of inflation. The decline of wage increases since 1981 also appears to be greater than was generally expected by forecasters. We have fit the conventional form of the wage regression to quarterly data to see whether another step—this time to a lower rate of wage increase—occurred in recent years.

The conventional regression is the following:

$$w = a_1 + a_2 \frac{1}{U} + a_3 \left(\frac{1}{U} - \frac{1}{U_{-1}} \right) + a_4 p_{-1} + \text{dummy variables}$$

where w is the change in a wage index, $1/U$ is the reciprocal of the unemployment rate, $1/U - 1/U_{-1}$ is the change in the unemployment reciprocal since the previous quarter, p_{-1} is the rate of inflation over some number of preceding quarters ending one quarter prior to the present, which serves as a proxy for market adjustments to rising prices, and dummy variables allow for shifts that would occur if no dummies were included in the regression. The a's are constant regression coefficients. The reciprocal of unemployment is used to approximate an assumed convexity in the magnitude of its effect on wages. Various fits of this regression to the data are reported in accompanying tables.[4]

Shifts in the relation when the dummies are excluded have been variously attributed to changes in price expectations, structural changes in the labor force affecting unemployment, and wage controls or guidelines. A dummy variable is included here for each business cycle to estimate these shifts. After allowing for past shifts in this way, we may test whether a shift has occurred in the latest cycle. The regressions begin one quarter after the cycle peak of 1953, which excludes the post–World War II and early Korean War periods on the grounds that they are less applicable to recent experience. A separate dummy covers each subsequent cycle from one quarter after a cycle peak to the next peak. The 1960s and 1970s dummies coincide with shifts in the regression identified in another study.[5]

We first fit the equation in two versions up to the first quarter of 1980, the cycle peak immediately following the announced change in monetary policy in October 1979. Simulations of these two regressions from the second quarter of 1980 to the first quarter of 1983 are compared with the actual wage changes in figure 1.

The actual wage changes generally exhibit more cyclical fluctuation than can be explained by the regressions. In particular, wage changes began to decline in 1981 and since the fourth quarter of 1981 have fallen well below the predictions of either regression. A datum for the second quarter of 1983, which was not available when the statistical work for this paper was completed, is added to figure 1. This latest datum reinforces the impression of a greater deceleration of wages than the past behavior would suggest. The two regressions differ in the measurement of the inflation variable. Many studies use the inflation rate for the past year. One of the equations in figure 1 does therefore average the annualized inflation rates for four quarters,

FIGURE 1

ACTUAL AND PREDICTED WAGE INCREASES, 1980II–1983II

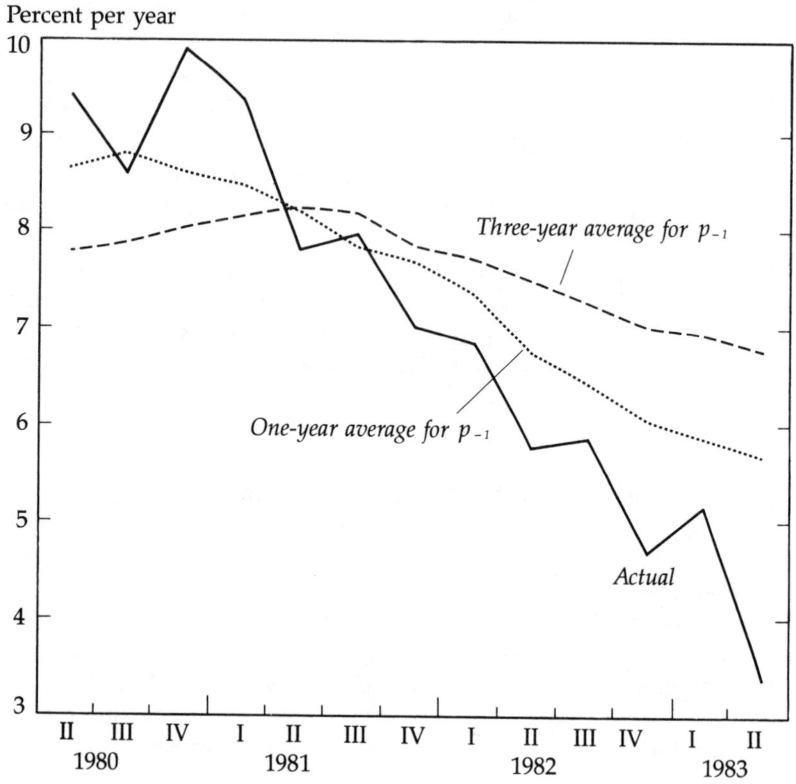

Percent per year

SOURCE: Table 3, equations 7 and 8.

ending with the previous quarter. But one year may be too short to cover the past inflation rate to which wages respond; furthermore, the one-year inflation rate can spuriously reflect recent wage changes or other cyclical variables that may be correlated with the dependent variable. To assess an alternative formulation that partially avoids these difficulties, the inflation variable in the other regression in figure 1 is an average of the rates for twelve quarters.

It is the deviations of actual from predicted wage changes beginning in the fourth quarter of 1981 that suggest a further shift in the relationship, in this case downward. In table 1 the equations are extended to the first quarter of 1983, including cycle dummies as well as a special dummy for the recent period, the fourth quarter of 1981 to the first quarter of 1983. The cycle dummies[6] point to an upward step in wage changes in the 1970s and again in the first cycle of the 1980s,

TABLE 1
WAGE CHANGE REGRESSIONS 1-4,
1953QIII-1983QI

Dependent Variable: w	Coefficients (and absolute value of t)			
	1	2	3	4
Constant	3.0(5.8)	3.4(4.3)	3.0(5.8)	3.1(3.7)
$1/U$	15.7(6.4)	19.0(7.4)	15.7(6.3)	18.8(7.3)
$1/U - 1/U_{-1}$	12.7(2.5)	7.7(1.4)	12.5(1.8)	14.3(1.7)
p_{-1}				
one year	0.3(4.8)		0.3(4.7)	
three years		0.2(1.8)		0.2(2.1)
Individual cycle dummies[a]				
1953QIII-1957QIII	−2.2(3.6)	−3.5(4.2)	−2.2(3.5)	−3.2(3.7)
1957QIV-1960QII	−2.3(4.5)	−3.2(4.8)	−2.3(4.5)	−3.0(4.4)
1960QIII-1969QIV	−2.8(5.6)	−3.7(5.3)	−2.8(5.6)	−3.5(4.7)
1970QI-1973QIV	−0.9(2.4)	−1.6(3.5)	−0.9(2.4)	−1.5(3.2)
1974QI-1980QI	[b]	[b]	[b]	[b]
1980QII-1981QIII	0.3(0.7)	0.8(1.4)	0.3(0.7)	0.6(1.1)
Cycle contractions			−0.02(0.1)	0.4(1.1)
Recent period, 1981QIV-1983QI	−0.8(1.92)	−1.5(2.7)	−0.8(1.65)	−1.8(2.8)
$\bar{R}^2$	.80	.77	.80	.77
SE	.87	.94	.87	.94
DW	2.01	1.81	2.01	1.85

NOTE: $\bar{R}^2$ is the adjusted correlation coefficient squared; SE the standard error; and DW the Durbin-Watson statistic for first-order correlation of residuals.

a. From the quarter after the National Bureau of Economic Research reference peak to the quarter of the next peak.

b. Omitted dummy.

SOURCES: See note 4.

as previous studies have noted, though the last one is based on too few quarters to be statistically significant. The t statistic for the dummies indicates whether each is statistically different from the omitted dummy. This statistic is derived on the assumption that the regression error terms are serially uncorrelated. The presence of serial correlation, however, would mean that a string of deviations in the same direction was not unusual. While some serial correlation is undoubtedly present in these regressions, the Durbin-Watson (DW) statistic suggests that it is serious in only one regression noted below.

The dummy variable for the last period beginning with the fourth quarter of 1981 is negative, which indicates a downward shift compared with the omitted dummy for the comparison cycle 1974–1980 and with the positive dummy for the previous cycle 1980–1981, and is on a par with the 1970–1973 dummy. The t statistic for the 1981–1983 dummy indicates borderline significance[7] when the inflation variable covers one year (regression 1) and high significance when it covers three years (regression 2). The reason for the difference in significance is clear. The inflation rate declined sharply in 1981–1983, and the one-year average came down more rapidly than the three-year average did. Hence the former appears to account for more of the deceleration of wages than the latter does, leaving less of the decline to be assigned to the dummy variable for this period.

In a sense both inflation variables tell a similar story. The rapid deceleration of wages in 1981–1983 can be attributed either to a rapid decline in market responses to inflation represented by the one-year average rate or to a shift in the entire equation compared with previous cycles. On either interpretation a change in the response of wages to current developments occurred: given the one-year inflation variable, price expectations affecting wages fell rapidly because inflation did, and the shift in the relationship is only marginally significant. Given a three-year inflation variable, the deceleration of wages reflected a significant increase in their response to the business contraction and only partly to a public perception of reduced inflation. The two interpretations differ, however, in the following, somewhat overstated implications: The first interpretation implies that wages decelerated in part because prices did; the second implies that prices decelerated in part because wages did and that wages decelerated mainly because of the decline in output.

The tables report some other regressions to show whether certain alternative forms make an important difference. Regressions 3 and 4 include a special dummy for the periods of all business cycle contractions, to see whether the latest decline simply reflects the fact that wage changes are normally larger in contractions than in expansions. The result is to reduce the significance of the latest decline somewhat so that it is now only marginally significant in regression 3 by a one-tail test though still strongly significant in regression 4. The significance of the 1981–1983 dummy is slightly understated, however, since the contraction dummy also covers 1981–1983 along with the earlier contractions.

In table 2 the cycle dummies are consolidated to cover the 1950s and 1960s in one dummy and to cover the 1970s through 1981 in another dummy, since the differences within these periods appear minor. These consolidations simplify the regressions without chang-

TABLE 2

WAGE CHANGE REGRESSIONS 5–6,
1953QIII–1983QI

Dependent Variable: w	Coefficients (and absolute value of t)	
	5	6
Constant	2.6(5.6)	1.8(2.9)
$1/U$	12.9(6.3)	15.2(6.7)
$1/U - 1/U_{-1}$	11.9(2.4)	9.6(1.8)
p_{-1}		
one year	0.4(9.3)	
three years		0.5(7.4)
Consolidated cycle dummies		
1953QIII–1969QIV	– 1.7(5.8)	– 1.6(4.2)
1970QI–1981QI	a	a
Recent period,		
1981QIV–1983QI	– 0.7(1.6)	– 2.1(4.3)
$\bar{R}^2$	.79	.75
SE	.91	.99
DW	1.76	1.53

a. Omitted dummy.
SOURCES: See note 4.

ing the results importantly. (The dummy for 1953–1969 is reduced in value compared with its components in regressions 1 and 2 because the omitted dummy for 1970–1981 includes 1970–1973, which separately has a negative dummy.) The consolidation does, however, cause the DW statistic in regression 6 to drop, which is corrected by the Cochrane-Orcutt method in regression 11 in table 3. Regression 12 uses a slightly different set of consolidated cycle dummies in order to compare the entire period after the fourth quarter of 1979 with previous periods. No significant shift in the regression is recorded for this longer recent period 1980–1983.

Regressions 9 and 10 in table 3 use Perry's unemployment rate, which he adjusted for structural changes in the labor force. Its effect is to reduce slightly the shifts recorded by the cycle dummies, but the shift for the recent period is hardly affected.

Finally, we should note that, if one is so inclined, these results can be given a contrary interpretation. Because the recent period experienced the highest unemployment rates in the entire period of fit, some function steeper than the reciprocal of unemployment would

15

TABLE 3
WAGE CHANGE REGRESSIONS, 7-12
1953QIII-1983QI

Dependent Variable: w	Coefficients (and absolute value of t)					
	7	8	9	10	11	12
	1953QIII – 1980QI		1953QIII – 1983QI		1953QIII – 1983QI	
Constant	3.1(5.5)	3.4(4.1)	3.5(7.0)	4.1(5.3)	1.7(2.3)	2.4(5.3)
$1/U$	15.8(6.2)	18.8(7.2)	8.9(6.1)[a]	11.1(7.4)[a]	15.1(5.4)	13.5(6.3)
$1/U - 1/U$	12.4(2.3)	8.4(1.5)	9.1(2.5)[a]	4.1(1.1)[a]	12.2(2.0)	12.4(2.4)
p_{-1}						
one year	0.3(4.1)		0.3(4.7)			0.4(8.6)
three years		0.2(1.7)		0.2(1.7)	0.5(6.1)	
Individual cycle dummies[b]						
1953QIII-1957QIII	-2.3(3.4)	-3.4(4.0)	-1.6(2.7)	-2.9(3.7)		
1957QIV-1960QII	-2.4(4.3)	-3.2(4.6)	-1.9(3.9)	-2.8(4.4)		
1960QIII-1969QIV	-2.9(5.3)	-3.7(5.0)	-2.6(5.2)	-3.6(5.2)		
1970QI-1973QIV	-1.0(2.4)	-1.6(3.4)	-0.8(2.1)	-1.5(3.5)		
1974QI-1980QI	c	c	c	c		
1980QII-1981QIII			0.4(0.8)	0.9(1.7)		
Recent period, 1981QIV-1983QI			-0.8(1.86)	-1.4(2.5)		
Consolidated cycle dummies						
1953QIII-1969QIV					-1.5(3.2)	-1.7(5.4)

1970QI–1981QI						
1970QI–1979QIV						
Recent period,						
1980QI–1983QI					−2.0(3.4)	−0.2(0.6)
1981QIV–1983QI					0.2(2.6)	
rho						
$\bar{R}^2$	.78	.75	.81	.77	.76	.78
SE	.90	.96	.87	.94	.97	.92
DW	2.00	1.82	1.97	1.81	2.05	1.74

a. Uses Perry's adjusted unemployment rate.

b. From the quarter after the National Bureau of Economic Research reference peak to the quarter of the next peak.

c. Omitted dummy.

SOURCES: See note 4.

"fit" the recent data points without any shift in the equation. Certainly a linear function (of the level not reciprocal) of the unemployment rate will do so, as we have verified without reporting it. Besides its inability to fit at low unemployment rates, however, a linear function implies, as is well known, that a policy of rapid disinflation would be no more costly in terms of total worker months of unemployment than would a gradualist policy—a proposition generally thought to be untrue.

It would be unconvincing to claim that the relevant relation is convex up to some point and becomes linear beyond that point. The claim would be based on the arbitrary choice of one among numerous functions that have the property of approximating a certain convexity in one segment and linearity in another. We do acknowledge that further observations at higher unemployment rates will be necessary to determine the validity of the standard convex interpretation.

Conclusion

We are inclined to the view that the data indicate somewhat more disinflation *per unit of slack* (unemployment) so far in 1981–1983 than one might have guessed from analogous quantitative reasoning applying to the 1970s. We do not claim that the data have by now led to conclusive results in this regard, but we do believe that at the present writing (August 1983) recent wage behavior is indeed suggestive of this direction of a shift. To this extent the more convincing policy posture—more consistent and more credible disinflation promises of policy makers in the early 1980s—may well have made some difference, after an initial lag, by exerting an influence on market expectations and thus on the speed and costs of adjustment.

Notes

1. Arthur M. Okun, "Efficient Disinflationary Policies," *American Economic Review*, vol. 68 (May 1978), pp. 348–52. But see also Robert J. Gordon and Stephen R. King, "The Output Cost of Disinflation in Traditional and Vector Autoregressive Models," *Brookings Papers on Economic Activity* 1982:1, pp. 205–42.

2. William Fellner, *Towards a Reconstruction of Macroeconomics* (Washington, D.C.: American Enterprise Institute, 1976). The reader will find the discussions of the costs of disinflation and of the question of how the credibility of an anti-inflationary policy might influence these costs in many issues of the *Brookings Papers*.

3. See, for example, George L. Perry, "Inflation in Theory and Practice," *Brookings Papers on Economic Activity* 1980:1, pp. 207–60, and Otto Eckstein and James A. Girola, "Long-Term Properties of the Price-Wage Mechanism in

the United States, 1891 to 1977," *Review of Economics and Statistics,* vol. 60 (August 1978), pp. 323–33.

4. *U* is the total unemployment rate in percent, and *p* the rate of change of the consumer price index for urban households in percent per year; *w* is the rate of change in percent per year of average hourly earnings adjusted for interindustry shifts and overtime in manufacturing. The Bureau of Labor Statistics, which is the source of the data, has published only an annual version of the wage series for the pre-1964 period. Before the latter annual extension became available, a quarterly series for pre-1964 years was constructed by Robert J. Gordon ("Inflation in Recession and Recovery," *Brookings Papers on Economic Activity* 1971:1, pp. 105–58, Appendix C), which Perry used and kindly made available to us. We adjusted it to conform to the new BLS annual series. The adjustment is not major, and the results are essentially the same using the Gordon series without the adjustment. In equations 9 and 10 in table 3, we have used Perry's adjusted unemployment rate, which he also made available and we updated. Perry, "Inflation in Theory and Practice."

5. See Perry, "Inflation in Theory and Practice."

6. Each cycle dummy coefficient gives the difference in the constant term between the period covered by the dummy and the period for which a dummy is omitted. For example, in regression 1 the constant term is 0.9 lower in 1970–1973 than in 1974–1980.

7. Five percent significance for a one-tail test (has the regression shifted downward or not?) requires a *t* of 1.66 or greater, and for a two-tail test (has the regression shifted in either direction or not?) requires a *t* of 1.96 or greater.

Monetary Policy and Subduing Inflation

Phillip Cagan

Summary

*In October 1979 a change in the Federal Reserve's operating procedure sig-
naled a new attack on escalating inflation. Although the high inflation rates
of 1979 were expected to recede as the increase in world oil prices stabilized, a
restrictive monetary policy was primarily responsible for cutting the inflation
rate by substantially more than the rise attributable to oil prices. In a little
more than two years, by early 1982, the inflation rate was cut almost in half
from the rate of early 1979 just before the oil price increases. In previous years
much discussion of the difficulties of subduing inflation had assessed past
experience and had emphasized not only how large the economic costs were in
terms of reduced output but also how a gradual disinflation that was widely
expected might smooth the transition and largely eliminate the costs. As it
turned out, this disinflation was not gradual, smooth, or remotely costless.
Monetary growth, though declining overall, was highly variable; the economy underwent two recessions, the second quite severe; interest rates remained high in real terms, crippling business, farmers, and thrift institutions
and exasperating everyone but lenders; and the foreign exchange rates of the
dollar appreciated, depressing exports, intensifying pressures for foreign trade
protectionism, and (along with high interest rates) requiring bail-outs of
heavily indebted countries.*

*This essay assesses the role of monetary policy in the decline of inflation,
the expected consequences and unexpected developments, and the problems to
be faced in pursuing further disinflation.*

*The first recession, covering the first half of 1980, largely reflected the
imposition of credit controls, which produced a sharp decline in retail sales,
consumer credit, and monetary growth, all of which were reversed in the
second half of 1980. During that year the inflation rate declined, mainly
because the oil price shock of 1979 ended its upward push on the price system.
Monetary growth was cut sharply again in the second half of 1981, producing
a severe and prolonged decline in activity from fourth quarter 1981 to fourth*

I am indebted to Eduardo Somensatto and Maryam Homayouni for research assistance.

21

quarter 1982. Although the cyclical peak in economic activity is dated earlier, in July 1981, activity was essentially flat in the second two quarters of 1981, which resembled the plateau in activity following the oil shock of 1973. In both cycles an initial decline in real money balances owing to exogenous price increases not fully accommodated by monetary growth exerted an early contractionary pressure on economic activity.

The major decline in the core rate of inflation came in 1982, reflecting the sharp monetary contraction after mid-1981. The disinflation generally followed the classic pattern. Monetary contraction raised real interest rates temporarily and depressed aggregate demand, and the ensuing reduction in inflation increased the demand to hold money and appreciated the foreign exchange rates. Interest rates remained exceptionally high long after the temporary effects of reduced monetary growth subsided, because the usual financial adjustments to expectations of declining inflation lagged (just as in the 1970s these lags made real interest rates negative when inflation escalated) and because business, illiquid with considerable short-term debt on hand after a shift away from bonds during years of inflation, had to borrow heavily to weather the low cash inflows of a severe recession. The large federal deficits in fourth quarter 1981, though only fractionally due to the disinflation, added to the accompanying financial stringency.

Although expectations of declining inflation had little immediate effect in reducing interest rates or the costs of unemployment, such expectations helped appreciate the dollar and appeared to increase the demand for money in 1982 as inflation subsided. Ironically, these effects of expectations made the economy's adjustments to disinflation more, not less, difficult.

The Federal Reserve decided to ease the disinflationary pressure in mid-1982 when a hoped-for business recovery did not appear, political opposition to high interest rates mounted, and the international credit situation deteriorated. The Fed had been hesitant about easing because of the danger that such action might precipitate market expectations of an inflationary resurgence and raise interest rates. The rates turned down in July 1981, however, as business borrowing leveled off, whereupon monetary growth was expanded without fear of raising interest rates. In fact the rates declined sharply. The decline in intererst rates, along with disinflation, could be expected to increase the public's willingness to hold money balances. An analysis here of the demand for money does indeed point to an upward shift in demand in the first quarter of 1982, which largely offset an earlier downward shift in mid-1974.

The Federal Reserve attributed the shifts to financial innovations, such as the introduction of NOW accounts. The two shifts can also be viewed as responses to a change in expectations of inflation that have not been captured by the conventional demand equation. Because of the shifts and because of a desire to have more flexibility in conducting policy, the targeting of M1 was abandoned in October 1982 as its growth expanded rapidly. This growth combined with the cyclical contraction in business activity to produce an unusually large decline in monetary velocity in the second half of 1982. The analysis here finds no evidence of a shift in money demand after early 1982 but rather a predictable increase in demand from a large decline in interest-rate differentials. Otherwise, velocity would have been esssentially flat, not exceptional for a period of recession. Nevertheless, the actual decline in velocity was seen as exceptional and reinforced the doubts about M1 as a target. Whether M1 would be reinstated as a target later was unclear.

Despite uncertainty over how rapidly M1 could continue to grow to stimulate the business recovery without reviving inflation, it seemed clear that the 14 percent annual M1 growth from July 1982 through June 1983 could not be prudently sustained and would have to be cut back appreciably. The fight against inflation in 1983 was only half won, as was widely recognized, but it was not lost, as many observers pessimistically concluded on the grounds that the nation would not accept another two years like 1981–1982 in order to wring the remaining three to four points out of the inflation rate. Once inflation is on a declining course, such as was attained in 1982, the downward trend can be sustained, even with an economic recovery if it is not excessive, through the deceleration of unit costs both as productivity improves and as wages incorporate lower cost-of-living adjustments. Continuing disinflation, however, requires corresponding declines in monetary growth. Overstimulation that leads to a resurgence of inflationary pressures would mean relinquishing the costly gains. The issue as 1983 unfolded was how far the Federal Reserve would pursue a more restrictive policy and how serious the consequences for domestic and international financial markets and business conditions would be.

The Cycles in Inflation and Economic Activity

The Rise and Decline of Inflation since 1972. Figure 1 shows the course of inflation since 1972, as represented by three series for the consumer price index (CPI) and a fourth for wages. The first of the CPI series is for all items; the second excludes energy prices, and the third mortgage interest, two particularly abnormal components in recent years. The fourth series is average hourly earnings adjusted for interindustry shifts and overtime in manufacturing. The series show changes monthly for the preceding half year,[1] expressed as annual rates. Since 1972 there have been two large waves in the inflation rate associated with two major increases in oil prices by the Organization of Petroleum Exporting Countries (OPEC), a quadrupling in 1973 and a further doubling in 1979.

Both waves nevertheless began with an intensification of inflationary pressures before oil prices increased. After the business recession of 1969–1970, the economy recovered slowly during 1971 and more rapidly during 1972. By the end of 1972, the United States and other

23

FIGURE 1
RATE OF CHANGE OF CONSUMER PRICE INDEX AND AVERAGE HOURLY EARNINGS, MONTHLY, 1972–JUNE 1983

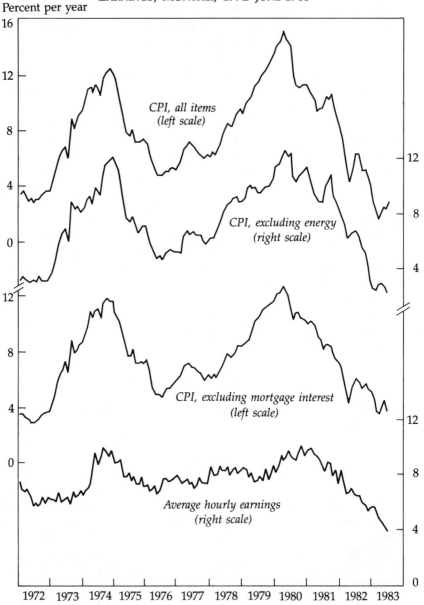

Percent per year

NOTE: Average hourly earnings are adjusted for interindustry shifts and for overtime in manufacturing.

SOURCE: Bureau of Labor Statistics.

24

major industrial countries had reached nearly full-employment levels. During 1973 an explosion of world grain and metals prices preceded the quadrupling of oil prices by OPEC in the final months of the year. The annual inflation rate of the CPI for all items, which was below 4 percent during 1972 when price controls were in effect, rose to 8 percent in September 1973, after the controls were relaxed but a few months before oil prices increased. The shock wave from oil prices then carried the CPI rate to a peak of 12½ percent in November 1974. The relaxation of price controls allowed suppressed prices to recover and so may have shifted one or two percentage points of the inflation rate from 1972 to 1973.[2] According to the CPI, excluding the energy component, the OPEC price shock did not spread significantly to the other components until September 1974, almost a year later. Then the other components rapidly joined the escalation, and the first two versions of the CPI moved together from 1975 until 1979.

The sharp drop in business activity after October 1974 brought the inflation rate down dramatically to below 5 percent by mid-1976. The rate then reversed part of its decline and stabilized during 1977 in the 6 to 7 percent range, at about half the 1974 peak rate. Wage increases traced a similar pattern. They had been rising about 6½ percent per year in 1973, had accelerated to almost 10 percent in late 1974, and then settled down to a 7 to 8 percent rate in 1976–1977. In 1977, at the end of the first inflationary wave, wage and price increases remained well above the 1972 rate, even if we allow for the elimination of price controls in 1974.

In 1978 a second inflationary wave began. Gathering inflationary pressures raised the CPI rate for all items during 1978 from 6½ to 9½ percent, or to 8½ percent excluding mortgage interest. Then during 1979 the second oil shock hit. The average cost of petroleum to U.S. refineries increased 80 percent, and the annual CPI rate rose to a peak in March 1980 of 15 percent for all items and to 12½ percent excluding mortgage interest. The rise in the CPI rate, excluding the energy component, peaked a quarter later, in June 1980, at 12 percent, appreciably lower than the peak rate for all items. Wages accelerated to a peak rate even later, in November 1980, which at 10 percent per year was on a par with the peak rate reached in 1974. The direct contribution of higher oil prices to the overall inflation rate was less important than the indirect effects. The oil increases passed through as higher input costs to other prices and as cost-of-living adjustments for wages, which fed back to increase prices further and so on.

Despite the cost-push effects, however, aggregate demand was strong when the oil shocks occurred in 1973 and 1979. It would not have been possible to sustain such enormous increases in the price level if aggregate demand had not been strong and monetary policy had not partially accommodated the higher level of prices.

Insofar as cost-push influences raised the inflation rate for a time above the supporting growth of money, the public found itself with lower real money balances than were desired, which led to adjustments that raised intererst rates and contracted aggregate expenditures. Thus the oil price increases were temporarily inflationary, and, because of less than full accommodation in the money supply, were at the same time contractionary for real sales and output.

The second inflationary wave has subsided in three steps so far since 1980. In the first step it declined sharply in the second quarter of 1980 during the short business recession. Most of this reduction in inflation reflected the end of the oil price effects, since the nonenergy prices show a smaller temporary deceleration that was largely reversed during the recovery of business in the second half of 1980. In the first half of 1981, the inflation rate contracted a second time to 9½ percent for all items and to 8¼ percent excluding mortgage interest, though the contraction in the nonenergy components was substantially reversed in the third quarter of 1981. Then, shortly after business activity peaked in July 1981, a third step cut the inflation rate in half by early 1982. Despite some reversal later during 1982, the average rate for the year was 5½ percent for all items and 5¾ percent excluding mortgage interest. In 1983 the rate declined further, to 3 percent in the first half for all items.

Prices of basic commodities underwent a radical deflation. The International Monetary Fund index of commodity prices[3] began falling sharply after November 1980. At its low point two years later, the index had declined 29 percent. Although the appreciation of the dollar helped, the deflation of these prices also reflected and contributed to a worldwide decline in inflation of all prices. An index of consumer prices in twenty-three countries (excluding the United States)[4] decelerated from a rate of 13½ percent per year in early 1980 to 8 percent per year at the end of 1982, a decline only slightly less than that in the United States. Basic commodity prices are highly sensitive to business prospects and partially recovered in 1983 with the end of the U.S. recession.

The deceleration of U.S. wages, in contrast to that in the CPI, started later and continued without major interruptions. From a 10 percent peak annual rate in November 1980 and 9 percent as late as August 1981, they decelerated to 5 percent in December 1982, an unusual and remarkable decline. This decline of four percentage points during the recession exceeded the three-point decline in 1974–1975 and brought the rate down below the level of 1973. Moreover, the rise in unemployment in 1973–1975 of almost four percentage points was greater than the 3½ point rise from September 1980 to December

FIGURE 2
RATE OF CHANGE OF REAL GNP AND UNIT LABOR COSTS, QUARTERLY,
1972–1983II

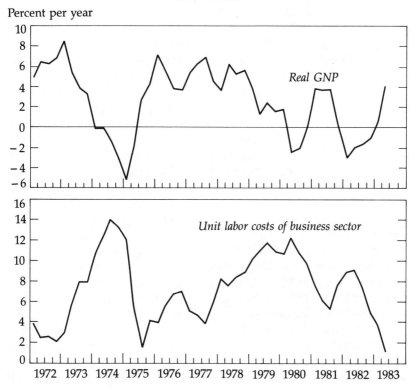

SOURCE: Bureau of Economic Analysis.

1982. There is some statistical indication of a more flexible wage response to the later recession, possibly attributable to a reduction in
inflationary expectations (see the essay by Cagan and Fellner in this
volume).

The prices of most finished goods and services have usually departed very little from unit costs of production (composed mainly of
labor costs). Unit labor costs are often cited to indicate the core rate of
inflation, since they are less affected than are most prices by temporary cycles in demand and largely set the trend of prices over the long
run. As shown in figure 2, the rate of increase in unit labor costs for
the business sector rose in 1978 and 1979 to more than 10 percent. The
rate declined to 7 percent in the second half of 1980 and early 1981 and
then declined considerably further in 1982, reflecting a slackening of
wage increases and an improvement in productivity growth. Prior to

this improvement, productivity growth had been virtually stagnant for several years, and it remained to be seen whether the improvement would continue. Even with favorable productivity growth, the key to continued disinflation depends on further deceleration of wages.

The decline of inflation has clearly exceeded what could be expected from subsidence of the 1979 oil price shock. The two business recessions after 1979 reflected the strong contractionary forces at work on the inflation. The period of disinflation as a whole bore the classic pattern produced by a decline in monetary growth, but it also exhibited some characteristics that were not generally foreseen. These were the brevity of the first recession and the length and severity of the second, the rising foreign exchange rates of the dollar, and the high interest rates, all of which importantly influenced the conduct of monetary policy.

The Business Recessions. When in October 1979 the Federal Reserve announced stricter measures to fight inflation, a recession in activity was not unexpected. That had been the consequence of previous episodes of monetary restraint in 1966 (a minirecession in early 1967), in 1969 (a recession in 1970), and in 1973 (a severe recession in 1974 that lasted until May 1975). What was not foreseen in 1979 was that two back-to-back recessions were in store[5] and that the second one would be quite severe. The first in 1980 was very short; it is dated from January to July and appeared largely to reflect the period of consumer credit controls from March to May, which curtailed retail sales. Apart from the credit controls, the role of monetary policy in this recession (discussed below) appears limited. The second recession from July 1981 to November 1982 was severe but had a smaller decline than that of 1973–1975. In 1981–1982, as compared with 1973–1975, the unemployment rate rose slightly less, though to a higher level (reflecting an upward trend during the 1970s), and both industrial production and real GNP fell less.[6] The widespread impression to the contrary is due to the fact that the 1973–1975 recession, though it lasted just as long as did that of 1981–1982 (sixteen months), was deep for only a short period, whereas the later recession became deep a quarter after the cyclical peak. The later one also started from a lower level of activity and consequently reached a slightly lower level of capacity utilization. The prolonged severity of the 1981–1982 recession has been attributed to several special influences in addition to a tight monetary policy. The special influences were the increases in foreign exchange rates of the dollar, in federal deficits, and in interest rates. The first and third, which could be attributed to the disinflation, were important. The second was not contractionary and cannot be held responsible for the overall weakness of the economy.

The average foreign exchange rate (trade weighted) of the dollar began to rise in late 1980 and in the next two years rose more than 40 percent up to November 1982 (see figure 1, in the essay by Gottfried Haberler, page 104, this volume). The rise stemmed from capital inflows attracted by the actual and prospective decline in U.S. inflation and by high interest rates. The high interest rates were not solely responsible, however, because when they declined after mid-1982, the exchange rate continued rising until November and remained high through most of 1983. The rise in the exchange rate steadily reduced the net foreign trade balance; from the third quarter of 1980 to the fourth quarter of 1982, exports minus imports declined in constant dollars by one-half. More than a third of the decline in real GNP from third quarter 1981 to fourth quarter 1982 was attributable to the trade balance. The shift in foreign trade aggravated the long-run weakness in the steel and automobile industries particularly. The combined effect of the recession and rising exchange rate pushed these industries into a major depression. The effect of the recession on individual industries and regions, consequently, was quite uneven.

Increases in the federal deficit and the associated Treasury borrowing were much talked about as a depressing influence on the economy but on net were most likely mildly expansionary. The federal budget deficit in the national income and product accounts ran just under $60 billion in both 1980 and 1981. It began increasing in fourth quarter 1981 and in the first half of 1982 doubled to a $119 billion annual rate as a result of tax reductions and continued expenditure increases. Such a large deficit could be expected to stimulate aggregate demand, though with a lag for the part due to reduced taxes because private expenditures typically respond gradually to changes in disposable income. Any stimulation from the deficit was not noticeable during 1982, however, apparently because of the overriding decline in business activity. It could also be that stimulative effects were largely crowded out by reductions in private investment owing to high real interest rates (figure 3), held up in part by the heavy Treasury borrowing. Yet, despite the rise of the deficit, interest rates fell sharply in July 1982 prior to an easing of monetary policy. As the economy expands, projected large deficits will be important for interest rates and private investment, but increased deficits are not in their net effect contractionary and so do not explain the severity of the 1981–1982 recession.

High interest rates until mid-1982 were a symptom of the strong contractionary forces in the economy that accounted for the length

FIGURE 3

RATE OF CHANGE OF CONSUMER PRICE INDEX AND TREASURY BILL RATE,
MONTHLY, 1972–JUNE 1983

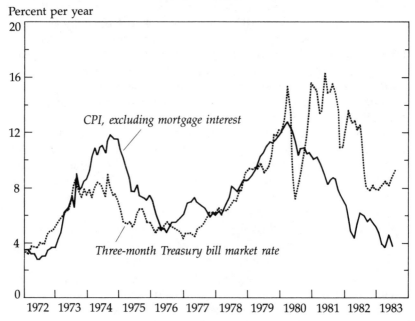

SOURCES: Bureau of Labor Statistics and Board of Governors of the Federal Reserve System.

and severity of the recession. High nominal rates produced severe disintermediation in thrift institutions, carrying many over the brink of viability. The high nominal rates became high in real terms as inflation declined, which helped depress the housing and automobile industries. Business bankruptcy rates surpassed typical levels during the recession because of the high real costs of borrowing.

It was unusual for interest rates to remain high in nominal and real terms for more than a year after business peaked in July 1981. Federal deficits commonly rise as business activity contracts, so an increase in Treasury borrowing during this recession was not unusual. What was unusual was the continuing strong demand for credit by business, reflecting widespread illiquidity. Table 1 shows that short-term business borrowing from large banks atypically remained high during this recession compared with the preceding year.[7] In all the recessions since 1950, except for the first part of the 1973 downturn, business borrowing had slackened after the peak. The increased growth in the year after the 1981 peak can be related to the inflation-

TABLE 1

CHANGE IN COMMERCIAL AND INDUSTRIAL LOANS OF
LARGE BANKS IN BUSINESS CYCLES
(percent per year)

Business Peak	Year before Peak	Year after Peak	Peak to Trough of Business Cycle
July 1953	8.1	−5.2	−5.3
July 1957	11.4	−7.3	−7.4
April 1960	11.0	2.4	2.5
November 1969	16.2	10.4	10.4
November 1973	21.2	26.0	17.8
(October 1974[a]	26.2	−8.2	−0.5)
January 1980	22.7	10.4	8.9
July 1981	14.1	18.8	12.8

NOTE: Large weekly reporting member banks.
a. Alternative to November 1973 peak, dated at end of plateau in business activity.
SOURCE: Board of Governors of the Federal Reserve System.

ary environment. As bond and equity financing was abandoned during the 1970s in the face of escalating and unpredictable inflation rates, business firms moved toward short-term financing (bank loans and commercial paper). The ratio of short-term debt to total credit market debt of nonfinancial corporations rose from 35 percent in 1971 to 48 percent in 1981.[8] Yet, because of the risks involved in continually rolling over short-term debt, and also because of the high rates, many firms must have reduced their borrowing to the minimum. To the extent that they did, the decline in their cash flow in the 1981–1982 recession caught them short and forced them to borrow more for survival at any cost. When firms were finally able to contract operations and to reduce distress borrowing, the demand for funds fell and short-term interest rates declined. Business borrowing from banks slackened in mid-June and peaked in early October, and interest rates started declining in the first week of July 1982. Before the high rates came down, they slowed the upswing in housing and related industries that normally spark cyclical recoveries.

Distress borrowing contributed to the length of the recession, and rising foreign exchange rates to its depth, but they fall short as complete explanations, and neither one can account for the onset of the last two recessions. The generally accepted explanation for these recessions as well as for the pervasive effects of declining inflation is monetary policy, but it did not follow the usual pattern.

Monetary Policy since 1979

Monetary Growth and the Recessions. Although the change to stricter monetary targeting in October 1979 has been criticized for failing to reduce fluctuations in monetary growth, monetary policy did eventually turn highly restrictive and was responsible for the decline in inflation and for the two recessions and overall weakness in business activity. The precise contribution of monetary policy is obscured, however, by the unclear role of new monetary instruments, which make interpretation of the monetary data especially difficult, and by the credit controls imposed from March to May 1980.

The growth rate of transactions money—the narrow M1 definition—fluctuated from 1977 through 1979 largely within a range of 7 to 9 percent per year (see figure 4). Its average rate of 7 percent from November 1979 to February 1980 appears insufficient to produce a business downturn. Still, monetary restraint was probably greater than is shown by M1 growth. First, an expanded M1 including overnight repurchase agreements (RPs) and Caribbean Eurodollar deposits (EDs), which substitute for demand deposits, shows a large deceleration after October 1979, to a 5½ percent annual rate between November 1979 and February 1980 from more than 10 percent during most of 1979. This deceleration can be attributed to the imposition in October 1979 of a marginal reserve requirement on increases in managed liabilities[9] that curtailed their supply. Second, the oil price increases of 1979 sent an inflationary wave through the economy that, because it was generated independently of monetary growth, reduced money balances in real terms. The resulting upward pressure on interest rates from the decline in real balances had a contractionary influence on economic activity. Whether these influences by March 1980 had reached the point of precipitating a business recession, or whether they would have done so in several more months, is unclear, because the credit controls imposed in March 1980 overrode all other influences in the business downturn of March to May. They led to a sharp curtailment of consumer credit that reduced retail sales and bank financing, and as a result business activity and monetary growth contracted together.

This contraction in business activity was short. After removal of the controls in May 1980, monetary growth and business activity recovered rapidly. By the end of 1980, the inflation rate (excluding energy, figure 1) and interest rates (figure 3) had returned to previous peak levels. Still, this resurgence too was short lived. Signs of economic weakness began to appear in the second quarter of 1981 when real GNP growth faltered (figure 2) and the inflation rate declined further. The economy remained on a plateau for half a year before

FIGURE 4

MONETARY GROWTH AND TREASURY BILL RATE, MONTHLY, 1972–JUNE 1983

Percent per year

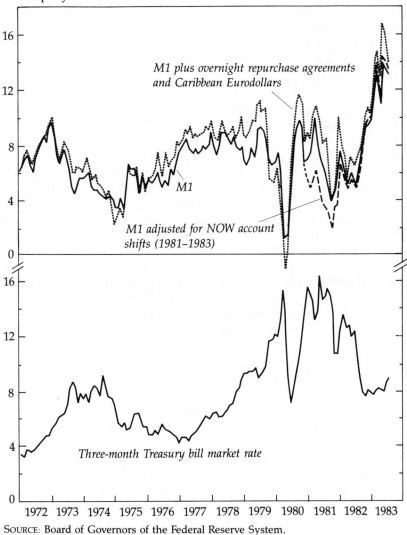

SOURCE: Board of Governors of the Federal Reserve System.

contracting sharply in the fourth quarter, even though the peak was reached the preceding July.

A similar pattern showing economic activity sliding off a plateau also pertains to 1974, when activity plummeted in October after being flat since the preceding November peak. During 1974 escalating inflation combined with declining monetary growth to produce a sizable decline in real money balances, which was contractionary for aggregate demand. Similarly, in the 1981–1982 recession, M1 balances deflated by the CPI fell more than 10 percent from the end of 1978 to the second quarter of 1981, reflecting a higher inflation rate as a result of the OPEC oil price increases. In contrast to experience in 1974, however, M1 growth in 1981 did not decline much below previous trend rates until midyear, which is true as well of an expanded M1 including overnight repurchase agreements and Caribbean Eurodollars. (A third series with an adjustment for NOW accounts, which is also shown in figure 4, beginning in 1981, declines considerably but, as explained below, apparently overstates the decline.) A major decline in monetary growth began only one month prior to the July business peak, too short a time for a monetary contraction to affect business activity. The decline in monetary growth after midyear was sharp and thus explains the fall in real GNP in the fourth quarter. The plateau in business activity in the second and third quarters can be attributed instead to the prior decline in real money balances, to high interest rates, and to deterioration of the foreign trade balance.

After the contraction in economic activity in the second half of 1981, monetary growth remained low much longer than was usual for a business recession in terms of any of the three series in figure 4. Monetary growth did not begin to increase until November, four months after the business peak, and even then, after a short three-month spurt to February 1982, it contracted again until July 1982, a full year after the business peak. If we compare the first year of business recessions with the year preceding the business peak (table 2), we see that monetary growth not only declined after the 1981 peak, as it also had in the two previous recessions, but declined by appreciably more than it had in any of the previous post–World War II recessions.

Money and the 1983 Recovery. A year after the business peak, in third quarter 1982, monetary policy eased and, in the fourth quarter, turned quite expansive. We can only conjecture about the motivation for this belated policy shift, since monetary growth was near the top of its target range all during the year and no change in policy was announced, except for a statement later in the year that M1 growth had been increased to accommodate demand shifts. Clearly, however, the main reason for the change in policy was the economic situation in late summer. When it became evident during the summer that the recession would be longer and deeper than had been forecast earlier,[10] political pressure mounted to bring down the level of interest rates, which remained high despite reduced inflation. In addition to concern about deteriorating economic conditions at home, many develop-

TABLE 2
M1 GROWTH IN BUSINESS CYCLES
(percent per year)

Business Peak	Year before Peak (1)	Year after Peak (2)	Difference (2) – (1) (3)
November 1948	– 1.2	1.0	0.2
July 1953	2.8	1.3	– 1.5
July 1957	0.7	1.0	0.3
May 1960	– 0.7	2.3	3.0
November 1969	3.8	4.6	0.8
November 1973	6.0	4.8	– 1.2
(October 1974[a]	5.0	4.8	– 0.2)
January 1980	7.7	6.6	– 1.1
July 1981	7.9	5.8	– 2.1

a. Alternative to November 1973 peak, dated at end of plateau in business activity.

SOURCE: Milton Friedman and Anna J. Schwartz, *Monetary Statistics of the United States* (New York: National Bureau of Economic Research, 1970), table 1 (to 1959), and Board of Governors of the Federal Reserve System for years thereafter (early 1983 version without NOW account adjustment).

ing countries in heavy debt to Western banks were struggling to continue payments, because of high interest rates and declining exports, which in the case of Mexico mainly reflected the decline in oil prices. The Federal Reserve at first expressed caution that a stimulative monetary expansion could revive inflationary expectations and could send interest rates even higher.[11] The worry that an easier monetary policy might, contrary to its usual effects, raise interest rates because of inflationary expectations was finally relieved when interest rates started declining in early July. It appears that the initial decline in interest rates reflected a flattening of loan demand and not an easing of monetary policy. The monetary base was flat through July, until August. With interest rates heading down, and the fear of raising them allayed, a strong expansion in monetary growth ensued.

From August through the end of 1982, the annual growth rate of M1 was 19 percent, which carried it far above its target for the year. In October, Paul A. Volcker, chairman of the Federal Reserve Board, announced that M1 was for technical reasons no longer a reliable indicator of monetary policy and would be temporarily disregarded.[12] The reason given was that the expiration of All-Savers Certificates (savings deposits with one year tax exemption of interest authorized by the Tax Reduction Act of 1981) and other financial developments were affecting the demand for checkable deposits to an unpredictable extent.

35

Volcker claimed that these developments heightened the risk that the original target for M1 growth was too low. It is also clear, however, that disregarding the M1 target gave the Federal Reserve flexibility to pursue a more stimulative policy to bring down the high level of interest rates and to support a business recovery without at the same time explicitly raising the monetary target. The reasons given for overshooting the M1 target were a roundabout way of claiming that higher M1 growth would not be inflationary. Rather than justify a new higher target on the grounds that the previous one was considered lower than necessary to subdue inflation, the Federal Reserve abandoned the M1 target until further notice. In the meantime, targets for M2 and M3 as well as for other variables, such as interest rates, became the chief guides for policy.

Volcker insisted that the Federal Reserve's commitment to a disinflationary policy remained unaltered. Although most members of the business and financial community were relieved by the easing of policy, some observers saw a danger that the original intention of reducing monetary growth gradually year by year could be delayed or perhaps never reinstated and that monetary policy, without a clear long-run goal, would be a hostage of short-term developments. By 1983 the Federal Reserve faced a problem: how to contain the explosive growth of M1 to avoid a resurgence of inflation while at the same time preserving the economic recovery.

The Evidence of Money Demand Shifts. Chairman Volcker pointed to shifts in money demand (mainly upward) as evidence that monetary targets could not be relied upon to guide monetary policy. Earlier there had been strong evidence of a downward shift in 1974. The chairman was referring, however, to new shifts since 1979. A source of shifts in money demand is the development of new kinds of financial instruments. Some of these were brought into M1 under a redefinition published in 1980. Conventional money demand equations do not account for new financial arrangements or other developments that shift the equation, as indicated by its prediction errors. The prediction errors of a standard version of the money demand equation, with alternative definitions of money, are shown in table 3. The statistical details of fitting the equation to the data are given in appendix table A. We may examine the prediction errors for evidence of shifts since 1974 and particularly since 1979. As explained below, a substantial shift can be seen in 1974 and again in 1982, but no others appear in other years.

Part 1 in tables 3 and A is based on the standard equation that was widely used before the mid-1970s. In this equation real money balances (using the GNP deflator) are regressed on real GNP, an interest

TABLE 3
ERRORS OF MONEY DEMAND EQUATIONS

Money Variable	Standard Error of Regression (percent of M/P)	Regression Coefficient of Lagged Dependent Variable	Simulation Error Root Mean Square (percent of M/P)	
			1979 IV– 1981 IV	1982 I– 1983 I
	1. Period of regression fit, 1955 I to 1974 II			
1. M1	0.41	0.64	11.8	9.5
2. M1 + savings deposit shift	0.41	0.64	8.8	8.6
3. M1 + RP + ED	0.40	0.64	9.6	5.8
4a. M1 + savings deposit shift + RP + ED	0.40	0.64	6.0	2.6
4b. M1 + savings deposit shift + RP + ED + NOW adjustment	0.40	0.64	6.8	4.9
	2. Period of regression fit, 1955 I to 1979 III, with shift variable, 1974 III and afterward			
1. M1	0.45	0.84	1.4	1.5
2. M1 + savings deposit shift	0.44	0.73	2.3	1.8
3. M1 + RP + ED	0.45	0.76	1.5	2.8
4a. M1 + savings deposit shift + RP + ED	0.45	0.66	1.3	2.7
4b. M1 + savings deposit shift + RP + ED + NOW adjustment	0.45	0.66	1.7	0.5
	3. Period of regression fit, 1955 I to 1979 III, with ratchet interest rate			
1. M1	0.51	0.97	1.3	3.0
2. M1 + savings deposit shift	0.50	0.88	3.1	2.7
3. M1 + RP + ED	0.54	0.89	1.6	1.9
4a. M1 + savings deposit shift + RP + ED	0.50	0.61	1.2	3.1

(Table continues)

TABLE 3 (continued)

Money Variable	Standard Error of Regression (percent of M/P)	Regression Coefficient of Lagged Dependent Variable	Simulation Error Root Mean Square (percent of M/P)	
			1979 IV– 1981 IV	1982 I– 1983 I
4b. M1 + savings deposit shift + RP + ED + NOW adjustment	0.50	0.61	1.6	1.1

NOTE: Errors (predicted minus actual) are derived from dynamic simulations in which the lagged dependent variable and autocorrelation part of the error term are the predicted values for the preceding quarter. Regarding the savings deposit shift, see appendix table A (note). (RP + ED) is overnight repurchase agreements plus overnight Caribbean Eurodollar deposits. The NOW adjustment is the Federal Reserve estimate for 1981 of the amount of new NOW accounts that did not replace other checkable deposits (see John A. Tatom, "Recent Financial Innovations: Have They Distorted the Meaning of M1?" Federal Reserve Bank of St. Louis *Review*, vol. 64 [April 1982], pp. 23–35, table 1). Other variables and form of regression are defined in appendix table A.

SOURCE: Equations shown in appendix table A.

rate pertinent to households (the savings deposit rate) and to businesses (the commercial paper rate), and a lagged value of the dependent variable to allow for partial adjustments in the balances held. All the variables are in logarithms, and a correction is made for serial correlation of the residual error term. Using M1 as then defined, numerous studies found that this equation fit the quarterly data for the mid-1950s to mid-1970s fairly well.[13] The standard error of the regression for that period is less than a half percent of real money balances. In the years since this equation was originally used, the definition of M1 has been expanded to include new kinds of checkable deposits (mainly NOW accounts) that pay interest. These revisions of M1 are included here, though they are of no quantitative importance until the late 1970s. The measurement of the two interest rates in the equation has also been redefined here as the differential of these rates over the average rate paid on money balances.[14]

When these fitted demand equations are used to predict real money balances in later quarters, the predicted values minus the actual real balances are the simulation errors of the equation. The errors of the standard equation began getting large in mid-1970, indicating that actual real money balances were increasing less rapidly than the predicted amounts. When we inspect these errors (not shown), it is clear that a sharp decline in the accuracy of the equation occurs in mid-1974. The date of the shift identified by numerous studies is the first half of 1974,[15] and so the regressions in part 1 of the tables were terminated in second quarter 1974. The simulation errors reach a plateau of about 10–12 percent by 1977 (not shown). The error for two periods after the change in Federal Reserve policy beginning in fourth quarter 1979 is reported in table 3. For M1 the overprediction continued to be about 10 percent.

To what extent can this overprediction be attributed to new financial instruments or arrangements? One development was a change in regulations allowing small businesses and state and municipal agencies to hold savings deposits, previously restricted to individuals. Beginning in mid-1975 a sizable shift occurred from demand to savings deposits by these new holders, which was estimated to have totaled $16½ billion by mid-1977.[16] A second development was the significant growth in recent years of overnight repurchase agreements and overnight Caribbean Eurodollar deposits, which appear to be important substitutes for holding checking deposits. Finally, the rapid buildup of NOW accounts in 1981, which are included in the redefinition of M1, may have reflected an increase in the demand for money balances that the equation is unable to describe. To account for this possibility, the Federal Reserve published an adjustment of the NOW account data for 1981 to exclude the amount of new NOW accounts that were not replacing other checkable deposits.[17] Table 3 and appendix table A allow for these three developments by providing alternative definitions of money. These alternatives, except for the NOW account adjustment, reduce the simulation errors of the equation.

Since none of these or other known adjustments of money balances fully accounts for the large simulation errors after the mid-1970s, it appears that the public also developed various arrangements for minimizing money balances in response to high and rising interest rates. The reductions in money demand can be described fairly well by either a lasting reduction all at once in third quarter 1974 or a gradual reduction over a series of years. The former is represented in part 2 of tables 3 and A by adding a dummy variable for third quarter 1974 and after, and the latter in part 3 by a ratchet interest rate. The ratchet interest rate is a transformation of the market rate on five-year Treasury securities by which the rate is kept at its highest previous level whenever the market rate is lower. The ratchet rate is intended to approximate the effect of new cash management procedures that, once developed in response to high interest rates, are still effective even after interest rates decline.[18] Although the shifts in money demand can be *described* by these additions to the regressions, the *explanation* given for them in terms of more sophisticated cash management is unproven yet plausible. It is plausible on the argument that the sharp escalation of inflation in 1973 acted as a catalyst for the expansion and development of interest-bearing substitutes for non–interest-bearing transactions balances. Parts 2 and 3 of the tables allow for these earlier shifts in order to verify whether new shifts occurred after 1979.

Either of these shift adjustments eliminates a large part of the simulation errors. Between the fourth quarters of 1979 and 1981, the simulation error for M1 averages less than three times the standard error of the equation (1.4 percent with the dummy variable and 1.3 percent with the ratchet variable, compared with a standard error of 0.5 percent for both equations, line 1 of parts 2 and 3). The acceptability of these adjustments of the equation depends, however, on their success not only in reducing the size of errors but also in leaving the coefficients of the equation largely unchanged (on the assumption that behavior represented by the coefficients has not changed). The regression for M1 with the dummy variable has an unrealistically higher coefficient for the lagged dependent variable (table 3) and differences in the other coefficients (see appendix table A, page 52) as compared with its fit ending in second quarter 1974. The same is true of the regression with the ratchet variable. The only equation having essentially the same values of all coefficients as its counterpart in part 1 is equation 4 of part 2, which includes all the adjustments of the money supply listed, suggesting that, except for a shift in mid-1974, these adjustments of money otherwise provide a demand equation that is the same over the full period until third quarter 1979. Since this equation describes more consistent behavior over the full period, it is tentatively to be preferred.

The simulation error for equation 4 in table 3 includes all NOW accounts on line 4a and the NOW account adjustment (which begins first quarter 1981) on line 4b. In the first period between fourth quarters 1979 and 1981, the error without the adjustment is smaller. It is smaller for the root mean square, as shown in table 3, and also for the mean of unsquared errors not shown there (which for part 2 is 0.5 for line 4a as compared with 1.4 for line 4b, indicating less bias as well as smaller deviations). The smaller error for equation 4a strongly suggests that the NOW account adjustment is not needed and that the equation best predicts a demand for which all NOW accounts are included.[19] (The error in the later period between first quarters 1982 and 1983 is discussed below.)

In figure 4 monetary growth with the NOW account adjustment showed a sharp decline for the first half of 1981, which would imply a strong contractionary effect on the economy, unlike the other two money series shown, which did not decline much until mid-1981.

Although the Federal Reserve stressed the need for adjusting the data on NOW accounts, it viewed the estimated adjustment as unreliable and apparently as exaggerated. If it had not, such a sharp monetary contraction in 1981 as is implied by the NOW account adjustment would be hard to justify without a major effort to moderate the contraction, which policy did not undertake.

If the NOW account adjustment is largely not needed and should be disregarded, however, monetary growth did not decline appreciably until mid-1981. This timing is in fact consistent with the movements in economic activity. In spite of the business peak in July, activity remained on a plateau in the second and third quarters of 1981 (which was attributed above to other influences on aggregate demand) before plummeting in the fourth quarter, following the sharp monetary contraction beginning midyear.

The simulation error for the preferred equation 4a in table 3 increases substantially for the later period between first quarters 1982 and 1983, reflecting a sudden increase in real money balances in first quarter 1982, which is not explained by any of the equations.[20] When equation 4a is fitted to the entire period between first quarters 1955 and 1983, with an additional dummy variable to measure a shift in 1982 and afterward, the estimated shift is upward by 1.4 percent.[21] The explosive growth in money in the second half of 1982 and the introduction of super-NOW accounts in 1983 cannot explain such a prior shift beginning in early 1982. The unexplained shift in money demand, called an "increased demand for liquidity" by the Federal Reserve, led to the abandonment of M1 as a target.

The behavior of money demand is depicted in figure 5, which compares the predicted values of equation 4a (footnote 21) and the actual values, expressed as velocity ratios. That is, both series use actual real GNP in the numerator as a ratio to the predicted and the actual real money balances. The difference between the series is therefore the discrepancy between predicted and actual real money balances. The predicted values as fitted, however, have been adjusted to remove the contributions of the 1974 and 1982 dummy shift variables in order to highlight their effects. Consequently, the predicted series shows a lower velocity than the actual velocity after 1974, whereas this discrepancy is appreciably narrowed by the opposite shift in 1982. Although the development of new financial instruments has been stressed as making monetary targeting unreliable, the timing of the two shifts in 1974 and 1982 appears unrelated to new instruments. What the two years have in common is a previous major change in the inflation rate: a sharp escalation preceding 1974 and an equally sharp reduction preceding 1982. It is plausible that changes in expectations of inflation were involved, which shifted the demand downward (ve-

41

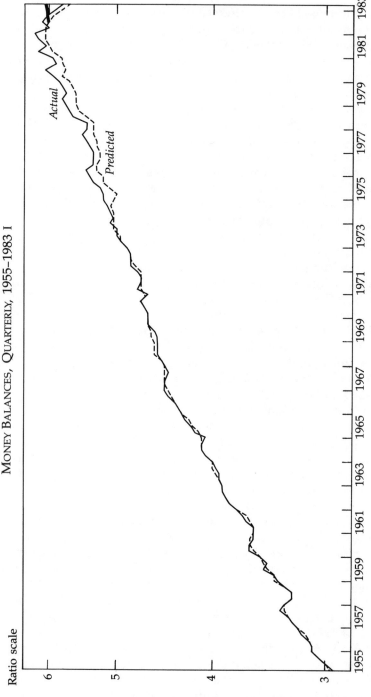

FIGURE 5

VELOCITY RATIOS OF ACTUAL REAL GNP TO PREDICTED AND ACTUAL REAL
MONEY BALANCES, QUARTERLY, 1955–1983 I

Ratio scale

NOTE: The heavy curve shown for 1982II–1983I presupposes that there is no change on interest-rate differentials after 1982II.

SOURCE: Equation in note 21, for M1 and savings deposit shift and RP + ED; contributions of dummy shift variables beginning 1974III and 1982I have been removed from predicted series.

locity upward) by 2 percent in 1974 and shifted demand upward (velocity downward) by 1½ percent in 1982. The 1974 shift was apparently not reversed in 1975–1977 when inflation temporarily moderated.

Since the equation underlying the predicted series in figure 5 predicts money balances rather than the velocity ratio, it does not purport to explain all cyclical variations in velocity, in which short-run changes in money and GNP diverge. Changes in real GNP respond to prior changes in money and other influences and in turn affect the demand for money balances only gradually over time. Only over the long run does the equation imply, if interest rates are unchanged, that growth in real GNP will produce a proportional growth in real money demand and velocity.[22] Nevertheless, the equation helps to explain the contribution of money demand to some changes in the velocity ratio.

A particularly dramatic and widely noted decline in velocity occurred in fourth quarter 1982 and first quarter 1983, as shown in figure 5. This was by far the largest two-quarter decline at least since 1953 and appeared to support the Federal Reserve's decision to downgrade the targeting of M1.[23] The Federal Reserve suggested that the decline may have reflected the decline in interest rates and the payment of interest on a growing volume of transactions balances. It was generally thought that such developments made money demand unpredictable and unreliable as a target.[24]

We may estimate the effect of interest rates on money demand by supposing for the equation in footnote 21 that the rates did not change while the other variables including the error terms changed as they actually did. If the interest rates in the equation for second quarter 1982 are held constant thereafter, the equation predicts a slight decline in real money demand in the next three quarters contrary to its actual increase. In that event velocity would rise 0.4 percent in third quarter 1982 and another 0.4 percent in first quarter 1983 instead of falling 5 percent in those quarters. This hypothetical behavior of velocity that assumes no change in interest rates is also shown in figure 5. The decline in interest rates was thus responsible for the decline in velocity in those quarters, and otherwise velocity would have risen slightly. It still would have risen much less than its long-run trend growth, but such slackening is characteristic of velocity in cyclical contractions when real GNP is stagnant or declining.

The reason why the rise in money demand in those quarters was so much larger than in previous recessions is that, in addition to the large decline in interest rates generally, the differential rate on savings deposits relative to the average rate on money, which has a large coefficient in the equation but usually changes slowly, also had a rapid decline. Its unusual decline reflected the importance of money market mutual funds, which have flexible rates, unlike traditional savings deposits, and the growing importance in M1 of NOW accounts, which pay interest. Hence the average rate of interest on M1 was growing, reducing its differential vis-à-vis savings deposits and money market funds. With the introduction of money market deposit accounts in January 1983, this greater importance of interest-rate movements on money demand and velocity can be expected to continue.

It will take time to assess fully the nature of the 1982 shift in money demand and the subsequent decline in velocity. It is clear that the volatile changes of an inflationary environment complicate the conduct of monetary policy. The preceding analysis of money demand suggests that its behavior has not been as inconsistent with past experience as was thought and that it can still serve as a guide for monetary policy. Whether it would be reestablished as a target was an open issue in 1983.

Monetary Growth and Interest Rates. Interest rates rose to very high levels in late 1979 and, except for a large dip in the 1980 recession, remained high until mid-1982 (figure 3). As the inflation rate gradually declined during this period, the high rates translated into extremely high real rates of interest. In the first half of 1982, when Treasury bill rates were 12–13 percent and the bank prime rate was above 16 percent, the fall in the inflation rate to 5–6 percent made the real rate of interest 6–8 percent for bills and 10–11 percent for prime bank loans. Following the business downturn in July 1981, the nominal bill rate fell below 11 percent for only two months and otherwise remained above 12 percent for another year. The persistence of high real short-term rates of interest for so long after a business downturn was unprecedented and, as discussed earlier, could be attributed to distress borrowing by businesses. In addition to the delayed fall in the interest rates in the 1981–1982 recession, their continued high level in nominal terms since the late 1970s and rise in real terms as inflation subsided was unexpected and prompted a variety of explanations.

The explanations most widely advanced for the high interest rates have varied over the period. In 1979 high nominal rates were attributed to fears of escalating inflation following the doubling of oil prices. A rampant inflationary psychology took hold in gold, silver, and commodity markets in February and March 1980 and precipitated a dramatic collapse of the bond market with soaring yields. The panic in financial markets was broken by the imposition of credit controls in mid-March, and interest rates dropped sharply. The rates rapidly recovered, however, reaching new highs in late 1980. When this recovery in rates occurred, even though inflation was clearly subsiding, the explanation shifted to the prospective increase in federal deficits. In

1980 and most of 1981, the prospect of large future deficits could have raised bond yields, but not short-term rates, before the deficits materialized in fourth quarter 1981. Yet large deficits remained the chief explanation for high interest rates, especially after business peaked in July 1981, when the rates could normally have been expected to fall.

It was also said that the variability of monetary growth and interest rates since 1979 had increased uncertainty regarding their future movements, adding a substantial risk premium to the level of rates in real terms.[25] This effect seems unlikely, however. A risk premium typically exists in yields on long-term securities relative to short-term securities to balance the disadvantages to lenders of long-term commitments against the benefits to borrowers of financing long-term capital at a maturity equal to the life of the investment. In contrast, the uncertainty over future inflation rates is a risk to both lenders and borrowers, and which one receives a premium for this risk (and it may be that neither does) depends on the weight each attaches to this disadvantage and to the alternatives. Such uncertainty produces a decline in long-term lending and borrowing, as it did during the 1970s, and long-term rates are determined by borrowers and lenders who remain in this market. Moreover, whatever its effects on long-term rates, it is hard to see why uncertainty would directly affect short-term rates, where unanticipated real capital gains and losses are minor.

The puzzling failure of both long- and short-term interest rates to decline for some time after inflation subsided appears to have reflected a combination of influences rather than a single one. In addition to the distress borrowing noted above, two traditional influences undoubtedly were important. First of all, interest rates generally lagged behind the escalation of inflation in the 1970s and were frequently negative in real terms. At the beginning of the 1980s, therefore, they had some catching up to do. Moreover, given the lagging behavior of rates in the 1970s, it is not surprising to find them lagging behind the reduction in inflation in the 1980s, thus producing high positive real rates as the counterpart of the negative real rates in the 1970s. Although the adjustment of interest rates to inflation, previously quite slow and incomplete for most of the post–World War II period, has speeded up in recent years, it is doubtful that financial markets can make such adjustments without some delay.[26]

A second important influence on interest rates during this period was an upward pressure from monetary tightness, like that which had previously occurred in 1966, 1967, and 1973–1974. Figure 4 shows that the declines in monetary growth in late 1979 and again in late 1980 were associated with increases in interest rates to new highs. This relationship is consistent with a long-noted inverse effect of monetary growth on interest rates.[27] The inverse effect is temporary, of course, and cannot account for all of the increases or for the high average level of intererst rates during the period from October 1979 to July 1982. After the removal of credit controls in May 1980, for example, interest rates rose rapidly to their previous high levels while monetary growth was expanding sharply. These high rates reflected a further adjustment to expectations of higher inflation rates.

The behavior of interest rates in recent years is a dramatic example of how inflation upsets financial markets and thereby further distorts economic activity. Since World War II, short-term intererst rates have typically declined at the onset of a business downturn. After the 1981 downturn, the decline in rates was delayed because of distress borrowing. The illiquid financial condition of many firms, the distress borrowings, and the high interest rates are mutually reinforcing and prolonged the stagnation of the economy. The imposition of disinflation on financial markets that have partially adjusted to high inflation thus sets in motion a reverse adjustment that disrupts the transition to price stability.

Postmortem on the First Stage of Disinflation, 1979–1983, and the Problems to Be Faced in the Second

The renewed determination to subdue inflation, signaled in October 1979 by the adoption of monetary targeting after numerous previous failures with interest-rate targeting, proved successful. By early 1983 the annual inflation rate had fallen below 5 percent, and for the time being a re-escalation appeared unlikely. Further progress in reducing the rate was possible if monetary policy avoided overstimulus.

Yet the success so far had departed from the ideal path of a gradual and steady reduction in monetary growth and the inflation rate; the path indeed had been extremely volatile. An unhelpful experiment with credit controls in early 1980 brought first a sharp contraction in monetary growth and then a sharp reversal, so that by mid-1981 little overall reduction in monetary growth had occurred. The progress against inflation until mid-1981 could be attributed to the tapering off of the oil price increases of 1979. It was the extended decline in monetary growth and economic activity in 1981–1982 that successfully reduced the core rate of inflation. The side effects of this reduction in inflation were that output was virtually flat from 1979 to third quarter 1981 and then declined severely until the end of 1982. These developments largely conformed to prior predictions of the disinflation process and therefore reinforced the view that a painful adjustment cannot be avoided.

The severity of the dislocation to the economy in 1981–1982 was greater than the (stated) intentions of policy makers. Initially, the administration seemed to think the path of disinflation could be smooth and not highly disruptive, and a belief in the importance of policy credibility fostered the optimistic view that market expectations of disinflation would make the process much easier than previous experience suggested. Although disinflation in some prices and wages was enhanced by changes in expectations, these made only a marginal difference at best in reducing the severity of the decline in output.

Other expectational effects ironically made the disinflation more difficult for policy. First, the foreign exchange rates of the dollar appreciated sharply in 1981–1982. This effect could be ascribed to capital inflows from abroad attracted by the rise in interest rates but also, in view of the decline in interest rates in the second half of 1982, by prospects of reduced U.S. inflation. The appreciation of the dollar depressed U.S. exports and, along with high nominal and real interest rates and world recession, substantially increased the burden on heavily indebted countries of servicing their dollar debt. The problem of international debt undoubtedly weighed heavily in the Federal Reserve's decision in mid-1982 to relax the restrictive policy. Second, an upward shift in money demand in 1982, likely due to a change in inflationary expectations, complicated the conduct of monetary policy. The Federal Reserve concluded from this shift that M1 was unreliable as a target and withdrew its commitment to monetary targeting. The very success of a policy of controlling monetary growth thus led to its abandonment.

With recovery from the 1981–1982 recession, the campaign to subdue inflation enters a crucial second stage. The first stage covered the reduction in output from a cut in monetary growth and the underlying inflation rate. The first stage is easy to initiate—simply cut monetary growth—but is difficult to endure. The second stage that began in 1983 can combine a revival of economic growth and productivity with further disinflation, but overstimulus to aggregate demand must be avoided. The second stage calls for steady but moderate growth in the relevant monetary aggregates. It need not be disruptive and is deceptively easier to bear, except that it requires difficult maneuvers by policy to keep recovery on track without reigniting inflationary pressures.

In these maneuvers the Federal Reserve is now hampered by uncertainty regarding the indicators of policy. Interest-rate targeting has been a failure; it requires a stable financial environment that has not yet been reestablished. The intermediate monetary aggregates, such as M2 and M3, are plagued by distortions from shifts in money market balances, and the broader aggregates, such as total liquid assets or debt, are untried. Monetary policy cannot sensibly avoid attention to transactions balances, which the traditional M1 approximates. The analysis here suggests that the distortions in demand for M1 balances were less than was thought. Successful maneuvering through the second stage to achieve monetary stability will require, first, a large reduction in the explosive growth of M1 that began August 1982 and continued through the first half of 1983 and, second, a proper interpretation of M1 behavior and appropriate setting of its growth path for 1984 and later years. Monetary velocity will trend upward as real GNP expands, and could rise even faster if interest-rate differentials increase, thus adding to the stimulus of monetary growth on aggregate demand. If recent years are any guide, the road ahead will be bumpy. What was lacking in past second stages in which recession inroads against inflation were subsequently lost was the conviction that subduing inflation and preventing its reemergence require top priority. Any lower priority has not been enough.

Notes

1. The rates of change in these series and others shown or cited are calculated by a method devised by Geoffrey H. Moore to reduce short-run volatility with a minimum of smoothing. They are calculated by taking the ratio of the current month to an average of the preceding twelve months. The span of the ratio is equivalent to six and one-half months and so is raised to the 12/6.5 power for conversion to an annual rate. For quarterly data in figure 2, the span of the ratio is equivalent to two and one-half quarters and is raised to the 4/2.5 power.

2. Robert J. Gordon, "The Response of Wages and Prices to the First Two Years of Controls," *Brookings Papers on Economic Activity*, 1973, no. 3, pp. 765–78, and Michael Darby, "The U.S. Economic Stabilization Program of 1971–74," in *The Illusion of Wage Price Controls* (Vancouver, B.C.: Fraser Institute, 1976).

3. Dollar spot prices of thirty-five basic commodities exported by primary producing countries, not including gold and petroleum, compiled by the International Monetary Fund.

4. Compiled by the Organization for Economic Cooperation and Development.

5. It may not be a coincidence that the two recessions that broke the momentum of inflation in the 1950s (1957–1958 and 1960–1961) were also separated by a short expansion.

6. From November 1973 to March 1975, as compared with July 1981 to November 1982, the unemployment rate rose 3.7 and 3.5 percentage points, and industrial production fell 13.7 percent and 12.3 percent. Real GNP fell 4.8 percent from fourth quarter 1973 to first quarter 1975 and 3.0 percent from third quarter 1981 to fourth quarter 1982. Capacity utilization in manufactur-

ing, mining, and utilities was 71.1 percent at its lowest in 1975 and was only slightly lower, at 69.6 percent, in November 1982. Even then, utilization started much higher in the earlier cycle and fell more than in 1981–1982. On the other hand, civilian nonfarm employment fell less in the earlier contraction (1.3 percent) than in the later contraction (1.8 percent). For the world economy, however, the later recession was more severe according to most indicators.

7. Similarly, funds raised through bank loans by nonfinancial business, shown in flow-of-funds accounts, increased substantially in the first year of the 1981–1982 recession and were two-thirds greater in the first half of 1982 than in the first half of 1981. In the third quarter of 1982, the increase finally slackened, and in the fourth quarter, funds raised through bank loans by these borrowers declined by $12½ billion at an annual rate. Commercial paper issues of nonfinancial corporations slackened earlier and declined in the final three quarters of 1982.

8. Based on flow-of-funds accounts. Also see article by Murray Foss in this volume.

9. The initial requirement was 8 percent of increases in managed liabilities (mainly large time deposits, Eurodollar borrowings, repurchase agreements, and federal funds borrowed from nonmember institutions) over a base amount. The requirement was raised to 10 percent in April 1980, was reduced to 5 in June, and was eliminated in July.

10. The median forecast made early in 1982 by the professionals surveyed by the American Statistical Association for the final three quarters of 1982 was for 2½ percent annual rate of real GNP growth. The actual figure was a rate of decline of 0.5 percent. (See National Bureau of Economic Research, *NBER Reporter*, summer 1982.) These forecasters also misjudged the strength of the 1983 recovery. The median forecast made in February 1983 for real GNP from fourth quarter 1982 to third quarter 1983 was 3.8 percent (*NBER Reporter*, spring 1983). It was clear by midyear that the recovery would be much stronger.

11. "The Federal Reserve would be short-sighted to abandon a strong sense of discipline in monetary policy in an attempt to bring down interest rates. . . . The more important influence on interest rates—particularly long-term interest rates—is the climate of expectations about the economy and inflation. . . . An effort to drive interest rates lower by the creation of money in excess of longer-run needs and intentions would ultimately fail and would threaten to perpetuate policy difficulties and dilemmas of the past" (Paul A. Volcker, statement before the Joint Economic Committee, June 15, 1982, reprinted in *Federal Reserve Bulletin*, July 1982, p. 408).

12. Paul A. Volcker, speech before the Business Council at Hot Springs, Virginia, October 9, 1982, excerpted in *Federal Reserve Bulletin*, November 1982, pp. 691–92.

13. See Stephen M. Goldfeld, "The Demand for Money Revisited," *Brookings Papers on Economic Activity*, 1973, no. 3, pp. 577–638, and John P. Judd and John L. Scadding, "The Search for a Stable Money Demand Function: A Survey of the Post 1973 Literature," *Journal of Economic Literature*, vol. 20 (September 1982), pp. 993–1023.

14. The average rate on money is negligible until the late 1970s. The rate on savings deposits is an extension of the passbook savings rate used in previous studies. It does not cover the rate on small time deposits, which were increasingly held by households during the 1970s and which began to pay rates competitive with money market funds. Preliminary examination suggests that these high rates paid on small time deposits may have had important effects on the demand for money in recent years, which deserves further study.

15. Goldfeld, "The Demand for Money Revisited," and Judd and Scadding, "The Search for a Stable Money Demand Function." See also Lawrence J. Radecki, *Structural Shift versus Specification Error in the Demand for Money*, Research Paper 8104 (New York: Federal Reserve Bank of New York, February 1981), who uses statistical extrapolations to conclude that a shift occurred in 1974. See also Congressional Budget Office, *Mid-1982 Report*, appendix A, p. 81, which places the shift in second quarter 1974. Robert L. Hetzel ("The Stability of the Demand for Money in the 1970s," typescript [Richmond: Federal Reserve Bank of Richmond, April 1982]) argues for two segments of shifts, however, one downward from third quarter 1966 to third quarter 1972 and a second upward from second quarter 1973 to second quarter 1978.

16. See appendix table A, note regarding the savings deposit shift.

17. See table 3, note regarding the NOW adjustment.

18. Developed by Thomas D. Simpson and Richard D. Porter ("Some Issues Involving the Definition and Interpretation of the Monetary Aggregates," *Controlling Monetary Aggregates III* [Boston: Federal Reserve Bank of Boston, October 1980], pp. 161–234), who test various complex forms of a ratchet rate.

19. John A. Tatom ("Recent Financial Innovations: Have They Distorted the Meaning of M1?" Federal Reserve Bank of St. Louis *Review*, vol. 64 [April 1982], pp. 25–35) also finds that the NOW account adjustment is not needed in view of the behavior of the currency-deposit ratio.

20. The error for equation 4b in table 3 is smaller for this period only because its previous overprediction of real money balances is eliminated by its underprediction in 1982. Its NOW account adjustment does not explain this underprediction.

21. This regression equation is the following, which also includes a dummy for first quarter 1980 to allow for the unusual error produced by the credit controls. It is a refitting of equation 4a of table 3, part 2, first quarter 1955 to first quarter 1983 (t statistics appear without signs in parentheses).

$$\ln \frac{M}{P} = \underset{(5.8)}{.82} + \underset{(9.7)}{.25} \frac{GNP}{P} - \underset{(7.6)}{.10} \ln (r_{SD} - r_M) - \underset{(7.9)}{.02} \ln (r_{SP} - r_M)$$

$$+ \underset{(10.7)}{.57} \ln \left(\frac{M}{P} \right)_{-1}$$

$$- \underset{(8.1)}{.021} \text{ (dummy variable for 1974 III and afterward)}$$

− .028 (dummy variable for 1980 I)
(5.4)

+ .014 (dummy variable for 1982 I and afterward)
(5.0)

Standard error = .0049 DW = 1.97   rho = .18
(1.6)

22. The long-run elasticity of money demand with respect to real GNP implied by the equation in footnote 21 is 0.25/(1 − .57) = 0.58. The predicted long-run trend of velocity is therefore 42 percent of real GNP growth. In past years, interest rates have risen. Consequently, the growth of velocity was higher.

23. Monetary growth was greater over this period if we include RP and ED than if we exclude them (see figure 4), which made the drop in velocity when we include them in figure 5 even greater.

24. The decline also appeared, however, in the velocities of the broader financial aggregates, including total debt. See Richard W. Kopcke, "Must the Ideal 'Money Stock' be Controllable?" *New England Economic Review* (Federal Reserve Bank of Boston), March/April 1983, pp. 10–23, chart 3.

25. See Allan H. Meltzer, "The Results of the Fed's Failed Experiment," *Wall Street Journal*, July 29, 1982, editorial page, and Zvi Bodie, Alex Kane, and Robert McDonald, *Why Are Real Interest Rates So High?* (Cambridge, Mass.: National Bureau of Economic Research, Working Paper 1141, June 1983).

26. See Phillip Cagan, "Two Pitfalls in the Conduct of Anti-inflationary Monetary Policy," in William Fellner, ed., *Contemporary Economic Problems: Demand, Productivity, and Population* (Washington, D.C.: American Enterprise Institute, 1981), pp. 19–52, esp. pp. 37–40.

27. See Phillip Cagan, *The Channels of Monetary Effects on Interest Rates* (New York: National Bureau of Economic Research, 1972).

Appendix

TABLE A
Estimates of Money Demand Equations

Dependent Variable ln M/P, M:	Constant	ln $\frac{GNP}{P}$	ln $(r_{SD} - r_M)$	ln $(r_{SP} - r_M)$	ln $\left(\frac{M}{P}\right)_{-1}$	Dummy Shift Variable 1974 III and Afterward	Ratchet Interest Rate	Rho	Standard Error of Regression	Durbin Watson Statistic
1. Period of fit, 1955 I to 1974 II										
1. M1	0.72 (2.9)	0.20 (3.8)	-0.08 (2.8)	-0.02 (6.3)	0.64 (6.2)			0.37 (2.5)	0.0041	1.85
2. M1 + savings deposit shift	0.72 (2.9)	0.20 (3.8)	-0.08 (2.8)	-0.02 (6.3)	0.64 (6.2)			0.37 (2.5)	0.0041	1.85
3. M1 + RP + ED	0.64 (3.1)	0.21 (4.3)	-0.08 (3.2)	-0.02 (6.9)	0.64 (7.0)			0.26 (1.8)	0.0040	1.88
4. M1 + savings deposit shift + RP + ED	0.64 (3.1)	0.21 (4.3)	-0.08 (3.2)	-0.02 (6.9)	0.64 (7.0)			0.26 (1.8)	0.0040	1.88
2. Period of fit, 1955 I to 1979 III										
1. M1	0.28 (2.5)	0.09 (5.7)	-0.02 (2.3)	-0.02 (7.7)	0.84 (23.4)	-0.02 (6.2)		0.15 (1.4)	0.0045	1.95
2. M1 + savings deposit shift	0.52 (3.3)	0.15 (5.4)	-0.05 (3.3)	-0.02 (8.0)	0.73 (12.5)	-0.02 (5.5)		0.23 (2.1)	0.0044	1.96

3. M1 + RP + ED	0.40 (3.6)	0.14 (7.9)	-0.05 (4.8)	-0.02 (7.9)	0.76 (20.0)	-0.02 (8.0)	0.06 (0.6)	0.0045	1.97
4. M1 + savings deposit + RP + ED	0.59 (3.8)	0.21 (6.4)	-0.08 (4.6)	-0.02 (8.0)	0.66 (10.3)	-0.02 (6.2)	0.21 (1.8)	0.0045	1.96

3. Period of fit, 1955 I to 1979 III

1. M1	-0.02 (0.2)	0.03 (1.7)	0.02 (2.0)	-0.02 (5.1)	0.97 (25.6)	-0.01 (1.6)	0.41 (3.7)	0.0051	2.01
2. M1 + savings deposit shift	0.24 (1.0)	0.07 (2.2)	0.01 (0.3)	-0.02 (5.0)	0.88 (11.7)	-0.02 (1.6)	0.49 (3.7)	0.0050	2.05
3. M1 + RP + ED	0.19 (0.9)	0.07 (2.7)	0.004 (0.3)	-0.01 (3.8)	0.89 (14.3)	-0.02 (1.8)	0.47 (3.8)	0.0054	2.04
4. M1 + savings deposit + RP + ED	0.84 (2.5)	0.20 (3.6)	-0.06 (2.1)	-0.01 (3.2)	0.61 (5.1)	-0.03 (1.9)	0.68 (5.3)	0.0050	2.09

SOURCE AND NOTES: Signs of t statistics have been omitted. Regression fits were made by the Cochrane-Orcutt method, where rho is the coefficient of the lagged error term. All variables are in natural logarithms (ln). M1 is the published version as of March 1983, just as in table 2. The savings deposit shift is the linear interpolation of the following additions to M1: $0.336 billion in June 1975, $9.453 billion in June 1976, and $16,405 billion in June 1977 and thereafter (from "A Proposal for Redefining the Monetary Aggregates," Federal Reserve Bulletin, January 1979, pp. 13–42, table 2). (RP + ED) is overnight repurchase agreements plus Caribbean Eurodollar deposits. GNP is gross national product. P is the implicit deflator for GNP. r_{SD} is a weighted average of rates paid on savings deposits in commercial banks and thrift institutions and on money market mutual funds. r_M is a weighted average of rates paid on "other checkable deposits" and, when included, on RP and ED (rates were kindly supplied by Paul Spindt of the Federal Reserve staff). In earlier quarters some rates are approximations. The variable r_{CP} is the three-month commercial paper rate. Ratchet interest rate is the highest level reached on five-year Treasury securities up to the current quarter since 1955 I (based on Thomas D. Simpson and Richard D. Porter, "Some Issues Involving the Definition and Interpretation of the Monetary Aggregates," Controlling Monetary Aggregates III [Boston: Federal Reserve Bank of Boston, October 1980], pp. 161–234).

Monetary and Fiscal Policy in a Disinflationary Process: Justified and Unjustified Misgivings about Budget Deficits

William Fellner

Summary

*The disappointing experience of recent decades has convinced many econo-
mists that demand policies should be aimed not directly at "real" objectives,
such as employment goals, but at a practically noninflationary average rate of
nominal demand creation during the business cycle. The cost- and price-
setting practices in the markets can adjust to such a policy at normal levels of
resource utilization. A consistent and credible policy of this type can be guided
over shorter periods by money-supply target ranges, and it can condition
market expectations to noninflationary demand management. This is the case
even if, after many years of inflationary experience, no policy of disinflation
can avoid the difficulties of a transition period during each stage of which the
level of resource utilization remains subnormal by the usual standards applicable to that stage of the business cycle. The essential point here is that
authorities directing their policies consistently at nominal demand creation
can make it clear to the market participants that the behavior of the real
magnitudes in the economy will depend on how well the cost- and price-
setting practices of the market participants fall in line with the policy objectives.*

*This study starts out by contrasting a policy line so described with past
policies generating the expectation that, for the sake of growth and employment objectives, the authorities will accommodate inflationary processes. Inflation has proved stimulative only as long as its acceleration was accommodated; and since this cannot be done without major interruptions, the actual*

For clarifying the subject matter of this study in my own thinking, I found discussions
with Professor Phillip Cagan, with Mr. Eduardo Somensatto, and with Miss Maryam
Homayouni very helpful, and I am indebted to Miss Homayouni also for help in
carrying out the research itself. On the role of Mr. Somensatto in the project in general,
see the introduction to this volume.

result of these policies was the now-notorious "stop and go," resulting in a generally poor performance of the economy.

From this problem the study turns to the role of monetary and of fiscal policy in bringing about the needed disinflation. Whereas the assumptions underlying the approaches nowadays labelled as "Keynesian" lead in many respects to different conclusions from those usually labelled as "quantity theoretical" (or monetarist), both types of approach suggest that normally the effects on nominal demand of budget deficits as well as those of an enlargement of the money supply will prove expansionary. As will be seen in this chapter, it is possible to formulate specific assumptions on which budget deficits would restrain rather than stimulate nominal demand, but these are not the assumptions that normally prove realistic. The question whether any given additional nominal demand is generated by a larger increase in the money supply and a smaller budget deficit (even a surplus) or is generated alternatively by a lesser increase in the money supply and a larger deficit exerts a significant influence on the composition of output, that is, on the consumption-investment mix. The negative effect of deficits on private investment develops through an effect of the deficits on real rates of interest.

In principle the maximum level the deficit could reach without either debt-repudiation through legislative measures or repudiation in real terms through inflation is set by the gross savings that are available for being diverted from investment to deficit-financing. But essential difficulties connected with the reduction of productive investment would start developing at a much earlier stage.

The investment-reducing effect of deficits for any given aggregate nominal demand has often been crudely overstated in presentations taking no account of the possibility that savings as usually defined may well increase in circumstances in which deficits grow to a large size. The qualifications deserving serious consideration have to do in large part with the changes in saving ratios brought about by revaluations of the public's real net worth that have in fact accompanied our deficits. An analysis of the problem of how deficits, and thus the "monetary-fiscal mix," affect investment therefore leads into an examination of the more general problem of the effect on savings of the revaluation of the asset-and-liability positions of households. That analysis is here followed by a discussion of the extent to which capital inflows may also reduce the effect of deficits on domestic capital formation.

While the factors qualifying the investment-reducing effect of budget deficits are not of negligible importance, my specific quantitative appraisals will lead to the conclusion that the qualifying factors are far too weak to carry the main thrust of the argument. The main thrust of the argument is carried by the statement that given the nominal income of an economy—that is, given a monetary policy that offsets any additional expansionary or restraining effect of fiscal policy—deficits do channel savings away from investment. If, therefore, at the present writing the deficits estimated for future years are considered to be of troublesome size—a view to which I subscribe, along with many other economists—then these misgivings must be based on the judgment that it is undesirable to finance government expenditures by methods that are particularly apt to reduce productive investment. This is, indeed, a widely held judgment, but if this is the reason for attempting to reduce the estimated deficits of "good years" in our future cyclical sequences, then the measures taken for achieving this objective should be directed at tilting the consumption-investment mix back toward investment. Insofar as these measures need to be additional taxes, they should be broadly based consumption taxes.

The Relation of Money-Supply Target Ranges to Desirable Nominal Demand Objectives

The main objective of a demand policy conscious of the dangers of creating the inefficiencies of an inflationary environment is to achieve nominal demand creation at the appropriate rate over the cycle. This is a rate to which it is useful to gear market expectations and thereby the cost- and price-setting practices in the markets. It is a rate of demand creation that leaves room for a normal average growth rate of output over cycles as a whole at an approximately stable price level.

A policy so oriented differs essentially from a demand policy that aims directly for desirable real-growth and employment levels. It differs essentially from policies based on what for a while had become the neo-Keynesian orthodoxy in postwar macroeconomics—an approach in which the conception of a long-run Phillips trade-off between inflation and output loomed large. The assumptions underlying that approach have not stood up well at all, because inflationary policies cannot be kept stimulative for more than a very limited period. The reason is that after a while market expectations catch up with the intentions of the authorities, and, hence, the inflationary stimulus can be kept up only by accommodating an unexpected steepening of inflation. This cannot be done for long unless the process is to get out of hand at an early stage. Thus, a policy oriented toward a long-run trade-off between inflation and output (or employment) inevitably results in harmful stop-and-go sequences around steepening inflation and usually also along a rising unemployment rate. Such a policy can by now safely be said to have *failed*, at least in countries in which the political authority lacks the powers to enforce a comprehensive system of direct wage and price controls. The United States is fortunate enough to belong in this category of countries. We thus have experienced a renewal of interest among economists and other observers in a demand policy that attempts to condition market expectations and cost and price trends to nominal demand creation at a rate compatible with practically noninflationary normal growth. The market participants would then be aware that the outcome in real terms depends on their own behavior, given a reasonably predictable line of demand policy that generates nominal demand at a noninflationary rate.

No reasonable person could expect the transition from an inflationary era to practical price stability to be completed without an intervening period of uncomfortable adjustments. The question this raises at the level of politics is whether during the adjustment period the policy makers will be capable of resisting the temptation to resort to direct wage and price controls. As long as the political institutions work by and large the way in which ours have been working, such direct controls would prove counterproductive even by their own standards (which, of course, are not those of market economies). The political-institutional changes required for making them effective are exceedingly uncomfortable to contemplate. Wage and price controls that are "effective" (by their own standards) require a political system in which the central authority is powerful enough to enforce them.

It is occasionally suggested that instead of relying on wage and price controls proper, a demand policy directed at "real" objectives could be supplemented with tax rewards and penalties for inducing a general wage trend corresponding to guidelines compatible with general price stability. This policy, however, has all the characteristics of an unpromising device. In the first place, it is unlikely that market participants would respond positively to such financial incentives instead of assuming that a policy of this sort will accommodate inflationary cost developments, including the tax penalties, in an effort to achieve its real objectives. To the extent that the public might nevertheless respond to the incentives and behave according to the cost guidelines, the policy would introduce a substantial degree of rigidity into the cost and price *structure* of the economy. Such a policy would do this during a disinflationary transition period, the success of which depends crucially on structural adjustments within the general cost and price system. Involved devices for getting around this difficulty have been discussed, but in the appraisal of most economists, including myself, they are unrealistic.

The view here expressed suggests that a monetary authority attempting to disinflate after an inflationary era and thereafter to establish practically noninflationary normal growth needs to aim consistently for nominal demand objectives with which the cost trends generated by intelligent market participants will have to fall in line. In the United States, for example, it would be reasonable to aim for approximately *a 5 percent average annual increase of nominal GNP over cycles as a whole,* after completion of the disinflationary adjustment process.

Nominal demand is not, however, well suited to guiding the short-run routine operations of the monetary authority, because movements in nominal demand are very strongly influenced by the course of the business cycle. It would be an overambitious undertaking to try to "fine-tune" the policy operations in the sense of trying to suppress the cyclical variations of velocity and the nominal demand variations associated with it. Once one takes for granted cyclical variations of the velocity of money—or of the reciprocal of velocity, that is, of the money demand per unit of expenditures—it becomes inadvisable to specify nominal GNP targets over *short* intervals during each cycle.

This is the justification for specifying money-supply target ranges, that is, target ranges in terms of M aggregates. Specifying target *ranges* rather than rigid targets for these aggregates, ranges within which we may move in view of the variations of velocity, expresses a compromise between complete abstention from efforts to compensate for velocity variations (as would be implied in rigid money targets) and a commitment to efforts at systematic compensation for such variations (as would be implied in short-term nominal GNP targets). Given the limitations of our knowledge concerning serial correlations and policy lags, it does seem reasonable to choose such a compromise.

The Dilemma Caused by the Behavior of Velocity in 1982

As I have stressed on other occasions, consistency of the disinflationary monetary policy in spite of the difficulties of the adjustment process is crucial to establishing the credibility of a policy that depends on its credibility for success. Such a policy can achieve its purpose only if it succeeds in conditioning market expectations and thereby in decisively influencing cost trends at satisfactory levels of activity. Even those of us taking a strong position on consistency and credibility should admit, however, that at a rather early stage of the recent adjustment effort—during the recession year 1982—policy makers became faced with difficulties calling for the balancing of various considerations. This year, intended to fall in the transition period from high inflation *toward* practically noninflationary conditions, brought an extraordinarily large downward deviation of velocity from its usual course.

From the cyclical peak year 1953 to the peak year 1979 (five cycles later), the average annual compound rate of increase of the GNP velocity of $M1$ was 3.1 percent. Within this span the lowest peak-to-peak average yearly growth rate during any cycle as a whole was 2.5 percent, the highest 3.8 percent. The *maximum* yearly deviation from the 3.1 percent long-term velocity growth rate occurred in the first of the five cycles that developed in this period[1]—hence, a long time ago—and that maximum yearly velocity deviation was 4.7 percentage points. Until very recently all other yearly deviations were very much smaller. Yet for 1982 the deviation from the 3.1 rate was a downward deviation in excess of 8 percent—a deviation of record height. High downward deviations developed in 1982 also for the velocity of other M aggregates.

While consistency and credibility of the conduct of monetary policy are indeed essential conditions of success, it must not be overlooked that all target *ranges* for money creation are set by policy makers *with the usual ranges of velocity variations in mind*. This is so despite the fact that a policy of target ranges is not pursued with a pretense that enough is known about serial correlations and policy lags to undertake systematic compensatory efforts successfully. Yet, the unusually large velocity deviations of 1982 lasting into 1983 created conditions significantly different from those the authorities had reason to expect when setting their target ranges for the year. This had to do *inter alia* with institutional changes and deregulation which made it possible to earn interest on deposits carrying checking privileges.

That the Federal Reserve exceeded its 1982 M targets in these circumstances is not, in itself, objectionable to me. What I do regard as regrettable and potentially very damaging, however, is that the authorities have not made a more convincing effort to relate their behavior to the objective of gradually reducing the increase of nominal GNP to a noninflationary rate. Determination to achieve this objective within a span of several years should have been expressed forcefully, regardless of the unusual behavior of velocity. I expressed this criticism earlier, and I continue to consider it a valid proposition that deserves to be emphasized. But in the present context I should repeat also my conviction that circumstances do exist in which it is reasonable to engage in more velocity-compensating monetary-policy action in one or the other direction than is created by the normally sufficient money-target ranges. In other words, circumstances do exist in which it is advisable to widen the ranges beyond the limits within which money creation should *usually* remain.

Thinking one's way through the possibilities suggests that the proper interpretation of the case for deviating upward in 1982 would have led to expressing the intention of returning subsequently to the course of gradually declining money-growth rate targets with the possibility left open that the past upward deviations may have to be offset by a substantial downward deviation. I do not feel that the official pronouncements would so far have been consistent with this diagnosis, which implies that behind money targeting there is the objective of moving with perceptible speed toward noninflationary demand creation. The official pronouncements often give the undesirable impression that the authorities primarily have in mind a continued and appreciable upward deviation from the earlier contemplated money-growth target ranges.[2] But at the present writing it is not yet too late to establish a credible line of monetary policy leading gradually to noninflationary growth.

Summary of Two Propositions to Be Justified in the Subsequent Two Sections

We have not yet considered the question whether authorities using the money supply as a means of influencing nominal demand should consider the emergence of large budget deficits as an expansionary (demand-raising) or a contractionary (demand-reducing) factor. This chapter will develop an argument from which two propositions can be derived, and each will be outlined quite briefly in this section. These two propositions need to be stressed because of the disillusionment with macroeconomic propositions on which inflationary posture policies were based. This disillusionment is fully justified when directed at the long-term trade-off between inflation and employment, but by now doubts have arisen in many minds about the content of macroeconomic theory in general, including other conventional propositions of much older standing. In regard to the two propositions—(a) and (b)—to which we now turn, these doubts are on the whole unfounded; or, at least, they could acquire importance only in exceptional circumstances.

(a) First, not only is it true on any reasonable set of assumptions that expanding the money supply is expansionary in terms of nominal demand (and vice versa), but it is also true that on normal macroeconomic assumptions—expressed *either* in "Keynesian" *or* in "quantity theoretical" terminology—deficits are *expansionary*. In other words, with respect to aggregate demand, deficits work in the same direction as an increased money supply. This is true as long as our reasoning moves on what deserve to be regarded as normal macroeconomic assumptions. Hence, on these assumptions a contradiction exists between two fears that some critics of disinflationary programs have recently been expressing: First, the fear of these critics that, in terms of aggregate demand objectives, monetary policy had been too restrictive, and second their fear that in terms of the same objectives, our prospective deficits are too large. To be sure, it is possible to argue that if one goes through the content of these arguments with some care, one is apt to arrive at the conclusion that even more faith deserves to be placed in the normal macroeconomic assumptions concerning the expansionary consequences of an increased money supply than in the analogous "normal" assumptions concerning the expansionary consequences of deficits. At least in my appraisal, a difference in degree does exist in this regard, but, even as concerns the expansionary demand-effects of deficits, the circumstances in which there is reason to modify the usual assumptions should be regarded as distinctly exceptional. The proposition that deficits are expansionary in terms of nominal demand deserves to retain its place among the standard propositions of macroeconomics (none of which is, after all, valid in literally *all* conceivable cases unless it is a truism). This problem will be further discussed later in this chapter.

(b) We now turn to the second proposition to be outlined in the present section and elaborated upon subsequently. Even in analysis based on normal macroeconomic assumptions—including the assumption that both an enlarged money supply and an increased deficit tend to *raise* nominal demand—it is essential to bear in mind that the composition of the output will be tilted more toward consumption, that is, away from investment, if the same aggregate demand develops with a larger deficit and tighter money than the other way around. This is the conclusion derived from the normal (usual) macroeconomic assumptions, and here again it needs to be understood that while any straightforward, simple reasoning based on these assumptions is indeed subject to qualifications, a reasonable policy needs to be based on the normal assumptions rather than on the qualifications. This problem will be discussed in the sections following those concerned with the overall expansionary effects, which on normal assumptions develop not only from an increased money supply but also from deficits.

The "Conventional" or "Normal" Assumptions Concerning the Demand Effects of Money Creation

The normal macroeconomic assumptions on which we may conclude that raising the money supply will increase nominal GNP (and reducing the money supply will have the opposite effect) include all assumptions other than those postulating that the demand for money is infinitely elastic to interest rates. This latter exceptional case is that in which Keynesian liquidity preference is "absolute," and the economy therefore finds itself in the "liquidity trap."

How much importance Keynes attributed to "absolute" liquidity preference continues to be a controversial question in the history of economic thought. My own inclination is to interpret the Keynes of the *General Theory* as having visualized absolute liquidity preference as what might well describe the typical long-run situation of advanced

Western economies at some future date—quite possibly a future date lying not very far out in the future when seen from the vantage point of the mid-1930s. This prediction seemed unconvincing to many of us even at that time, but it would be unfair to interpret Keynes as asserting that absolute liquidity preference was the normal situation in which Western economies found themselves in his own time. Even as concerns his own time, however, he did make allowances for the occurrence and recurrence of absolute liquidity preference (the "liquidity trap") in adverse phases of cyclical development—perhaps depending on what kind of business-cycle policy would be adopted in these various cyclical phases.

Only in the circumstances in which an economy is caught in the liquidity trap will an increase (decrease) in the money supply result in no increase (decrease) in nominal demand for goods and services but exclusively in an increase (decrease) of money held per unit of expenditure. In quantity-theoretical terminology this is expressed as a situation in which all changes in the money supply carry with them fully offsetting changes of velocity in the opposite direction.

To argue that recent American experience points to the existence of this condition would be very unconvincing. As Keynes has rightly argued, this condition requires that the purchase of additional securities by the monetary authority should not have an effect on interest rates that would make it more rewarding to investors to borrow and invest. This would be the case if the rate of interest had already declined to a floor level, giving the owners of securities merely the required compensation for the risk of a decline in security prices. In that case the security purchases of the monetary authority would lead the public merely to substituting money holdings for security holdings but not to making additional investment expenditures.

Even on the assumption that rates of interest had already declined to a floor level below which risk considerations prevent them from declining, this reasoning leaves some questions unanswered. But the main point here is that the recent record of the American short-term rates includes rates on three-month Treasury bills consistently exceeding any reasonable short-term inflation estimate by several percentage points. This would make it exceedingly unconvincing to argue that, because of the risk of the decline of security prices, additional security purchases of the monetary authority could not have reduced the real short rates, and thus would not have led to additional borrowing and spending and to additional nominal demand creation but merely to the accumulation of additional "idle" money deposits. The additional security purchases in question might very well have led to rising *nominal* rates of interest. Yet this result clearly would not have occurred by inducing the public to accumulate more idle deposits but, on the contrary, by generating additional expenditures and a steepening of the trend of the nominal GNP.

A brief way of summarizing this analysis is to state that as concerns the effect of money creation on nominal demand we can safely place confidence in the normal macroeconomic assumptions. These point to the conclusion that additional money creation steps up the rate of nominal GNP and that reducing the rate of increase of the money supply restrains the nominal GNP. To *what extent* changes in the money supply affect nominal demand remains a question of movements in velocity or in its reciprocal (that is, in the ratio of money holdings to expenditures). We have seen that concerning the behavior of velocity from completed business cycle to completed business cycle, certain regularities have come through rather well over a number of cycles since the Korean War, though the unusual behavior of velocity in 1982, which continued into 1983, created the difficulty discussed earlier in this study. What needs to be stressed in the present context, however, is that one would have to go out of one's way in making unconvincing assumptions if one wanted to deny that by raising or by reducing the rate of money creation a larger or a smaller rate of demand generation can be achieved. In this regard qualifications of the normal macroeconomic assumptions deserve practically no attention.

The "Conventional" or "Normal" Assumptions Concerning the Expansionary Effect of Deficits

The normal macroeconomic assumptions also stand up well concerning the effect of budget deficits on aggregate nominal demand, given the money supply, though in this regard I would pay somewhat more attention to possible exceptions. The normal assumptions suggest that, given the supply of money, deficit per se tends to *raise* nominal demand.

In Keynesian terminology this is expressed by attaching a positive multiplier to government expenditures, and by recognizing that no offset results from reduced after-tax income when the government expenditure represents deficit spending. Indeed, on specific assumptions even the balanced budget multiplier has been shown to be unitary rather than zero.[3]

In quantity-theoretical terminology, given the supply of money, deficit spending has a nominal demand-raising effect because it increases the velocity of money by increasing the quantity of money-substitutes available to the public. This is often expressed in terms of the interest-elasticity of the demand for money, in which case the proposition focuses on the fact that supplying more government securities raises interest rates. Hence in this analytical framework it may also be argued that given the money supply, even tax-financed government expenditures are apt to be demand-raising, through the interest-raising effect of the taxing of funds that would be partly saved. At higher interest rates it becomes more profitable to accept the transactions costs and risks of moving in and out of security markets over time intervals that at lower interest rates would be too short to justify such an in-and-out policy.

In the analysis of the demand for money—hence, of velocity—attempts to explore measurable effects of interest rates along these lines have led to quantitative estimates that proved useful for some periods but misleading for others. A broader proposition is, however, undeniably appealing, and it too implies a process working through interest-rate effects. The broader proposition whose claim to general reasonableness is indeed strong can be expressed by stating that greater abundance of interest-bearing securities convertible into money at any moment—convertible with practically no risk of default or of capital loss—is apt to induce the owners of such securities to hold less money per unit of their incomes and expenditures. On normally valid assumptions, deficits reduce investment relative to consumption; but, given the money supply, they have an expansionary effect in terms of aggregate demand.

To mention first an exception raised by some participants in recent debates, *future* deficits may increase the *present* long-term real rates of interest because, unless the present rates rise, the buyers of long-term securities are not compensated for a capital loss they expect to suffer as a result of a future rise of the rates. This means that the negative demand-effect on investment develops "now"—and, indeed, a recession may develop "now"—while the positive demand-effect of the government expenditures will develop merely at some future date.

If not carried further, this *objection* to the conventional reasoning about the positive demand-effect of deficits—this *turning around* of the conventional conclusions—fails to explain why in the assumed environment the present short real rates should also rise to unusually high levels as has in fact been the case in the environment in which some participants in the contemporary debates started referring to the potentially demand-reducing *present* effect of *future* deficits. On the assumptions just outlined, the lenders would be unwilling to acquire long-term securities except at high real rates at which the loan-demand of borrowers is as yet small, but this does not explain why, in order to overcome the preference of lenders for idle money deposits, the real rates on Treasury bills and other short-term securities also have to rise to high levels. The lenders have no reason to expect noteworthy capital losses on three-month Treasury bills and the like;

and in the environment so described, one would therefore expect short-term real rates to be at very low levels, *while this has clearly not been the case in the environment in which this qualification of the normal assumptions has recently been injected into the debate.*

Another argument pointing to the unconventional conclusion that budget deficits may turn out to be demand-reducing could be based on the proposition that the classical economists—believers in Say's law—presumably had in mind when suggesting that partial overproduction may acquire the symptoms of general overproduction (without being that). To support this proposition in the present context it is not necessary to draw a sharp distinction between future and present deficits but merely to take account of the fact that our deficits have been rising. Once we take account of this fact and remember that deficits channel savings away from investment by a mechanism involving higher real rates of interest, we need to recognize that higher deficits become associated with additional structural shifts. Not only are resources shifted from the investment goods, as usually defined, to other goods, but also from industries whose products are largely acquired on credit to industries not falling in this category. Large resource shifts from specific sectors to others may degenerate into general economic underutilization because of the intervening lags, which market expectations *can* but *need not always* prevent from resulting in the underutilization of resources *in general.* It is possible to develop a logically tenable argument along these lines. What such an argument plays down, however, is the fact that Western economies have, on the whole, a remarkably good record of overcoming the difficulties caused by needs to rearrange the structure of production.

I think it fair to suggest the following summary. Essentially indefensible assumptions are required for denying the validity of the conventional conclusion that in our present environment aggregate demand is increased by money creation and is decreased by reduced money creation. Somewhat more attention deserves to be paid to the assumption required for denying the validity of the conventional conclusion that, given the money supply, deficits increase nominal demand. Yet, on further reflection, in our present circumstances the high, real, short rates weaken one version of the argument pointing in the unconventional direction of deficit-induced depressive effects. These rates weaken the version stressing possible depressive effects of future deficits. And the other version, stressing the possibility that adjustment lags turn partial overproduction into substantial general underutilization, is significantly weakened by most phases of modern Western economic history, which point to a high degree of adjustability of the structure of production.

The Monetary-Fiscal Mix: Do Deficits Absorb Savings Despite Revaluations of Real Net Worth?

A proposition stated in the preceding section and now to be analyzed in some detail hinges on the assumption that a public acquiring the government securities resulting from deficits interprets these security acquisitions as part of its net savings serving the desired purpose of increasing the saver's real net worth. The proposition that hinges on the assumption of a perceived increase of the public's real net worth when it acquires additional government securities is the proposition that deficits reduce investment relative to consumption. In the analysis of this proposition it is advisable to take the aggregate demand (rather than the money supply) as given, that is, to assume that any expansionary effect that deficits would have at a given money supply is *compensated by tightening the money supply.* If this assumption is made, the proposition that budget deficits reduce investment *relative to consumption* automatically becomes simplified to the proposition that deficits reduce investment—channel savings away from investment—since by assuming the aggregate demand as given we avoid *merging* the problem of the adverse specific effect of deficits on investment with their expansionary effect on demand for all goods.[4] What the proposition we are now considering amounts to is that the composition of any given output by consumption and investment goods depends on whether a given increase in demand along the growth path of the economy is brought about by a more expansionary monetary policy and by a smaller deficit (greater surplus) or vice versa. This is the proposition that hinges on a perceived increase of the public's net worth when it buys government securities.

Deficits cannot simply be said to divert savings away from investment—and the monetary-fiscal mix cannot, therefore, have the effect just described—if the public fails to regard the acquisition of the deficit-induced addition to the government security holdings as resulting in an increase in its real net worth. In that case the public does not perceive these security acquisitions as achieving the purpose for the sake of which savings are made. Even in that case, however, the acquisitions in question do enter into the public's "savings," as these are conventionally defined (that is, into after-tax income minus consumption). Why we should limit ourselves here to *personal* savings will be explained in the section beginning on page 73.

Situations in which the public does not regard the government securities reflecting the deficits as representing an increase in its net worth have two characteristics in common. In the first place, the public does not, in these situations, regard the deficit-financed government expenditures as public "investment" yielding the corresponding flow of future yields. This goes without saying, and I will from here on take it for granted that we are concerned with deficit-financed government expenditures such as are not in the nature of equivalent capital formation in the public sector.

Second, situations in which the public does not regard the government securities reflecting such deficits as increments to its real net worth also have the characteristic that the positive effect on net worth of asset accumulations in the form of these securities is, in the public's perception, associated with an offsetting (or canceling) *net-worth diminishing* effect. It would be wrong to assume that whenever the deficit-financed government spending is not in the nature of public investment, the buyers of the government securities will always interpret their purchases of these securities as being associated with an offsetting (or canceling) downward revaluation of real net worth. But in the event that in the public's perception the positive effect on net worth of asset accumulations in the form of government securities *is* associated with an offsetting downward revaluation of the public's real net worth, then the public increases other savings correspondingly. This is why, in that case, the deficits will not, on balance, channel savings away from investments.

In other words, personal savings as conventionally defined—the difference between disposable income and consumption—include the acquisition of government securities. Savings as conventionally defined are apt to increase if the public associates deficits with a perceived downward revaluation of the buyers' accumulated *real* net asset positions. For the same reason, savings are apt to decrease if the public associates deficits with a perceived net upward revaluation of the buyers' accumulated *real* net asset position. Revaluations reflecting merely the rise of the general price level—say of the PCE deflator—have approximately the same proportionate effect on the current-dollar value of disposable income as on that of consumption and that of net worth.[5] Hence, revaluations reflecting merely the rise of the general price level cannot be expected to have any major effect on the relation of income to wealth or to savings. We shall also disregard in this discussion any increase in domestic savings that *may* be brought about by a deficit-induced increase in interest rates. Higher interest rates involving more future income per unit of present income *may*, on balance, have this consequence despite the fact that they also make the same future income available from reduced savings (and this latter effect, considered by itself, works in the savings-reducing direction). We shall not try to weigh these two effects and to estimate the net effect that may develop in one of the two directions.

However, the considerations to which we have referred call attention to the effect on savings of *asset-liability revaluations,* and within this category to revaluations that are "real" in the sense that they *exceed or fall short of the revaluations corresponding to changes in the general price level,* as measured by the PCE deflators. Note that when so defined, real revaluations of net worth from any year to the next—that is, *to* the year for which we wish to observe the effect of these revaluations and of other explanatory variables—are expressed each time in terms of the prices of the second of the two years (not in the prices of an arbitrarily chosen base year). The analysis directs attention to the question whether introducing these real revaluations of net worth into regressions relating consumer outlay to disposable income improves that relation. Consumer outlay and disposable income are each time expressed in the prices of the same year as our revaluations. I have not tried to identify the effect on consumption of the level of wealth itself, or of the ratio of net worth to disposable income, in addition to trying to identify the effect of real revaluations of net worth. From the mid-1950s to the end of the 1970s or to the early 1980s—the span with which we will be largely concerned—the ratio of the net worth of households to their disposable income declined moderately (from 3.7 to 3.3 when we compare 1982 with 1954).[6]

In the preceding pages we had reason for raising the relevant question in this form: Have the processes that have led to the direct or indirect ownership by the public of additional government securities at the same time resulted also in a *perceived real downward revaluation of the public's accumulated net worth,* and have these processes therefore led the public to save a correspondingly larger proportion of their incomes in the usual sense of the word "saving"? Should we therefore conclude that to this extent deficits do not "channel away" savings from investment?[7]

We shall now examine two lines of argument suggesting why negative effects on net real asset positions (downward revaluations) may in fact accompany deficit financing. Along these lines of argument it has been suggested that the deficit-induced "channeling away" of savings from private investment is *wholly* (according to one argument) or *partially* (according to the other) *avoided.* A discussion of these two lines of argument follows in the next two sections.

This deliberately leaves aside the question whether from the domestic point of view any channeling-away that does nevertheless take place via the interest-rate mechanism is not largely offset by a capital inflow from abroad. To that question I will return later. This is, of course, a different question from that to which we turn in the next two sections, namely, the question whether deficit financing becomes associated with an increase in the saving rate.

The two suggested reasons for an increase of the saving rate—this kind of offset—will now be discussed in succession.

Tax Liabilities as Offsets: The Equivalence Theorem

It is, of course, a valid proposition that government securities have not merely an "asset" aspect but also a "liability" aspect. Already David Ricardo called attention to the fact that it is possible to formulate rationality assumptions from which it would follow that the buyers of government securities do not regard these as an addition to their net wealth. The essential point in his argument was that in the event of deficit financing, the discounted value of the future flow of tax liabilities created by the government debt equals the tax liability that in the event of tax financing would develop "now." A logical case can therefore be made for the *equivalence* of debt financing with tax financing where the latter, by reducing disposable income, reduces *mainly* consumption rather than savings.[8]

Another way of putting it is to say that the present value of additional future tax liabilities cancels the addition to wealth created by the government securities representing the deficits. Along these lines one might thus place the emphasis on the fact that the deficit financing under consideration creates no net wealth for a nation as a whole, and, given this point of departure, one may then conjecture that this fact must carry over into the perception of the wealth-holding public. From these premises one may, in turn, arrive at the conclusion that the amount of "savings" (in the conventional sense of this term) that goes into government securities will not displace any investment but will, instead, give rise to correspondingly more other savings such as are *true* net savings in the sense of not being offset by the present value of additional tax liabilities.

Ricardo was, however, aware of the dependence of these propositions on intergenerational transfers. The tax liabilities in question will in large part be borne by future generations, and to say that the present generation's assets consisting of government-security holdings are offset by tax liabilities therefore implies that the present generation will increase its bequests correspondingly in order to leave its heirs as well off as they would be if the tax burden had been imposed on the present generation. Ricardo did not believe that the required conditions were satisfied in the real world. After developing the argument underlying the equivalence theorem, he thus expressed the view that the theorem would lead to unrealistic conclusions.[9]

Indeed, it takes no stretching of one's imagination to describe situations in which the required intergenerational conditions are not satisfied. To use a few strong illustrations: Some may plan to leave nothing to the next generation when that generation is assumed not to be burdened by additional taxes. Some also may leave nothing when the presumption develops that it will be burdened by the taxes corresponding to a present deficit, though they might well have made a bequest if the future tax burden were expected to become even larger than it is expected to become. Others might leave a bequest with the possibility in mind that their heirs will turn out to belong in the tax-exempt, low-income group; and they might not increase their bequest merely because the present deficits will increase a tax burden imposed upon their heirs if these should turn out to belong in higher income groups. Again, others might attribute a high probability to an indefinite postponement of the tax burden—a postponement beyond present horizons—due to the possibility of servicing the debt by future borrowing, as long as the interest burden does not continue to absorb an ever increasing proportion of output and income.[10.]

To put it briefly: It is a valid but in the present context inconclusive proposition that, whenever deficit-financed government spending does not lead to capital formation in the public sector, the "savings" placed in government securities are not part of the flow of net savings from the viewpoint of a country as a whole. True though this is, it is inconclusive in the present context because the concept of a country as a whole merges the creditor with the debtor positions of different generations, and of individuals with different incomes within each generation. Hence, the fact that as a result of such merging the number of dollars *owned* and *owed* will wash out for an "immortal" country as a whole does not imply that the *effects* of the *owning* and those of the *owing* will wash out. Belief in the intelligence of a well-informed public does not in itself create a presumption that the behavioral results of asset acquisitions by specific individuals in specific generations will be offset by the burden that arises to other individuals in other generations through the service charges of the numerically equivalent debt. And as for the strength of evidence derivable from empirical approaches, to these the orders of magnitude are unfavorable. Quantitatively the problem tends to get lost in a much larger complex of problems.

So far we have been concerned with the problem of the effect on savings of those specific revaluations of real net worth that develop from deficit-induced future tax liabilities. This is merely one element within a large set of problems. That large set can be described as the *effect on savings* of the revaluations of real net worth in general.[11]

Why is it difficult quantitatively to identify within this broader problem the problem of the effect on savings of deficit-induced future tax liabilities?

In the first place the post–Korean War period includes a long span—1953 to 1973—during which the cumulated change in the real value of the government securities as assets, and thus of the public debt as a liability, is reduced to small size by the inflationary downward revaluation of the real worth of these assets and of the corresponding liabilities.[12] In these circumstances it does not seem promising to try to devise a method by which it would be possible to identify the effects of any awareness on the part of the public that the assets aspect of the government securities is offset by the liabilities aspect of the debt. During these two decades the rising trend of the price level was a good enough offset to any growth of the significance of the assets aspect, and this was a powerful offset even for a public that may have been uninfluenced by speculations about the future tax liabilities developing from the debt and thus may not have regarded such liabilities as offsets. Attributing the role of offsets to both these factors would obviously result in double counting.

For more recent spans, such as that extending from the cyclical peak year 1973 to the peak year 1979, we do observe a more significant increase in the aggregate real value of the public debt and of the corresponding liabilities. This is so regardless of how these magnitudes are defined within reasonable limits. Hence for the 1973–1979 period, more pronounced difference exists between the assumption on the one hand that the public regarded merely the inflationary reduction of the real value of government securities as an offset to these asset-acquisitions and the assumption on the other hand that, along the lines of the equivalence theorem, the public regarded the value of the assets represented by the government securities as *fully* offset by prospective tax liabilities. We shall soon see, however, that for the cyclical peak-to-peak period 1973–1979, a significant *decline* of the saving ratios is observed as compared with earlier periods, which is the contrary of what the equivalence theorem leads one to expect for a period of rapidly rising real public indebtedness. The data to which I am referring do not, of course, provide conclusive evidence against the effect of perceived future tax liabilities on savings, because the comparisons to which I referred are not based on any adequate control of a number of other potentially important explanatory variables. Yet it remains noteworthy that the significant reduction of the saving ratio observed for the recent period of high deficits needs to be "explained away" in any reasoning developed along the lines of the equivalence theorem, and there comes a point at which such efforts become increasingly less convincing when the hypothesis stressing the role of perceived future taxes is one whose inherent weaknesses were recognized already by Ricardo.

At any rate, more definite statements can be made about the *gen-*

eral problem of the effects on saving rates of real net-worth revaluations in general to which we now turn. Some effects belonging in the category of general revaluation effects have, to be sure, all along developed from government securities that remain fixed in nominal value and hence are revalued downward in real terms when the price level rises. But this is merely part of a much more comprehensive problem of real net-worth revaluations when this problem is posed in a manageable way. Posing the revaluation problem in a manageable way implies disregarding the intractable question of what the public's guesses might conceivably be about future tax liabilities developing from present deficits.

When this intractable question is disregarded, we are left with a problem for the analysis of which data are available, namely, the problem of the year-to-year revaluation in real terms—revaluation relative to movements in the general price levels—of assets and liabilities for which we have estimates based on observed developments in markets. Inflation clearly does place government securities in the much more inclusive category of assets that are systematically subject to such revaluations.

We now turn to the question whether there are indications that real revaluations of assets and liabilities in general, and thus among these assets the revaluation of government securities in particular, have had an effect on saving rates.

The Effect on Saving Ratios of Real Revaluations of Net Worth: General Indications of an Effect

The savings to be explored here will be *personal* savings expressed as ratios of disposable *personal* income. If saving ratios are to be related to revaluations, then including corporate savings into the savings would involve substantial double-counting. Under the "ideal" conditions of simplified models, net corporate savings would reflect themselves precisely in the revaluation of corporate stock. In the real world these conditions are not precisely satisfied, but it nevertheless would be wrong procedure to include into savings the corporate savings when the dependence of savings on net-worth revaluations is explored.

Turning to the quantitative exploration of the relation of savings to real net-worth revaluations, I feel disinclined to place much faith in the apparently precise results of measurements for which the exploration of revaluation effects on savings would ideally call. Later I will nevertheless submit some results of such a strictly quantitative effort. But before doing so, I will call attention to more modest indications.

The hypothesis of a relation of savings to real revaluations passes a "qualitative" test—more precisely a test relating to the *direction of movements* of variables—which is suggestive, even if it cannot claim to be more than that. The hypothesis earlier discussed of a positive effect of budget deficits on saving rates does not pass even this "qualitative" test.

The "qualitative" test in question—the test relating to the direction of movements, which is the hypothesis suggesting a relation of revaluations to savings passes successfully—can be described as follows. Over the periods listed in table 1, the cycle-to-cycle *increases* in the algebraic value of the total real *revaluations* shown in column 2 are quite consistently associated with *decreases* in the column 1 *saving ratios*, and vice versa. However, as concerns budget deficits, it was already seen that for the most recent cycle-to-cycle change covered by the table, the analogous conjecture based on the equivalence theorem is strongly contradicted. Instead of observing for a large increase in the deficit an increase in the saving ratio, we observe for the last cycle-to-cycle change a large decrease in the saving ratio—a decrease from 7.8 to 6.8 percent. And now we see that, by these criteria, counterindications are obtained from table 1 also for most other periods even when we examine merely such a "qualitative" conjecture concerning the substitution of additional savings for the deficits.[13] At this level it "works" for the relation of total real net-worth revaluations to savings, but not for budget deficit in relation to savings.

As for the favorable indications obtained for the relation of total real revaluations to savings, the question arises which components of the total revaluations are mainly responsible for this favorable result. If, relying on table 2, we take a look at the composition of the total real net-worth revaluations—the composition of the totals included in table 1 and repeated in column 2 of table 2—we find that the qualitative test, which the relation of savings to total real revaluations passes flawlessly, is passed also with respect to the real revaluation of corporate equities in *all* cycle-to-cycle transitions. That is, a comparison of the direction of the change in column 4 with that in column 1 in table 2 shows that a rise in the algebraic value of the corporate equity entry in column 4 is always associated with a decline in the saving ratio entry in column 1, and vice versa. The same test is almost always passed by the relation of changes in the saving ratio (column 1) to changes in the real revaluation of net fixed-dollar positions (column 5).[14] In contrast to the relation of savings to the real revaluation of corporate equities, the relation of savings to the real revaluation of net fixed-dollar positions does not pass the test literally *always*: it does not pass the test for the change from the penultimate to the last cycle, at which time increasingly unfavorable real revaluations of the net fixed-dollar positions became associated with a reduction rather than with a rise in the saving ratio. But for this last cycle-to-cycle change, the physical asset revaluations listed in column 3 do pass the test along with corporate equities. That is to say, during that period of steepening inflation, a sharp rise in the real upward revaluation of physical assets occurred along with a decline in the real downward revaluation of corporate equity, and this was sufficient to produce an increase in the algebraic value of the total real net-worth revaluations and to produce a corresponding decrease in the saving ratio.[15]

To express the upshot of the matter first in these somewhat formalistic terms, among the three revaluation components listed in columns 3, 4, and 5 of table 2, we always find two that move in the right direction relative to savings, in the sense that movements to higher revaluations were associated with movements to lower saving ratios, and vice versa. This is always confirmed for two of the components of the total revaluations as well as for the total. While by these standards changes in one of the three revaluation components always went in the wrong direction, the fact that two of the three components were always well behaved in relation to savings was sufficient to ensure for all periods the observed good behavior of changes in the total real net-worth revaluation when these changes are conjectured to have contributed to changes in saving ratios. This is how the changes listed in column 2 always go in the right direction in relation to column 1.

One may *make sense* of the story in these terms by (1) identifying a flattening of inflation (observed in table 2 only for the first cycle-to-cycle comparison) as a factor usually conducive not only to *lesser real devaluations* of the fixed-dollar items but also to *favorable real revaluations* of corporate equity and, correspondingly, as a factor conducive to a reduction of the saving ratio; and by (2) identifying a steepening of inflation (observed in all subsequent cycle-to-cycle comparisons) as a factor increasing tax distortions as well as increasing the degree of uncertainty, and thereby usually exerting an unfavorable influence on the real revaluations of equity in addition to those of the fixed-dollar items. The real revaluations of physical household assets and of noncorporate equity have, however, consistently risen and declined along with the rate of inflation, but this factor has not been sufficient to determine the direction in which total real revaluations have moved.

Details aside, the emphasis in this kind of analysis belongs on the simple fact that in table 2, the column 2 figures on *total* real net-worth revaluations *always* move in the opposite direction from that of the column 1 figures on saving ratios. Some of these details do deserve attention, however, particularly because they point to a pattern in which various components of the total revaluations tend to move to-

TABLE 1
Cycle Averages of Saving Ratios, Real Revaluations of Household Wealth, and Budget Deficits, 1954–1979

| | (1) | (2) | (3) | (4) | Addendum |
| | | | | | (5) |
Periods Making Up Successive Business Cycles (defined as beginning with years of trough and ending with years of peak)	Personal Saving, as % of Disposable Income	Total Real Revaluations of Net Worth, as % of Disposable Income	Federal Government's Surplus, as % of Disposable Income	Federal Plus State and Local Governments' Surplus, as % of Disposable Income	Disposable Income (billions of dollars)
1954–1957	6.8	9.6 (10.9)[a]	0.6	0.2	1,133.62
1958–1960	6.4	11.2 (12.8)	−0.8	−1.1	1,009.45
1961–1969	6.7	7.3 (8.3)	−0.5	−0.4	4,368.74
1970–1973	7.8	1.4 (1.6)	−1.6	−0.6	3,171.86
1974–1979	6.8	7.1 (8.7)	−2.9	−1.4	7,726.94

NOTES: This chronology omits the unusually short expansion period that, according to the National Bureau of Economic Research, started in the third quarter of 1980 and ended about a year later and was associated with atypically little cyclical expansion of output.

No account is taken in column 2 or elsewhere in the paper of real revaluations of life-insurance and pension-fund reserves, nor of social security claims. Nor is account taken of the revaluation of consumer durables. The real revaluations of each year are revaluations as compared with the net worth of households that they would have had if their net worth had been revalued in proportion to the year-to-year change in the PCE deflator (and would not have included the year's personal savings). For the figures placed in parentheses, see footnote below.

All surpluses and deficits are those shown in the National Income Accounts.

a. In column 2 the main series of figures, beginning with 9.6, is based on the revaluation estimates of the Flow of Funds statistics. The figures in parentheses beginning with 10.9 are constructed by adding to the net worth revaluations derived from the Flow of Funds statistics the so-called "discrepancy" by which the savings implied in the Flow of Funds statistics exceed the savings as shown in the National Income statistics (that is, exceed them after allowances for the deliberate conceptual differences). The reason for listing these parenthetical figures is that *in all other respects* we are relying on data derived from the National Income statistics; and if for the sake of consistency the savings shown in National Income statistics are accepted as "correct," then one possible reason for the "discrepancy" is that to that extent the Flow of Funds has underestimated the revaluations along with overestimating the savings. The parenthetical figures include an adjustment for this possible underestimate.

In the regressions to be discussed later we shall, however, remain at the conceptual level of the main series in column 2 rather than moving to the conceptual level of the parenthetical figures. This is because even if the savings shown in the National Income Accounts are accepted as the precise measures of that concept, it does not necessarily follow that the Flow of Funds has underestimated the revaluations by the amount by which it in this case has overestimated the savings. Another possibility would be that the Flow of Funds has overestimated net worth in each period by the amount by which it has overestimated savings. That would imply no underestimate of revaluations. What remains an indisputable fact is that the large "discrepancies" pointed out here cast some amount of doubt on any quantitative statement in this area of research. *Yet the regularity discussed in the text applies regardless of whether we consider the main series in column 2 or the series of numbers placed in parentheses.* See in this context also my article "The High-Employment Budget and Potential Output" in *Survey of Current Business*, November 1982, mainly p. 32.

SOURCES: National Income and Product Accounts of the Bureau of Economic Analysis and the Balance Sheets prepared by the Flow of Funds Division of the Board of Governors of the Federal Reserve System.

TABLE 2

Cycle Averages of Saving Ratios and of Real Revaluations of American Household Wealth by Components of the Latter, 1954–1979

Periods Making Up Successive Business Cycles (defined as beginning with years of trough and ending with years of peak)	(1) Personal Savings, as % of Disposable Income	(2) Total Real Revaluations of Net Worth, as % of Disposable Income	(3) Physical Assets and Noncorporate Equity, as Component of (2)	(4) Corporate Equity, as Component of (2)	(5) Assets Minus Liabilities Fixed in Nominal Terms, as Component of (2)	Addendum (6) Percentage Increase of PCE Deflator from Peak Year to Peak Year such as 1953–57 (annual compound rate in parentheses)
1954–1957	6.8	9.6	3.6	6.9	−1.0	7.3(1.8)
1958–1960	6.4	11.2	1.5	10.6	−0.9	6.0(2.0)
1961–1969	6.7	7.3	3.0	5.3	−1.0	22.9(2.3)
1970–1973	7.8	1.4	8.6	−5.4	−1.9	19.6(4.5)
1974–1979	6.8	7.1	10.9	−0.9	−2.9	53.7(7.2)

NOTES: Real revaluations are defined as in table 1. Columns 3, 4, and 5 add up to column 2, aside from rounding errors. In the text the items in column 5 are often referred to also as "net fixed-dollar positions." See the notes to table 1 also on the omission of various items including consumer durables.

SOURCES: National Income and Product Accounts of the Bureau of Economic Analysis and the Balance Sheets prepared by the Flow of Funds Division of the Board of Governors of the Federal Reserve System.

gether, and this greatly increases the difficulty of separating their individual effects on saving ratios.

Some Specifics about Substitution Ratios of Inflationary and Other Real Revaluations for Savings

The regression technique provides a more ambitious, if not very reliable, way of tracing the effect on consumption and saving of the real net-worth revaluations of households. These real revaluations are defined here too as net-worth revaluations in relation to a frame of reference in which the revaluations of net worth would reflect merely movements of the PCE deflator. Although it is gradually becoming a commonplace comment of skeptics that the next investigator will come up with an alternative model yielding different regression results, I think that the data to be submitted nevertheless do suggest that these revaluations have had an effect on consumption and savings. Yet given the orders of magnitude, one would consider the effect quite moderate.

When total real net-worth revaluations are introduced into a consumption function estimated for the United States from yearly data for the period 1954–1982, we obtain the following, with correction for first-order autocorrelation but with no major changes brought about by that correction (though $t = 2.8$ for rho):

$$C = -6006.5 + 0.9370Y + 0.0189TR + 0.0279TR_{-1} + 0.0234TR_{-2}$$
$$(-1.6) \quad (248.1) \quad (2.4) \quad (3.7) \quad (2.4)$$

$\bar{R}^2 = 0.999$
$DW = 2.1$
SEE (normalized) $= 0.0072$

With the variables measured in millions of dollars, C is consumer outlay, Y is disposable income, TR is total real net-worth revaluation as defined above, and TR_{-1} and TR_{-2} are lagged values of the last-mentioned variable (lagged once and twice, respectively). The lagged TR terms beyond these two would lack statistical significance, as conventionally viewed, by a large enough margin to suggest omitting these. The inclusion of the three TR terms here used does, however, reduce the normalized standard error, since without any of the three TR terms the normalized measure of SEE would be 0.0081 instead of 0.0072.[16]

For the entire period 1954–1981 or 1954–1982, the joint value of the three explanatory revaluation variables TR, TR_{-1}, and TR_{-2} is between $3.56 trillion and $3.26 trillion depending on whether we end the period in 1981 or in the recession year (unfavorable year) 1982. *This* *amount of $3.56 trillion to $3.26 trillion is the algebraic sum of the* TR *terms for overlapping three-year spans.* In our analysis this *cumulated value* of successive *three-year sums of real valuations*—rather than simply the single-year sum of these[17]—needs to be taken into account because our regression suggests that in each year significance has attached to the real revaluations of three years. These sums will often be referred to as *cumulated, overlapping, three-year revaluations* (for example, for 1954 the revaluations of 1952, of 1953, and of 1954, and for 1955 those of 1953, of 1954, and of 1955).

In view of the coefficients of the three revaluation variables in the regression, no large error is made in the analysis of these results if they are interpreted as pointing to a revaluations-induced rise in consumption over the 1954–1981 or 1954–1982 period as a whole by 2 to 3 percent of $3.56–3.26 trillion, that is, by about $70–90 billion.[18] Interpreting this as an amount that in the event of $TR = TR_{-1} = TR_{-2} = 0$ would have been a deduction from the consumer outlay of almost three decades, and thus would have been an addition to that period's savings—an addition to the period's actual personal savings of $1.45 trillion for 1954–1981 or of $1.58 trillion for 1954–1982—we obtain the suggestion that the total revaluations reduced these personal savings by 5–6 percent.

This numerical appraisal, however, suggesting a 5–6 percent saving-reducing effect, is, of course, not based exclusively on the estimated coefficients in our regression but also on the small size of the cumulated three-year total real revaluation ($3.56–3.26 trillion) relative to the disposable income of the 1954–1981 period ($21.3 trillion) or of the 1954–1982 period ($23.4 trillion). Expressed differently, our cumulated overlapping three-year total real revaluations were on the order of 15 percent of the period's disposable income, and the cumulated overlapping three-year real revaluations were about twice the period's cumulated personal savings. Thus, it took cumulated overlapping three-year real revaluations in excess of twice the personal savings themselves to reduce the savings by about 5 to 6 percent. This is a small *substitution ratio of savings for total real revaluations,* and it would remain small even if we wanted to relate the 5 to 6 percent reduction of savings not to the sum of cumulated three-year real revaluations but to the sum of single-year real revaluations (which fell somewhat short of the sum of the savings rather than exceeded twice the savings). Nevertheless, what in view of the coefficients estimated for the regression expresses the essentials of the matter most clearly is that three years' worth of cumulated real revaluations seem to have raised consumption and to have reduced savings by 2–3 percent of the cumulated real revaluations themselves.

I do not find the low value of the substitution ratio of savings for real revaluations particularly astonishing. In the first place, what makes the real revaluations of the period a positive figure at all is mainly the specific component consisting of physical assets and of noncorporate equity, that is, largely real estate. Without that component the balance of the remaining real revaluations would be a negative magnitude. As for the physical assets and the noncorporate equity (owners of real estate who do not want to become homeless or to give up their business), the upward revaluations of the physical assets and noncorporate property, which make the total a positive figure, are in many respects not "available" the way liquid savings plus corporate equity are.[19] Second, and perhaps more important, the real revaluations varied a great deal from cycle to cycle and even from year to year in relation to disposable income, which is another way of saying that in an essential sense these real revaluations have been very undependable. In view of these considerations it is not astonishing that the substitution ratio of savings for real revaluations should be low.

Having concluded this much concerning the proportionate savings *reduction* due to the observed positive total real revaluations, one should keep in mind that nothing follows from these conclusions directly concerning the effect on savings-*raising* effects of the inflationary *downward* real revaluations of net fixed-dollar positions (including government).

Any claims that could be made for quantitative results based on a decomposition by individual components of total revaluations, including net fixed-dollar positions, would be very shaky. The discussion presented above in connection with table 2, along with other indications, leaves little doubt that the various components of total revaluation come in packages. Nevertheless, the footnotes to which we are referring in this sentence provide indications that the substitution ratio of savings for the real revaluation of net fixed-dollar positions and of corporate equity are in excess of the substitution ratio of savings for *total* real revaluations (hence, the revaluations of physical household wealth may be pulling down the total substitution ratio).[20] For the cumulated three-year real revaluation of *fixed-dollar positions plus corporate equity* we obtain about minus $0.4 trillion, and the (positive) effect on savings appears to be about $20 billion, yielding a ratio that does not change much if we end the period in 1981 instead of in 1982. The *total* revaluations gave us a distinctly lower substitution ratio of savings for real revaluations. Earlier we obtained a $70–90 billion effect on savings from cumulated three-year *total* revaluations of more than $3 trillion.

Substitution of Capital Inflows for Domestic Savings

From this analysis it follows that one would need to stretch one's imagination quite a bit to consider it likely that more than a small part of the savings-diverting effect of budget deficits is compensated by the savings-augmenting effect of adverse revaluations of real net worth. One consequence of large deficits normally to be expected is a decrease in aggregate demand for a given supply of money (an increase in velocity). Another consequence is an increase in real rates of interest by which private savings are diverted from investment, and *thus the output-mix becomes tilted away from investment toward consumption.* As for the qualifications, the savings-increasing effect of adverse influences on real net worth deserves to be taken into account but does not deserve to be weighed heavily.

Yet more quantitative importance attaches to the supposition that a major part of the interest-rate raising and savings-diverting effects of deficits will in some circumstances be offset by capital inflows from countries in which deficits are smaller relative to private savings. Indeed, an extreme case exists in which practically all deficit-induced diversions of savings from domestic investment will predictably be offset by the savings of other countries for investment in the high-deficit country. This is the case in which (1) the high-deficit country is small and in which (2) the international mobility of capital is very high, and the emergence of appreciable interest-rate differentials is therefore prevented by the interest-equalizing consequences of capital imports into the country whose interest rates tend to rise relative to the outside world. If only the second of these conditions—the capital-mobility condition—is satisfied, that is, if we are concerned with the "large country" problem, then, as a result of the weight of the country in question in the international community, real rates of interest will rise appreciably abroad as well as at home. Also, savings will become diverted from investment to an appreciable extent throughout the international community *including* the country we are considering.

The United States is, of course, a prominent example of a large country, and the mobility of capital is sufficiently far from "perfect" to permit noteworthy international interest-rate differentials to develop. Hence, as concerns the United States, capital imports would by no means wholly prevent a shift of the output mix away from investment, in response to forces raising real rates of interest such as would develop from large American deficits. International capital movements would presumably nevertheless reduce the shift away from domestic capital formation, but the domestic investment resulting from this would develop at a cost to the country, since the capital and the income flowing from it directly would be foreign-owned. Yet the fact remains that, as input, capital is complementary with labor, and the capital formation resulting from capital imports would strengthen American real-wage trends regardless of who earns the yield flowing from the investment. One of the difficulties not to be overlooked, however, is that if the domestic effect of high budget deficits should in large part be offset by capital imports, then the state so described implies a correspondingly large current-account deficit for the country importing the capital. In such circumstances, staving off protectionist pressures in the capital-importing country would become a particularly difficult task.

A Consistency Requirement for Tax Policy

In the preceding pages I have argued that for the appraisal of the effect on demand creation of monetary expansion or restraint and of budgetary deficits or surpluses, the "normal" or "conventional" assumptions are reasonably adequate. The problem that has called for the present investigation, and should call for others, arises not so much in connection with these effects as with the effect of budget deficits on the *consumption-investment mix.* Sweeping conclusions concerning the negative effect of budget deficits on the investment component—that is, concerning the crowding-out effect—need to be qualified in several respects, but the qualifications turn out to be of very moderate weight for quantitative analysis. It follows that if worries about the high prospective size of deficits in cyclically favorable years should lead to additional taxation, it would be a requirement of consistency to try to shape the additional taxation in such a way as to tilt the consumption-investment mix away from consumption toward investment.

This, of course, leaves open the question why the effect of large prospective deficits on the consumption-investment mix should be considered worrisome. I think the main reason is that the chances of preserving the institutions of our society are very much better if, in spite of the short-term sacrifice required, we succeed in restoring favorable trends in labor productivity and in the standard of living.

I have little confidence in the various quantitative estimates of the significance of investment in generating a rising trend in labor productivity and real wage rates. I believe also that in the context of productivity analysis the relevant variables include the replacement of old with new capital goods as well as with *net* savings and *net* capital formation. But at the present writing most estimates suggest the likelihood that in the absence of new measures preventing such a budgetary outcome, *even the deficits of those future years favorably located in the business cycle will significantly exceed past record heights in relation to net or to gross savings.* The resulting displacement of investment clearly involves the risk of major adverse productivity effects, which it would be highly desirable to avoid. Within the framework of any consistently devised policy, the measures suitable for avoiding this risk must restrain consumption rather than investment at the levels of aggregate demand that the policy makers attempt to achieve.

Notes

1. The first of the five cycles in question was bordered by the peak years 1953 and 1957. The average yearly compound rate of increase of GNP velocity of $M1$ from 1953 to 1957 was 3.2 percent, and the maximum yearly deviation from that was 4.7 percentage points. See my "Criteria for Useful Targeting: Money versus the Base and Other Variables," *Journal of Money, Credit, and Banking,* November 1982, part 2.

2. See Chairman Paul A. Volcker's statement on February 16, 1983, before the Committee on Banking, Housing, and Urban Affairs of the United States Senate in Board of Governors, Federal Reserve System, *Monetary Policy Report to Congress Pursuant to the Full Employment and Balanced Growth Act of 1978,* February 16, 1983. See also his statement on July 20, 1983 before the same committee.

3. An early and clear explanation of this proposition is found in Henry C. Wallich in his "Income Generating Effects of a Balanced Budget," *Quarterly Journal of Economics,* November 1944.

4. For an analysis of the problems that are merged if aggregate demand is not assumed as given and for the extensive literature on this subject, see Benjamin M. Friedman, "Crowding Out or Crowding In? Economic Consequences of Financing Government Deficits," *Brookings Papers on Economic Activity,* 1978:3, pp. 593–654.

5. This statement, which is true "approximately," disregards indirect consequences of inflationary processes. As for the constants in the relevant regressions, these were found to lack significance.

6. These numbers imply including into net worth those items the revaluation of which is taken into account in the tables and regressions. See the notes to the tables in this chapter.

7. Raised in different analytical contexts than those here, and thus explored on different assumptions, the general problem of wealth effects and of capital gains effects on consumption and savings has an extensive literature. For a penetrating analysis of that general problem see Don Patinkin, *Money Interest Prices,* 2d ed. (New York: Harper and Row, 1965), passim and pp. 653 ff (1st ed. 1957). In the second edition of this work references are found to John J. Arena's Yale doctoral thesis, "The Wealth Effect on Consumption: A Statistical Inquiry," published in *Yale Economic Essays,* Fall 1963. Among more recent contributions, see Joe Peek, "Capital Gains and Personal Saving Behavior," *Journal of Money, Credit, and Banking,* February 1983.

8. See David Ricardo, *Principles of Political Economy and Taxation* (1817; third and last edition, 1821), chap. 17; and in the more recent literature, see

particularly Robert J. Barro, "Are Government Bonds Net Worth?" *Journal of Political Economy,* November-December 1974.

9. For a detailed discussion of the intergenerational aspect of the problem, see the analysis in Barro, "Are Government Bonds Net Worth?" which, however, has a much less skeptical tenor as concerns the required conditions.

10. For the maximum level the deficit could in principle reach without debt-repudiation, see the summary to this chapter.

11. The concept of revaluations excludes, of course, value increments brought about by the current savings themselves (that is, by failure to consume part of one's after-tax income).

12. Whether a small increase or a small decrease in real values is obtained for this span as a whole depends on decisions such as whether merely the federal debt is considered or the state and local debt is added, and whether we concentrate on government securities owned by American households directly or on the entire net liability position of the government.

13. Only from the 1961–1969 to the 1970–1973 period is a rise in the deficits with a rise in the saving ratio associated. The three other cycle-to-cycle comparisons provide counterindications.

14. For an explanation of the terminology used, see the notes to table 2.

15. For the earlier cycle-to-cycle transitions, the physical assets viewed in isolation (column 3) do not pass the test in question; that is, their real upward revaluation declines when the saving ratio declines, and their real upward revaluation rises when the saving ratio rises.

16. Without the three TR terms this is a regression of C on Y that yields almost identical results if in an alternative formulation we deflate both C and Y for changes in the price level. For a comment on the regression coefficients, when the TR terms are included *and the explanatory variables are deflated for the size of the population,* see note 18.

17. The simple sum of the yearly real revaluations was $1.10 trillion for 1954–1981 and $0.83 trillion for 1954–1982.

18. The mean value of the three TR coefficients is very similar (in the 2 to 3 percent range) regardless of whether we estimate the values for 1954–1981 or for 1954–1982. Nor does dividing C and Y and the TR terms by population make much difference.

19. It is possible to take out second mortgages and to borrow in various other ways on residential buildings and other noncorporate physical property, but the ease of these operations is not the same as that of drawing down a bank balance or selling securities in the market.

20. The total real revaluations being positive, and the real revaluations of corporate equity plus the fixed-dollar positions being on balance negative, the effect of the total on savings is negative, while the effect of the corporate plus fixed-dollar real revaluations is positive. The quantitative reasoning in the text is based on the following. At a somewhat disaggregated level the relatively most satisfactory regression results were obtained from yearly data for the 1954–1982 period by using as explanatory variables of consumer outlay the following two real revaluation variables, in addition to disposable income: physical assets including noncorporate equity and the *sum* of net fixed-dollar positions and of corporate equity. These two revaluation variables were used

as simultaneous variables and lagged once and then twice. It was reasonable to conclude from this regression that a coefficient of 0.04 to 0.05 applies to the cumulated three-year value of the sum of net fixed-dollar positions and corporate equity, and this exceeds the 0.02 to 0.03 range suggested by the regression that aggregates all revaluations and was discussed earlier in this section.

The regression discussed in this footnote is:

$$C = \underset{(-2.9)}{5440.3} + \underset{(345.2)}{0.9358Y} - \underset{(-0.4)}{0.0065\ Rev.Phys} + \underset{(2.3)}{0.0489\ Rev.\ Phys._{-1}}$$

$$+ \underset{(1.1)}{0.0263\ Rev.\ Phys._{-2}} + \underset{(4.6)}{0.0461\ Rev.\ (Fix\ plus\ Corp)}$$

$$+ \underset{(5.4)}{0.0454\ Rev.\ (Fix\ plus\ Corp)_{-1}} + \underset{(4.2)}{0.0411\ Rev.\ (Fix\ plus\ Corp)_{-2}}$$

$\overline{R}^2 = 0.9999$
$DW = 1.7$
SEE (normalized) $= 0.0063$

C is consumer outlay measured in millions of dollars, as are all other variables, Y is disposable income, $Phys$ is physical household assets including noncorporate equity, and $(Fix\ plus\ Corp)$ is net fixed-dollar positions (that is, fixed-dollar net creditor positions) plus corporate equity. The subscripts express lags. $Rev.$ stands for real revaluation.

The International Monetary System in the World Recession

Gottfried Haberler

Summary

This paper has two parts. Part one, in three sections, describes the scope and briefly analyzes the causes of the recession from which the world economy now seems to be emerging. It was the severest and longest global recession since World War II. Despite the many warnings that the world economy is in a mess and is sliding into a deep depression, it is, or was, definitely a recession and not a depression, if by depression we mean a contraction remotely resembling the Great Depression of the 1930s or earlier depressions. Some global statistics and figures from leading industrial countries are cited to prove the point.

Five views, three from prominent noneconomists and two from leading economists, are cited to illustrate the widespread view of the seriousness of the situation and the alleged inability of economists to explain it and to suggest remedies. Actually, the recession was predictable and had been predicted. It was caused by the policy of disinflation that major industrial countries were forced to adopt. It is well known that a serious inflation cannot be stopped without causing transitional unemployment and recession.

In the second section the contribution of the two oil shocks to world inflation and recession is briefly analyzed. It is argued that the role of the oil price rise imposed by OPEC has been greatly exaggerated. The first oil shock of 1973 was preceded and accompanied by a highly inflationary commodity boom, which, in turn, was superimposed on an inflationary groundswell. Nor was the second oil shock of 1979-1980 the major factor in world inflation and recession.

The third section briefly takes up one aspect of the world debt problem, which is widely regarded as a major danger that may plunge the world into deep depression. It is argued that even if some large debtor countries default and several large international banks get into difficulties, this would not plunge the world into a deep depression, provided a sharp contraction of the money supply is avoided. Protection of bank depositors and no bail-out of the banks or of the defaulting countries would be required.

It would, of course, be much better if defaults of large debtor countries could be avoided. It would be better for everybody, including the debtor countries themselves, if they restored their credit worthiness by putting their houses in order and accepting the austerity programs prescribed by the International Monetary Fund.

Part two, discusses the international monetary system. The international monetary system is still one of widespread managed floating. All major currencies float, though approximately 100, mostly small countries peg their currencies to the dollar, to the D-mark, to the French franc, or to some basket of currencies or special drawing rights. There is, furthermore, the European Monetary System (EMS), whose nine members maintain a precarious stability of their exchange rates and float jointly against the dollar and other currencies.

Section four discusses how floating was forced on reluctant policy makers by spells of weakness of the dollar. The dollar had ruled supreme and was regarded "better than gold" until the late 1960s. At that time U.S. inflation began to soar because the Johnson administration was financing the rising cost of the war in Vietnam and the equally expensive Great Society programs through inflationary bank credit rather than through higher taxes. Gradually, an inflation differential between the United States and some low-inflation countries, notably Germany, Japan, and Switzerland, developed, and the dollar came under increasing pressure. In August 1971 the gold convertibility of the dollar was suspended, and in December 1971 the dollar was devalued, by about 8 percent, against all major currencies in the Smithsonian Agreement.

The new pattern of exchange rates did not last long. Early in 1973, after futile attempts to prop up the dollar by massive interventions in the foreign exchange markets on the part of foreign central banks, the Bretton Woods system of "stable but adjustable" exchange rates broke down, and managed floating of all major and many minor currencies started.

In 1974 the U.S. inflation rate reached its highest level, 12.4 percent. It was brought down to below 5 percent in 1976. But when the Carter administration switched course from fighting inflation to new expansion, the rate of inflation climbed again into the two-digit range. Again an inflation differential between the United States and the low-inflation countries developed, and the dollar came under heavy pressure.

It has often been said that in 1979 the exchange rate "overshot," that the dollar fell too low. But it was a beneficial overshooting; it forced the Carter administration to appoint Paul Volcker chairman of the Federal Reserve and to give him a free hand to start the process of disinflation in October 1979. The foreign exchange market calmed down, and after the election of Ronald Reagan the dollar began its dramatic rise.

Predictably, the sharp fluctuations of the exchange rates of major curren-
cies, especially of the dollar, have revived the criticism of floating exchange
rates. Even some former advocates of floating have become alarmed by recent
swings, and the dollar is widely regarded as grossly overvalued with sharply
depressive effects on the U.S. economy and inflationary effects abroad.

In the fifth section, I analyze the criticism of floating of two leading
academic economists, Ronald McKinnon and Peter Kenen, and of three promi-
nent officials and former officials, Fred Bergsten, Otmar Emminger, and
Alexandre Lamfalussy. The sixth section is devoted to an analysis of the
"overvalued" dollars.

Much of the criticism of floating and all the forecasts of gloom and doom
of the world economy were robbed of much of their relevance by the fact that,
despite the "overvalued" dollar, high interest rates, and the large U.S. trade
deficits, the U.S. economy has staged a strong rebound, and the world econ-
omy seems to be emerging from the recession.

Apart from advocates of the gold standard, hardly anyone recommends a
return to fixed exchange rates or fixed but adjustable rates.

Now that the Gold Commission has rendered its report, it is no longer
necessary to explain why a return to the gold standard is out of the question.
But I show that the basic rule of the gold standard can be found in recent
policy proposals, expressed, of course, in modern terminology, and transposed
to the inflationary conditions of our times.

The key problem is the "overvalued" dollar, which is widely regarded as a
flagrant case of malfunctioning of the exchange markets under floating. In the
United States it is attacked as a depressive factor; abroad, especially in France,
it is assailed for its inflationary effect.

The explanation of the rise of the dollar is comparatively uncontroversial.
It is due to two mutually supporting factors—high interest rates in the United
States and the fact that, for political and economic reasons, the United States
has again become an attractive haven for foreign investors. The high U.S.
interest rates in turn are caused by large budget deficits and lingering doubts
that inflation has definitely been curbed and will not be reignited by the
ongoing recovery. Whatever the comparative strength of these factors, there is
no doubt that the rise of the dollar and the large U.S. trade deficits have been
powerful depressive factors in the United States and inflationary factors
abroad.

This is not the case of malfunctioning of floating, for it can be shown that,
given high interest rates in the United States and the attraction for foreign
capital of the U.S. economy, foreign countries would be much worse off under
fixed exchanges than under floating. Under fixed exchanges the capital flow
into the United States would be much heavier than under floating because the
exchange risk would be absent. Thus, foreign countries would suffer large
losses of international reserves and be put under strong deflationary pressure.

Although the strong dollar and the large trade deficits have been powerful depressive factors in the United States, they were also potent anti-inflationary factors. Consider what would have happened if the dollar had not gone up because, say, foreign investors had lacked confidence in the future of the dollar. A powerful anti-inflationary factor would have been lost. Assuming that inflation has to be curbed, the Federal Reserve would have had to step harder on the monetary brake, and the recession would be pretty much the same as it was with the strong dollar.

Now change the scenario. Suppose the United States had followed the advice offered at home and even more strongly abroad, especially by France, and had tried to keep the dollar down by massive intervention in the foreign exchange market, by buying D-marks, yen, and French francs and by selling dollars. A sharp distinction has to be made between "nonsterilized" interventions on the one hand, and "pure" or "sterilized" interventions on the other. Under the system of nonsterilized interventions, sales and purchases in the foreign exchange market are allowed to have their full effect on the domestic supply of money. If the Fed sells dollars and buys D-marks, it creates dollars and increases the money supply. No doubt this would, sooner or later, bring down the dollar, at the high cost of undercutting the anti-inflation policy. But it is not certain that nonsterilized intervention would improve the competitive position of U.S. industries abroad. To be sure, a lower dollar would help American exporters and import-competing industries. But rising costs due to inflation would work in the opposite direction. It is by no means sure that the favorable force would be the stronger except in the short run.

Under the system of sterilized interventions the central bank offsets or sterilizes the effect of the interventions in the foreign exchange market on the money supply by countervailing operations on the domestic security market. Thus, when the Fed buys D-marks with dollars, it sells an equal amount of Treasury bills, so that the money supply remains unchanged. That this has a weaker effect on the exchange rate than nonsterilized interventions, or no effect at all, follows from the fact that the sale of Treasury bills tends to raise interest rates, which in turn attracts more capital from abroad. The sale of dollars for marks depresses the dollar, but the additional capital imports boost the dollar. This latter effect is absent under the system of nonsterilized intervention.

There is fairly general agreement among experts that under certain circumstances sterilized intervention would have some effect on the exchange rate, though an uncertain and a weak one. It would require sterilized interventions on a truly massive and impractical scale to achieve the desired results.

In the next section, I discuss a recent policy shift of the United States on interventions in the foreign exchange market. On August 1, 1983, it was announced that, at the urging of European countries and Japan, the United States had agreed to a policy of "internationally coordinated interventions," *selling dollars for D-marks and possibly other currencies. The new policy has been described by a high U.S. official as a case of "correcting disorderly market conditions." This is rather odd, for there is nothing disorderly about the persistent rise of the dollar, which the interventions are supposed to slow down. The policy is better described as a gesture of good will toward the European countries, which have been rather unhappy about the soaring dollar. U.S. critics of the new policy would call it "appeasement" of foreign critics of the policy of non-intervention. The volume of the interventions has not been divulged, but estimates of knowledgeable sources are between $2.5 billion and $3 billion for the total during the first eight days of the new policy.*

Fears have been expressed that the new policy may put the United States under inflationary pressure. I argue that these fears are unfounded. The reason is that the interventions by the United States and other important countries are of the sterilized kind. That means that the money supply is not changed. Thus, sterilized interventions have no direct inflationary effect. It could even be argued that the policy is slightly anti-inflationary, because the sales of Treasury bills tend to raise interest rates. It could also be argued that the policy may be indirectly inflationary if it slows down or possibly reverses the rise of the dollar. Reasons are given for the expectation that this effect is likely to be minimal.

The final section sums up the conclusion about floating. Floating is here to stay, though in a sense it is only the second best solution. The best solution would be fixed exchanges, provided it were possible to maintain fixed exchange rates without exchange control and without imposing too much inflation on some countries and too much unemployment on others.

This would require, among other things, very close international coordination of macroeconomic, especially monetary, policy. If proof were needed that in our imperfect world this is rarely possible between sovereign countries, it is provided by the EMS.

From the economic point of view, the EMS has been a failure. It has been characterized by frequent realignments of exchange rates, preceded and accompanied by large, destabilizing, speculative capital flows. The second largest member of the EMS, France, has an oppressive system of exchange control, involving searches at the border, censorship of the mail, and tight allocation of foreign currencies for travel abroad—a system reminiscent of what was known as the Schachtian regime in Nazi Germany. The EMS is a heavy burden for France's partners, especially West Germany, and is kept alive for political reasons, to prevent France from leaving the European Economic Community (EEC). If the Europeans who are united in the EEC—which has developed a huge international bureaucracy for the purpose of coordinating policies and integrating their economies—cannot operate a fixed rate system, how can it be done on the international scale?

Because of the enormous growth of the public sector and of large bureau-

cracies in all countries since the days of the gold standard, and because each country has its national tradition and idiosyncrasies, it is awfully hard to coordinate policies between our modern "mixed" economies. In a free market economy, it would be much easier.

Fortunately, there are important exceptions. As mentioned, quite a number of countries peg their currencies to the dollar or to another major currency. These countries have to adjust their macroeconomic policies, especially their monetary policy and inflation rates, to that of the country or countries to whose currency they peg their currency, if they wish to keep their currencies fully convertible without controls.

If the EMS were dissolved, some of its members—say, Belgium, the Netherlands, and perhaps Denmark—would probably join Austria and peg to the D-mark. From the economic point of view, such a mark block would be a much better arrangement than the EMS. But politically it would hardly be acceptable.

PART ONE
The State of the World Economy

Scope and Causes of the World Recession

The world economy seems to be just emerging from the severest and longest recession of the postwar period. The strong rebound of the U.S. economy undoubtedly plays a major role in the global recovery. Despite the often-heard warning that the world has already started, or is just about, to slide into a deep depression, it must be stressed that the recent decline has been a recession and not a depression, if by depression we mean a decline in economic activity approaching the magnitude of the Great Depression of the 1930s or earlier depressions.[1]

Some data will show that the recent decline has been mild compared with that of the 1930s, and I shall argue that, despite certain dangers ahead, it is unlikely that a major depression will develop.

First, let us look at some global data. In the Great Depression, 1929–1933, the value of world trade in terms of gold dollars fell by about one-half and in real terms by about one-third, the difference reflecting the terrific decline in the price level, especially of internationally traded goods. In sharp contrast in the recent recession, according to the latest statistics of the General Agreement on Tariffs and Trade (GATT), in 1982 the volume of world trade fell by about 2 percent from the level of 1981, declining to about the volume prevailing in 1979. In U.S. dollars the decline of world trade from 1981 to 1982 was 6 percent.[2]

A glance at the economies of the industrial countries leads to the same conclusion, that they suffer from a recession but not a depression. In 1982–1983 U.S. unemployment reached 10.8 percent compared with 25 percent in the Great Depression. Moreover, because of generous unemployment benefits, unemployment today is a lesser evil than it was in the 1930s. Today's unemployment figures contain a much larger portion of spurious, voluntary unemployment than those of the 1930s, and the hardship on the jobless is much less than it was fifty years ago. From 1929 to 1933 real GNP fell by 30 percent compared with 1.8 percent from 1973 to 1975 and −1.1 percent from July 1981 to March 1983.

The recession in Europe seems to be more severe and persistent than in the United States. Germany has the highest unemployment rate (10 percent) since the German economy rose from the ashes of the Third Reich. In France, Mitterrand's socialist government follows in the footsteps of the popular front (socialist) government of Léon Blum almost fifty years ago (1936)[3]—combining an expansionary ("Keynesian") policy with price- and wage-boosting measures and nationalization of banks and industries. The predictable result was the same—rising unemployment and inflation and huge balance of payments deficits.

Both in France and in Germany, the present difficulties are definitely a recession and not a depression. For example, unemployment in Germany at the nadir of the Great Depression, in 1932, was 43 percent, much higher than it was in the United States, and four times higher than it is in 1983.[4] In France the contrast between 1983 and the 1930s is certainly much smaller.

It would not be necessary to dwell on this if it were not for the widespread atmosphere of gloom and pessimism, not only in political circles and the media, but also among professional economists. This pessimism concerns the severity of the recession, the prospects as well as the ability, or inability, of governments to do anything about it, and the competence, or incompetence, of economists to provide an acceptable explanation or cure. Five examples of this pessimism, three from prominent noneconomists and two from well-known economists, should be sufficient.

Henry Kissinger writes in an article titled "Saving the World Economy":

John Maynard Keynes wrote that practical men who believe themselves quite exempt from intellectual influences are usually the slaves of some defunct economist. Politicians these days certainly have many economic theories to choose from, most discordant, not a few of them defunct. No previous theory seems capable of explaining the current crisis of the world economy.[5]

Ralf Dahrendorf, a political scientist, former prominent member of the German Free Democratic Party and now director of the London School of Economics, writes in an article titled "Die Arbeitsgesellschaft ist am Ende": "Whoever promises that he has a cure for unemployment, says an untruth."[6]

Somewhat pathetic is the statement of Pierre Mauroy, the socialist prime minister of France. At a meeting of seven socialist nations in Paris before the Williamsburg summit, according to news reports he said: "The world recession is the crisis of a system that is not ours—it is the crisis of the capitalist system."[7] The French situation may be serious enough to be called a crisis, but the world recession is not.

Following are two appraisals of the present state of the world economy by economists that are much too alarmist to my mind.

Peter Kenen writes:

> The world is mired deeply in a macroeconomic mess, and it is getting worse. Forecasts of recovery recede before our eyes. But governments are paralyzed by myths that they [read: their economic advisers or mentors] created. It is impossible, they say, to cut taxes or to increase public spending, because budget deficits are too large. It is impossible, they say, to speed up monetary growth, because it will rekindle inflation immediately.[8]

Since Kenen wrote, the cyclical recovery, which he saw receding before his eyes, has started and gathered momentum in the United States and in other industrial countries too.

Lester Thurow comes to a similar depressing conclusion:

> If one thinks of the economics profession as a navigator charged with achieving a high rate of economic growth without hitting the icebergs of inflation or unemployment, the profession has clearly failed. The world economy is sinking, yet the profession is unable to reach any consensus on what should be done. In the resulting confusion, policy makers wander at random from policy to policy, but nothing seems to work.[9]

Both authors recommend "Keynesian" policies of monetary-fiscal expansion, jointly undertaken by major industrial countries, fortified by some sort of incomes policy.[10]

Actually, the explanation of the world recession and its relative severity is easy; it was predictable and was predicted. The basic reason for the recession is that the major industrial countries were forced to bring inflation down by monetary restraint. The recession in the

United States and in other industrial countries was relatively severe for two reasons: inflationary expectations have become deeply entrenched by long inflationary abuse,[11] and the economy, especially wages, is becoming increasingly more rigid.

Two other factors often mentioned as being largely responsible for the recession, oil shocks and exchange rate volatility, will be considered below. But first a few observations about the basic reason.

It is simply impossible to stop an inflation without a transitional period of higher unemployment, in other words, without a recession. The size and duration of unemployment, which unavoidably accompanies the process of disinflation, depend largely on wage behavior. It stands to reason that the more rigid wages are, the more unemployment will be created by disinflation, leaving open the controversial question whether perfect wage flexibility could avoid unemployment altogether.

In recent years more and more economists have reached the conclusion that a full and sustained recovery from the present recession will require a moderate reduction of real wages, in all industrial countries (with the possible exception of Japan) to bring about a shift in the income distribution from wages and salaries to profits for the purpose of stimulating investment and growth.

I cite three examples of this trend of thought. Two years ago a group of prominent German economists, several of them monetarists, issued a statement urging a temporary wage freeze. Since there was still a significant rate of inflation at that time, a temporary freeze of money wages would have brought about the required reduction in real wages. The plea of the economists was not heeded, however; wages continued to rise, and unemployment has reached the two-digit level.

Herbert Giersch, a monetarist, has argued in several important articles that all industrial countries suffer from excessively high real wages and too low profits. He thinks it will take several years to bring about the necessary adjustment in the income distribution.[12]

The theme has been taken up by *The Economist* (London) in two excellent articles.[13] *The Economist* asks for a substantial cut in *money* wages to bring about an increase in profits for the purpose of stimulating investment, growth, and employment. Predictably, this has shocked many of *The Economist*'s Keynesian readers.[14]

The main argument against cutting money wages as a recovery measure is that it reduces total spending by reducing money income of labor, and thus is a deflationary factor that would intensify the recession. This argument is, however, fallacious and rests on a misunderstanding of what a wage cut is supposed to achieve. The purpose is not to reduce effective demand (nominal GNP); if such a reduction is necessary, it should be done by restrictive monetary-fiscal measures. The purpose of cutting money wages is to boost profits and stimulate investment, employment, and growth. Suppose hourly wage rates are cut by 10 percent—that does not necessarily mean that the wage bill and spending power of labor is reduced. If the elasticity of demand for labor is greater than unity (as it almost certainly is in the medium run), employment (in terms of hours) will rise by more than 10 percent, and the wage bill and spending will rise. True, if employment rises by less than 10 percent, labor income will decline; but that does not mean that total incomes and spending, too, will decline. A shift to profits will stimulate investment, employment, and growth. This tendency could be assisted by monetary expansion; the reduction of the unit labor cost would ease the inflationary danger of easier money.

What these three statements of the problem have in common is that they assume that market forces will, in due course, bring about the necessary restructuring of the economy to achieve substantially full employment, provided a moderate cut in the wage level is achieved, and macroeconomic levers are set right. The first of the two articles in *The Economist* cited above brings that assumption out very clearly. It argues that entrepreneurs would find hundreds of ways to substitute labor for capital if labor costs were reduced, just as they found ways to substitute capital for labor when wages went up.

This optimistic conclusion will be challenged by the "structuralists." In the 1930s it was widely believed that part of the unemployment problem was that labor-saving inventions had reduced the demand for labor, or that the "structure of production" had been distorted in some other way. In other words, it was argued that a large part of unemployment was "technological" and "structural," requiring large-scale reallocation of factors of production, a time-consuming, painful process. There can be no doubt that subsequent developments were entirely at variance with that structuralist theory. Experience has shown that as soon as deflation was stopped, the huge structural distortions that had been diagnosed by theorists during the depression had shriveled as quickly as they had surfaced earlier. What was called "secondary deflation" turned out to be a much more important cause of high unemployment than structural distortions that may have started the deflationary spiral. In other words, the great bulk of unemployment was "Keynesian" (or monetarist, if you like), not structural or "Hayekian."

Extreme structuralist views can be heard again today. It is said that robots and other "smart" machines have put human labor in the same position as horses were when tractors came into wide use. This is, however, a very misleading analogy. Tractors replaced not only horsepower but also manpower. But unlike horses, human labor could be shifted to producing tractors.

This is not to deny that it is possible that technological progress may require reallocation of factors of production that may cause some structural unemployment until the transfer and retraining of labor has been carried out. As we have seen, a modest decline of the share of labor in the national product is probably required now. But it is most unlikely that a large reduction of the marginal productivity of labor, an intolerable drop in the real wage, and a massive decline of the share of labor (and salaries) would occur, as the analogy with the horses suggests. As far as we can tell, the share of labor in the national product has remained remarkably stable—apart from cyclical fluctuations—despite the tremendous technological changes, including mechanization and automation, that have occurred since the industrial revolution in England.

I conclude that the present-day gloomy forecasts that disaster will befall us unless radical reforms are undertaken, involving massive redistribution of income to spread work, will turn out to be totally unfounded. These forecasts will share the fate of earlier, similar gloomy prophecies, which regularly made their appearance in periods of depression, from those underlying the Luddite movement to the most famous, Karl Marx's theory of increasing misery of the working classes—prophecies that were completely disproved and discredited by subsequent developments.

The Role of the Oil Shocks

The two oil shocks, the quadrupling of the crude oil price in 1973 and doubling in 1979–1980, have been widely held primarily responsible for the world inflation and the recession. In my opinion this is a great exaggeration. The first oil shock was preceded and accompanied by a highly inflationary commodity boom, which, in turn, was superimposed on an inflationary groundswell that encompassed the whole postwar period and went into high gear in the 1960s.[15] For the United States the additional oil import bill due to the first oil shock was about $20 billion a year. This was about 1.22 percent of the GNP at that time, or less than half of the normal annual increase in GNP. It follows that a once-for-all small decrease of about 1.22 percent in the wage level would have taken care of the problem, or, assuming that money wages were rigid downward, a once-for-all increase in the price level of about 1.22 percent would have solved the problem. An additional increase in inflation by 1.22 percentage points is a matter of minor importance in a period of two-digit inflation.

For other industrial countries the oil levy was a greater burden than for the United States, because they depend more heavily on imports. The jump in the oil import bill from 1973 to 1974 was about 4.31 percent of GNP for Japan, 3.96 percent for Italy, 3.73 percent for the United Kingdom, and 2.17 percent for Germany.[16] This is not a negligible burden, but it is not an intolerable one. For all Organization for Economic Development and Cooperation (OECD) countries as a group it was less than one year's normal growth. Hence, ideally, suspension of wage (income) growth for less than a year or a mild once-for-all rise in the price level would have taken care of the problem.

The conclusion I draw is that if one wants to assign to the oil price rise a major role in inflation and recession, it must be done by stressing *indirect* effects, for example, by assuming what J. R. Hicks has called "real wage resistance"—workers resisting not only money wage decreases but also real wage decreases, which could be brought about by widespread indexation of wages (and other incomes).

This theory has been widely applied to the second oil shock. Karl Otto Pöhl, president of the German Bundesbank, in a wide-ranging speech attributed "the present difficulties"—high inflation and unemployment—"to the delayed effect of the second oil price shock," in the sense that "all segments of society defend their acquired income levels and living standards against the dictates of OPEC."[17]

While in the first oil shock the OPEC crude oil price was quadrupled, in the second one it was "merely" doubled. For the United States the increase in the net oil import bill, the oil levy imposed by OPEC, amounted to about 0.52 percent of GNP. This can hardly be regarded as a major factor in the U.S. inflation or recession. For Germany the increase in the levy from 1979 to 1980 amounts to something like 0.86 percent of GNP. This factor can scarcely be assigned the major role in causing the German inflation or recession—a conclusion supported by the fact that Germany did not experience any noticeable improvement when the oil price tumbled in 1982. The same is true of Britain when it became a net exporter of oil.

The general conclusion is that the two oil shocks aggravated world inflation and thereby also the subsequent recession, but they were neither the initiating nor the major cause.

The International Debt Problem

A word must be said about the international debt problem, for it is widely feared that default by some of the large debtor countries— Mexico, Brazil— would topple a number of large international banks and thus plunge the world economy into a deep depression. This would justify, it is said, a bail-out of the banks or of the defaulting countries at almost any cost to the taxpayers of the United States and of other industrial countries.

I will not discuss this danger and the likelihood of its happening but will address a narrower question: If there are a few defaults and a large number of international banks get into serious trouble, would that have the same deflationary effect on the United States and other industrial countries as the collapse of the banking system and deflation had in the 1930s?

My answer is no. This relatively optimistic conclusion is based on the assumption that it is an established fact that the exceptional severity of the Great Depression of 1929–1933 was due to a contraction of the money stock by about 30 percent. One need not be an extreme monetarist to accept that proposition. Joseph A. Schumpeter, who was definitely not a monetarist, said that the waves of bank failures in the early 1930s "turned retreat into rout"; what otherwise would have been a regular or perhaps a relatively severe cyclical recession became a catastrophic slump.

It is unthinkable today that the monetary authorities would stand idly by and let the money supply contract by 30 percent as the Federal Reserve did in the 1930s. What would be necessary to avoid a sharp contraction of the money supply is not to protect the managers or shareholders of the banks, nor to bail out the defaulting countries, but to protect the depositors.

To sum up, a default of large debtor countries would be most unfortunate. It would be much better, also for the countries concerned, if they restored their credit-worthiness by putting their houses in order and by carrying out the austerity programs prescribed by the IMF. The default and its repercussions on the lending banks would put a damper on the recovery from the recession, but it would not plunge the industrial countries into a deep depression. If the major industrial countries keep their economies on an even keel, the rest of the world, too, will avoid a severe depression.

PART TWO
The International Monetary System

How Floating Originated—The Decline of the Dollar

The international monetary system, or nonsystem as some experts like to call it, is still one of widespread managed floating. All major currencies and many minor ones float, most of them with frequent interventions by central banks in the foreign exchange market.

There are, however, some areas of stable rates. Approximately 100, mostly small countries peg their currencies to the dollar, the German mark, the French franc, special drawing rights, or some other basket of currencies; and the nine members of the European Monetary System try to keep the exchange rate of their currencies in precarious stability, floating jointly against the dollar and other currencies.

It is not surprising that the recession caused exchange rate fluctuations, which in turn were and are widely regarded as excessive and as a sign of malfunctioning of floating exchange rates. As during the whole postwar period, the U.S. dollar is the center of discussion.

It will be useful to sketch very briefly the evolution of the international monetary system in the postwar period. Special reference will be made to how floating originated, because this is in danger of being forgotten.

During the early postwar period the dollar was generally accepted as "better than gold." This is underscored by the great popularity in the 1940s and 1950s of the theory of the "permanent" dollar shortage, which was especially popular in Britain, where even giants among economists such as J. R. Hicks and D. H. Robertson embraced it, though not in such a crude form as many others espoused it.[18]

The rapid recovery of Europe and Japan and the devaluation of the British pound and of many other currencies in 1949 confronted U.S. industries with increasing competition. The dollar lost some of its bloom and became "more equal." But up to the mid-1960s, the U.S. inflation was one of the lowest in the world, and the strength of the dollar remained unquestioned.

This began to change after 1965 when the Johnson administration started to finance the escalating war in Vietnam and the equally expensive Great Society programs at home through inflationary borrowing. Gradually, the emergence of a significant inflation differential between the United States and other industrial countries, primarily the three strong-currency countries, Germany, Switzerland, and later Japan, became noticeable. In 1969 the German mark and in June 1971 the Swiss franc were revalued. On August 15, 1971, the gold convertibility of the dollar was suspended, and the major currencies de facto floated. On December 18, 1971, in the Smithsonian realignment of exchange rates, the U.S. dollar was formally devalued, and most major currencies were revalued in terms of gold.

The Smithsonian Agreement did not last long. In June 1972 the British pound was set afloat, and early in 1973 the realignment became unstuck. After huge interventions in the foreign exchange markets by foreign central banks in the vain attempt to prop up the dollar, all major currencies were set afloat. Thus in 1973 the Bretton Woods regime came to an end. The adjustable peg system simply could not cope with the strains and stresses on the balance of payments caused by high global inflation.

That floating was imposed by events on reluctant policy makers is demonstrated by the fact that in 1974, a year after widespread floating had started, a prestigious Committee on Reform of the International Monetary System (Committee of Twenty) wrote in its report to the governors of the IMF, "The [reformed] exchange rate system will remain based on stable but adjustable par values."[19] According to insiders, the repeated statements by the committee that the reformed system would be one of stable but adjustable pegs "made the work of the Committee look increasingly unreal."[20]

In 1970 one dollar was worth 4.31 Swiss francs, 3.65 German marks, and 360 yen. Two years later the rates were 3.81 Swiss francs, 3.81 German marks, and 303 yen. Since then there have been fairly large fluctuations, but even after the recent surge of the dollar, its value in terms of the three strong-currency countries did not come anywhere near the 1970 level, though the average effective exchange rate vis-à-vis fifteen major countries (as measured by Morgan Guaranty Trust Company of New York) was about the same in early 1983 as in pre-June 1970.

Five years later, in 1975, the dollar had another spell of weakness, which again was the consequence of a large inflation differential between the United States and the strong-currency countries. The year 1974 was one of high global inflation. Even Switzerland had a 10 percent inflation rate. In the United States the inflation rate reached 12 percent but was brought down to a little below 5 percent by the end of 1976. It started to rise again and reached the two-digit level in 1979 when the Carter administration prematurely shifted emphasis from fighting inflation to stimulating the economy.[21]

The three strong-currency countries, in contrast, continued the anti-inflation policy. Switzerland brought its rate of inflation down to practically zero. As a consequence of this disinflation policy, the three countries had a slower recovery from the recession than the United States; they accepted a temporarily lower rate of growth of output and employment to bring inflation down, while the United States impatiently reflated the economy.

The divergent growth and price trends, the result of a divergent policy stance, produced a heavy deficit in the U.S. trade and current account balance, which was widely regarded as an alarm signal. The trade deficit was $9.3 billion in 1976, $30.9 billion in 1977, and $33.7 billion in 1978. The current account balance had a surplus of $4.6 million in 1976 and a deficit of $14 billion in 1977 and $13.5 billion in 1978. No wonder that market participants, both private and official (foreign central banks), became increasingly pessimistic about the fu-

101

ture of the dollar and started to diversify their currency holdings. In October 1978 the foreign exchange markets became quite jittery, and on November 1, 1978, President Carter announced a sharp reversal of economic policy, the so-called (first) dollar rescue operation, consisting of a tightening of monetary policy and the mobilization of a $30 billion fund of foreign currencies for interventions in the foreign exchange market.

The response of the markets was dramatic. From October 31, 1978, to December 8, 1978, with the assistance of central bank interventions, the mark declined against the dollar by 8.2 percent, the Swiss franc by 12.9 percent, and the yen by 3.7 percent. The dollar appreciated overall by about 7.9 percent. The monetary restraint did not, however, last very long. Before the middle of 1979 the monetary aggregates resumed their rapid climb. The dollar again declined, and the markets became unsettled. At the annual meeting of the International Monetary Fund in Belgrade, according to news reports, Paul Volcker, the newly appointed chairman of the Board of Governors of the Federal Reserve System, was put on notice by some of his European colleagues that they would stop supporting the dollar if the United States did not take decisive steps against inflation. Volcker left the meeting hurriedly, and on October 6, 1979, the second dollar rescue package was announced, consisting of a sharp rise in the discount rate, higher reserve requirements for certain types of liabilities, and a shift in the operating procedures of monetary policy from emphasis on interest rate targets to emphasis on monetary aggregates.[22] Since then, the growth of monetary aggregates has slowed, and interest rates have risen sharply.

The policy shift of October 1979 was a real turning point. At last the process of disinflation had started. The response of the foreign exchange market was again favorable, though the steep ascent of the dollar got under way only a year later, after the election of Ronald Reagan.

The Rise of the Dollar since 1980 and the
Recent Criticism of Floating Exchange Rates

The dramatic rise of the dollar, since 1980, as measured overall by the trade-weighted effective rate and vis-à-vis the Swiss franc, the German mark, and Japanese yen, is depicted in figure 1. The chart also shows large fluctuations. The dollar appreciated also in real terms as measured by the real exchange rate (the nominal effective rate adjusted for inflation in the countries concerned), both overall and against the three countries mentioned. This means that the recent appreciation of the dollar, unlike its depreciation in the early 1970s, cannot, at least not fully, be explained by inflation differentials or purchasing power parity changes.

Before taking up possible explanations, I will discuss various criticisms of floating exchange rates that were induced, revived, and intensified by the appreciation of the dollar.

We have seen that in official circles floating was accepted very reluctantly and with a very costly delay.[23] In academic circles, too, much aversion to flexible exchange rates and a deep-seated nostalgia for fixed rates quickly developed.

It is natural that advocates of the gold standard deplore floating, though it seems that some of them are ready to settle for stable but adjustable rates à la Bretton Woods. Now that the Gold Commission has issued its report, it is hardly necessary to set out the reasons why a return to the gold standard and fixed rates is entirely out of the question.

It is interesting, however, and should give satisfaction to the advocates of the gold standard, that the basic rule of balance of payments adjustment under the gold standard inevitably emerges again and again in present-day discussions—in modern terminology, of course, and transposed to the inflationary conditions of our times. This rule can be stated as follows: A deficit country that loses gold should let its money supply decline by the full amount of the gold loss or by more. A country in surplus should let its money supply expand by the full amount of the gold gain or by more. This will bring downward pressure on money incomes and prices in the deficit country, and upward pressure in the surplus countries, and thus restore equilibrium in the balance of payments.[24]

To translate the rule into modern terminology, substitute the broader concept of "international reserves" for the gold stock and reflect that the policy of the central banks under the gold standard to buy and sell gold at the gold export and import points, respectively, to keep exchange rates stable can be described as "nonsterilized interventions." (More will be said on the distinction of "sterilized" or "pure" and "nonsterilized" interventions later in this chapter.)

To transpose the gold standard rule to the inflationary conditions of our times, substitute "changes in monetary growth targets" for "absolute changes in the money supply." Countries in deficit should lower their monetary growth targets; countries in surplus should raise their monetary growth targets.

I cite two examples of the recent reappearance, in modern dress, of the basic role of the gold standard. Ronald E. McKinnon in a widely noted paper, "Currency Substitution and Instability in the World Dollar Standard," argues that the instability of the world dollar standard stems from the fact that the United States and many other countries

FIGURE 1
MOVEMENTS IN EXCHANGE RATES, 1975–1983

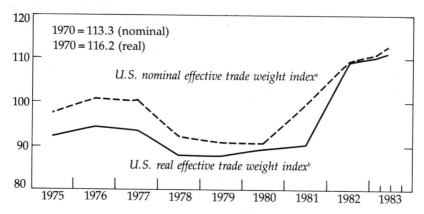

1970 = 113.3 (nominal)
1970 = 116.2 (real)

U.S. nominal effective trade weight index[a]

U.S. real effective trade weight index[b]

a. 1980–1982 = 100. The index measures the currency's trade-weighted value vis-à-vis fifteen other major currencies. Annual figures are averages of months. Trade weights based on 1980 bilateral trade in manufactures.

b. 1980–1982 = 100. Index of the nominal effective exchange rate adjusted for inflation differentials, which are measured by wholesale prices of nonfood manufactures.

SOURCE: World Financial Markets, August 1983, Morgan Guaranty Trust Company of New York.

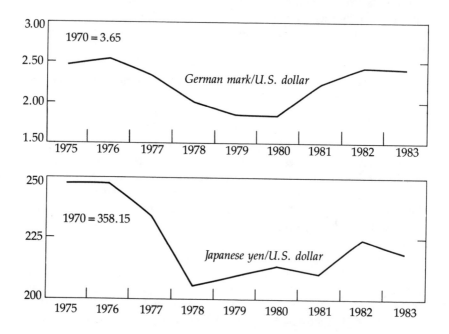

1970 = 3.65

German mark/U.S. dollar

1970 = 358.15

Japanese yen/U.S. dollar

FIGURE 1 (continued)

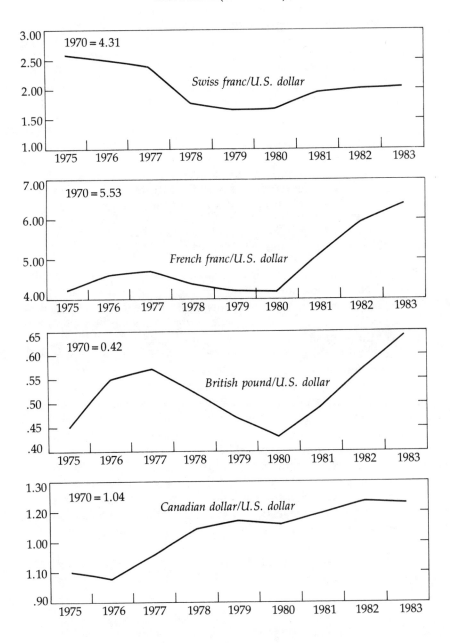

NOTE: Data for 1983 are averages of data from the first and second quarters of 1983.
SOURCE: Federal Reserve Board, Exchange Rate Release G-5.

"define [their monetary] policy targets in terms of growth rates of purely domestic monetary aggregates."[25] He claims that "even for the United States itself, this [his] tentative measure of changes in the world money supply explains the great (dollar) price inflations of 1973–74 and 1979–80 much better than does any domestic American aggregate."[26]

What the author is really saying is best understood by turning to the last section of his paper, entitled "Policy Implications." The author says that

> the solution to international currency instability is straightforward: the Federal Reserve System should discontinue its policy of passively sterilizing the domestic monetary impact of foreign official interventions. Instead, a symmetrical non-sterilization rule would ensure that each country's money supply mutually adjusts to international currency substitution in the short run without having official exchange interventions destabilize the world's money supply.[27]

He suggests that for all practical purposes "Germany, Japan, and the United States are capable of jointly bringing the world's supply of convertible money under control through a mutual non-sterilization pact and agreed-on rates of domestic credit expansion by each of the three central banks."[28]

To recognize that this is equivalent to the basic rule of balance of payments adjustment under the gold standard, only in modern dress, it should be recalled that gold sales and purchases by the central banks to keep the exchange rate stable can be described as a policy of nonsterilized intervention. This is exactly what McKinnon prescribes.

The other key concept is that of domestic credit expansion (DCE) as distinguished from an expansion of the money supply. This brings me to the second example of the resurrection of the basic rule of the gold standard where the concept of the DCE plays the key role.

William H. White of the IMF has drawn my attention to the fact that the IMF, at the suggestion of J. J. Polak, has recommended in a number of cases the use of DCE for setting the proper target for monetary policy in open economies.

In 1969 Britain accepted the advice of the Fund, and the new policy was lucidly set out by the Bank of England in its *Quarterly Bulletin*:

> Put briefly, DCE may be viewed as the total arrived at after adjusting the increase in the money supply to take account of any change in money balances directly caused by an external surplus or deficit. DCE is thus approximately equal to the increase in the money supply plus those sterling funds accru-

ing to the authorities by their provision of foreign exchange, from one source or another, for the accommodation of an external deficit or, conversely, minus the sterling finance required to accommodate an external surplus.[29]

To understand that this is equivalent to the gold standard rule, consider that in countries suffering from an external deficit, DCE indicates a larger monetary growth than does the money supply figure; it follows that restraining measures should be taken. In surplus countries, in contrast, DCE shows a *smaller* expansion than money supply figures; hence, expansionary measures should be taken.

This is, of course, part and parcel of the "monetary approach" to the balance of payments, which was independently developed by the IMF staff, J. J. Polak, Marcus J. Fleming, and their associates, and by academic economists Harry G. Johnson, Jacob A. Frenkel, and others.[30]

Two giants in the area of international monetary economics— Charles Kindleberger and Randall Hinshaw—have always been critical of floating. The latter recently gave expression to his feelings by giving the title *Global Monetary Anarchy* to the latest volume of his famous series of conference volumes.[31]

Another prominent member of the fraternity of the international monetary specialists, Fred Bergsten, who describes himself as a "traditional supporter" of the system, said that "the system of flexible exchange rates has now produced—or at least permitted—a disequilibrium situation at least as great as that which emerged during the final years of the Bretton Woods system." The dollar has become substantially overvalued, "by an average of 20–25 percent and by much more against the German mark and Japanese yen." As a consequence, "the price competitiveness of the U.S. economy has severely deteriorated" and so have the trade balance and current account balance.[32] Bergsten was thus one of the first to stress the depressive effect of the alleged overvaluation of the dollar on the U.S. economy. "Since the first quarter of this year [1982], the fall in net exports accounted for almost 80 percent of the total decline in real U.S. GNP in the second quarter, and more than explains the entire drop in the third quarter."[33]

This view has been widely accepted. The gloom cast by that theory has been lifted, however, by the U.S. economy's healthy recovery from the cyclical recession, despite the alleged overvaluation of the dollar and large trade deficits.

Except for the advocates of the gold standard, hardly anyone recommends a return to stable but adjustable, let alone fixed, exchange rates. What is widely recommended is a more vigorous policy of official interventions in the foreign exchange market to counteract what is regarded as excessive volatility of exchange rates. I will briefly discuss the views of three prominent experts, two officials and one academic.

In an important, wide-ranging speech, republished a year later in an updated version, Otmar Emminger pleads for an active exchange rate policy and judicious interventions on the foreign exchange market.[34] He distinguishes two types of cases where official interventions are justified and when judiciously executed have often been successful.

First,

> foreign exchange markets, if left entirely to themselves, are notoriously volatile and erratic, at least on occasion . . . . They are very sensitive to psychological and political influences. Strong upward or downward movements have a tendency to feed upon themselves and become exaggerated (bandwagon-effect). Smoothing out wild, erratic fluctuations [by judicious interventions]—without trying to "stabilize" a specific rate, and without operating against basic trends—may give the market a helping hand . . . . In the past, many of these smoothing-over interventions proved to be self-reversing, and in my experience, when a currency was oversold or overbought, it needed often relatively small amounts of intervention to restore calm and reason.

He here refers to what is often called "disorderly market conditions."

The second, much more important type of malfunctioning of the foreign exchange market is this:

> When a large fundamental disequilibrium in the balance of payments develops, floating exchange rates often have a tendency not only to overshoot but to overcorrect. Some overshooting, i.e., a movement beyond relative cost and price trends, may be necessary and useful in order to bring about the required adjustment of the payments balance on current-account. But sometimes exchange rate swings go clearly beyond such useful overshooting, beyond what can be justified by the underlying payments situations.

In such cases official interventions in the exchange market are justified.

Emminger makes it clear, however, that no attempt should be made to hold stable a "specific rate of exchange," and he emphasizes that the dollar presents a special case: "For the U.S. dollar there is certainly no other solution than free floating, be it with or without occasional intervention in the exchange market. There is no other currency the dollar could hang on to," and it does not seem "practical" to peg it to a "currency basket." Emminger thinks that "deliberate exchange rate policies" of countries other than the United States are "compatible with the present U.S. administration's policy not to intervene at all in the foreign exchange market except in emergency situations, provided that the administration does not object to other countries intervening as they see fit."

Clearly, Emminger is opposed to a return to a Bretton Woods system, and he gives short shrift to the idea of resurrecting the gold standard: "All the King's horses and all the King's men cannot put Humpty-Dumpty together again."

The difficulty of a policy of intervention that goes beyond the attempt at smoothing out very short-term oscillations ("disorderly market conditions") is that at any time it is impossible to be sure whether the long-run equilibrium has been undershot or overshot. True, with the benefit of hindsight, it is often possible to reach an agreement that overshooting has occurred in the sense that the market has reversed itself within a relatively short period of time. But even in retrospect problems remain. Not every reversal of the market can be regarded as a case of overshooting that should have been prevented by official interventions. It may have been due to events unforeseen by the market as well as by the authorities. Moreover, as Emminger says, some overshooting may be desirable to bring about the required adjustments in the balance of payments and, we may add, in the policies of the authorities.

The contrast between ex post facto and ex ante is neatly illustrated by Emminger's paper. Although in 1981 he was quite sure in his judgment that the dollar was undervalued in 1977 and 1978 and the yen in 1979, he said, "it *might* be that the *present* depreciation of the D mark . . . will later also turn out as a case of overcorrection" (italics added). A year later his uncertainty about 1981 had disappeared. In his brilliant pamphlet, *Exchange Rate Policy Reconsidered*, he said:

> American observers, official and unofficial, sometimes poked fun at the Europeans because they always seemed to complain about the dollar: in 1978 that it was far too low and in 1981 that it was far too high. But it is likely that the Europeans were right in both cases, i.e. that a rate of DM 1.70 to the dollar was just as much out of line with all fundamentals as at DM 2.50. It is indeed extremely unlikely that the fundamental factors determining the equilibrium rate between the dollar and the Deutschemark could have justified a change of 50 percent within three years.[35]

I suggest that even in restrospect the case is not at all clear. Since the under- or overvaluation of the mark is the mirror picture of the under- or overvaluation of the dollar, it will be convenient to recall why the dollar declined sharply from 1977 to 1979 and rose sharply in 1980 to 1982–1983.

Emminger explains the decline of the dollar in terms of the large current account deficits in 1977 and 1978—$14 billion each year.[36] But we have seen that these deficits as well as the decline of the dollar can be traced to inflation and growth differentials that developed between the United States and Germany, Japan, and Switzerland, when the Carter administration embarked on expansionary policies, and inflation rose to the two-digit level.

The decline of the dollar made the two dollar-rescue operations necessary. The *first* one, in 1978 under Fed Chairman G. William Miller, at first calmed the markets but then proved ineffective because the disinflation was not carried through. The *second*, in October 1979 under Fed Chairman Paul Volcker, proved to be a real turning point. It is highly doubtful that the unavoidable disinflation would have been carried through if the decline of the dollar had not scared the politicians. Call it overshooting if you like; but it was a beneficial one. Floating once again showed its disciplinary capability.

Whether the dramatic rise of the dollar since 1980 has been a pernicious overshooting that should have been prevented will be discussed presently. The intrinsic uncertainty of the judgment that overshooting has occurred is often expressed by the question, why should the judgment of the monetary authorities be better than that of the market? Alexandre Lamfalussy in two important speeches rises to the challenge of this question.[37]

Lamfalussy deplores the great volatility of exchange rates in recent years and pleads for "greater stability" through "official action," including vigorous interventions in the foreign exchange market, though he makes it clear that he is not advocating a return to pegged exchanges.[38] "Floating among the dollar, the D-mark and the yen seems to be the only practical way of letting exchange rate changes play their indispensable role in the balance of payments adjustment process."

What, then, is Lamfalussy's answer to the question why should the authorities' judgment of what is the appropriate exchange rate be better than that of the market? In his words,

> Why should the authorities be better than other market participants in forecasting the future? The answer is, simply, that they are "market participants" of a special kind . . . . The authorities know, or at least are supposed to know, what policy they are pursuing and therefore by intervening in the exchange market they signal their policy stance. In other words, intervention means that the authorities are putting their money where their mouth is.

This sounds like a plea for nonsterilized interventions. A little later Lamfalussy indeed speaks of interventions that have their "full

110

effect on the domestic money markets." But Lamfalussy is not a monetarist. His conception of a "country's main policy thrust" comprises
"interest rate policy" and "fiscal policy," not merely changes in the
money supply. He illustrates his position by "the example of a sharply
deteriorating currency. It clearly would be a waste of money to try to
prop up [by intervention in the exchange market] their currency if the
government's fiscal and monetarist policies are more expansionary
than those of other countries." Interventions are useful only if "the
direction in which intervention goes is compatible with the country's
main policy thrust." This applies, he says, "even to 'pure' interventions, i.e. to interventions which have no effect on the domestic
money supply" (sterilized intervention) and "a fortiori" to nonsterilized interventions.

As a set of principles, this sounds plausible: With optimal adjustment policies, carried out persistently, interventions would contribute
to stability. Unfortunately, governments frequently lack persistence in
carrying out their plans, especially in an election year. Moreover, the
accuracy of their assessment of how the proposed policies will work
out and how individual measures will affect demand and supply of
foreign exchange and the exchange rate is not always correct, to put it
mildly. It follows that there is a good chance that, contrary to what
Lamfalussy says, the forecast of the markets will be more accurate
than that of the authorities.

In his London speech of February 1983, Lamfalussy repeats the
reason why, in his opinion, the authorities' judgment of the appropriate exchange rate may be better than that of the market, which justified vigorous intervention or, more generally, exchange rate policies.
No additional comments are required on this part of his interesting
speech.

He points also to recent developments that, in his opinion, signify
a glaring malfunctioning of floating and of the uncontrolled foreign
exchange market. Lamfalussy, correctly, points out that the depreciation of the D-mark in recent years is just the other side of the
appreciation of the dollar. Both the appreciation of the dollar
and the depreciation of the D-mark are in *real* terms; in other words,
the exchange rate "overshot" the purchasing power parity and the
inflation differential. He concludes:

> To fight inflation imported through the depreciation of the
> real effective exchange rate, interest rates will have to serve
> exchange rate objectives rather than stimulating a depressed
> economy. This is not text-book theorizing, but a description of
> what happened in the Federal Republic of Germany in 1980–
> 81; it is only more recently, since the intra-EEC exchange rate
> adjustments, that the problem has lost its acuteness for Ger-

many. It is the irony of history that floating, which has been proposed as an effective way of freeing domestic policy from external constraints, has in fact, precisely in the German case, imposed such a constraint on the freedom of policy makers.

The problem will be taken up presently when I discuss the alleged overvaluation of the dollar and what can and ought to be done about it. But three comments are called for here.

First, that the inflationary effect of the rise of the dollar on Europe is not due to a malfunctioning of the market under floating becomes clear if one reflects on what would have happened under fixed exchanges (gold standard or Bretton Woods). It can be shown that under fixed rates the Europeans would have suffered much more than under floating. The reason is that high interest rates in the United States would have attracted much more capital (and gold) under fixed exchange rates than under floating. This in turn is due to the fact that under floating foreign investors in dollars have an exchange risk; they cannot be quite sure that the market has not overshot the mark and will reverse itself. Under fixed rates, this risk is absent. This is the well-known reason why fixed rates, especially stable but adjustable rates, are so vulnerable to destabilizing speculation. The upshot is that the Europeans would be put under heavy deflationary pressure and would have to raise interest rates to protect the par value of their currencies.

Thus, there is nothing ironic about the fact that floating cannot protect a country from *real* influences from abroad, such as the oil shocks or, more generally, changes in international demand and in the terms of trade; nor does it protect a country from shifts in capital flows, as the one just discussed. But fixed rates are no protection either in such cases.

It has been explained many times, however, that floating can ward off *monetary* shocks from outside. So let it be repeated once more that in the early 1970s and again in 1978–1980, floating enabled Germany, Switzerland, and Japan to enjoy a much lower inflation rate than the United States and that in the 1930s floating (or devaluation) made it possible for a number of countries to extricate themselves from world deflation long before the U.S. economy emerged from the depression. In other words, floating shielded countries from imported inflation and deflation.

Second, to speak of a "collapse" of the theory of purchasing power parity as Jacob Frenkel does is an exaggeration. But there is probably agreement that neither purchasing power parity calculations nor inflation differentials are reliable indicators of equilibrium exchange rates in the short and medium run. Since it is based on international price comparisons the real effective exchange rate, like purchasing power parity and inflation differentials, is an uncertain guide to the equilibrium exchange rate in the short term.

Third, it is odd to say that the EMS has alleviated Germany's economic difficulties. From the economic standpoint, the EMS has been a great failure. Frequent exchange realignments, preceded and accompanied by waves of destabilizing speculation, have demonstrated once again that stable but adjustable exchange rates are not a suitable arrangement in the present world. The EMS has been an economic burden for Germany and is kept alive, at great cost, for political reasons—to forestall France's exit from the European Community. *Frankerich's Uhren Gehen Anders.*[39]

The following is an example of a prominent academic economist who has become disenchanted with floating. Peter Kenen says:

> Looking back on our experience with floating rates and at the behavior of particular currencies, I have begun to wonder whether this trip was necessary. I am therefore increasingly interested in target zones and crawling pegs as second-best solutions to a difficult problem. I am likewise intrigued by Bergsten's suggestion that a temporary reinstatement of Japanese capital controls could help with the most serious exchange-rate problem facing the world right now.[40]

This is hardly convincing. Looking back at the turbulences of the 1970s, I find it difficult to disagree with what Otmar Emminger said in 1980: "No other system but floating could have coped with the enormous short-term swings in the U.S. balance on current account—from a surplus of $18 billion in 1975 to deficits of $14 billion in each of the years 1977 and 1978 . . . .," and with two oil shocks, we may add.[41] The remedies mentioned by Kenen strike me as third-best of the band-aid variety. But since the whole problem has been largely defused by the rapid recovery of the U.S. economy from the recession despite the "overvalued" dollar and larger trade deficits, it is not necessary to repeat again the arguments against the suggested measures.

The Problem of the "Overvalued" Dollar

The dramatic rise of the dollar since 1980 can be explained by two mutually supporting factors, high interest rates in the United States and the fact that the U.S. economy again offers a confidence-inspiring atmosphere for foreign investors.

The high interest rates can be traced back to large current and projected budget deficits, in relation to the flow of private saving, and to lingering doubt that inflation has been definitely curbed and will not be reignited by the ongoing cyclical recovery.

The U.S. economy is a safe haven for foreign investors for several reasons, economic as well as political ones: political and economic stability, absence of controls on international transactions, and the existence of a large, efficient capital market.

Whatever the correct explanation, it is certainly true that the appreciation of the dollar and the large trade deficits have a significant depressive influence. This fact has disturbed some experts who say that it has cost the economy several percentage points of real growth.

This is, however, a very shortsighted argument. In the *first* place, it ignores the fact that despite the appreciation of the dollar and the large trade deficits, the U.S. economy has staged an unexpectedly vigorous expansion. Many experts believe that the expansion has been too fast to be sustainable. If that is accepted, by slowing down the pace of the expansion, the appreciation of the dollar and the trade deficit may well have a positive effect on real GNP growth in the longer run.

In the *second* place, and even more important, the argument overlooks the fact that the appreciation of the dollar and the trade deficits are also potent anti-inflationary factors. Some counterfactual theorizing will reveal the far-reaching implications of this fact.

Suppose the dollar had not gone up in the foreign exchange market because, say, market participants had lacked confidence in the future; in this case a powerful disinflationary factor would have been lost. It follows that, assuming we wish to bring down inflation, the Fed would have had to step harder on the monetary brake. Therefore, the recession would have been about the same as it actually was.[42] It is hardly necessary to point out that if the Fed had not stepped on the brake, the recession would have been merely postponed and would have later reappeared in an aggravated form.

Now let us change the scenario. Suppose the Fed or foreign central banks[43] had tried to prevent the dollar from rising by massive interventions in the foreign exchange market, as has been widely and even vociferously demanded, especially in weak-currency countries.[44]

There is no doubt it would have been easy for the Fed to prevent the dollar from rising, or to bring it down, by nonsterilized interventions, that is, by selling dollars and buying German marks, Japanese yen—and French francs—and by letting the money supply go up in the process at the high cost of reaccelerating inflation.

What remains in doubt is, *first*, whether such a policy would improve the competitive position of U.S. industries and thus reduce the trade deficit, and, *second*, whether interventions in the foreign exchange market, without an increase in the money supply—in other words, whether pure or sterilized interventions—would do any good. I discuss these two issues in turn.

114

The *first* question can be put as follows: The decline of the value of the dollar relative to other currencies, in other words, the decline of the trade weighted effective rate per se, undoubtedly stimulates exports and restrains imports and thus tends to improve the trade balance. But does not the inflation caused by the increase in the money supply operate in the opposite direction? Is there a reason to believe that the two opposite effects will offset each other, or that the one or the other will dominate the outcome?

Martin Feldstein, in a recent paper, reached the conclusion that "the essential impact of a change in the money stock [resulting from interventions] in the foreign exchange market is to alter only the *nominal* rate. Any decline in the real exchange value of the dollar would be only temporary." The result "therefore" would be "to leave the incentive to import and export unchanged." [45] This implies that the opposite effects mentioned above tend to offset each other exactly.

This conclusion is based on the assumption that inflation would accelerate quickly, in other words, that we do not live in a Keynesian world where output could be expanded without large price increases.

Many economists would probably agree that the economy is now much closer to the "classical" extreme than to the Keynesian. The elasticity of aggregate output (real GNP) with respect to an increase in aggregate nominal demand is low, despite the relatively high unemployment rate. There are two reasons for that. First, inflationary expectations have been sensitized by a long period of inflation, and, second, much of the unemployment is structural and requires time-consuming relocation of labor. The implication is to support Feldstein's conclusion: An inflationary intervention policy to bring down the value of the dollar relative to other currencies would probably improve the competitive position of the U.S. industries only slightly and temporarily.

I come to the *second* open question concerning the effectiveness or ineffectiveness of pure or sterilized interventions—a question that has received a good deal of attention recently. Under this system the Fed creates money by selling dollars in the foreign exchange market and then offsets (sterilizes) the additional dollars by selling Treasury bills in the domestic security markets (or by raising the discount rate or increasing reserve requirements of the banks). This is, however, only one half of the whole transaction. The other half relates to how the Fed disposes of the foreign currency, say D-marks, which it acquires in the foreign exchange market. If the intervention is to be fully sterilized, it must be assumed that the D-marks are invested in D-mark denominated securities, for if the Fed kept the marks the German effective demand (MV) would be reduced. This becomes clear if we consider what happens if the intervention is carried out by the Bundesbank selling dollars for marks rather than by the Fed. The final outcome must be the same. But there is this difference: If the Bundesbank sells dollars for marks, the stock of marks (M) declines; if the Fed acquires marks, the velocity of circulation of money (V) declines. In both cases effective demand (MV) declines, which makes the transaction a case of nonsterilized intervention. To sterilize the effect the mark must be invested in mark-denominated securities.

There is, I believe, general agreement that sterilized interventions are much less effective, many would say totally ineffective, compared with nonsterilized interventions in influencing the exchange rates.[46] Why this is so becomes clear when we consider that, unlike nonsterilized interventions, sterilized interventions (1) do not change the money supply and (2) tend to raise interest rates in the country whose currency is sold, compared with the country whose currency is bought. In our example, when the Fed sells Treasury bills, it tends to boost U.S. interest rates. When it buys mark-denominated securities, it tends to depress German interest rates. The incipient interest differential will attract capital from abroad. These additional capital imports constitute demand for dollars. The net effect, if any, of the whole operation on the exchange rate will depend on the comparative strength of the two forces operating in *opposite* directions: Sales of dollars in the foreign exchange market weaken the dollar; sales of Treasury bills tend to strengthen the dollar.[47] If the additional demand for dollars resulting from capital inflow exceeds the additional supply of dollars resulting from the sale of dollars, the dollar will strengthen, which means that the whole operation was counterproductive. The opposite will be true if the additional demand falls short of the additional supply; in that case the whole operation has the desired effect of weakening the dollar. If the two forces are of equal strength, the intervention has no effect on the exchange rate.

Whether sterilized interventions have an effect on exchange rates depends on whether or not the public regards securities of different currency denominations as perfect substitutes. In our example, if market participants were indifferent to whether they held mark- or dollar-denominated securities, sterilized interventions would have no effect on the exchange rate, for the slightest interest differential would lead to capital shifts from marks into dollars. Hence, an additional supply of dollars resulting from sales of dollars in the foreign exchange market would be matched by increased demand resulting from capital imports.

The assumption of perfect substitutability of securities denominated in different currencies is obviously unrealistic. The reason is that there is always an exchange risk, especially under floating. This implies that sterilized interventions have some effect, as becomes clear if one considers that sterilized interventions alter the relative size of the stock of outstanding securities of different currency denominations. If the Fed intervenes, the stock of dollar-denominated securities increases. If the Bundesbank intervenes by buying mark-denominated securities to offset (sterilize) the decrease in the money supply, the stock of mark-denominated securities decreases. In either case the ratio of the stock of dollar-denominated to that of mark-denominated securities increases. To induce the market to accept the changed portfolio, an interest differential and/or a change in the actual or expected exchange rate is required. We can, then, take it for granted that sterilized interventions will have some effect.

What is still uncertain is the magnitude of the effect. It is generally assumed, rightly in my opinion, that, considering the huge volume of outstanding securities denominated in major currencies, sterilized intervention would have to be of truly massive proportions to have a significant effect—massive, that is to say, compared with the volume of interventions that have actually been made. Indirectly sterilized interventions may have an effect, for example, if they give market participants the impression that the authorities are determined to take stronger measures, if necessary, to bring about the desired change in the exchange rate—in other words, if sterilized interventions are regarded as the precursor of nonsterilized interventions.

The Recent Policy of "Coordinated Interventions" in the Foreign Exchange Market

On August 1, 1983, it was announced in Washington, with considerable fanfare, that at the urging of European countries and Japan the United States had agreed to joint "coordinated interventions" in the foreign exchange market. On the face of it, this is a sharp reversal of the present administration's policy of interventions. To describe it as a case of "correcting disorderly market conditions," as a high official put it, is rather odd. The Europeans certainly do not see it that way. They want a lower dollar. The persistent rise of the dollar may be exaggerated and undesirable, but there is nothing disorderly about it. The change in policy is better described as a gesture of good will; some would call it "appeasement." Actually, as we shall see, the U.S. concession does not amount to much.

As usual, the French were in the forefront of the critics of U.S. policy. French Minister of Finance M. Jacques Delors "sharply criticized" U.S. policy for "high interest rates and the hausse of the dollar," for "showing no concern for European interests," and for "ignoring the decisions of the Williamsburg Economic Summit." He demanded joint action and more "solidarity."[48] The minister evidently wants other countries to jump on the inflationary bandwagon to let France off the hook.

Since August 1, sizable interventions have been taken by the United States, by West Germany, and by other countries. As usual, the magnitude of interventions was not divulged, nor were the currencies involved. But according to informed sources, the total of all interventions for the first eight days or so was between $2.5 billion and $3 billion, and they have all involved sales of dollars for marks and other currencies.

Most interventions have been of the sterilized kind. When the New York Fed sells dollars, it almost simultaneously sells Treasury bills for the same amount so that the money supply is not affected. That the German interventions, too, are sterilized follows from the fact that the German minister of finance and the president of the Bundesbank have stated that interest rates will not be raised because of the fragility of the German recovery.[49] Nonsterilized interventions would do just that—raise interest rates. The Swiss National Bank, too, has intervened by selling dollars for marks; how much was not stated. The operation was officially described as "neutral with respect to Swiss monetary growth" and the president of the Swiss National Bank, Fritz Leutwiler, while expressing the view that joint action of several central banks can be useful in certain situations, has emphasized the "priority of monetary policy."[50]

Fears have been expressed that the policy of internationally coordinated interventions to stop or reverse the rise of the dollar will have inflationary effects in the United States. These fears are unfounded so long as the interventions are sterilized. Sterilized interventions have no direct inflationary effect because the money supply remains unchanged. The rise of interest rates resulting from the sale of Treasury bills may even be said to be slightly anti-inflationary. Indirectly, the policy possibly may have an inflationary effect if it succeeds in reducing the external value of the dollar, for we have seen that the high dollar is an anti-inflationary factor.

But this qualification is unimportant because, as we have seen, there is fairly general agreement that sterilized interventions have little, if any, effect on the exchange rates. True, it has been shown that if market participants are not indifferent with respect to the currency composition of their assets, sterilized interventions will have some effect on the exchange rate. It should be noted that this argument involves portfolio considerations, which makes the *stock* of assets relevant. It follows that the effect on the exchange rates is likely to be minimal in view of the enormous size of outstanding assets in relation to the magnitude of interventions.

The upshot is that the effect of the whole operation is likely to be negligible. It has been argued that it may even have a negative effect. The almost daily announcements that this or that central bank will intervene, followed as they usually are by a further rise of the dollar, may fortify bullish expectations of market participants about the future course of the dollar. Since the rise of the dollar sooner or later (probably sooner than later) will come to an end or even reverse itself somewhat, not much harm will be done.

The whole operation must look very attractive to the participating central banks. When the rise of the dollar stops, they can claim that their interventions turned the tide. And it will never be quite certain whether the intervention prolonged or shortened the rise of the dollar. These conclusions are based on the assumption that the interventions continue to be fully sterilized.

Concluding Remarks on Floating: Summing Up

I will start with some general observations. Floating should be regarded as a second best. The best system would be fixed rates— provided at least three basic conditions are fulfilled. *First,* monetary policies (or more generally macroeconomic policies) in participating countries have to be closely coordinated. National inflation rates must be roughly the same. *Second,* there must be a certain amount of wage flexibility, also in the downward direction, which means that no country would have to submit to periods of general Keynesian unemployment because of its balance of payments.[51] These conditions were fulfilled in the heyday of the gold standard. Wages were much more flexible, also in the downward direction, than they are now, and the common link to gold and the rules of the gold standard game assured close coordination of monetary policy and roughly equal inflation rates in all countries. *Third,* there must be no exchange control of any kind.[52]

Unfortunately, today the conditions for fixed (or semifixed) exchange rates exist only in exceptional cases. They do not exist between the leading industrial countries—the United States, Japan, Germany, Great Britain, France, and Italy. Real exceptions are the numerous, mostly small countries that peg their currencies to the dollar, the D-mark, or some other currency or basket of currencies, provided these countries maintain their fixed exchange rates without exchange control and without intolerable unemployment or inflation. Examples are Austria, Taiwan, Venezuela, and Kuwait.

The European Monetary System is no exception. Inflation differentials between member countries are large; exchange rate realignments occur frequently, preceded and accompanied by very large speculative capital flights; and one country, France, was forced to

119

introduce tight exchange control involving searches at the border, censorship of the mail, and tight rationing of foreign exchange for travel abroad—a system reminiscent of what used to be called the Schachtian system during the Nazi period in Germany—in clear violation of the spirit if not the letter of the IMF charter and the Treaty of Rome by which the EMS was set up.[53] From the economic point of view the EMS has been a costly failure. It has imposed a heavy burden, especially on Germany, and is kept alive largely for political reasons, to prevent France from isolating itself even more from the European Community. If the EMS were dissolved, some of its members—the Netherlands, Belgium, and Luxembourg, possibly also Denmark and Ireland—would peg to the D-mark as Austria does. From the economic point of view, an open-ended D-mark bloc would be a better arrangement than the EMS.

The conclusion is that floating is here to stay; a global return to fixed or semifixed exchanges is out of the question.

The principal advantage claimed for floating in our imperfect world is that it protects countries from inflationary and deflationary shocks from abroad. Thus, in the 1970s it enabled Switzerland, Germany, Japan, and some other countries to reduce their inflation rate way below the level they would have had if they had kept the link with the dollar. In the 1930s, floating (or at that time devaluations) made it possible for a number of countries to extricate themselves from the deflationary spiral long before the U.S. economy turned up.

But floating is no panacea. It has been explained many times that floating shields a country only from *monetary* shocks from abroad. Specifically, no country can be forced under floating, as it often happens under fixed exchanges, to expand or to contract the money supply more than it finds acceptable. Floating does not protect from *real* shocks from abroad. The concept of real shocks has to be defined broadly—it covers not only clearly exogenous shocks, such as the oil shock,[54] but also changes in the terms of trade that usually accompany the business cycle and can be regarded as having been caused by monetary forces. Thus in the depression of the 1930s, prices of primary products fell sharply, which implied a catastrophic deterioration in the terms of trade of less developed countries. Floating obviously does not protect a country from adverse changes in the terms of trade.

Critics of floating often assert that the insulating power claimed for floating exists only if there are no capital flows. There are, indeed, various scenarios that seem to support that assertion. One such scenario was analyzed above: We have seen, in the United States in recent years, that floating does not protect a country from the adverse effects of capital exports and depreciation of its currency caused by high interest rates abroad.[55] But it has been demonstrated that in such a case a country would be even worse off under fixed exchanges. Hence, floating can be credited with mitigating the damage.

The following is another scenario. A relatively inflationary country develops a current account deficit that is financed by capital imports of different kinds, including losses of official reserves. So long as this goes on, it reduces inflationary pressure in the deficit country and increases it in the surplus countries. The deficit country can be said to "export" its inflation to the surplus countries. Sooner or later the country will find it difficult to finance its deficit. If its currency is then set afloat, its exchange value will go down, and inflationary pressure will increase; prices of traded goods will rise, and the aggregate domestic expenditures will decline. It can then truthfully be said that floating has "caused" inflation. What has happened is better described, however, by saying that inflationary pressure has been shifted from the victims of the pre-existent situation, the surplus countries, to the culprit, the inflationary deficit country.

This can also be described by saying that under floating each country has to swallow the inflation it generates because it cannot export it to others. This has increasingly been recognized by central bankers and policy makers, which in turn should be a strong inducement to resist inflation. Thus floating has a certain disciplinary effect of its own. I cannot resist quoting my observations on an earlier occasion: "The fact that floating provides an inducement for the monetary authorities to step on the brakes does not guarantee that inflation will in fact be curbed. A strong inducement to disinflate can always be overwhelmed by an even stronger propensity to inflate." [56] The same can be said about the vaunted disciplinary effect of the gold standard.

Finally, I will add a few more words about overshooting and official interventions in the foreign exchange market designed to "calm down" the market and to correct its alleged frequent overshooting. Until the recent policy shift, discussed in section VII above, the present U.S. administration has pursued a strict hands-off policy. Interventions in the foreign exchange market are to be taken only "in extraordinary circumstances to counter serious market disorders." One of the few interventions occurred after President Reagan was shot on March 30, 1981, when the Federal Reserve intervened by selling a paltry sum of $76 million in foreign currencies.

The nonintervention policy has been laid down by the U.S. Treasury. It is not quite clear whether the Federal Reserve System fully supports that strict policy of nonintervention. In fact, it is no secret that the Federal Reserve Bank of New York, the operating arm of the system as far as international transactions are concerned, is in favor of a much more active policy of intervention. That attitude seems to reflect habits formed in the good old days of stable but adjustable exchange rates, when, especially in the closing years of the Bretton Woods era, almost continuous large interventions plus frequent emergency meetings of central bankers were the order of the day.

The same is true of central bankers in most other countries. They seem to be itching to act. Before I explain the reasons for doubting the wisdom of frequent interventions, let me repeat that these doubts are not meant to apply to the many countries that peg their currency to the dollar or some other currency or basket of currencies. I can see no economic objection to such a policy—provided, first, that the country keeps its currency fully and freely convertible in the market (absence of exchange controls), and, second, that it does not pay too high a price in terms of inflation or unemployment. On the second condition each country has to make its own judgment.

What, then, are the reasons for doubting the wisdom of frequent large interventions under floating? It is the great difficulty of diagnosing the existence and of estimating the extent of overshooting. Overshooting can be defined as the deviation of the spot exchange rate from the long-run equilibrium level. But what is the equilibrium exchange rate? The modern portfolio-asset market approach to the problem of exchange rate behavior under floating has highlighted the extraordinary complexity of the problem.[57]

Things were simpler, though not without problems, under the Bretton Woods regime and under the gold standard. It will be recalled that the Articles of Agreement of the IMF said that in case of a "fundamental disequilibrium" a change of the par value was in order. The concept of fundamental disequilibrium is not defined in the IMF charter, but it was usually interpreted either in terms of some purchasing power parity or loss of international reserves.

The theory of purchasing power parity appears to be going out of fashion.[58] To speak of a "collapse" seems to me exaggerated; large deviations from the purchasing power parity are still a symptom of disequilibrium, and so are large inflation differentials. But what is large? Neither purchasing power parity nor inflation differentials are suitable measures for the degree of overshooting.

Changes in official reserves obviously play a different role under floating than under fixed exchanges. If under floating the authorities use reserves to intervene in the foreign exchange market, they must have made up their minds that the market has overshot. The judgment that there is a disequilibrium must be based on other grounds than the loss of reserves.

It is true, however, that the loss of reserves may well be taken by the private market participants as a signal from the authorities or an indication of how the authorities judge the situation and how they are likely to act. This introduces expectations into the picture. Expectations play, indeed, a central role in the portfolio-asset market approach to the exchange rate problem.

Other factors that have always been regarded as influencing exchange rates and are widely watched as possible danger signals are the current account of a country and comparative monetary growth rates.[59] The asset market theory of foreign exchange rates under floating explains how these factors and events and the market participants' expectations concerning future events and government policies interact in a very complex fashion. Overshooting is not excluded, but there are no easy guides to recognizing the existence of overshooting, let alone estimating the magnitude.[60]

The upshot of this discussion is that diagnosing overshooting is a more difficult task than many policy makers and their advisers seem to realize. It follows that interventions that go beyond ironing out strictly short-run fluctuations easily can do more harm than good.

Notes

1. The sharp distinction between recession and depression is of comparatively recent origin. But in the earlier literature a roughly similar distinction was made between "Kitchin" and "Juglar" cycles (Joseph Schumpeter), "minor" and "major" cycles (Alvin Hansen), and "mild" and "deep" depression cycles (Milton Friedman). The National Bureau of Economic Research ranks as especially severe the cyclical downswings of 1937–1938, 1929–1933, 1920–1921, 1907–1908, 1893–1894, 1882–1885, and 1873–1879. These cyclical downswings can be regarded as depressions. See Geoffrey H. Moore, ed., *Business Cycle Indicators*, vol. 1 (Princeton, N.J.: Princeton University Press, 1961), p. 104, table 3.6.

2. How a 6 percent decline in terms of dollars translates into a smaller (2 percent) decline in real terms in a period of inflation is a little puzzling. The reason is that, because of the recession and the appreciation of the dollar, prices of many internationally traded commodities, including oil, have sharply declined in terms of dollars, despite the ongoing inflation (rising CPI) in all industrial and developing countries.

3. Blum's policy was patterned after Roosevelt's New Deal. As a recovery policy the New Deal was unsuccessful. True, there was a long period of expansion—1933–1937, but the upswing was marred by rising prices, which led to the short but extremely vicious depression of 1937–1938. After six years of the New Deal, unemployment was still over 10 percent, and it took the war boom to restore full employment.

4. See Walter Galenson and Arnold Zellner, "International Comparisons of Unemployment Rates," in *The Measurement and Behavior of Unemployment*, a Conference of the Universities, National Bureau Committee for Economic Research (New York, 1957), pp. 455, 467.

The figure of 43 percent mentioned in the text refers to 1932, the nadir of the cycle. In 1931 the unemployment rate was 34.3 percent, more than three times as high as now. This is important because it contradicts a widely quoted, pessimistic statement by Helmut Schmidt, the former minister of finance and chancellor of the Federal Republic of Germany. At a World Forum in Vail, Colorado, sponsored by the American Enterprise Institute on August 28, 1983 (see the *New York Times*, August 29, 1983), Schmidt said unemployment in West Germany now is as high—3 million—as it was in 1931, two years before Hitler came to power. Actually, it was over 4 million in 1931, compared with 2.2 million in June 1983. Moreover, to compare absolute numbers now with those fifty years ago is misleading because of large territorial differences and vast changes in the composition of the labor force (female labor, guest workers, etc.) Unemployment expressed as a percent of the labor force conveys a much better impression of the severity of the decline now and fifty years ago.

5. *Newsweek*, New York, January 24, 1983, p. 46.

6. *Die Zeit*, nos. 48 and 49, December 3 and 10, 1982.

7. Reported in the *New York Times*, May 20, 1983.

8. Peter Kenen, "Concluding Remarks," in *Essays in International Finance, No. 149, December 1982, From Rambouillet to Versailles: A Symposium* (Princeton, N.J.: International Finance Section, Princeton University Press, 1982).

9. Lester C. Thurow, "An International Keynesian Yank," *Challenge*, March/April 1983, p. 36.

10. I put "Keynesian" in quotation marks, because we have learned from T. W. Hutchison and Axel Leijonhufvud that the word has to be distinguished from the "economics of Keynes." Thurow admits that "Keynesian expansion" was tried by Mitterrand, but it failed, presumably because France did not have the right kind of incomes policy.

11. Kenen also wrote that "inflationary expectations have subsided." He is surely overoptimistic. Kenen, "Concluding Remarks."

12. See Herbert Giersch, "Prospects for the World Economy," *Skandinaviska Enskilda Banken Quarterly Review* (Stockholm, 1982), pp. 104–110.

13. "Work on a Pay Cut," *The Economist* (London, November 27, 1982), pp. 11–12, and "Wage Cuts," *The Economist* (London, December 18, 1982), pp. 14–15.

14. For samples of the dissenting letters, see *The Economist*, December 18, 1982. *The Economist* rightly argues that Keynes, if he were alive, would support its position and not that of its critics. It is one thing to say, as Keynes did in the 1930s, that a deflationary spiral should be stopped by expansionary measures rather than by wage reduction, and an entirely different thing to urge in a period of persistent, severe stagflation that the level of money wage rates must not be touched. One year after the publication of his *General Theory*, Keynes had urged a shift in policy to fight inflation. As I have mentioned already, we have to distinguish between Keynesian economics and the economics of Keynes.

15. See "International Financial Statistics," *Supplement on Price Statistics*, no. 2 (Washington, D. C.: International Monetary Fund, 1981).

16. Based on OECD data. See Organization for Economic Cooperation and Development, *Economic Outlook*, no. 17 (July 1973), p. 56, table 21.

17. See Karl Otto Pöhl, "Remarks on the National and International Monetary Scenario," *Deutsche Bundesbank, Auszüge aus Presseartikeln*, no. 101, No-

vember 19, 1981.

18. J. R. Hicks, "The Long-Run Dollar Problems: Inaugural Lecture," *Oxford Economic Papers*, June 1953. D. H. Robertson, *Britain in the World Economy*, London, 1954. For further references see P. T. Bauer and A. A. Walters, "The State of Economics," *Journal of Law and Economics*, vol. 18, no. 1 (April 1975), p. 5.

19. See *International Monetary Reforms: Documents of the Committee of Twenty* (Washington, D. C.: International Monetary Fund, 1974), p. 11.

20. See Thom de Vries, "Jamaica or the Non-Reform of the International Monetary System," *Foreign Affairs*, vol. 54 (April 1976), p. 587. The story is told in detail in Robert Solomon's authoritative monograph *The International Monetary System 1945–1981: An Updated and Expanded Edition of the International Monetary System 1945–1976* (New York: Harper & Row, 1982).

21. That this shift in policy was a grave mistake has later been frankly admitted by the administration's chief economic spokesman, former secretary of the Treasury Michael Blumenthal. See *Washington Post*, October 30, 1979.

22. For detailed analysis of the monetary policy shift, see Phillip Cagan, "The New Monetary Policy and Inflation," in *Contemporary Economic Problems 1980*, William Fellner, Project Director (Washington, D.C.: American Enterprise Institute, 1980), pp. 9–38.

23. Foreign acquisitions of enormous dollar balances through massive official interventions to prop up the dollar in the dying days of Bretton Woods, resulting in an inflationary increase in international liquidity, was one of the costs of resisting the float.

24. Even in the heydays of the gold standard there were frequent violations of the basic rules of the game. The introduction of the gold exchange standard constituted a major violation of the basic rule; it no longer applied to the reserve currency countries, the United States and the United Kingdom. These countries were thus liberated from the disciplinary effect of the gold standard. That was duly noted and criticized by staunch advocates of the gold standard and by others, by Jacques Rueff and Robert Triffin, to mention two names.

25. *The American Economic Review*, vol. 72, no. 3 (June 1982), pp. 320–33.

26. Ibid., p. 320. This claim has been challenged, convincingly in my opinion, by Henry Goldstein, "A Critical Appraisal of McKinnon's World Money Hypothesis" (mimeographed), Federal Reserve Board of Chicago, 1982.

27. Ibid., pp. 331–32.

28. Ibid., p. 331.

29. Bank of England, Quarterly Bulletin, September 1969, pp. 363–64.

30. The most important IMF papers, which go back many years, are collected in *The Monetary Approach to the Balance of Payments: A Collection of Research Papers by Members of the Staff of the IMF* (Washington, D. C.: International Monetary Fund, 1977).

31. See Randall Hinshaw, ed., *Global Monetary Anarchy* (Beverly Hills, Calif.: Sage Publications, 1981).

32. See Fred Bergsten, "Statement before the Subcommittee on International Trade, Investment and Monetary Policy, Committee on Banking, Finance and Urban Affairs, U.S. House of Representatives," November 4, 1981.

See also "The Villain Is an Overvalued Dollar," interview with C. Fred Bergsten in *Challenge*, March-April 1982, pp. 25–32. He has restated his position in "From Rambouillet to Versailles: A Symposium," *Essays in International Finance*, no. 149 (Princeton, N.J.: Princeton University Press, December 1982), pp. 1–7.

33. Bergsten, "Statement before the Subcommittee on International Trade, Investment and Monetary Policy."

34. See "Exchange Rates, Interest Rates, Inflation," remarks by Otmar Emminger, September 28, 1981, Bankers' Forum, Georgetown University, Washington, D. C. (mimeographed). A year later the paper appeared in an enlarged and updated version: Otmar Emminger, *Exchange Rate Policy Reconsidered*, Occasional Papers 10 (New York: Group of Thirty, 1982). The quotations come from the original version, except where indicated.

35. Emminger, *Exchange Rate Policy Reconsidered*, p. 17.

36. Ibid., p. 8.

37. See Alexandre Lamfalussy, "A Plea for an International Commitment to Exchange Rate Stability" (Paper presented at the 20th Anniversary Meeting of the Atlantic Institute for International Affairs, Brussels, October 1981). A more elaborate and updated version can be found in Lamfalussy's speech "Some General Policy Conclusions for Tempering the Excesses of Floating" (Address to the Financial Times Conference on "Foreign Exchange Risk—1983," delivered in London, February 16, 1983). Excerpts reprinted in *Deutsche Bundesbank, Auszüge aus Presseartikeln*, March 13, 1983. The quotations are from the 1981 version, except where indicated. For an excellent presentation of what may be called the point of view of the Bank for International Settlements, see the interesting paper by Helmut Mayer, *The Theory of Floating Exchange Rates and the Role of Official Exchange-Market Intervention*, BIS Economic Papers No. 5, February 1982 (Basle, Switzerland: Bank for International Settlements, Monetary and Economic Department, 1982).

38. He looks back with nostalgia at the system of stable but adjustable rates, though "a return to a new Bretton Woods" would "not be practical politics." It is "arguable," in his opinion, that "the system of pegged but adjustable exchange rates could have been saved, if the par value of the main currencies and the price of gold had been adjusted in time and in sufficient proportion." This is difficult to accept in view of the fact that it was a basic defect of the adjustable peg (namely, "the Graham effect," which makes the system extremely vulnerable to destabilizing speculation) that brought down the Bretton Woods system and forced floating on reluctant policy makers. What Otmar Emminger said in 1980 is still true: "On the occasion of the first oil shock, Mr. Witteveen, then the managing director of the IMF, said in a major policy speech in January 1974: 'In the present situation, a large measure of floating is inavoidable and indeed desirable.' I think this is still valid today, after the second oil shock" (*The International Monetary System under Stress: What Can We Learn from the Past?* AEI Reprint No. 112 [Washington, D.C.: American Enterprise Institute, May 1980], p. 16).

39. The title of a famous book by the Swiss historian Herbert Lüthy, which means, freely translated, *France Marches to a Different Drummer*. That the second largest member of the EMS, France, has a most oppressive system of

exchange control, involving searches at the border, censorship of the mail, and tight rationing of foreign currency for travel abroad further highlights the failure of the EMS to provide a well-functioning regional system of stable exchange rates.

40. Kenen, "Concluding Remarks," p. 38.

41. Emminger, *The International Monetary System under Stress*, p. 7.

42. One could perhaps argue that the effect of the recession on traded and nontraded goods would have been somewhat different. I do not think that this is an important qualification, however, because there is such a large overlap between traded and nontraded industries. To be sure, protectionists are using the high dollar and the trade deficits as an argument. But the basic cause of protectionist pressure is unemployment and the recession. And that would not be different.

43. Only those foreign central banks that hold a large reserve of dollars (or gold) or a credit line could do it.

44. For example, the French minister of finance was reported to have "accused Washington of irresponsibility toward the needs of Western Europe. He also warned that the dollar's rise could lead to more belt-tightening in France." He said: "America's partners had rallied round to help when the dollar's weakness in 1978 disturbed the world economy. With the phenomenon now reversed, Washington should do the same in return" (*Washington Post*, April 22, 1983).

45. See "Gains from Disinflation," testimony by Martin Feldstein, chairman, Council of Economic Advisers, before the Joint Economic Committee, U.S. Congress, Washington, D. C., April 22, 1983.

46. See, for example, Michael Mussa, *The Role of Official Intervention*, Occasional Paper 6 (New York: Group of Thirty, 1981), and Martin Feldstein, "Gains from Disinflation." The *Official Report of the International Working Group on Exchange Market Intervention* comes to the same conclusion, though in somewhat veiled and guarded language, which one expects from an international body.

47. It is instructive to consider that in the case of nonsterilizing interventions, the effects of the foreign and domestic parts of the operation—that is, the sale of dollars in the foreign exchange market and the increase in money supply—operate in the *same* direction; both tend to weaken the dollar.

48. See *Deutsche Bundesbank, Auszüge aus Presseartikeln*, no. 75, August 4, 1983, p. 2.

49. See *Deutsche Bundesbank, Auszüge aus Presseartikeln*, no. 77, August 13, 1983, p. 1.

50. See *Deutsche Bundesbank, Auszüge aus Presseartikeln*, no. 75, August 4, 1983, pp. 1-2, 4-5.

51. This statement requires a qualification with respect to *structural* unemployment. A comparison with regional adjustments makes that clear. See note 52.

52. It is instructive to reflect that these conditions are fully realized between regions in each country. For example, all Federal Reserve Banks in the United States follow the same policy. Thus inflation rates are practically the same in the east and west, north and south. Wage rigidity and wage push, if

any, are also roughly the same. (Unemployment rates may, of course, differ between regions because of structural differences.) These are the main reasons why we do not hear of balance of payments adjustment problems of regions and why there are no exchange rate problems between regions.

Other factors are often mentioned that facilitate regional adjustment, such as interregional mobility of labor and capital and automatic or discretionary official income transfers from relatively prosperous to relatively depressed regions via government taxes and expenditures. But the two conditions mentioned above are basic. If they are fulfilled, the world is the "optimum currency area."

These problems have been extensively discussed in the voluminous literature on the optimum currency area. For an excellent survey, see Edward Tower and Thomas Willett, *The Theory of Optimum Currency Areas and Exchange Rate Flexibility*, Special Papers on International Economics No. 11 (Princeton, N.J.: International Finance Section, Princeton University Press, 1976).

53. The French controls apply ostensibly only to capital transactions permitted by the Articles of Agreement of the IMF. But experience has shown again and again that effective capital controls require de facto control of current transactions.

54. It is, however, a misunderstanding when some critics of floating said or implied that OPEC's "persistent" balance of payments surplus is a "disequilibrium," which in the opinion of advocates of floating should have been eliminated by floating. The *global* OPEC surplus could and should not have been eliminated by floating (or by any other means). But since different oil importing countries were not equally burdened by the oil shock, and since policy reactions to the oil price rise differed from country to country, floating had to play an important role in the adjustment to an oil price rise. On this point, see my chapter "The Dollar in the World Economy: Recent Developments in Perspective," in *Contemporary Economic Problems 1980*, pp. 160–65, and the literature cited there.

55. Since a change in the terms of trade is involved, it is not unreasonable to regard this and similar scenarios as involving *real* factors, and therefore not constituting exceptions from the rule that floating protects from monetary disturbances from abroad. But this is a purely semantic question, which need not detain us.

56. See my paper "The Future of the International Monetary System," *Zeitschrift für Nationalökonomie*, vol. 34 (1974), pp. 391–92. Available as Reprint No. 30 (Washington, D.C.: American Enterprise Institute, 1975). See also "The Dollar in the World Economy," pp. 151–52.

57. For an excellent, brief discussion of the "asset market approach," see Mussa, *The Role of Official Intervention*, pp. 3–12 and the literature cited there.

58. See Jacob A. Frenkel, "The Collapse of Purchasing Power Parities during the 1970s," NBER Reprint No. 193, National Bureau of Economic Research, and *European Economic Review*, vol. 16, no. 1 (May 1981), pp. 145–65 (Amsterdam: North-Holland, 1981). See also the interesting comments by Roland Vaubel, "Comments 'The Collapse of Purchasing Power Parities during the 1970s by Frenkel," *European Economic Review*, vol. 16, no. 1 (May 1981), pp. 173–75.

59. Both concepts must, of course, be carefully defined. For example, a large and persistent U.S. current account deficit will cause suspicion, because the United States is generally regarded as a "natural" capital exporter, while a large current account deficit of a developing country in good financial standing may be regarded as quite appropriate. Monetary growth rates ought to be adjusted for real GNP growth to make them comparable.

60. On this point see Michael Mussa, "A Model of Exchange Rate Dynamics," *Journal of Political Economy*, vol. 90, no. 1 (1982), pp. 74–104.

The External Effects of U.S. Disinflation

Sven W. Arndt

Summary

After a period marked by rising inflation and a depreciating dollar, the United States embarked on a program of disinflation. The Federal Reserve changed its operating procedures in 1979 and thereafter pursued an increasingly credible policy designed to break inflation. While the monetary authorities were shifting down, fiscal policy became increasingly expansionary.

In the early 1980s the U.S. inflation rate declined in absolute terms and in comparison with the inflation rate in some countries; it remained higher than inflation rates in countries such as Japan, Germany, and Switzerland. If relative price movements were the dominant factors in the determination of exchange rates, the dollar should have depreciated against the currencies of those countries. Instead, it appreciated.

Nominal interest rates remained high in the United States, and their coexistence with a high and rising dollar suggests tight credit conditions. Conventional calculations of real interest rates confirm this view. The elevated real dollar impaired the international competitive position of U.S. producers of traded goods. The economy passed through an unexpectedly deep and protracted recession. The trade balance deteriorated.

In the public discussion the dollar has been criticized as overvalued, and the large trade balance deficit has been blamed for the loss of jobs in traded goods industries. The high value of the dollar is, however, consistent with overall conditions in the U.S. economy; the currency is thus neither overvalued nor undervalued. The trade deficit is a result of U.S. economic policies rather than an independent cause of sectoral unemployment. These distinctions are important if appropriate remedies are to be found.

The "cause" of economic developments during this period is the policy package containing disinflationary monetary policy and budget deficits that are both sizable and expected to persist. High interest rates, the strong dollar, the recession, the trade deficit, the foreign repercussions, as well as the defeat of inflation, are the joint products of those policies. Unwarranted inferences about causal relations between any pair of these outcomes are likely to suggest inappropriate and ineffective remedies.

131

Several policy options are available to policy makers wishing to bring down the dollar. Some, including monetary expansion, whether achieved by monetization of the deficit or by unsterilized exchange market intervention, will deflate the dollar but only at the expense of reinflating the economy. Sterilized exchange market intervention will not work, especially over extended periods. An immediate and lasting reduction in the budget deficit will bring down the dollar and improve the trade balance but is politically improbable. A credible commitment to future budget cuts will bring down the dollar at once and improve the trade balance in due course; it may also be politically feasible.

The recent experience shows convincingly that floating exchange rates fail to insulate a country from disturbances originating in the United States when economies are subject to wage and price rigidities and to factor immobilities. Moreover, policies of the type pursued in the United States coupled with the dominating influence of the United States on exchange rates generate pressures abroad that can be simultaneously inflationary and recessionary.

The policy package in question was adopted for reasons not primarily related to exchange rates and trade balances. Indeed, it has been the official policy of several U.S. governments that determination of exchange rates shall be left to the market, a policy that commends itself in light of the inability of governments to fashion consistent macroeconomic policies. The recent experience suggests, however, that leaving nominal exchange rates to the market does not give a government license to ignore the effects of its policies on real exchange rates.

Introduction

This chapter examines the effects of recent U.S. policies on such "external" variables as exchange rates and the balance of trade. It also examines their repercussions for America's principal trading partners. The focus is on adjustment in the short run and on the role of price and wage rigidities in bringing about the observed results. The chapter begins with a brief review of the major developments and then proceeds to an analysis of the relevant interrelations. An appendix provides a more formal treatment of the major analytical issues.

A Review of Recent Developments

Prices had been rising steadily in most industrial countries when in late 1979 the Federal Reserve embarked on a policy of monetary restraint designed to bring down the rate of inflation. The weighted GNP deflator for all industrial countries, which had risen an average of 4.2 percent in the period 1963–1972, rose by 7.6 percent in 1978, 8 percent in 1979, and 9 percent in 1980. Comparable figures for the

TABLE 1
NOMINAL AND EFFECTIVE EXCHANGE RATES, SELECTED INDUSTRIAL
COUNTRIES, 1976–1982

	1976	1977	1978	1979	1980	1981	1982
Nominal exchange rates[a]							
France	4.78	4.91	4.51	4.25	4.23	5.43	6.57
Germany	2.52	2.32	2.01	1.83	1.82	2.26	2.43
Italy	832	882	849	831	856	1137	1353
Japan	297	268	210	219	227	221	249
Switzerland	2.50	2.40	1.79	1.66	1.68	1.97	2.03
United Kingdom	0.56	0.57	0.52	0.47	0.43	0.50	0.57
Effective exchange rates[b]							
France	97.3	91.0	87.8	87.5	87.9	82.2	74.9
Germany	127.6	136.4	142.2	148.3	149.3	142.8	148.3
Italy	61.6	56.0	51.8	49.8	48.2	43.4	40.0
Japan	112.0	124.1	151.3	140.0	134.7	153.5	144.7
Switzerland	151.0	154.1	189.0	191.6	189.1	191.6	205.9
United Kingdom	64.4	61.3	61.4	65.5	71.3	72.2	68.6
United States	87.6	87.0	79.2	77.1	77.1	87.0	96.0

a. National currencies against the dollar; average of daily rates.

b. 1970QI = 100; average of daily rates.

SOURCE: Organization for Economic Cooperation and Development, *Economic Outlook*, July 1983, p. 171.

United States were 3.5 on the average between 1963 and 1972, 7.4 percent in 1978, 8.6 percent in 1979, and 9.3 percent in 1980. Similarly, consumer prices rose on the average at a compounded annual rate of 3.9 percent for all industrial countries and 3.3 percent for the United States during 1963–1972, at 7.2 percent and 7.7 percent, respectively, in 1978, at 9 percent and 11.3 percent in 1979, and at 11.8 percent and 13.5 percent in 1980.[1]

The years preceding the change in Federal Reserve policy had seen steady increases in nominal interest rates in the United States, where the Treasury bill rate rose from an average of 5 percent in 1976 to 10 percent in 1979 and the yield on medium-term government bonds rose from an average of 6.7 percent to 9.7 percent.[2] At the same time the effective exchange rate of the dollar fell from an average of 87.6 in 1976 to 77.1 in 1979; the dollar declined against the currencies of all the countries in our sample except Italy, as table 1 makes clear.

In the years following the policy shift, nominal short- and long-term interest rates continued to rise for a time, and even after they

TABLE 2
SHORT-TERM INTEREST RATES, SELECTED INDUSTRIAL COUNTRIES,
1976–1982

	1976	1977	1978	1979	1980	1981	1982
	Nominal interest rates						
United States	5.0	5.3	7.2	10.1	11.4	14.0	10.6
Japan	7.0	6.1	5.1	5.9	10.7	7.7	7.1
France	8.6	9.1	8.0	8.9	12.2	15.2	14.9
Germany	4.2	4.4	3.7	6.7	9.5	12.1	8.9
Italy	17.8	14.8	11.0	13.5	15.9	19.6	19.4
United Kingdom	11.1	7.7	8.5	13.0	15.1	13.0	11.3
Switzerland	—	—	—	—	5.2	7.8	3.9
	Real interest rates[a]						
United States	−0.2	−0.5	−0.2	1.3	1.9	4.2	4.4
Japan	0.5	0.4	0.4	3.2	7.7	4.9	4.9
France	−1.1	0.1	−1.3	−1.2	0.3	2.9	2.5
Germany	0.8	0.7	−0.5	2.5	4.9	7.6	3.9
Italy	−0.2	−3.6	−2.5	−2.1	−4.0	1.0	1.6
United Kingdom	−3.1	−5.6	−2.2	−1.8	−3.4	0.7	3.1

a. Approximated by using annual changes in GNP deflators to adjust the nominal rates.
SOURCES: IMF, *World Economic Outlook, 1983*, p. 227; and IMF, *International Financial Statistics*, May 1983.

began to recede, they remained high by historical standards (see tables 2 and 3). Moreover, real interest rates began a steady climb, reaching 4.4 percent for short-term rates and 6.7 percent for long-term rates. The experience of other countries was quite similar, with nominal and real rates rising and remaining high by historical standards. The major exception, at least with respect to real rates, was Italy. Major shifts in interest differentials also took place (see table 4).

Inflation rates receded almost everywhere. In the United States, the GNP deflator rose by 6.0 percent in 1982 while consumer prices advanced by 6.2 percent. Only Italy and France, among the countries in our sample, continued to have rising inflation rates; elsewhere a period of disinflation had truly set in.

Exchange rates experienced a turnaround that was nothing short of remarkable. In 1982 the effective exchange rate of the dollar reached an average of 96.0, and in bilateral terms the dollar had either recouped much of the ground lost between 1976 and 1979 or actually gained in relation to its position in 1976.

Indeed, appreciation of the dollar vis-à-vis other countries' cur-

TABLE 3
LONG-TERM INTEREST RATES, SELECTED INDUSTRIAL COUNTRIES, 1976–1982

	1976	1977	1978	1979	1980	1981	1982
Nominal interest rates							
United States	7.6	7.4	8.4	9.4	11.5	13.9	13.0
Japan	8.7	7.3	6.1	7.7	9.2	8.7	8.1
France	9.2	9.6	9.0	9.5	13.0	15.7	15.4
Germany	7.8	6.2	5.7	7.4	8.5	10.4	9.0
Italy	12.7	14.7	13.1	13.0	15.3	19.4	20.2
United Kingdom	14.4	12.7	12.5	13.0	13.8	14.7	13.0
Switzerland	5.0	4.1	3.3	3.5	4.8	5.6	4.8
Real interest rates[a]							
United States		2.3	1.5	1.0	0.7	2.0	4.1	6.7
Japan		2.1	1.5	1.4	5.0	6.2	5.9	5.9
France		−0.6	0.6	−0.4	−0.7	1.0	3.3	2.9
Germany		4.3	2.4	1.4	3.2	3.9	6.0	4.0
Italy		−4.5	−3.7	−0.7	−2.5	−4.5	0.8	2.3
United Kingdom		−0.2	−1.2	1.4	−1.8	−4.5	2.2	4.7

a. Approximated by using annual changes in GNP deflators to adjust the nominal rates.
SOURCES: IMF, *World Economic Outlook, 1983*, p. 228; and IMF, *International Financial Statistics*, May 1983.

rencies exceeded changes in relative prices and costs and thus meant a deterioration in the competitive position of American producers of tradable goods. Table 5 traces the "real" appreciation of the dollar for manufacturing in terms of labor costs, wholesale prices, and export unit values.

During this period of disinflation real GNP growth declined in the United States and then turned negative; unemployment rose to double-digit levels, and capacity utilization collapsed. In many other countries similarly contractionary conditions prevailed, although they often followed developments in the United States with a lag.

Although monetary policy was relatively tight, especially in the early phases of this period, U.S. fiscal policy was decidedly expansionary. Between 1979 and 1982 the impulse (on a national income accounts basis) of state, federal, and local government moved from a surplus amounting to 0.6 percent of gross national product to a deficit of 3.8 percent of GNP while the federal deficit increased from 0.04 percent of GNP to 4.8 percent.[3] According to the Organization for Economic Cooperation and Development (OECD), this expansionary

TABLE 4
SHORT-TERM INTEREST RATE DIFFERENTIALS, SELECTED INDUSTRIAL
COUNTRIES, 1976–1982

	1976	1977	1978	1979	1980	1981	1982
Nominal interest rates							
United States	−1.4	−0.7	0.7	1.0	−0.1	1.2	0.1
Japan	0.6	0.1	−1.4	−3.2	−0.8	−5.1	−3.4
France	2.2	3.1	1.5	−0.2	0.7	2.4	4.4
Germany	−2.2	−1.6	−2.8	−2.4	−2.0	−0.7	−1.6
Italy	11.4	8.8	4.5	4.4	4.4	6.8	8.9
United Kingdom	4.7	1.7	2.0	3.9	3.6	0.2	0.8
Real interest rates[a]							
United States		0.2	0.3	0.4	0.2	−0.4	−0.1	0.4
Japan		0.9	1.1	1.0	2.2	5.4	0.6	1.0
France		−0.7	0.8	−0.8	−2.3	−2.0	−1.4	−1.5
Germany		1.2	1.4	0.1	1.5	2.5	3.3	—
Italy		0.2	−2.9	−2.0	−3.1	−6.3	−3.3	−2.3
United Kingdom		−2.6	−4.9	−1.6	−2.8	−5.7	−3.6	−0.9

NOTE: Difference between each country's rate and a weighted average for the five largest industrial countries.

a. Approximated by using inflation differentials (based on GNP deflators) to adjust nominal differentials.

SOURCES: IMF, *World Economic Outlook, 1983*, p. 229.

impulse was due not only to the automatic response of built-in stabilizers but also to discretionary actions. In Europe and Japan, however, discretionary policies tended to be generally contractionary and in some cases managed to swamp the stimulus emanating from built-in stabilizers.[4]

Analytical Aspects

The period beginning late in the 1970s was characterized, as we have seen, by high short- and long-term interest rates in the United States and elsewhere, by a strong dollar, by recessions in the United States and elsewhere, and by a deficit in the U.S. trade balance.[5]

These developments have sparked a lively debate over their probable causes. High interest rates, for example, have been variously attributed to tight monetary policy (because it raises the cost of credit), to loose monetary policy (because it raises inflationary expectations,

TABLE 5
Relative Competitive Position in Manufacturing, Selected Industrial Countries, 1977–1982

	1977	1978	1979	1980	1981	1982
Relative normalized unit labor costs[a]						
United States	106.6	99.0	97.5	100.0	117.4	130.8
Japan	118.0	132.7	113.9	100.0	108.9	99.7
France	93.1	93.3	97.7	100.0	92.3	88.9
Germany	99.3	102.6	103.9	100.0	89.4	89.9
Italy	94.8	92.5	96.8	100.0	97.4	98.6
Switzerland	94.7	109.1	105.5	100.0	98.4	105.1
United Kingdom	65.9	70.3	81.4	100.0	106.7	104.3
Relative wholesale prices						
United States	107.5	100.0	99.3	100.0	115.7	124.0
Japan	104.3	116.3	108.1	100.0	107.9	98.8
France	90.3	92.6	96.4	100.0	93.8	89.7
Germany	103.7	104.7	105.6	100.0	92.1	95.6
Italy	97.4	96.0	97.8	100.0	94.8	94.2
Switzerland	100.2	114.4	109.5	100.0	97.3	101.7
United Kingdom	76.2	79.5	87.7	100.0	101.6	99.1
Relative export unit values						
United States	106.7	99.5	102.0	100.0	119.7	131.2
Japan	104.0	114.3	103.8	100.0	108.9	103.1
France	98.0	97.9	99.6	100.0	92.6	89.8
Germany	104.8	107.9	105.5	100.0	89.7	92.6
Italy	97.2	91.8	94.2	100.0	96.9	95.9
Switzerland	98.7	111.5	106.8	100.0	99.7	104.1
United Kingdom	78.9	84.7	89.6	100.0	98.1	92.5

a. Compensation of employees per unit of real output corrected for cyclical swings in productivity.
SOURCE: IMF, *International Financial Statistics*, May 1983, p. 48.

which get built into interest rates), and to budget deficits (because the government's borrowing requirements drive up the cost of credit).

The strong dollar has been attributed to high interest rates in the United States, but interest rates were relatively high in the period preceding the change in policy regime while the dollar remained quite weak. Consequently, high nominal interest rates alone cannot explain the dollar's strength. Moreover, the dollar has been strong not only in nominal terms but in real—that is, in price- and cost-adjusted—terms.

This departure of the dollar from purchasing power parity means that the international competitive position of American producers of tradable goods has been sharply eroded. Some observers have interpreted this as an overvaluation of the dollar and have called on the government to intervene in foreign exchange markets, presumably to push the nominal exchange rate back to a level approximating purchasing power parity.

This is a noteworthy proposition because it asserts that nominal exchange rates should be determined in commodity markets and that governments should maintain currency values near their purchasing power parities; that is, governments should pursue real exchange rate targets. It is a proposition sharply at odds with the modern asset view of exchange rates, which holds that they are first and foremost determined in financial markets.

These are clearly important issues bearing on the behavioral characteristics of modern economies and on the role and efficacy of macroeconomic and intervention policies. It may therefore be useful to examine the consequences of certain policies in greater detail.

Monetary Policy. The importance of monetary policy is directly related to its influence on "real" variables such as employment, output, the real trade balance, and the real exchange rate. This influence is minimal in a world of high price flexibility and factor mobility, where a monetary impulse gives rise to equiproportionate changes in "nominal" variables, such as money prices, money wages, and the nominal exchange rate, while leaving real variables unaffected. In such a world shifts in monetary policy produce matching variations in nominal exchange rates and in the ratio of home to foreign prices, thereby maintaining purchasing power parity. Consequently, departures from purchasing power parity of the kind observed in recent years are improbable, partly because the real interest rate changes needed to provoke them are improbable.

Monetary neutrality presupposes high degrees of price and wage flexibility and of factor mobility, which suggests that the influence of monetary policy on the real economy is likely to diminish as the adjustment period lengthens. In the short run, however, factor mobility is often limited, and prices and money wages are subject to control by contract and by law. Physical capital is largely immobile, that is, sector specific, in the short run, and the geographic and occupational mobility of workers is limited.

In the financial sector, financial capital is highly mobile, and asset prices are generally responsive to shifts in demand and supply. These differences in market response patterns lead to the distinction between *contract* markets, characterized by slow and gradual adjustment and by significant departures of prices and wages from their market-clearing levels, and *auction* markets, characterized by efficient adjustment processes that move prices rapidly to their market-clearing levels. The sluggishness of contract markets means that *expectations* concerning their eventual responses play a key role in the early phases of an adjustment process. Hence decisions in auction markets must take into account anticipated responses in contract markets.

To examine the consequences of monetary policy in the presence of such rigidities, we adopt the extreme but analytically convenient assumption that prices and money wages are completely unresponsive and that labor and capital are completely immobile in the short run. The policy change in question is a reduction in the degree of monetary stimulation, that is, a shift from a highly inflationary to a less inflationary monetary policy. It is a policy of disinflation, one that reduces the rate of inflation.

Since our assumption precludes an immediate response in the actual rate of wage and price inflation, the new policy's initial effect is on the *expected* rate of inflation, as well as on liquidity in the financial sector. The two forces exert conflicting influences on nominal interest rates, the liquidity effect tending to raise, and the drop in inflationary expectations tending to reduce, nominal interest rates. The net effect of a credible reduction in monetary laxity is to reduce nominal interest rates, where the effect on the term structure of interest rates depends on the market's perceived time profile of expected inflation rates. The net effect on the real rate of interest is to increase it.

The policy's effects on exchange rates are in the first instance again mainly the result of shifts in expectations. If market participants believe that exchange rates are influenced by relative inflation rates at home and abroad, a reduction in the expected inflation rate at home in relation to rates expected abroad reduces the expected change in currency values. If, as a result of the policy shift, the expected domestic inflation rate falls below the rate of inflation expected in another country, the home currency will be expected to appreciate with respect to that country. If, however, the policy of disinflation merely reduces the excess of domestic over foreign inflation, the home currency will be expected to depreciate at a diminished rate. Hence the policy of disinflation reduces the expected rate of currency depreciation and may even bring an expectation of appreciation.

A shift in the expected movement of exchange rates alters expected rates of return on foreign relative to domestic assets and hence provokes portfolio adjustments. A tendency for nominal (expected) rates of return on comparable home and foreign assets to differ by more than the sum of expected exchange rate changes and certain undiversifiable risks sets in motion portfolio shifts that return the

TABLE 6

DISCOUNTS OR PREMIUMS ON THREE-MONTH FORWARD EXCHANGE RATES,
1978–1982

	1978	1979	1980	1981	1982
Japan	9.87	5.26	7.00	6.46	1.87
Germany	7.88	5.66	8.17	3.16	3.28
France	5.26	2.19	5.85	—	−3.54
Italy	−2.41	−4.71	−3.14	−9.23	−18.25
Switzerland	11.85	8.86	10.09	5.23	6.12
United Kingdom	−0.89	−2.18	3.34	−1.51	−0.99

NOTE: Minus sign indicates discount.
SOURCE: IMF *International Financial Statistics*, May 1983, p. 46.

yield differential to acceptable bounds. In the course of this adjustment, both forward and spot exchange rates are likely to change. In
the case of a policy of disinflation that does not reverse the expected
inflation differential, the rate of (spot and forward) currency depreciation declines, but the currency continues to trade at discount in the
forward market.

This was true during the period in question for the dollar's position vis-à-vis the currencies of Japan, Germany, and Switzerland,
whose actual—and presumably expected—inflation performances
were largely superior (see table 6). If, however, the expected domestic
inflation rate falls short of the expected foreign rate, a forward premium emerges, as in the case of Italy. Finally, where the actual—and
presumably the expected—inflation differential fluctuates and reverses sign, as it did with respect to France and the United Kingdom,
the relation between spot and forward exchange rates fluctuates between premium and discount.

The Real Exchange Rate. To summarize financial sector adjustment
thus far, the nominal rate of interest declines, and the degree of exchange rate depreciation is reduced. Indeed, if the policy shift was
entirely unanticipated, the spot rate must initially appreciate to correct
positions based on earlier and now outdated expectations; thereafter,
the movement of exchange rates reflects the market's revised expectation's regarding domestic inflation.

A change in the movement of nominal exchange rates that is not
matched by movements in the actual inflation differential constitutes a
change in real exchange rates.[6] If, for example, the movement of nominal exchange rates reflects the new policy regime while actual prices

and money wages continue to be driven by pricing rules and cost-of-living formulas reflecting the earlier policy regime, the real value of the home currency will rise in terms of relative prices and wages (see table 5). Thus short-run imperfections in the response of wages and prices to changes in policy regimes provide one explanation for fluctuations in a country's international competitive position. Given the substantial lags in quantity adjustment in international trade, however, this deterioration in competitiveness is unlikely to affect the allocation of resources and the volume and pattern of trade unless it becomes protracted.[7]

With the passage of time pricing decisions in commodity and labor markets come to reflect the new policy regime, and the rate of price and wage inflation begins to recede. In this phase of the adjustment process, difficulties associated with disparities in the response of prices and wages may emerge. If prices are more responsive, the rate of price inflation will fall faster than that of wages, giving rise to real wage increases, which, if protracted, reduce employment and output. This factor appears to have played some role in the period under examination.

The Budget Deficit. The federal deficit rose from $16.1 billion in 1979 to $147.9 in 1982 while the financial position of all government (including state and local) changed from a surplus of $14.3 billion to a deficit of $116.1.[8] A deficit injects spending into the economy and thereby contributes to the eventual expansion of output and employment as well as prices. Under the assumed wage and price rigidities, the deficit's initial effect tends to fall on employment and output, price and wage adjustment coming later. These results, however, occur gradually, and the division between quantity and price effects depends on the degree of excess capacity in the economy. A protracted deficit is likely increasingly to crowd out private investment.

The effects of the deficit on the financial sector are immediate and are associated with efforts to finance the deficit and with expectations regarding the implications of current and expected future deficits for asset prices and other variables. If the debt issued by the Treasury is not monetized by the Federal Reserve, the deficit raises the proportion of government securities to be held in private portfolios, and this can be accomplished only with an increase in interest rates. Nominal interest rates rise and with them real interest rates.

Moreover, if the deficit is expected to persist or even increase, the government's future borrowing requirements must be expected further to enlarge the stock of securities. If the expected rate of growth of outstanding government bonds exceeds the rate of growth of private demand for bonds (which depends on the private rate of saving and the wealth elasticity of demand for government bonds), market participants will expect bond prices to fall. This expectation provokes attempts to move out of bonds, an attempt that depresses current bond prices and drives up interest rates.

The combination of current and expected future government borrowing thus tends to push up nominal and real interest rates. These forces also move the nominal exchange rate, the result depending on substitution elasticities among domestic and foreign assets. The ultimate effect on the exchange rate depends on the details of specification, but under a broad range of plausible assumptions, the currency appreciates.[9]

The immediate effect of a deficit that is expected to last and that is not expected to be monetized is thus to increase nominal and real rates of interest and to raise the international value of the currency. Since the deficit represents a net claim on resources, it raises the danger of crowding out private investment, a danger that rises as the economy approaches full employment. In a closed economy, the real rate of interest must move to maintain balance between domestic saving, on the one hand, and private investment and the government deficit, all in relation to GNP, on the other.

An open economy possesses an extra degree of freedom represented by the trade balance and its implied access to foreign resources. The trade balance deteriorates in response to the budget deficit, thereby releasing pressure on the real rate of interest and diminishing the danger of domestic crowding out. At the same time, however, this outcome raises the possibility that one country's budget deficit may cause real interest rates to rise and investment to be crowded out in another. The danger of "external crowding out" is likely to be small when foreign economies suffer from excess capacity but is bound to become a problem as those economies approach full employment.[10]

Variations in Real Exchange Rates. The evidence reviewed in an earlier section noted the degree to which the exchange rate has deviated from purchasing power parity. Its deviations have produced substantial shifts in the competitiveness of tradable goods sectors. The sustained strength of the dollar in real terms has hurt exporters and producers of import-competing products in the United States while bringing benefits to their counterparts in many other countries.

It is this departure of the real exchange rate from purchasing power parity that has raised concern in some quarters about the "overvaluation" of the dollar. It is entirely plausible in this context to argue that, if exchange rates were determined solely in commodity markets, the dollar would have depreciated against the currencies of the three low-inflation countries, appreciated against the lira, and fluctuated without changing significantly against the French franc and sterling. But exchange rates reflect other aspects of a country's foreign economic relations as well. Indeed, in the short run they are driven principally by financial market developments, and in this regard relatively higher (real) interest rates in the United States have played a major role.

As the analysis in this section makes clear, interest rates and exchange rates are jointly determined in the financial sector. The analysis suggests that an inflationary monetary expansion will raise nominal interest rates as well as the exchange rate and a budget deficit will raise nominal interest rates and reduce the exchange rate. A shift to less expansionary monetary policy produces a one-time adjustment, lowering nominal interest rates and the exchange rate, and a diminished rate of currency depreciation thereafter. The combination of monetary expansion and budget deficit maintains upward pressure on nominal and real interest rates while raising the international value of the currency. This outcome is especially likely if large (and rising) future deficits are expected. Hence the exchange rate appreciates in spite of a U.S. inflation rate that exceeds inflation in several major trading partners.

The real exchange rate that is the result of this policy package is consistent with overall conditions in the U.S. economy; the dollar is from this perspective neither overvalued nor undervalued. It nevertheless presents a policy problem in that it diminishes the competitiveness of producers of traded goods, who may respond with pressures for protection. A short-lived elevation in the dollar's real value is likely to cause little more than discomfort, but its persistence eventually becomes a signal for the reallocation of resources away from traded goods. If such a reallocation was not intended by policy makers, the policy mixture needs to be reexamined.

The analysis further suggests that deterioration of the trade balance is one of the consequences of forces set in motion by the policy package. The rise in real interest rates, the appreciation of the dollar, the deterioration of the trade balance and the loss in competitiveness and eventually in employment in the traded goods sector are part of the multifaceted outcome of a specific set of policies. Viewed from this perspective, claims that the trade balance has "caused" the loss of jobs in traded goods production are not only misplaced but likely to lead to the wrong "solutions."

A Question of the Policy Package. In the context of the present analytical framework, several avenues are open for policy makers wishing to "bring down" the real dollar and thereby to remove the unintentional and undesirable consequences of the existing policy package. Increasing the degree of monetary stimulus, either by monetizing the deficit or by unsterilized exchange market intervention, would bring the dollar down, but only at the cost of returning the United States to the kind of inflation from which it has been working to escape.

Reducing current and future budget deficits would reduce nominal and real rates of interest, reduce the nominal and real value of the dollar, and improve the trade balance. If reductions in the current deficit are politically difficult, a credible commitment to future deficit cuts would also lower nominal and real interest rates as well as the nominal and real value of the dollar without, however, providing the strong trade balance improvement associated with cuts in the current deficit. A credible commitment to future budget cuts has the attraction of producing immediate results while permitting tax increases and expenditure cuts to be phased in. It has the further virtue of reducing government's claim on resources in future periods when a continuing recovery is bound to increase the danger of internal and external crowding out.

Sterilized exchange market intervention is a deliberate attempt to shift the equilibrium in financial markets. It may provide fleeting relief, although even this depends on the market's perceptions, but it cannot "solve" the problem if the conditions created by the original policy package remain unaltered.

Foreign Repercussions. It is helpful to think about the effect of U.S. policies on foreign economies as being transmitted through changes in interest rates, in prices, and in output. The rise in U.S. interest rates sets in motion an arbitrage process that places upward pressure on foreign interest rates. Such an increase may or may not be consistent with prevailing economic conditions; it will be unwelcome if foreign economies are already suffering from demand deficiencies. Further, the externally caused real depreciation of foreign currencies exerts upward pressures on prices and thereby adds to whatever inflationary pressures may already exist abroad. Finally, the decline in output and employment in the United States weakens demand for foreign products.[11]

Hence the initial effect of a policy package combining disinflationary monetary policy with budget deficits is to raise pressures on foreign interest rates and prices while depressing foreign output and employment. This outcome underscores the inability of flexible exchange rates to insulate countries from external disturbances when short-run adjustment is inhibited by wage and price stickiness and by factor immobilities. It presents policy makers with a major dilemma,

forcing them to deal simultaneously with inflationary and recessionary tendencies.

Foreign Options

The situation faced by foreign governments in this period included (1)
depreciating currencies in both nominal and real terms; (2) continuing
but generally declining rates of inflation; and (3) weakening demand
from abroad, contributing to rising unemployment.

The policy responses of governments are influenced by their goals
and objectives. A government attempting to maintain exchange rate
targets would make efforts to match the macroeconomic restrictions
being imposed on the U.S. economy. Interest rates at home would
have to increase, but the resulting tighter credit would be contractionary.

If the objective were to stabilize nominal interest rates, the appropriate policy would depend on the forces that were causing interest
rates to rise. In countries with relative price stability, rising nominal
rates would reflect rising costs of credit and would call for monetary
expansion. Japan, Germany, and Switzerland are the only countries
in our sample for which this may have been true. In high-inflation
countries, such as Italy, monetary contraction would have been the
appropriate policy for a government intent on pursuing an interest
rate target. In either case, however, a successful interest rate policy
would, in the face of influences emanating from the United States,
widen the interest rate differential, increase the capital outflow, and
add to pressures depreciating the domestic currency.

An interest rate target may be merely an intermediate objective,
the ultimate target being employment and output. A government
may, of course, focus directly on employment and output, in which
case the appropriate response would be expansionary macroeconomic
policies, the monetary-fiscal package depending on specific conditions in that country.

A final focus of government policies abroad may be price stability.
A government may be battling domestic inflationary tendencies; it
may respond to a depreciating currency either because it sees the
depreciation as the result of relative home inflation or because it fears
the cost-raising influences of a depreciation. Under these circumstances, macroeconomic contraction would be the appropriate response.

In the major European countries industrial production began a
pervasive slide in 1980 while national output either stagnated or declined. Yet the fiscal impulse was, on the whole, contractionary, as

TABLE 7
DISCRETIONARY AND AUTOMATIC CHANGES IN GENERAL GOVERNMENT
FINANCIAL BALANCES, SELECTED INDUSTRIAL COUNTRIES, 1980–1982

	Change in Actual Balance[a]	Built-in Stabilizers[b]	Discretionary Change[c]
United States			
1980	−1.7	−1.3	−0.4
1981	0.3	−0.7	1.0
1982	−2.8	−1.7	−1.1
France			
1980	1.0	−0.6	1.6
1981	−2.2	−1.1	−1.1
1982	−0.7	−0.9	0.2
Germany			
1980	−0.5	−0.1	−0.4
1981	−0.8	−1.0	0.2
1982	0.1	−1.4	1.5
Italy			
1980	1.6	0	1.6
1981	−3.7	−1.3	−2.4
1982	−0.3	−1.5	1.2
Japan			
1980	0.5	−0.1	0.6
1981	0.5	−0.1	0.6
1982	−0.1	−0.2	0.1
United Kingdom			
1980	−0.3	−1.4	1.1
1981	0.8	−2.0	2.8
1982	0.5	−1.3	1.8

NOTE: A positive (negative) sign signifies a surplus (deficit) and hence a move toward restriction (expansion).

a. Year-to-year changes in financial balances.

b. The automatic reaction of budgets to changes in economic activity, measured as variations in real GDP around the trend growth of productive potential.

c. Reflects deliberate policy intervention and fiscal drag.

SOURCE: OECD, Economic Outlook, various issues.

table 7 indicates. The monetary impulse tended to vary and had relatively restrictive phases, especially in Japan and Germany. Short- and long-term interest rates, both nominal and real, rose, as we have seen.

Conclusion

Recent macroeconomic developments in the United States have encompassed high real interest rates, a strong dollar, and significant deterioration in the trade balance. They are the joint product of a policy package combining a disinflationary monetary policy with budget deficits that are large and expected to persist.

The strong and sustained real appreciation of the dollar is consistent with overall conditions in the economy, which means that the dollar is from that perspective neither overvalued nor undervalued. Its high level has nevertheless impaired the international competitive position of U.S. producers of tradable goods, which must be considered an unintended result of the aforementioned policies. It is also undesirable, because it raises immediate pressures for protectionist relief and issues probably inappropriate signals for the long-run reallocation of resources.

The massive deterioration of the trade balance is merely one consequence among many of recent economic policies and as such cannot be viewed as the "cause" of unemployment in traded goods industries. Treating it as the cause is likely to lead to the adoption of inappropriate remedies.

Recent experience has taught that flexible exchange rates will not insulate a country from external disturbances when short-run adjustment is inhibited by wage and price rigidities and by factor immobilities. A policy package of the kind adopted in the United States has the potential under some circumstances of generating both inflationary and recessionary pressures abroad.

Among the several options available to policy makers wishing to "bring down the dollar," a credible policy of future budget cuts offers some hope of an immediate improvement in the alignment of exchange rates and an eventual amelioration of the trade balance position.

Appendix

The interactions between financial and real sectors can be quite complex and depend in part on the nature of expectations. There is increasing agreement among analysts that the nominal interest rate and nominal exchange rate are determined in asset markets in the short run but that expectations about the results of more gradual and time-consuming adjustment in commodity and factor markets play a decisive role. There is less agreement and still less conclusive evidence on the precise linkages between financial and real adjustment.

FIGURE A-1

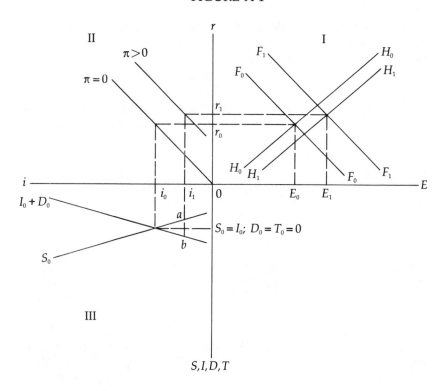

The complexity of these linkages may be formidable, but certain essential relationships can nevertheless be sketched with the aid of the following model of an open economy. Panel I of figure A-1 describes the financial sector, consisting of a market for domestic money, a market for foreign interest-earning assets, and a market for domestic interest-earning assets. The HH and FF schedules represent combinations of nominal interest rate (r) and nominal exchange rate (E, defined as the home-currency price of foreign exchange) that produce equilibrium in the money and foreign asset markets (and by Walras's law in the market for domestic assets), given foreign prices and interest rates, expectations concerning future changes, and income and wealth.

The HH schedule is positively sloped because a rise in the nominal exchange rate creates excess demand in the money market, a condition that is eliminated by a rise in the rate of interest. The FF schedule is negatively sloped because a rise in the exchange rate creates excess supply of foreign assets in residents' hands, a condition that is removed by a cut in the rate of interest.

In the second panel, nominal (r) and real (i) interest rates are related in the spirit of the Fisher condition along schedules giving various expectations about future price inflation (π). When expected inflation is zero (along schedule $\pi = 0$), the two interest rates are equal. When prices are expected to rise (fall), the π schedule shifts up (down), and the emerging gap between the two interest rates accommodates the inflation premium (discount).

The third panel depicts real sector interaction between saving (S) and investment (I) and the budget deficit (D), all expressed in relation to gross national product. The slopes of the curves reflect the interest elasticities of saving and investment—and perhaps government budgets—while changes in expectations, in exchange rates and prices, and in budgetary policy are among the factors that cause shifts in one or both schedules.

In the initial, noninflationary, balanced-budget equilibrium, the nominal exchange rate is at E_0, the two interest rates are equal at r_0 and i_0, respectively, and the saving rate (S_0) is matched exactly by the rate of investment (I_0), which implies a condition of balanced trade ($T_0 = 0$, where we ignore for the sake of simplicity the problem of net foreign factor earnings).

Monetary Policy. A monetary expansion shifts the HH schedule to the right, creating pressures for the nominal interest rate to fall and the currency to depreciate. If we suppose that actual prices and nominal wages do not adjust immediately because of short-term rigidities in commodity and factor markets, the policy gives rise to *expected* increases in prices and nominal wages, shifting the π schedule in panel II to the right. If, moreover, market participants believe that relative movements in home and foreign prices affect exchange rates, an expected rise in domestic prices relative to foreign prices generates an *expected* currency depreciation, which shifts the FF schedule to the right.

The FF shift adds to the pressures tending to raise the exchange rate but reverses the tendency for the nominal interest rate to fall. Short-run financial sector equilibrium is given at nominal interest rate r_1 and exchange rate E_1. The real rate of interest also falls (to i_1); its level is determined by the declining nominal rate of interest and by the size of the inflation premium. It is important to note, in this connection, that the movement of the HH schedule is governed by a liquidity effect tending to lower it and by an expectations effect tending to raise it. A sufficiently inflationary monetary policy can shift the HH schedule up, thereby adding to pressures on the nominal rate of interest.

At the new real rate of interest (i_1), a gap emerges between saving and investment, unless there are forces that would tend to shift the S

and $(I + D)$ schedules in compensating ways. Expected inflation, for example, may shift the S schedule up as consumers raise current expenditures in anticipation of rising prices; similar reactions among investors would shift the $(I + D)$ schedule down. These are two adjustments tending to widen the gap. The budget, however, may move into surplus as a result of automatic and discretionary responses of revenues and expenditures to the increase in nominal demand brought about by the monetary expansion. The net effect of these and other shifts depends on the details of specification and need not concern us here.

A shortfall of saving relative to investment and net government expenditures means that the trade balance must show a compensating deficit; in the case of the original schedules, the trade deficit at real interest rate i_1 is equal to $\overline{ab}$. The issue here is not the precise magnitude of the domestic expenditure gap and hence of the trade imbalance but the availability to an open economy—in sharp distinction to a closed economy—of the foreign sector as a resource. In a closed economy adjustments combining shifts in the S and $(I + D)$ schedules and movements in the real rate of interest (which imply adjustments in the financial sector beyond those sketched above) would have to occur to "clear" the real sector. In an open economy the burden of adjustment need not fall entirely on the real rate of interest but is shared by the trade sector.

An imbalance in trade means that the country is changing its holdings of the foreign asset over time; in the case of a trade deficit, the country is reducing its net claims on foreigners. This gradual decumulation of foreign assets causes the FF schedule in the first panel to drift gradually to the right, bringing with it pressures tending to raise the nominal rate of interest and to reduce the international value of the currency. This tendency for the nominal rate of interest to rise is translated into upward pressure on the real rate of interest, which in turn tends to reduce the domestic expenditure gap and hence the trade balance deficit.

In the long run, actual prices and nominal wages rise, the HH schedule shifts back up as the real value of cash balances declines, the π schedule shifts back to its original position, and nominal and real interest rates return to their original levels. Prices and nominal wages, as well as the nominal exchange rate, have risen in proportion to the rise in money supply, all this under assumptions approximating the neoclassical model. Real wages and real exchange rates remain unaltered.

The foregoing started with an economy in equilibrium and examined the effects of a monetary expansion. In the United States during the period under review, however, monetary policy became less ex-

FIGURE A-2

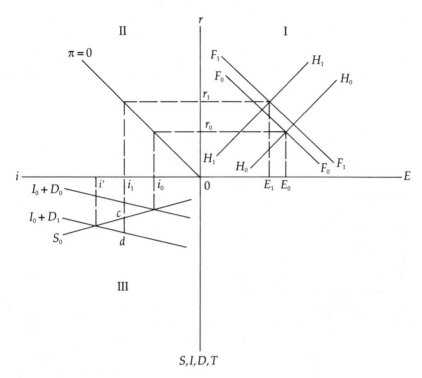

pansionary: it reduced inflationary pressures without completely eliminating them. The analogue in the present comparative-static framework is to compare two different expansionary policies. A less expansionary policy would produce a smaller expected rate of inflation and hence a smaller expected currency depreciation; it would mean a smaller fall in the real rate of interest and hence a smaller trade deficit.

Budgetary Policy. A budget deficit shifts the $(I + D)$ schedule down and to the right. In a closed economy restoration of real sector equilibrium would require a rise in the real rate of interest to i' in figure A-2, barring offsetting shifts in the S and I schedules. In an open economy with access to foreign saving, the interest rate need not rise by as much, leaving whatever gap remains to be financed by a trade deficit.

The real effects of the deficit do not appear immediately but take the form of gradual flow adjustments as the effect of net government expenditures is felt. In the financial sector, however, the deficit is likely to force immediate stock adjustments, their precise nature depending on how the deficit is financed and how market participants expect it to affect the economy.

In the present model the budget deficit will affect the real rate of interest to the extent that it alters expectations (and hence shifts the π schedule) and excess demands for assets (and hence shifts the HH and FF schedules). If, for example, the deficit is not expected by market participants to cause inflation, perhaps because they do not expect it to be monetized, the π schedule remains in its place, so that nominal and real rates of interest move in tandem. The deficit-induced sale of bonds to the public shifts up the HH schedule; its effects on the FF schedule are somewhat more uncertain and depend on the substitution elasticities among domestic and foreign monetary and nonmonetary assets. Under plausible assumptions, however, the net effect of these shifts is to raise the nominal rate of interest and the international value of the currency, say, to r_1 and E_1, respectively.[12]

The increase in the nominal rate of interest leads, in the absence of inflationary expectations, to an equal increase in the real rate of interest, a process that tends to reduce the domestic expenditure gap that must be accommodated by the trade balance deficit. The share of the burden of adjustment that falls on the trade balance also depends on the foreign repercussions arising from the initial disturbance, which in turn depend on country size. Such repercussions include changes in foreign interest rates and in foreign prices.

It is important to note the analogy in the open economy to the concept of crowding out in the closed economy. In the latter the real rate of interest rises to induce the private sector to relinquish resources to the public sector, especially when resources are fully employed. In the open economy the emerging trade balance deficit provides access to foreign resources. When foreign economies suffer from unemployment and excess capacity, crowding out is minimal, and the demand stimulus is highly welcome; but when economies abroad are running near capacity, real external crowding out occurs.

Notes

1. International Monetary Fund, *World Economic Outlook, 1983.*

2. Ibid.

3. See Council of Economic Advisers, *Economic Report of the President, 1983,* p. 192. See also IMF, *World Economic Outlook, 1983,* p. 35.

4. Organization for Economic Cooperation and Development, *Economic Outlook,* July 1983, p. 35.

5. The balance on goods and services showed a surplus of approximately $5 billion in 1979. That surplus expanded to $11 billion in 1981, as net incomes and fees and royalties from U.S. investments abroad soared, but receded in 1982. The current account, which includes remittances and unilateral trans-

fers, showed a small deficit in 1979, rose to a surplus of approximately $4.5 billion in 1981, and then fell to a deficit of more than $8 billion in 1982. See Council of Economic Advisers, *Economic Report of the President, 1983*, p. 276, and OECD, *Economic Outlook*, July 1983, p. 85.

6. The real exchange rate, e, is the product of the nominal exchange rate, E, and the ratio of foreign to home prices, that is, $e = E(P^*/P)$, where P and P^* may be comparable prices or price indexes at home and abroad or comparable cost indexes. Table 5 reports the inverse of the real exchange rate in terms of labor costs, wholesale prices, and export unit values. In dynamic terms, the rate of change of the real exchange rate is then given by the rate of change of the nominal exchange rate plus the difference between foreign and domestic inflation rates.

7. For a more detailed evaluation of a policy of disinflation, see the appendix.

8. Financial positions measured on national income accounts basis. See Council of Economic Advisers, *Economic Report of the President, 1983*, p. 192; 1982 figures preliminary.

9. For a detailed study of the role of substitution elasticities, see J. Bisignano and K. D. Hoover, "Monetary and Fiscal Impacts on Exchange Rates," *Economic Review* (Federal Reserve Bank of San Francisco, Winter 1982), pp. 19–36.

10. These and other aspects of budgetary policy are discussed in the appendix.

11. It is, of course, the net effect of these diverse and divergent pressures that matters. Thus the real depreciation of foreign currencies raises the demand for foreign products while the U.S. recession reduces it. Similarly, the rise in interest rates abroad reduces demand there for investment goods and consumer durables, thereby adding to recessionary tendencies. At the same time, currency depreciation raises the domestic prices of traded goods sold in those countries and thereby pushes up the general price index, producing changes that affect cost-of-living clauses and other aspects of the wage-setting process.

12. See Bisignano and Hoover, "Monetary and Fiscal Impacts."

Disinflation in the Housing Market

John C. Weicher

Summary

The rate of inflation has been the dominant factor in the housing market since the later 1960s. For about fifteen years, persistent, accelerating inflation generated a number of changes in housing patterns that were quite at variance with—in some cases, opposite to—those expected by most analysts. This period culminated in a speculative housing boom from 1977 to 1979. Then at the beginning of the 1980s, the rate of inflation declined sharply, with further unanticipated consequences.

This chapter analyzes the changes in the housing market resulting from disinflation. In many respects, however, these changes represent a slowing or reversal of the previous effects of inflation and can best be understood in a longer perspective. The chapter therefore describes events during the inflation, as well as the more recent trends.

Inflation and Housing Investment. *The important effects of inflation on housing derive from the fact that the housing stock is a tangible asset as well as the source of a continuing flow of services while it is occupied.[1] People sought and were able to use their housing as a hedge against inflation in the late 1960s and 1970s. The demand for housing as an asset—the investment demand—increased substantially as a result of inflation, and to a much greater extent than did the demand for the flow of services (the consumption demand). When inflation decelerated in the early 1980s, the investment demand declined markedly.*

This should not have been surprising. Newly constructed housing is treated as investment in the National Income and Product Accounts, and the existing stock is classified as a tangible asset in the national balance sheet. The standard theory of the effects of inflation on the economy, as it had been developed before the onset of inflation in the mid-1960s, held that housing

I would like to thank Carol Barnes and Alex Gemrich for research assistance, Douglas B. Diamond, Jr., for helpful comments on earlier drafts, and John C. Musgraves, James M. Poterba, James D. Shilling, and Robert Van Order for providing unpublished data.

becomes a preferred asset when prices rise.[2] On a popular level, the National Association of Home Builders and other trade groups have often asserted that "your home is the best investment you can make."

The microeconomic implications of inflation, however, were not well understood. As inflation accelerated, most housing policy discussions focused on the relationship between current costs or prices and current incomes, concepts more appropriate to the analysis of housing consumption. Toward the end of the 1970s, the tenor changed, partly in recognition of the findings of economists who were beginning to analyze contemporary housing market behavior in terms of investment and inflation, and partly because the consumption-oriented approach failed completely to predict what was actually happening in housing. Insofar as a shift in policy discussions can be dated, it occurred during 1978. At the Federal Home Loan Bank Board's annual forecasting conference in December 1977, for example, most participants stressed the problem of new home affordability and forecast a downturn in housing construction. Instead, the record production levels of 1977 were exceeded in the next year. During 1978, also, the first academic studies began to circulate.[3] At the 1978 conference, discussion centered on housing as a highly profitable investment, in an inflationary environment, with forecasts of continuing price appreciation and strong demand for single-family homes. It is ironic to note that, very shortly thereafter, the process of disinflation began, and this new general perception became outdated.

Discussions in the popular press generally have still not recognized the significance of inflation for housing. A 1977 cover story in Time lamented the high cost of housing and devoted only one paragraph in six pages to home-ownership as an investment. During the recession of 1981–1982, both Time and Newsweek described the collapse of the construction industry amid falling house prices.[4] Neither recognized the change in inflation as the key determinant of the change in the housing market.

Outline of the Chapter. This chapter traces the major effects of the inflation-induced increase in the investment demand for housing. The additional demand in large part took the form of a shift to owner-occupancy, countering demographic trends toward smaller households and more one-parent families, who historically have preferred to rent. It also manifested itself as an increase in investment. Housing became a larger share of household asset portfolios, along with consumer durables and other tangible assets. Buyers chose larger and better residences, and existing owners devoted more resources to home improvement and maintenance.

The increase in demand drove up both the nominal and real price of houses, generating much public discussion and concern. But inflation also reduced the real costs of ownership, particularly through its interactions with the housing finance system and the federal tax structure. The housing finance *system itself underwent severe stresses and began to change significantly in an effort to adapt to inflation.*

Most of these trends came to an abrupt halt with the advent of disinflation. In the early 1980s, homeownership, housing investment, and real house prices have declined, while the real cost of ownership has risen.

At this writing, it is difficult to forecast whether disinflation will continue or whether inflation will be allowed to resume. The study therefore concludes with an assessment of the probable changes in the housing market under each of these scenarios.

A Caveat. *It is necessary to be wary of attributing all of the recent changes to disinflation alone, even though they are consistent with it; there have been other contributing factors. In particular, disinflation has been occurring simultaneously with a severe recession, which would be likely to generate many of the same phenomena. Previous, less sustained periods of disinflation, such as 1974–1975, also coincided with recessions. Thus it is difficult to separate and quantify the relative importance of disinflation and recession, and this study should be regarded as preliminary and suggestive, rather than definitive.*

In order to have a clearer picture of the importance of disinflation, it will be necessary, or at least exceedingly helpful, for the process of disinflation to continue as the economy recovers from the recent recession. A low rate of inflation, concurrent with a low unemployment rate, would be beneficial to the economist trying to understand the effect of disinflation on the housing market, as well as to the economy in general.

The Effect of Inflation on House Prices

This section discusses the prices of single-family owner-occupied homes, which compose almost 60 percent of the total stock of occupied housing. Rising home prices have been the center of public concern about housing for the past fifteen years and the subject of much recent scholarly research. The section first briefly describes the behavior of nominal prices and then devotes more attention to the ways in which inflation and disinflation have affected real house prices. It concludes with some comparisons of the prices of houses with those of other tangible assets that have been considered a hedge against inflation.

Price Trends. The measurement of house prices is complicated by the heterogeneity of the housing stock. Houses are extraordinarily diverse; it is at most a slight exaggeration to say that no two are exactly alike, even ignoring location. Further, only a small fraction of the stock changes hands each year, so that prices of most houses cannot be directly observed. These problems are much less severe for other goods and services.

The most commonly cited house price data are simply medians for the homes actually sold in a period, with no adjustment for quality changes. Since size and amenities have gradually increased over time, the median overstates price changes. There are two indexes that attempt to adjust for quality differences and to report the change in price for the same house over time. These are the Census Bureau's "New One-Family Home Price Index" and the home purchase component of the consumer price index (CPI). The former is probably better, because it covers the entire price distribution of new homes sold, and more housing size and quality attributes are used to construct it. The CPI component is limited to homes insured by the Federal Housing Administration. Since there is a legislated ceiling on the mortgage amount that FHA can insure, the data exclude higher-priced homes, and during periods of inflation the upper tail of the sample distribution is further truncated until Congress raises the ceiling. The CPI component does, however, include existing homes, which the census index does not.

Table 1 contains the annual median prices for new and existing homes and the census new home price index, using the year 1967 as a convenient benchmark for the start of inflation.[5] It also contains the year-to-year percentage changes in each series. The median new home price is adjusted for the years 1969 to 1973, because during that period the federal government subsidized over 350,000 new homes for lower-income families under the Section 235 program. These homes were much smaller, and much less expensive, than the typical unsubsidized new home, and they therefore distort the median price in those years.[6]

The recorded price increases were startling by any previous experience. Both the new and existing home price nearly tripled from 1967 to 1979; the actual increases were 177 and 187 percent, respectively. These increases generated much concern about housing affordability, particularly for young families seeking to buy their first home.[7] Less widely noticed was the fact that median prices rose more rapidly than the price index until 1976. The typical new home built in the latter year was about 4 percent better than the 1967 home. Despite the price rises, therefore, people were able to buy better homes.

After 1976, however, the pattern was reversed. Between 1976 and 1979, the typical new home declined slightly in quality. This is somewhat surprising, because these were the boom years when inflation and inflationary expectations were strongest; in previous boom periods, quality improvements were the norm. There are some possible

TABLE 1
HOUSE PRICES, 1963–1982

	Actual Values			Percentage Change		
Year	Median new home price^a (dollars)	Median existing home price (dollars)	Census new home price index (1967 = 100)	Median new home price	Median existing home price	Census new home price index (1967 = 100)
1963	18,000	n.a.	90.2	—	—	—
1964	18,900	n.a.	91.1	5.0	—	1.0
1965	20,000	n.a.	93.2	5.0	—	2.3
1966	21,400	n.a.	96.6	7.0	—	3.6
1967	22,700	19,400	100.0	6.1	—	3.5
1968	24,700	20,000	105.3	8.8	3.1	5.3
1969	26,400	21,800	113.3	6.9	9.0	7.6
1970	26,500	23,000	116.4	0.4	5.5	2.7
1971	29,000	24,800	122.7	9.4	7.8	5.4
1972	30,400	26,700	130.7	4.8	7.7	6.5
1973	34,400	28,900	142.1	13.2	8.2	8.7
1974	35,900	32,000	155.4	4.4	10.7	9.4
1975	39,300	35,300	172.0	9.5	10.3	10.7
1976	44,200	38,100	186.7	12.4	7.9	8.5
1977	48,800	42,900	210.5	10.4	12.6	12.7
1978	55,700	48,700	241.1	14.1	13.5	14.5
1979	62,900	55,700	275.4	12.9	14.4	14.2
1980	64,600	62,200	305.7	2.7	11.7	11.0
1981	68,900	66,400	331.4	6.7	6.8	8.4
1982	69,300	67,800	339.8	0.6	2.1	2.5

NOTE: n.a. = not available.
a. New home prices are adjusted for subsidized Section 235 homes between 1969 and 1973, as explained in text.
SOURCES: U.S. Bureau of the Census, *Statistical Abstract of the United States, 1982–1983*, p. 749; *Price Index of New One-Family Houses Sold*, Construction Reports, Series C-27, February 1983, table 1; John C. Weicher, "The Affordability of New Homes," *American Real Estate and Urban Economics Association Journal*, vol. 5 (Summer 1977), p. 214; U.S. Department of Housing and Urban Development, *1967 Statistical Yearbook*, GS table 89.

explanations. One is that young families made up an unusually large share of homebuyers in these years; they had lower incomes and fewer assets than their elders and probably therefore could not afford

159

as expensive homes. It is also worth noting that the average sales price increased more rapidly than the median, or than the price index. This means that the quality distribution changed; there was a greater demand for more expensive (higher-quality) homes. Taken together, these changes suggest a housing demand consisting partly of young families seeking first, relatively inexpensive homes and partly of older families seeking exceptionally expensive homes. Both would be reasonable reactions to accelerating inflation.

Price trends changed still more abruptly at the beginning of the 1980s. Prices rose at a much reduced rate and decelerated much more quickly than the price index. This was especially true for new home prices, which increased less than half as much as the census index.

Measuring Prices during Disinflation. Before analyzing the implications of these price trends, it is worth noting that there are special measurement problems with the price series in the last few years. A variety of unusual financing arrangements were developed in response to the high nominal mortgage rates prevalent from late 1979 to mid-1982. These typically involved a below-market interest rate to the homebuyer. They are important in the present context insofar as the savings in mortgage payments arising from the below-market interest rate are capitalized into the price of the house, which would be expected in a competitive market. Therefore the reported sales price will overstate the "true" price, meaning the price that would be charged if the customary mortgage arrangements were used.

The following are the most important of these devices:

1. Loan assumptions allow the buyer to continue to make the payments on the seller's original mortgage, rather than taking out a new one. Often the buyer also takes out a second mortgage, because the value of the home has risen so much during the inflation that he or she has not saved enough for a down payment covering the difference between the value and the outstanding principal balance on the mortgage.

2. Using "creative" financing the seller becomes the mortgagee and receives some or all of the sales proceeds over time, rather than in a lump sum at settlement.

3. "Balloon notes" offer the buyer a very short-term mortgage (perhaps one to five years). At the end of the period, he or she has to refinance the outstanding principal balance, probably with a conventional mortgage. In many cases, the buyer pays only interest during the period of the balloon note. Much "creative" financing takes this form; it has been particularly prevalent in California.

4. With builder buydowns, the homebuilder makes part of the

mortgage payment during the first few years. For that period, the buyer pays the mortgage as if it carried some specified below-market rate, while the builder pays the difference between that amount and the monthly payment on a mortgage at the market rate; afterwards, the buyer pays the full amount. For example, if the mortgage rate is 15 percent, and the builder "buys it down" to 11 percent, then the buyer's monthly payment on a $50,000 mortgage is reduced from $640 to $490. The monthly saving is almost, but not quite, proportional to the interest rate reduction (in this case, 23.4 versus 26.7 percent).

The first three of these mechanisms apply exclusively or primarily to the existing home market; the last, to new homes. Thus the first three do not affect the Census Bureau's new home price index. Nor do they affect the CPI, because creative financing arrangements are not insured by FHA, and loan assumptions go unreported. They do, however, affect the median existing home price, perhaps substantially. Salkin and Durning have estimated that creative financing caused the reported median price in California to be overstated by 1.5 percent in 1980 and by 3.1 percent in 1981.[8]

If these figures apply nationally, then the median existing home price was $61,300 in 1980 and $64,300 in 1981, and prices rose by about 10 and 5 percent, respectively, in those years. This probably overstates the national effect, however, because creative financing arrangements were probably more common in California than elsewhere.

Builder buydowns have probably affected both the median new home price and the census index. Surveys by the National Association of Home Builders at about semiannual intervals provide the only data on their extent and magnitude.[9] It appears that more than half of all builders were offering them from mid-1980, when they first became common, until the sudden sharp drop in interest rates in mid-1982; since then, fewer than one-third have offered buydowns. The typical buydown has varied in the range of two to three percentage points for between two and five years. If it were fully capitalized into higher house prices, it would raise them by 5 to 6 percent. Informed professional opinion appears to be that about half has been capitalized; the other half has been absorbed by the builder.

Table 2 reports the median new home price and census index from 1979 to 1982, adjusted for builder buydowns on the assumption that they were distributed uniformly among all sales price brackets. It appears that the median price and the index were both overstated by about 1 percent in 1980, 2 percent in 1981, and 1 percent in 1982; the rates of increase were overstated by 1 percent in each of the first two years and understated by 1 percent in the last year. The effect of the

TABLE 2
ADJUSTED HOUSE PRICES, 1979–1982

Year	Median New Home Price		Median Existing Home Price		Census New Home Price Index	
	Reported	Adjusted	Reported	Adjusted	Reported	Adjusted
1979	$62,900	$62,900	$55,700	$55,700	275.4	275.4
	(2.7)	(1.7)	(11.7)	(10.0)	(11.0)	(10.0)
1980	64,600	64,000	62,200	61,300	305.7	302.9
	(6.7)	(5.5)	(6.8)	(4.9)	(8.4)	(7.3)
1981	68,900	67,500	66,400	64,300	331.4	324.9
	(0.6)	(1.6)	(2.1)	—	(2.5)	(3.5)
1982	69,300	68,600	67,800	n.a.	339.8	336.4

NOTE: Data in parentheses are year-to-year percentage changes; n.a. = not available.
SOURCE: Reported data, same as table 1; adjustments based on sources described in the text.

adjustment is to smooth out the pattern of disinflation in these three years; prices rose less rapidly in 1980 and 1981 than reported in the unadjusted indexes, and more rapidly in 1982. None of these adjusted figures are very precise, however, though they may be sufficient to indicate general trends.

Relative Price Changes. To a substantial extent, the price changes were only the manifestation within the housing market of the general inflation occurring throughout the economy. They attracted more attention in housing than elsewhere, probably in part because the dollar magnitudes were so much larger; a $3,000 increase in the price of a $50,000 house apparently is more noticeable than a three-cent increase in the price of a fifty-cent loaf of bread, even though the percentage changes are the same.

The percentage increases in housing were not the same as those for goods and services as a whole. Particularly as inflation accelerated, house prices increased significantly more rapidly. Figure 1 compares the census house price index to the cost of living, measured by a variant of the consumer price index that replaces the homeownership cost component with the rental value of owner-occupied housing (the CPI-U-X1 experimental series).[10]

In every year but two from 1967 through 1979, the price of a new home increased more than the CPI series, and the annual difference itself increased over time. Thus in 1977 and 1978, house prices rose at double the rate of the CPI. Then in 1980 the pattern changed. Inflation

FIGURE 1
INDEXES OF HOUSE PRICES AND INFLATION, 1967–1982

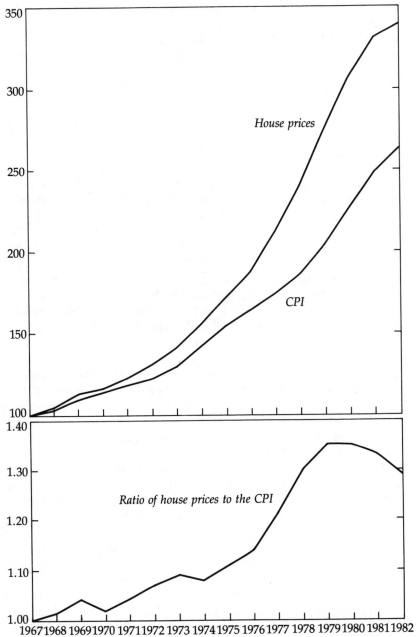

SOURCES: *Price Index of New One-Family Houses Sold*, Construction Reports, Series C-27, February 1983, table 1; and *Economic Report of the President*, February 1983, table B-56, p. 226.

continued to accelerate, while house prices rose at a slower rate than they did during the three previous years; for that year, house prices kept pace with inflation. (Adjusted for builder buydowns, house prices may have risen more slowly than inflation.) In 1981 and 1982, general inflation clearly exceeded house price increases, even though both rose at a decelerating rate. Over the three years, the relative price of a home declined by about 11 percent.

The rise and decline in the relative price of housing, particularly after 1976, was largely a consequence of inflation. By the later 1970s, many households had already experienced extraordinarily large windfall gains from their own homes and were realizing them in order to buy larger and better ones.

Some notion of the magnitude of these gains may be seen in table 3, which is based on estimates of asset values in the U.S. economy over time. House and land are reported separately, because they are calculated differently.[11] The gains for houses are measured as the difference between the current value of owner-occupied housing and the historical cost of construction. These data are calculated annually, and capital gains in any given year are the difference between that year and the previous one. Capital gains in land are estimated more crudely, on the simple assumption that they are proportional to the increase in value for the entire land area of the United States; thus any change in relative values is excluded.[12] This imprecise technique appears to be the best possible, given the limited information available on land values.

It is worth stressing that these are real capital gains, expressed in 1972 prices. Use of current prices, especially during the years of greatest inflation, would result in much larger nominal gains (about $140 billion in 1978, for example).

The table shows that very large capital gains, by historical standards, accrued in all of the cyclical upturns after inflation began in the mid-1960s. Further, gains were substantially greater in each cycle than in the one before. The importance of these gains may be grasped by comparing them with household assets: the $88 billion in gains in 1978 amounted to almost 1.5 percent of the net wealth owned by households in that year. The performance of housing contrasted sharply with financial assets during the same period. It is not surprising that more and more households sought to buy homes in the later 1970s, driving up real house prices in the process.

Then in late 1979, the inflationary climate changed abruptly: the Federal Reserve enunciated the goal of reducing inflation by restraining the growth of the money supply. This policy was not pursued steadily in the early 1980s, but both the growth rate of M1 and the overall rate of inflation did begin to decline.[13] This was apparently

TABLE 3
CAPITAL GAINS IN OWNER-OCCUPIED HOUSING, 1961–1982
(billions of 1972 dollars)

Year	Capital Gains		
	Houses	Land	Total
1961	− 2.4	5.1	2.7
1962	− 1.7	5.2	3.5
1963	− 8.3	2.6	− 5.7
1964	6.0	5.3	11.3
1965	0.8	6.6	7.4
1966	12.6	3.0	15.6
1967	4.4	2.9	7.3
1968	24.6	0.5	25.1
1969	14.0	− 2.8	11.2
1970	7.7	− 2.0	5.7
1971	17.0	− 0.1	16.9
1972	26.3	15.6	41.9
1973	43.0	16.0	60.0
1974	25.2	2.5	27.7
1975	6.7	7.7	14.4
1976	34.6	20.5	55.1
1977	46.2	11.4	57.6
1978	67.8	20.3	88.1
1979	8.1	1.2	9.3
1980	− 5.9	2.0	− 3.9
1981	0.6	− 16.6	− 16.0
1982	− 41.9	− 19.1	− 61.0

SOURCES: For houses: U.S. Department of Commerce, Bureau of Economic Analysis, *Fixed Reproducible Tangible Wealth in the U.S., 1925–1979*, tables A-11 and A-12; later data provided by John C. Musgrave of BEA. For land: Board of Governors of the Federal Reserve System, "Balance Sheets for the U.S. Economy, 1945–1981," issued in October 1982, tables 700 and 702. Capital gains calculated in the same manner as Phillip Cagan and Robert E. Lipsey, *The Financial Effects of Inflation* (Cambridge, Mass.: Ballinger, for the National Bureau of Economic Research, 1978), table 2-11, p. 41.

enough to begin the process of disinflation in the housing market. The decline in the relative price of housing, shown in figure 1, quickly translated into capital losses for homeowners. By the end of 1982, they had lost almost all of the gains accruing since 1977, and close to 20 percent of the gains since 1965. The figure is smaller for the more precisely measured house component, so the aggregate loss may be overstated, but it must still be substantial.

Other Factors Affecting Prices. The rate of inflation was, of course, not the only factor that contributed to house price movements. Most of the other important influences identified by housing analysts should, however, have contributed to a decline rather than to an increase in the real price of houses. This is especially the case for factors affecting demand. Demographic changes should have favored an increase in renting and a shift away from owner-occupancy, as the proportions of young households, one-parent families, and single individuals all increased during the 1970s. The rapid rise in the real price of energy after the 1973 Arab oil embargo was widely expected to trigger a sharp decline in demand for single-family homes, because of the increased costs of both heating and commuting.

Zoning, other land-use constraints, and building codes have been blamed for restricting the supply of new housing and for raising its costs and could have contributed to the real price increase. The best estimates indicate, however, that their effects on costs are much smaller than is assumed in much public discussion.[14] These are primarily local phenomena, and their importance varies quite substantially from one region to another. They may have contributed to the differences in inflation rates across the country; land-use constraints appear to be most severe in the West, which is also the region having the greatest price increases. But real price increases occurred in every region after 1965 and accelerated everywhere during the later 1970s.

Apart from these special situations, there is no reason to attribute the real price increase to problems of supply. Most analysts have concluded that the supply of new housing is perfectly elastic in the long run, meaning that additional houses can be supplied at the same real costs in response to any increase in demand; at most, there may be a temporary price increase that will dissipate in perhaps five years.[15] Thus some of the price increase during any cyclical upturn may result from the increased demand, but virtually none of the real increase over a period as long as a decade should be attributed to it.

The Relationship between Inflation and Prices. The process by which inflation affects house prices can be thought of as having two stages. First, as prices rise, households observe their increase and begin to expect further increases. Second, as these inflationary expectations for the future are formed, they are capitalized into current house prices. A number of economists have investigated one or the other step, theoretically and empirically.

There have been several attempts to measure inflationary expectations with respect to house prices, typically using either of two methodologies: inferring expectations from the term structure of interest rates,[16] or relating survey data on expectations to actual past inflation rates, and then projecting the estimated relationships for periods for which the survey data are not available.[17] There are a number of differences among the studies concerning the expected rate of inflation and even the timing of changes in expectations, but they agree that expected house price inflation rose during the 1970s, accelerating at a particularly rapid rate toward the end of the decade. By 1979, prices were expected to rise at 10 to 14 percent, compared with 4 to 6 percent a decade earlier.

Difficult as it may be to estimate the effect of current and past house prices on future inflationary expectations, it is still more difficult to estimate the effect of those inflationary expectations, once formed, on current house prices. To my knowledge, there have been only two systematic analyses of this problem, using quite different methodologies and yielding quite different results.

Poterba has constructed a partial-equilibrium dynamic model of the housing market, in which both prices and output respond to changes in expected inflation.[18] In his model, prices rise immediately in response to an increase in the expected inflation rate, but part of the increase is dissipated as output gradually increases over a number of years. The price response also varies with the tax bracket of the household, which implies that it varies by the price of the house, to a reasonably close approximation. To illustrate his model, Poterba has simulated the effect of the actual change in inflation experienced during the 1970s, on the assumption that the actual rate was the anticipated rate, at least at the beginning and end of the decade. These rates were 3 and 9 percent, respectively. For the 25 percent bracket, which is commonly used as the bracket of the typical first-time homebuyer, Poterba estimates an immediate real price increase of almost 20 percent if homeowners and buyers anticipate an increase in the supply of houses in response to inflation, and an increase of 35 percent if they do not. The former would appear to be more likely. For the 35 percent bracket, the increases are much larger, 32 and 71 percent, respectively. The actual real price increase in the decade was 29 percent, between these two estimates, suggesting that nearly all of the real price rise for housing in the 1970s was due to inflationary expectations alone. If there is no change in expected inflation, real prices would decline by perhaps 4 percent in the course of the 1980s; they would not rise further unless the inflation rate—not just the price level—itself increased. Poterba finds that the effect of inflation is quite similar, whether the change is assumed to be a one-time shock or a gradual acceleration.

An alternative approach has been developed by Diamond.[19] He analyzed actual changes in real prices between 1966 and 1982 in relation to changes in the volume of new home production, zoning and other land-use controls, and the rate of inflation. His preliminary estimates show that real house prices rose by about 25 percent during the later 1970s. Inflation accounted for only about a third, nine percentage points, of this. Also important were the cyclical increase in production, which peaked in the later 1970s, and a secular upward trend in prices unrelated either to output levels or to inflation, which Diamond suggests may represent unmeasured quality improvement.

An interesting feature of this analysis is its regional disaggregation of price changes. Diamond estimates that prices in the West rose by 25 percent in the later 1970s because of land-use restrictions imposed there at that time. This is the strongest evidence to date that supply constraints may have contributed to the rise in home prices, but it is a localized effect, accounting for between five and ten percentage points nationally.

These studies have quite different implications for disinflation. As noted previously, the real price of a home declined by 11 percent from 1979 through 1982. Poterba's simulations imply that this is not much more than half of the disinflation that would occur if inflation were expected to return to levels of the late 1960s which it actually did by early 1983. The inference is that most households do not believe that the recent disinflation is permanent. Diamond's results, however, suggest both that most of the decline is due to the recession and that most of the effect of disinflation has already occurred. Continued disinflation, combined with economic recovery, might result in rising nominal and even real prices in the next few years.

Houses versus Other Tangible Assets. A different perspective on the price changes for houses may be obtained by comparing them with other tangible assets rather than with other consumer goods. In this light, the house price increases during the 1970s were by no means uniquely high. This statement should be qualified, however; many of the problems in constructing a price index for houses apply with equal or greater force to other tangible assets. It is difficult to hold quality constant over time, and most of the few available measures of the prices of tangible assets do not seriously attempt to do so. One that does is an index of the prices of U.S. postage stamps compiled by the Scott Company, whose catalogues are the acknowledged standard price reference among philatelists in this country.[20] According to this index, stamp prices have been much more volatile than house prices, and real stamp prices have been much more responsive to inflation and disinflation. Indeed, in order to present stamps, houses, and general prices on the same scale, the substantial differences between the latter two must be sharply compressed (see figure 2). The annual rate of price increases for stamps averaged over 14 percent com-

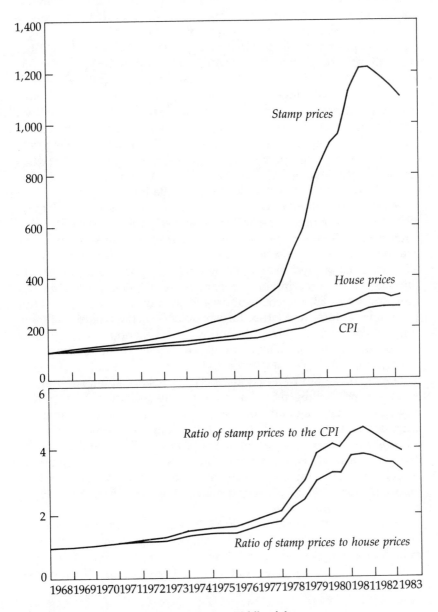

FIGURE 2

INDEXES OF POSTAGE STAMP, HOUSE, GENERAL PRICES, 1968–1983

Stamp prices

House prices

CPI

Ratio of stamp prices to the CPI

Ratio of stamp prices to house prices

1968 1969 1970 1971 1972 1973 1974 1975 1976 1977 1978 1979 1980 1981 1982 1983

NOTE: Prices at each year marker refer to the middle of the year.
SOURCES: *Price Index of New One-Family Houses Sold; Economic Report of the President,* February 1983; and *Scott's Stamp Market Update,* "U.S. Stamp Index," Spring 1983.

pounded between 1968 and 1976, compared with less than 7½ percent for houses; and the speculative housing boom of the late 1970s, with annual price rises of 14 percent, pales in comparison to the 40 percent increases in stamps during the same period. Stamp prices continued to rise in the early stages of disinflation: the Scott index rose by 50 percent from 1979 to mid-1981. Since then, however, it has fallen sharply, by 9 percent in nominal terms and by 16 percent in real value.

Estimated price indexes for other tangible assets, such as coins, paintings, jewels, and precious metals, show similar volatility.[21] Through most of the 1970s, these were much better hedges against inflation than houses. During the early 1980s, however, their prices dropped sharply, in some cases (such as silver) by far more than stamp prices. Dealers and experts in these assets have lamented the "havoc" wrought in their markets by disinflation.[22]

Despite their rapid price appreciation, collectibles and similar tangible assets were not an especially good investment vehicle for most households. There are problems of information, transactions costs, heterogeneity, and liquidity. Housing is by far the most durable asset with information and ownership widely diffused in our society. In 1965, about the time inflation began, the U.S. homeownership rate was more than 63 percent, comprising over 35 million households; and many renters were either former owners or the children of owners. By comparison, even the number of "serious" collectors of stamps—arguably the most common collectible—is quite small; one recent knowledgeable estimate is 150,000, at most.[23] Collectibles also usually involve high transactions costs: in postage stamps, for example, a dealer's selling price has traditionally been about double his buying price, although auction commissions for high-quality material are much smaller, between 20 and 25 percent. Transactions costs for housing are perhaps half as high. It is also difficult to protect collectibles against theft. Homeowners' insurance policies typically do not cover coins and stamps; it is necessary to buy a separate policy with a high premium and to photograph the entire collection in order to establish just what is owned.

Precious metals are also costly to store and to protect against theft. These disadvantages have been reduced to some extent, however, as inflation has progressed, with the spread of market innovations such as specialized gold or silver mutual investment funds. Nonetheless, precious metals remain a more esoteric form of inflation hedge than houses.

As a digression, it may be worth noting that one effect of inflation in the markets for collectibles has apparently been to generate an expansion of supply. Evidence of this change is essentially anecdotal but seems strong enough to warrant the conclusion. The expansion is most pronounced for collectibles: subscription series of porcelain figurines, china plates, and silver or gold medallions embossed with a specific theme were advertised in newspapers and magazines, especially during the late 1970s and early 1980s, as producers realized that earlier series had shared in the real appreciation enjoyed by collectibles and precious metals in general. Perhaps the *reductio ad absurdum* in this industry occurred when the Franklin Mint offered a series of uncirculated foreign bank notes, expensively framed, to investors— probably the first time that paper money has been promoted as a hedge against inflation![24]

Homeownership Costs

The dramatic rise in house prices has been the most noticed effect of inflation on the housing market, but other costs of homeownership have been affected as well. These include explicit costs such as the monthly mortgage payment, property taxes, and maintenance, and implicit ones such as depreciation and the forgone return on the owner's equity in the house. Inflation brings some of these costs down and makes homeownership less expensive, even as it drives up house prices, through its interaction with the federal income tax laws and the housing finance system.

This section describes these interactions. For expository convenience, it begins with the relationship between inflation and the tax system under the assumption that the real after-tax mortgage interest rate is unaffected by inflation. In reality, however, this is far from the case, and the inflation-induced changes in the real rate may have been especially important in explaining housing market behavior during the last two decades.

Taxes, Inflation, and the Cost of Capital. The main federal income tax provisions affecting owner-occupied housing are: (1) the deductibility of mortgage interest and property taxes for owners who itemize deductions; (2) the exclusion of the imputed rent on the home from taxable income; (3) the exclusion of capital gains arising from the sale of a home, as long as another home of equal value is purchased within a set period; and (4) since 1978, the one-time exclusion of capital gains up to $125,000 for households where the head is over fifty-five, regardless of whether another home is purchased.[25]

When prices are stable, these provisions encourage homeownership by lowering the cost of the capital invested in the home and exempting virtually all the returns from taxation. In addition, the progressivity of the tax system provides a greater ownership incentive

171

to higher-bracket households. Inflation accentuates both effects.

The effect of inflation on capital gains has already been discussed; this section, therefore, concentrates on the effect on capital costs. The largest component of these costs, and the most important one in the present context, is the monthly mortgage payment. The interaction between inflation, the tax system, and the mortgage rate therefore deserves special attention.

Until very recently, nearly all home mortgages were long-term, fixed-rate, level-payment, self-amortizing instruments: they were issued for twenty-five to thirty years, with the interest rate and the monthly payment fixed in advance for the full mortgage term. If inflation is anticipated at the time a mortgage is issued, then the mortgage rate will rise by the amount of the inflation rate, because lenders will insist on a rate that compensates them for the decline in the value of the dollars in which they will be repaid. Thus the real mortgage rate, as received by the borrower, will be unchanged. If, for example, the real rate is 3 percent, and inflation is expected to be 2 percent over the life of the mortgage, then the nominal rate will be 5 percent; if inflation is expected to be 5 percent, the nominal rate will be 8 percent.

The real after-tax rate paid by the borrower will, however, be reduced by inflation, because of the tax deductibility of mortgage interest. The tax deduction applies to the full nominal interest rate; the inflation rate is then subtracted from the after-tax nominal rate to derive the after-tax real rate. This effect of inflation may be conveniently shown for the examples of the previous paragraph, assuming that a taxpayer is in the 50 percent marginal tax bracket: if there is no inflation and the mortgage rate is 3 percent, the after-tax rate is 1.5 percent; if the inflation rate is 2 percent, then the after-tax nominal rate is 2.5 percent, and the real rate is 0.5 percent; if the inflation rate is 5 percent, then the after-tax nominal rate is 4 percent, and the real rate is −1 percent. Table 4 presents a range of real interest rates, depending on the marginal tax bracket and the rate of inflation, showing that the real after-tax interest rate is lower both as inflation rises and as the tax bracket of the household increases. The table is based on the common assumption of a normal real mortgage rate of 3 percent; in all cases, this is the rate earned by lenders. The proportion of this rate paid by the borrower, and by the taxpayer, however, varies with inflation. For a household in the 50 percent bracket, with no inflation, the borrower effectively pays 1.5 percent, and the taxpayer also pays 1.5 percent; but with a 2 percent inflation rate, the borrower pays only 0.5 percent, and the taxpayer 2.5 percent. At rates above 3 percent, the borrower's real rate is negative, and the taxpayer pays *more* than 3 percent.[26]

Several features of the table are especially noteworthy. Inflation

TABLE 4
INFLATION AND THE REAL AFTER-TAX MORTGAGE RATE
(percent)

Nominal Rate	Inflation Rate	Marginal Tax Bracket			
		30%	40%	50%	60%
3	0	2.1	1.8	1.5	1.2
4	1	1.8	1.4	1.0	0.6
5	2	1.5	1.0	0.5	0
6	3	1.2	0.6	0	negative
7	4	0.9	0.2	negative	
8	5	0.6	negative		
9	6	0.3			
10	7	0			
11	8	negative			

NOTE: Assumes real mortgage rate of 3 percent. After-tax rate calculated as: nominal rate (1 − marginal tax bracket) − inflation rate.

increases the advantages of homeownership in all tax brackets, but more so in the higher ones. The real mortgage rate turns negative for those in the 60 percent bracket at a rather low inflation rate of 3 percent; it becomes negative for those paying 30 percent only at an 8 percent inflation rate. For those in the higher bracket, real after-tax mortgage rates have been negative for more than fifteen years; for those in the lower bracket, rates were negative only in the late 1970s. (As of mid-1983, with the highest tax bracket being 50 percent and inflation less than 5 percent, the real after-tax mortgage rate is positive for all households.)

Perhaps a less obvious point is the effect of inflation on the real after-tax rate paid by a given household. This effect is twofold: the rate falls for a household in a given tax bracket, as the table shows; but if inflation continues for a few years, it pushes the household into a higher marginal tax bracket, increasing the value of the deduction. Thus, a household in the 30 percent bracket initially could reasonably expect to be in the 40 percent bracket after a few years of 5 percent inflation and thereby have its real mortgage rate more than cut in half. Despite higher house prices, inflation clearly encouraged home-ownership, especially for higher-income households.

Fully anticipated inflation makes homeownership more difficult in one way. The higher nominal interest rate compensates fully for the decline in the value of money over the life of the mortgage. The borrower thus pays the same real amount, before taxes, over the life of the mortgage. The time path of real payments is, however, "tilted" forward by anticipated inflation. With stable prices, the real value of the monthly payment is the same each month; with rising prices, a constant nominal payment has a higher real value in the early years of the mortgage, and a lower one later. This may not be fully offset by the decline in the real after-tax rate, especially for relatively low-income homebuyers, such as young families. These households may find the higher initial real payment too burdensome, when they would buy homes in the absence of inflation.[27] For this reason, an alternative mortgage instrument, the graduated payment mortgage (GPM), became popular during the mid-1970s. The GPM is a fixed-rate, but not level-payment, mortgage; it allows the buyer to make smaller payments initially, and larger ones later, presumably when income is higher.

Unanticipated Inflation and the Real Mortgage Rates. The foregoing discussion has been based on the assumption that inflation is fully anticipated by both homebuyers and mortgage lenders and that nominal mortgage rates therefore rise to leave real rates unchanged. Reality was quite different. Inflation was generally unanticipated, particularly by lenders. As a result, borrowers have received windfall gains, as they were able to make their mortgage payments in cheaper dollars than originally expected, and lenders correspondingly suffered windfall losses. The costs of ownership were lowered still more than indicated by table 4.

This section traces the movements in the real mortgage rate. Prior to the mid-1960s, the nominal mortgage interest rate commonly was about three to five percentage points above the inflation rate; in 1965, for example, they were 5.9 and 1.7 percent, respectively. The difference, the real mortgage rate, was 4.2 percent. As inflation began and accelerated, mortgage lenders failed to forecast its course with any degree of accuracy. Figure 3 compares nominal home mortgage rates with current inflation. It shows that throughout the 1970s, twenty-five-to-thirty year fixed-rate loans were being made at rates no more than three to four percentage points above the current inflation rate, even as the rate was rising. Lenders apparently did not react to the sudden acceleration of inflation in 1973–1975 and actually made loans at a negative current real interest rate, on the average, in 1974. (The inflation rate shown in the figure is the same CPI rental equivalent variant used in figure 1; the actual CPI shows a narrower spread in most years, and a negative one in 1975 as well as in 1974.) This behavior was sensible only if thrift institutions were assuming that the high current rate of inflation was a temporary aberration. The inflation rate did drop in 1976 and in 1977, apparently confirming that view.

FIGURE 3
MORTGAGE RATES AND CURRENT INFLATION, 1968–1982

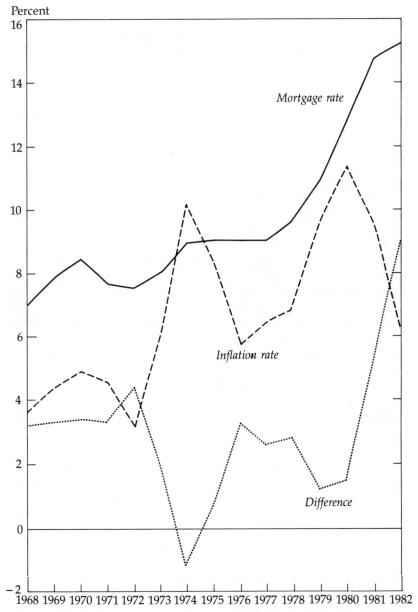

SOURCES: *Economic Report of the President*, February 1983; *Federal Home Loan Bank Board Journal*, table S.5.1, "Terms on Conventional Home Mortgage Loans Made: National Averages for All Major Types of Lenders," August 1977; and author's calculations.

Thus in the later 1970s, lenders once again did not react to the renewal of inflation and let the difference between the mortgage and current inflation rates narrow to about 1 percent by 1979.

In evaluating the behavior of lenders and borrowers, it is probably more appropriate to compare the mortgage rate with a measure of long-term expected inflation, rather than the current inflation rate. Figure 4 therefore shows the expected real mortgage rate, defined as the difference between the nominal mortgage rate and a measure of expected inflation for the next five years, developed by Dougherty and Van Order.[28] Five years is still a much shorter period than the life of the typical mortgage, but it is long enough to indicate whether a home is likely to be a profitable investment. The measure of expected inflation is based on a continuing survey of economists and thus does not necessarily represent the expectations of either borrowers or lenders, but it is the best long-term measure available over the past fifteen years. The expected real mortgage rate follows a similar but less pronounced pattern to the current real rate shown in figure 3: as inflation accelerates, the real rate drops below 4 percent at the beginning of the 1970s and remains there throughout the decade, with a particularly sharp decline in the mid-1970s.

No one has offered any plausible explanation for the failure of the nominal mortgage rate to adjust to inflation more rapidly, or, stated alternatively, for the apparent large difference in inflationary expectations between borrowers and lenders. Had they been more consistent, homeownership would have been a much less profitable investment in the 1970s, but owners would still have benefited from inflation.

Mortgage Rates and Disinflation. By the end of the 1970s, lenders were finally changing their expectations. From early 1979 to early 1980, the nominal mortgage rate rose from 10 to 13 percent; then it continued rising, reaching a peak of nearly 16 percent in early 1982. This movement in interest rates coincided with the process of disinflation. As it progressed, the nominal mortgage rate and the inflation rate moved sharply in opposite directions, and the real rate rose dramatically. By 1981, it was over 5 percent, measured against either current or expected inflation; in 1982, it was between 7 and 8 percent, which was almost certainly the highest real rate since World War II. (In the first half of 1983, both current and expected real rates have declined slightly; these data are not shown in the figures.)

The extraordinarily high nominal rates severely limited the ability of potential buyers to qualify for conventional mortgages on the homes that they wished to buy. In order to sell their homes, many owners therefore resorted to the "creative financing" techniques mentioned earlier. Often the seller became the mortgagee at a below-

FIGURE 4
Mortgage Rates and Expected Inflation, 1968–1982

SOURCES: *Federal Home Loan Bank Board Journal,* table S.5.1, August 1977; author's calculations; and unpublished data supplied by Robert Van Order.

market interest rate, holding a "balloon note" for a few years.

There is little data on the magnitude of seller financing, but it probably constituted a significant minor fraction of mortgage credit between 1979 and 1982. The figures compiled by Salkin and Durning for California indicate that sellers provided perhaps 17 percent of all mortgage credit in 1981.[29] This may be high for the nation as a whole, because creative financing was more prevalent in California prior to the late 1970s. A recent survey by the National Association of Realtors estimates that $32 billion in balloon mortgages will be coming due by 1987, half by 1985, and half in the subsequent two years.[30]

As interest rates remained high during disinflation, many policy analysts expressed concern that buyers would be unable to finance their mortgages when the balloon notes became due. The decline in mortgage rates in late 1982, however, has apparently largely forestalled this problem. Over $15 billion in home mortgages were refinanced at federally insured savings and loan associations between November 1982 and July 1983, as conventional rates dropped below 14 percent; at an annual rate, this would constitute the largest volume of refinancing on record. It seems likely that most of this refinancing involved balloon notes or other creative financing. Continued refinancing at the current rate for the balance of 1983 would permit refinancing of most balloon notes falling due through at least 1984 or mid-1985 and would greatly reduce the risk of widespread default arising from inability to refinance homes in the conventional mortgage market. Thus a potential problem in the transition to a lower inflation rate has probably been averted, unless interest rates rise more sharply than they did in mid-1983.

The high rates of the early 1980s also occasioned an intense legal and political controversy over mortgage loan assumptions and due-on-sale clauses. The latter require that a mortgagor pay the entire outstanding principal balance on the mortgage at the time he or she sells the house. In the absence of such a clause, the new buyer can assume the mortgage, continuing to make payments on it at the original interest rate. As interest rates rose, assumable mortgages became valuable assets for homeowners wishing to sell; as discussed earlier, some or all of the savings in monthly mortgage payments for assumable mortgages was capitalized into the price of the house.

Sellers subject to due-on-sale clauses therefore sought to prohibit their enforcement, in order to reap the same benefits as those with assumable mortgages. The issue pitted sellers and realtors against thrift institutions. The realtors argued that assumptions were essential to sales at the current high interest rates and that over half of all sales involved assumptions. Lenders claimed that valid contracts were being abrogated after the fact and that prohibition of due-on-sale was exacerbating the problems resulting from inflation. The rates they were paying for deposits were rising, while the low yields on old mortgages were being continued for the full twenty-five-to-thirty-year term of the mortgages, instead of the usual ten-to-fifteen-year period before prepayment.

In some eighteen states, courts prohibited enforcement of due-on-sale clauses in mortgages issued by state-chartered lenders; it has been estimated that in California alone, $100–300 million in wealth was transferred from savings associations to home sellers as a result.[31] On the federal level, the Supreme Court finally ruled in 1982 that due-on-sale clauses were enforceable in mortgages issued by federally chartered savings associations. Late in 1982, Congress overrode the state prohibitions, effective after a three-year "window period," as part of the Depository Institutions Act (the Garn–St. Germain bill). As interest rates came down at the end of 1982, however, the intensity of the issue gradually dissipated.

Trends in Homeownership Costs. The real mortgage interest rate, and the capital gains accruing to owners, are the most important components of real homeownership costs. They have combined to make ownership extraordinarily cheap during the inflationary 1970s, and extraordinarily expensive so far in the disinflationary 1980s. Dougherty and Van Order, for example, have calculated that expected capital gains in housing were consistently greater than the expected real mortgage rate from 1973 through 1980, meaning that the cost of capital to the homebuyer was actually negative, even in the absence of tax considerations; by early 1983, with high real rates and negative capital gains, the cost of capital was over 10 percent.

Measures of total real homeownership costs (including property taxes, depreciation, and maintenance) invariably parallel the movements of the real mortgage rate. Hendershott and Shilling have constructed such a measure for the longest time period, since 1951; they find that the cost of homeownership has declined almost continuously, slowly at first and then more rapidly after 1965, until by 1979 it was less than one-quarter of the original value; then it rose fivefold by 1982.[32] They also find a steady decline in the cost of owning relative to renting.

In the next section of this study, evidence will be presented to support the argument that real homeownership costs provide a better basis for understanding housing market behavior during the past fifteen years than the more widely noted nominal home prices. A subsequent section will discuss the rental housing market.

Homeownership

Inflation affected housing market behavior, as well as prices. It induced a pronounced shift in tenure: the ownership rate increased from 63.3 percent of all households in 1965 to 64.7 percent in 1976, and then to 65.6 percent by 1979, after the speculative housing boom of the preceding three years. These changes occurred while basic demographic trends were running in the opposite direction; as noted, there was disproportionate growth within categories of households that have traditionally been renters, such as single persons, one-parent families, and young married couples. It has been estimated that about four million more households became owners from 1965 to 1978 than would have been expected from demographic changes alone.[33] This is about 5 percent of all households.

While a number of analysts have noted that this increase in homeownership coincided with the decline in the real cost of owning, as mentioned in the previous section, only a few have attempted to construct a formal model of tenure choice, incorporating income and demographic changes as well as prices. The studies that do exist find that the real cost of ownership, which includes inflationary expectations, accounts for a large share of the tenure changes.[34] The range of estimated effects is wide, but it would seem that somewhere between 10 and 50 percent of the increase in homeownership might be attributed to income growth rather than to real price changes.

Ownership Changes among Household Categories. Within the population, ownership increased for nearly all identifiable groups during the decade of the 1970s. Table 5 shows changes by income class; all except the poorest rose, and the increases are strongly positively correlated with income. Ownership also rose in most demographic groups (see table 6), with by far the largest increase among young married couples. There were increases among two of the three major racial-ethnic groups in the United States, as well. (The slight decline among Hispanics may simply reflect increased immigration in the decade.)

Both tables show an interesting and perhaps disturbing pattern. Homeownership increased most among those groups for which it was already high; it increased less, or even decreased, among those who were more commonly renters to begin with. This suggests that inflation induced a shift toward homeownership among those who had the financial ability to own but had chosen to rent for reasons of personal preference. Thus inflation may have contributed to a closer alignment between housing tenure and income, or demographic sta-

TABLE 5

TENURE SHIFT BY INCOME CLASS, 1970–1980

(percent)

Income Class in 1970	Homeownership Rate	
	1970	1980
Under $5,000 (Under $10,000)ᵃ	50.0	45.4
$5,000-$7,000 ($10,000-$15,000)ᵃ	52.1	56.5
$7,000-$10,000 ($15,000-$20,000)ᵃ	61.3	65.5
$10,000-$15,000 ($20,000-$30,000)ᵃ	72.6	76.9
$15,000-$25,000 ($30,000-$50,000)ᵃ	80.5	88.2
Over $25,000 (Over $50,000)ᵃ	84.5	92.3

a. The numbers in parentheses are the 1980 income brackets approximately equivalent in real terms to the 1970 income values.

SOURCES: U.S. Department of Commerce, Bureau of the Census, and U.S. Department of Housing and Urban Development, *Annual Housing Survey: 1980*, Part A: General Housing Characteristics, tables A-1, A-7, A-9.

tus, helping to make renters in particular a more homogeneous group, with lower incomes and fewer married couples.

The clearest exception to this generalization is the dramatic increase among young married couples. These households chose to move more quickly to ownership status than they traditionally have. The median age of homebuyers, especially first-time buyers, declined throughout the 1970s; and the proportion of young families buying a home in any given year more than doubled, from about 6 to 8 percent in 1969–1970 to 16 to 20 percent in 1977–1978.[35]

Other Changes. The increase in homeownership manifested itself in several forms. Single-family home construction became an unusually large share of total new housing in the middle and later 1970s. The housing recession of 1974–1975 was especially severe in the multifam-

181

TABLE 6

TENURE SHIFT BY DEMOGRAPHIC GROUP, 1970–1980

(percent)

	Homeownership Rate	
Demographic Group	1970	1980
Married couples		
Head under age thirty	39.4	52.0
Head age thirty–forty-four	73.1	80.8
Head age forty-five–sixty-four	80.8	86.8
Head age sixty-five or more	78.4	84.9
Other male head		
Under age sixty-five	49.1	43.8
Age sixty-five or more	71.1	76.1
Other female head		
Under age sixty-five	42.7	41.7
Age sixty-five or more	69.9	73.2
One-person households, male		
Under age sixty-five	26.2	32.8
Age sixty-five or more	50.6	57.1
One-person households, female		
Under age sixty-five	39.3	38.2
Age sixty-five or more	55.2	59.2
All elderly	67.5	70.7
All whites	66.3	70.3
All blacks	41.6	43.9
All Hispanics	43.4	42.9
All households	62.9	65.6

SOURCE: Same as for table 5.

ily sector, and home production increased much more rapidly than apartments during the subsequent recovery. From 1965 to 1967, single-family homes amounted to about two-thirds of new housing construction. From 1975 through 1978, they were about three-quarters, and perhaps 20 percent of the new apartments were constructed under the Section 8 subsidy program.

There was also a shift toward homeownership within the existing stock. This occurred for every type of structure except small apartment buildings. Owner-occupancy in single-family detached houses increased from 81 to 85 percent; in town houses, from 58 to 62 percent; and in large apartment buildings (those with five or more units), from 5 to 8 percent. This last figure reflects a new form of housing ownership, the condominium. Condominiums have appealed to younger one- or two-person households in the upper half of the income distribution, enabling them to achieve the financial advantages of ownership, without the bother of maintaining a single-family house (and yard). By 1980, the Annual Housing Survey reported that there were more than one million owner-occupied condominium units; in 1970, they were not counted separately but were undoubtedly negligible.

Disinflation and Homeownership. The homeownership rate fluctuated between 64.8 and 65.8 percent from 1979 to 1981, reaching the higher figure in the third quarters of both 1979 and 1980.[36] This is probably the highest rate ever achieved in the United States. Ownership declined sharply, however, from 65.6 percent in the third quarter of 1981 to 64.5 percent by the fourth quarter of 1982. This is by far the largest decrease since quarterly data were first collected in 1964; declines in both 1970 and 1974 amounted to only 0.4 percent. About 900,000 households shifted tenure from owning to renting within fifteen months. Some, and perhaps all, of this decline appears to be the result of the recession; in the first quarter of 1983, the rate rose to 64.7 percent, where it remained in the second quarter.

Unfortunately, the income and demographic status of these households cannot be determined, because the latest available data are still only for the year 1980. A similar problem exists for the types of housing units in which tenure shifts are occurring, though fragmentary and anecdotal information indicates a decline in the demand for condominiums. In Washington, D.C., for example, apartments offered for sale declined by nearly 50 percent from 1981 to 1982. In addition, reversions to rental status constituted 15 percent of the total number of units offered for sale, and marketing was suspended in another 8 percent for reasons such as developer bankruptcy or construction loan foreclosure.[37]

Construction of new units shifted away from single-family homes. From 1980 through 1982, houses again accounted for only about two-thirds of new starts. Part of the relative strength of multifamily production may be due to the final wave of production under the subsidized Section 8 New Construction program, but any plausible adjustment for Section 8 would not affect this pattern.

Mortgage Delinquencies and Foreclosures. A minor but perhaps significant aspect of the relationship between inflation and homeownership has been the trend in mortgage defaults and foreclosures. As inflation creates capital gains, the owner's incentive to preserve his title is increased; with disinflation, the incentive is reduced. This means that mortgage default or foreclosure could respond to inflation; homeowners would alter their overall expenditure patterns to continue making mortgage payments as inflation accelerated, attempting to minimize the risk of losing their homes, and accept a greater risk when disinflation occurs.

Delinquency and foreclosure rates are strongly procyclical; typically, both peak at or shortly after a peak in unemployment.[38] This pattern has been repeated in the latest cycle: the ninety-day delinquency rate on conventional mortgages fell from 0.56 percent in 1976 to 0.46 percent by early 1979, then rose sharply to 0.65 percent as of the first quarter of 1983 before declining to 0.58 percent in the second quarter (the latest available data). A similar pattern occurs for FHA-insured mortgages. Because unemployment peaked in the fourth quarter of 1982, it is likely that the first quarter of 1983 will prove to be the peak for delinquencies in this cycle. Foreclosure rates, however, had not yet started to decline as of mid-1983.

There is also a secular trend toward higher delinquency and foreclosure rates over the postwar period, which can be attributed to the liberalization of mortgage terms, the rise in the divorce rate, and in the case of FHA, a downward shift in the income of mortgagors.[39] Thus when delinquencies and foreclosures are disaggregated by mortgage type (conventional, FHA, and VA), nearly all show postwar highs in early 1983.

Despite these strong influences, statistical analysis indicates that inflation has affected conventional and FHA foreclosure rates, though not VA rates or delinquencies. The accelerated inflation of the later 1970s may have depressed foreclosures by as much as a third, while disinflation in the 1980s may have raised them by a quarter. Thus the change in inflation may have exaggerated the cyclical effect of unemployment and contributed to the record foreclosures of 1982 and early 1983.

The Amount of Housing Investment

Household investment in housing has apparently been more sensitive to inflation than the incidence of homeownership. This would be expected, since investment includes quality improvements as well as tenure shifts. This section summarizes the available data and reports on a few selected forms of investment.

Total Investment. Table 7 shows the shares of personal disposable income devoted to various assets annually since 1955.[40] The housing

TABLE 7
HOUSEHOLD ASSET ACQUISITION AS A SHARE OF PERSONAL
DISPOSABLE INCOME, 1955–1982
(percent)

| Year | Housing | Tangible Assets | | Total Financial Assets |
		Consumer durables	Total	
1955	5.9	2.9	8.8	1.7
1956	5.2	1.6	6.8	3.8
1957	4.3	1.1	5.4	4.5
1958	3.9	0.1	4.0	5.3
1959	4.5	1.2	5.7	3.7
1960	4.0	0.9	4.9	3.3
1961	3.4	0.3	3.7	4.3
1962	3.2	1.2	4.4	4.3
1963	3.3	1.7	5.0	4.3
1964	3.1	2.0	5.1	5.4
1965	2.8	2.5	5.3	5.6
1966	2.3	2.5	4.8	6.8
1967	2.2	1.9	4.1	7.2
1968	2.3	2.4	4.7	6.2
1969	2.2	2.1	4.3	4.4
1970	1.8	1.1	2.9	7.4
1971	2.7	3.5	6.2	7.2
1972	3.4	4.2	7.6	7.1
1973	3.3	4.4	7.7	8.0
1974	2.5	2.8	5.3	8.5
1975	2.1	2.4	4.5	10.2
1976	2.9	3.3	6.2	8.1
1977	3.9	3.8	7.7	5.9
1978	4.3	3.8	8.1	5.7
1979	4.0	3.1	7.1	5.7
1980	2.6	1.8	4.4	9.2
1981	2.1	1.1	4.0	9.6
1982	1.3	1.7	3.0	10.2

SOURCES: Federal Reserve Board, *Flow of Funds Accounts, 1946–1975* (for 1955–1956); *Flow of Funds Accounts, Assets and Liabilities Outstanding, 1957–1980*; *Flow of Funds Accounts, Second Quarter 1981, Annual Revisions*; *Flow of Funds Accounts, Fourth Quarter 1982, Annual Revisions*.

share declined rather steadily until 1970, as the housing boom of the immediate postwar period tapered off and the birth rate began to decline after 1957. Investment then rose sharply during the 1970s.

There is a pronounced cyclical pattern in this decade, which seems to be magnified by inflation. The boom of 1977–1979 shows the highest levels of asset acquisition in two decades, for example; then the combination of recession and disinflation cut investment by 1982 to the lowest share in the entire postwar period.

Similar trends appear when housing is compared with other asset categories. There is a steady diminution in the relative importance of housing and consumer durables from 1955 to 1970, abstracting from business cycles; again this pattern is reversed during the 1970s, with tangible assets being particularly important relative to financial assets in the later 1970s. Financial asset investment displays a strong countercyclical pattern after 1970, reaching its peaks in the cyclical troughs of 1975 and 1982.

The data in table 7 refer to the annual flow of investment by households. This is a small part of their total wealth holdings. Table 8 presents two series on the value of the total stock of owner-occupied housing. The first column reports assets per capita, in 1972 dollars. The value of holdings increased steadily (but at a declining rate) until 1978, with minimal declines during some of the cyclical downturns. Since 1978, however, it has declined by about 4 percent in four years, with three percentage points coming in 1982 alone.

The data in the first column of table 8 are derived by deflating the current dollar value of the housing stock by the overall CPI. They thus overstate the value of the stock during the 1970s, because they omit the inflation-induced increase in the relative price of housing. Stated alternatively, the cost of reproducing the stock has risen by more than the CPI indicates. The second column of the table corrects for this relative price change. It measures the real value of the owner-occupied stock, deflated by its own price (the census new home price index, omitting land), as a ratio to real personal disposable income. This is a revised and updated version of a series developed by William Fellner and reported in the 1979 volume of *Contemporary Economic Problems*.[41]

The series shows that the value of the owner-occupied housing stock was noticeably greater before inflation began than during it. This unexpected finding should not, however, be stressed. There is a change in the housing deflator in 1964, when the census price index was first used; it appears that the pre-1964 deflator rose less rapidly than the census index.[42] Thus the data before 1964 may be slightly too high.

For the period since 1964, when consistent data are available, the decline in real housing assets occurs during the later 1960s, when inflation was just beginning. The value of the stock increased in the familiar cyclical pattern after 1970, reaching a post-1963 peak in 1978

TABLE 8
HOUSEHOLD WEALTH HELD AS OWNER-OCCUPIED HOUSING, 1955–1982

Year	Assets per Capita (1972 dollars)	Assets per Dollar of Personal Disposable Income[a]
1955	$1,958	$.880
1956	2,008	.874
1957	2,054	.888
1958	2,118	.924
1959	2,212	.934
1960	2,265	.945
1961	2,319	.955
1962	2,374	.949
1963	2,419	.944
1964	2,540	.936
1965	2,598	.915
1966	2,689	.910
1967	2,720	.887
1968	2,877	.908
1969	2,860	.881
1970	2,933	.871
1971	3,057	.887
1972	3,242	.913
1973	3,382	.906
1974	3,434	.931
1975	3,385	.907
1976	3,599	.929
1977	3,698	.925
1978	3,895	.941
1979	3,830	.911
1980	3,833	.906
1981	3,843	.893
1982	3,719	.859

a. Data are for residential buildings divided by their own implicit price deflator and by disposable income, which is deflated by the personal consumption expenditure deflator. Income data is adjusted to omit noncorporate business.

SOURCES: Federal Reserve Board, *Balance Sheets for the U.S. Economy, 1945–1981*; U.S. Department of Commerce, *The National Income and Product Accounts of the United States, 1929–1976*; *Survey of Current Business*, July 1982; *Survey of Current Business*, March 1983.

and declining to the lowest level in almost three decades by 1982. Thus the series roughly parallels the movements in the inflation rate and in measures of inflationary expectations, at least since 1970.

There are several reasons why the movement in real housing investment might not be closely related to inflation. As previously mentioned (and noted by Fellner in 1979), demographic trends in the 1970s favored rental housing. Also, the present consensus of econometric research on housing demand is that both price and income elasticities are slightly less than unity, which would impart a downward drift to real housing investment over time.[43] It is worth noting that investment in consumer durables, which is not subject to these influences, shows a much stronger correlation with inflation, including a sharper decline beginning in 1980.

There is little evidence about changes in the distribution of wealth, but some significant changes may have occurred. Households that were very young in the 1960s seem to have profited most from the inflation-induced increases in real estate values that occurred during the 1970s, and to have enjoyed the greatest overall increases in wealth. There have also been substantial gains in both total and real estate wealth for all young and middle age groups. Among household types, married couples experienced a similar relative gain.[44] Broadly speaking, those groups with the greatest wealth increases in the 1970s were those with initially high homeownership rates (excluding the very youngest households)—that is, owners have benefited relative to renters. This has probably skewed the wealth distribution in favor of those who were already relatively wealthy.

New Home Quality. The most detailed data on the composition of household investment in housing describe the attributes of new homes. These are only a small share of the stock at any time, but they are probably still indicative of general trends and more responsive to inflation (or other factors) than the entire existing stock.

Data limitations complicate the description of new home quality over time. Since the late 1960s there have been two changes in the concept of "new homes" covered in the Census Bureau data on size and amenities.[45]

A second problem is caused by the Section 235 federal homeownership subsidy program during 1969–1973. The homes built under this program were much smaller, with fewer amenities, than the unsubsidized homes built at the same time and skew the measures of size and quality. It is therefore not feasible to construct a set of quality indicators for the period since 1971, when consistent coverage of new homes begins.

For these reasons, the data on size and amenities, reported in table 9, should be treated only as general indicators of trends. The table includes an adjusted estimate for 1968, in an attempt to achieve rough comparability to the later data.

TABLE 9

CHARACTERISTICS OF NEW HOMES, 1968–1982

(percent)

	1968[a]	1975	1979	1982
More than 1,600 sq. ft.	43	45	53	45
Two or more bathrooms	53	60	74	67
Garage	62	67	73	65
Basement	43	45	42	31
Fireplace	44[b]	52	62	54
Central air conditioning	30	46	60	66

a. Data for 1968 are adjusted to account for changes in coverage in the new home data, as discussed in text.
b. This figure is for 1969 (earliest year available).
SOURCE: U.S. Bureau of the Census, *Characteristics of New Housing*, Construction Reports, Series C-25.

Even with these limitations, the data clearly show that new homes have become larger, with more amenities, as inflation accelerated and that the trend was reversed in response to disinflation. From 1968 to 1979, the size of the typical new home increased by about 10 percent. Marked increases were also recorded for all but one characteristic. The exception—basements—occurs because of a regional shift in construction toward the South and West, where basements are much less common; three of the four census regions show an increase. These regional shifts also understate the extent of the increase in homes with fireplaces. The reverse applies to central air conditioning.

Since disinflation began, there has been a sharp decline in size and amenities for new homes. The typical new home in 1982 was 1,550 square feet, down by over 100 square feet, or 6 percent, from the high of 1978. The 1982 size was about the same as 1975, also a year of recession, disinflation, and smaller homes. The incidence of several other characteristics also declined from peaks in 1978 or 1979 to about the levels of 1975, before the latest acceleration of inflation. Central air conditioning showed the only continuing increase, both nationally and in three of the four census regions as well.

Unexpectedly, lot size runs counter to the other characteristics. Data are available only since 1976, but they show a decline of about 550 square feet, or 5.5 percent, from 1976 through 1979, and a steeper decline of over 1,300 square feet, or almost 14 percent, from 1979 through 1982. Thus the downward trend during inflation is accentuated during disinflation. It is surprising, however, that lot size did not increase during the inflationary period, since land is the longest-lived asset of all and therefore presumably the best inflation hedge.

Maintenance and Improvement of Existing Housing. Changes within the existing stock are much harder to document. There are, however, data on maintenance, repair, and alteration expenditures from the Survey of Residential Alterations and Repairs (SORAAR) conducted quarterly by the Census Bureau, which suggests that owners of existing houses reacted to inflation in deciding whether to invest further in their homes. Total real expenditures rose by about 30 percent during the 1970s. The increase was concentrated in owner-occupied single-family homes and in basic improvements (additions, alterations, and major replacements), rather than in maintenance and repairs. Increases were greater in higher-valued homes and in those occupied by higher-income owners. From 1980 to 1982, real investment declined by more than 20 percent. The changes mirrored those of the 1970s, with the decline being largest in owner-occupied homes and in improvements. Real expenditures per home declined by almost 30 percent, to the lowest level since inflation began.[46]

There is a strong procyclical pattern to repair expenditures, which indicates that the increase in the later 1970s and sharp decrease in the early 1980s cannot entirely be attributed to changes in inflation. Expenditures also tend to follow sales with a lag, as new owners decide to modify the home to suit their own preferences. Still, the rise and decline in expenditures, especially since 1975, is much sharper than can be explained fully by these factors.

Rental Housing

Inflation and disinflation have caused significant changes in the rental market also, which are in many respects the complement of their effects on owner-occupied housing.

The Detrimental Effect of Inflation. While house prices were rising much more rapidly than the rate of inflation during the 1970s, rents were declining, in real terms, by almost 15 percent (1.7 percent annually). This pattern is consistent with the view that inflation generated a shift in demand toward owner-occupancy, which overrode demographic changes and resulted in both a rise in real house prices and an increase in homeownership, and conversely a decline in rents and rental tenure.

Available evidence indicates that the operating costs of rental housing rose more than rents during the decade, so that property owners suffered a decline in the real rate of return on their investments.[47] This by itself would have lowered the sales prices for rental property, in real terms, but inflation also affected profitability adversely in another way—through the tax system.

Owners of rental property have several tax advantages over homeowners. They can deduct other operating costs as well as mortgage interest and property taxes and can claim depreciation on their property at an accelerated rate in excess of true economic depreciation. They cannot, however, exclude rental receipts from their income, because the rent is realized rather than imputed. Also, their capital gains are taxed when realized; unlike homeowners, they cannot roll over the gain by buying a new building or escape taxation altogether by remaining in business until death. For each of these provisions, inflation either reduced the value of the tax benefit or increased the relative disadvantage of investment in real property. It reduced the real value of the depreciation deduction, because the deduction is calculated on the basis of the historic cost of the property, rather than its current value. It increased the effective tax rate on real capital gains, because the nominal gain, arising solely from inflation, is taxed as well as the real gain. It also raised the tax rate on net rental income. Rising marginal tax rates increase the value of the deductions for operating costs, as in the case of homeowners, and the increase may even be greater for landlords, if their marginal tax brackets are higher.[48] Their rental income is also raised by inflation. Thus, even if rents and operating costs are raised proportionately by inflation, the landlord's real after-tax return would be lower, because the nominal before-tax return would be taxed at a higher rate.

Changes in the tax laws between 1969 and 1978 worsened the rental property owner's position concomitantly with inflation. Accelerated depreciation was made subject to taxation as ordinary income rather than capital gains, if the building was sold for more than its depreciated value. A new minimum tax was applied to various tax preferences, including accelerated depreciation, affecting investors who received large amounts of tax-sheltered income. Investors were required to amortize the interest and taxes paid during the construction period of a rental project, rather than expensing them in the year they occurred.

DeLeeuw and Ozanne have calculated that these changes essentially offset the effect of inflation, leaving rental housing about as profitable an investment in the late 1970s as in the mid-1960s.[49] They assumed, however, that relative rents and construction costs were unchanged, whereas in reality rents rose less rapidly, so that landlords probably earned a lower return in the later period. This was in sharp contrast to owner-occupied housing, which had become much more profitable. This comparison is probably less meaningful for the potential investor in a large project than for the small landlord, but it may help to explain the diminishing importance of single-family homes in the rental stock during the 1970s.

Disinflation and Rental Housing. Since 1979, real rents have continued to decline, by about 1.5 percent annually; in 1982, however, they stabilized and may have begun to rise. This coincided with the reduction in the homeownership rate and with the higher proportion of multifamily starts, which are all apparently manifestations of disinflation.

Tax law changes in 1981 have increased the profitability of investing in rental housing, again serving to reinforce the effects of changes in the rate of inflation. Depreciation was liberalized in two ways. First, the period over which rental property must be depreciated was reduced from forty years to fifteen, as part of the Accelerated Cost Recovery System. Second, more rapid depreciation was permitted for existing rental housing (175 percent declining balance instead of 125 percent or straight-line depreciation), though a slower rate was required for new housing (175 percent instead of 200 percent or sum-of-the-years digits).

The effect of these provisions on the rental housing market may be quite substantial. Brueggeman, Fisher, and Stern have estimated that the price investors are willing to pay for rental property is likely to rise by 30 to 40 percent, in the short run, which will result in a long-run increase in the supply of rental housing (the magnitude of which they do not calculate) and a long-run reduction in the rents necessary for profitable investment of about 20 to 30 percent.[50] The demand for owner-occupied housing, and therefore its price, should decline if any substantial part of these rent reductions is realized.

The divergence between prices and rents has some interesting implications. House prices can be thought of as the present value of all of the future imputed rents the owner-occupant will receive. Thus if prices go up, a logical inference is that rents will rise in the future. With inflation, the higher nominal stream of future rental payments is capitalized into the price of the house, before the rents have in fact risen much. Apparently, the capitalization rate for owner-occupants increased substantially during inflation.[51] This implies that the imputed rent being received by the owner-occupant in the early years falls relative to his cash outlays and suggests that buyers during inflationary periods may face financial difficulties if their expectations of inflation fail to materialize. This may help to explain the recent rise in mortgage defaults.

The Housing Finance System

Inflation has subjected the housing finance system to especially severe strains and forced significant changes.[52] In 1966 Congress imposed a ceiling of 5¼ percent on the interest rate that savings and loan associations, traditionally the most important source of mortgage money, could pay for passbook account deposits. This action was taken as part of an extension and adjustment of interest rate ceilings on time deposits at banks as well as at savings and loans. In late 1965 the Federal Reserve had increased the ceiling rate on large certificates of deposits (CDs) at commercial banks, which had resulted in an outflow of funds from savings associations and a corresponding decline in mortgage lending and housing starts. The thrift institutions were allowed to pay twenty-five to seventy-five basis points more than banks, in the expectation that this would protect the housing market until interest rates returned to more "normal" levels. That still has not happened.

The ceilings clearly failed. Cyclical fluctuations in housing became increasingly severe after they were imposed, as inflation gradually drove up market interest rates. Households became increasingly aware of the widening spread between passbook and market rates and sought alternative investments. The volume of funds in passbooks was the same in 1974 as in 1965.

Savings associations have gradually been allowed to issue other types of deposits, in an effort to combat this disintermediation. In the early 1970s they began issuing longer-term higher-yield certificates of deposit; by 1974 these CDs constituted a larger share of deposits than the passbook accounts. But they were not enough to solve the problem. More important changes were brought about by the competition between savings associations and the new money market mutual funds, which enabled households to earn the same high interest rates as large investors, by investing in commercial paper and other market-yield assets. After an abortive experiment with market-rate "wild card" certificates in 1973, financial regulators finally permitted savings associations (and also banks) to issue six-month $10,000-denomination money market certificates (MMCs), carrying an interest rate pegged to the Treasury borrowing rate. These MMCs helped prevent disintermediation in 1978, and by 1981 they amounted to 40 percent of savings association deposits, more than passbooks and CDs combined. Money market funds also continued to grow, and in 1982 savings associations and banks were allowed to offer insured money market deposit accounts (MMDAs), permitting depositors to withdraw funds on demand while still earning market interest rates. Within three months, MMDAs constituted over 16 percent of all savings association assets.

These new deposit accounts have enabled thrift institutions to continue attracting funds, but only by paying higher interest rates; thus the favored position enjoyed by housing in competing for funds was gradually eroded. Higher deposit rates contributed to the rise in mortgage rates in the late 1970s, but thrift institutions had to pay more for most deposits, while receiving more only on new loans; older mortgages still yielded only the original rate, negotiated when inflation was lower. The disparity became particularly acute as interest rates rose and remained at unprecedented levels in the early 1980s. By mid-1982, savings associations were paying close to 11.5 percent for deposits, on average, but were earning less than that on well over half of their portfolio. The problem was exacerbated by the due-on-sale issue. Thus, many associations faced severe financial problems. A number were merged into more solvent institutions, with the federal government subsidizing the merger; others were allowed to borrow from the government, in effect, or from the public, with a government guarantee.

To meet this problem, savings associations have sought to shift at least part of the risk of interest rate fluctuations to mortgagors and have asked Congress for broader lending powers. In both areas, they have been successful.

After a decade of opposition from consumer groups, Congress in 1980 allowed federally chartered savings associations to issue adjustable rate mortgages (ARMs), on which the interest rate would vary with the cost of deposits. This happened only after other mortgage lenders, including state-chartered savings associations (particularly important in California) and banks had received similar authorization between 1975 and 1978. In 1982, ARMs accounted for more than 40 percent of new mortgage loans, but in early 1983 declined to about 30 percent. The consequences of this shift from fixed to variable rate mortgages will be discussed in the next section; here it is merely worth noting that relief came only after disinflation had begun, and actual rate adjustments have so far been downward rather than upward.

The same legislation permitted savings associations to make consumer loans (now amounting to 2 percent of assets), and in 1982 they acquired the further power to issue commercial loans. Although it is too soon to assess the quantitative importance of these new powers, there is concern that savings associations will be able to survive as institutions only by becoming more like banks and that, therefore, the supply of mortgage funds will be much reduced and the mortgage interest rate raised. This concern will be evaluated in the next section.

Conclusion

The record of the recent past described in this paper offers some guidance for understanding future housing market behavior. There are essentially two plausible macroeconomic scenarios: a continuation of the disinflation of the past few years or a renewal of the inflation of the 1970s. As of mid-1983, each scenario seems about equally likely. In this concluding section, therefore, it may be appropriate to speculate on the course of events in the housing market, given each scenario.

Although the future should have much in common with the past, at least two key factors affecting housing will not be the same: the underlying demographic trends and the housing finance system. It is useful to discuss these briefly, before turning to the two scenarios.

Demographic Trends. The basic demographic factor in the housing market is the maturing of the last wave of the postwar "baby boom" generation. The birth rate peaked in 1957. Thus the youngest members of that generation are now entering the prime household formation years. The most recent Census Bureau projections are that 17 million to 19 million more households will form in the 1980s, with growth concentrated in the twenty-five to forty-four year old age bracket.[53] This would be a larger increase than the 16.5 million of the 1970s. Based on these projections, a number of housing market analysts have forecast unprecedented new housing production, in the range of 2.2 million to 2.7 million units annually.[54]

The Census Bureau projections are essentially extrapolations from recent trends and have been the subject of debate among demographers. Some analysts have questioned whether household formation rates will continue to rise during the 1980s and have projected about 13 million to 15 million households.[55] In the past, it has proven quite difficult to predict changes in demographic behavior. Historically, the Census Bureau has underestimated household formations rather than overestimating them, but it need not continue to do so. Thus either, or neither, of these projections may turn out to be accurate. The low numbers, however, seem unlikely; they imply a dramatic reversal of postwar trends.

Whatever the level of production, most of the new units are generally expected to be single-family, owner-occupied homes, because of the growth of households in the prime homebuying age brackets. This is quite apart from any effect of inflation. Conceivably, these forecasts could be invalidated by economic conditions. It is worth remembering that demographic projections for the 1970s implied a strong demand for multifamily housing, which materialized only in the first three or four years of the decade; thereafter, inflation more than offset demographic trends. Nevertheless, the underlying population figures are so pronounced that the most likely outcome under any macroeconomic conditions still is increased homeownership.

The Mortgage Market. Regardless of the rate of inflation, the housing finance system will be different in the future; whether the housing market will therefore be different also is a subject of some debate. The most common opinion among housing analysts is that the real home mortgage interest rate will rise, because of the integration of the mortgage market with other capital markets; savings associations will use their new asset powers to diversify, and other lenders will be willing to enter the mortgage market only if the return is higher than at present. In addition, savings associations will increasingly utilize their power to issue ARMs. Some popular versions of this analysis are phrased in apocalyptic terms of "the end of an era" or "the fading dream" of homeownership.[56]

An alternative view has been expressed by Kane and by Van Order.[57] They note that the tax incentives to savings associations for investing in mortgages are unchanged and that, therefore, thrift institutions can earn more from mortgages than from other investments. They argue further that the existence of deposit insurance for savings associations eliminates their incentive to diversify their portfolios in order to minimize risk, because the price of insurance is unrelated to the probability that it will be needed (that is, to the riskiness of the association's portfolio). Deposit insurance also reduces the incentive to issue ARMs.

Disinflation. By the end of 1982, at the trough of the business cycle, the inflation rate had fallen to about 3 percent. Based on historical experience, one would expect it to rise in the course of the recovery; in noninflationary postwar cycles, the rate of inflation increased during recoveries by about two percentage points, on the average, and the largest increase was four points. Something less than average—perhaps an increase of only 1 to 2 percent—would be appropriate as an indicator of further secular decline in the inflation rate. Thus a reasonable definition of "continuing disinflation" might be an inflation rate rising to no more than 4 to 5 percent during the current cyclical recovery and falling to less than 3 percent in the next cyclical downturn.

Such a scenario need not imply much further adjustment in nominal house prices or interest rates. The most extreme plausible change in house prices during continued disinflation would be a return to the real price prevailing before inflation began. This would be predicted by the Poterba model, for example. From 1967 to 1979, the real price rose by about 36 percent; since then, it has fallen by 11 percent. But even a further decline of a full 25 percent over the next business cycle would be consistent with stable or slightly declining nominal prices. A smaller real price decline, such as that implied by Diamond's analysis, would allow nominal prices to rise in the next few years.

Nominal mortgage rates could continue their recent decline, rather than rising in the recovery. The traditional real rate of about 3 percent would imply a nominal rate of no more than 8 percent, if inflation were to rise to 5 percent. Even a 5 percent real rate, resulting from the integration of the housing finance system with other capital markets and the end of the traditional protected position for housing, would result in no more than a 10 percent nominal rate, compared with current rates of 13 to 14 percent.

Disinflation would also imply that the changes in the mortgage finance system would turn out to be less important in practice than seemed likely when they were enacted. There would be less reason for thrift institutions to utilize either the broader range of mortgage instruments or the expanded asset powers that they have recently acquired. The traditional fixed-rate mortgage would probably regain its dominant position. The issue of the due-on-sale clause would disappear, and there would be no reason to change the law.

The housing market would probably develop in a pattern somewhat like that of the 1950s. At that time, the rate of inflation declined from its early postwar high levels. This did not depress the housing market, however. Instead, there was an unprecedented rate of housing production, well above any prewar levels, concentrated in single-family owner-occupied homes. This resulted largely from demographic trends—high household formation rates and birth rates—and rising real incomes. A further parallel is the fact that the real mortgage interest rate was around 4 to 5 percent. Thus, even if the common view of the mortgage market in the 1980s is correct, experience suggests that the real rate will not be high enough to choke off the housing boom. It might, however, slow the rate at which housing quality improves.

Renewed Inflation. A recurrence of inflation is likely to heighten inflationary expectations quite rapidly. It would signal the collapse of the second attempt in five years to bring inflation under control. An administration of each party would have embarked on the path of price stability, endured a recession, and then concluded that the costs of disinflation were too great. Inflation would probably appear to be a permanent feature of the American economy, and the search for inflation hedges would begin again, with perhaps greater intensity.

The effect on the housing market would be marked. House prices would undoubtedly resume their upward movement in both real and nominal terms. The magnitude of the rise can only be estimated, but experience in the later stages of the 1970s inflation may offer a guide. From 1976 to 1979, house prices rose by about 5.25 percent annually, in real terms. A similar rise with renewed inflation in the near future would not be unreasonable.

For the same reason, nominal mortgage rates would probably rise, even though the real rate is at present about 9 percent. It is possible that mortgage rates would begin to rise sooner than house prices, since renewed inflation would be likely to affect financial markets before the markets for real goods and services.

In this scenario, the expanded range of mortgage instruments becomes important. Renewed inflation would quickly reduce the willingness of thrift institutions to continue making fixed-rate long-term loans. The adjustable rate mortgage, or some variant, would probably become the standard instrument.

For most, if not for all, homebuyers, therefore, the usefulness of their home as a hedge against inflation would be diminished. Its value would rise, but so also would the monthly mortgage payment. The investment advantages of homeownership would not be entirely eliminated, because the house would be a long-term asset, subject to special tax treatment, while the mortgage interest rate would become a series of short-term rates. Thus, a rise in the inflation rate would be fully capitalized immediately into the value of the house, while the mortgage rate and payment would rise only in response to the inflation during the current year. In addition, most ARMs do not permit contemporaneous and full response to interest rate changes; the contract rate is typically fixed for six months or a year and cannot vary outside a legally mandated range, regardless of market rate changes. Housing still would be a better hedge than financial assets, but the great capital gains and windfalls of the 1970s are unlikely to be repeated.

Even with these limitations, many homeowners might find it hard to meet the rising debt burden of an ARM, especially if their incomes do not increase as rapidly as inflation. This has been a common experience in other countries with variable rate mortgages. A number of governments have responded by subsidizing the mortgage payments of existing homeowners.[58] Thus the inflation-induced interest rate risk is shifted first from lending institutions to buyers, and then from buyers to the entire society.

The real effects of renewed inflation might not be easily discernible. Few upper-income, or even middle-income, renters remain, so there is little room for a significant rise in the rate of ownership beyond that stemming from demographic factors alone. Increases in house size, and quality improvements, would be likely, quickly reversing the 1979–1982 downtrends. A new boom in condominiums is another possible effect, perhaps reaching farther down in the income distribution than the first wave apparently did. The demand for ownership and the development of the condominium concept might combine to generate an unprecedented expansion of second homes.

Even renewed inflation would probably not be enough to prolong a housing boom into the 1990s, when the lower birth rates of the 1960s and 1970s would produce a much smaller increase in the adult population and a sharp reduction in the demand for additional units.

Final Comments. Unlikely as it may seem in the wake of the severe housing recession that the country has just experienced, the early 1980s offer the best opportunity for disinflation in the housing sector, with minimal damages to market participants. Disinflation has been occurring when demographic trends are strongly favorable for housing. Later in this decade, and beyond, they will be strongly adverse. In addition, disinflation at some later time—after a renewed inflation during the mid-1980s—will undoubtedly have to begin from a higher nominal mortgage rate than the 15 to 18 percent of the later 1970s and from a higher real house price level. This will make any future adjustment more difficult than the recent adjustment has been.

Notes

1. This distinction has been drawn in the economic theory of demand and consumption since the work of Frank Knight in the 1920s; see, for example, Frank H. Knight, "Economic Psychology and the Value Problem," *Quarterly Journal of Economics,* vol. 39 (May 1925), pp. 372–409.

2. For a summary of "the standard theory of the effects of inflation on the economy," see Phillip Cagan and Robert E. Lipsey, *The Financial Effects of Inflation* (Cambridge, Mass.: Ballinger, for the National Bureau of Economic Research, 1978), chap. 1. Cagan and Lipsey also apply this term to the literature that they summarize.

3. For example, John C. Weicher, "New Home Affordability, Equity, and Housing Market Behavior," *American Real Estate and Urban Economics Association Journal,* vol. 6 (Winter 1978), pp. 395–416; Kevin Villani, "The Tax Subsidy to Housing in an Inflationary Environment: Implications for After-Tax Housing Costs," in C. F. Sirmans, ed., *Research in Real Estate,* vol. 1 (Greenwich, Conn.: JAI Press, 1982), pp. 31–86; and Douglas B. Diamond, Jr., "A Note on

Inflation and Relative Tenure Prices," *American Real Estate and Urban Economics Association Journal,* vol. 6 (Winter 1978), pp. 438-50. Early versions of the first two of these papers were delivered at the Mid-Year Meeting of the American Real Estate and Urban Economics Association in Washington, D.C., in May 1978.

4. "Housing: It's Outasight," *Time,* September 12, 1977, pp. 50-57; "Housing's Roof Collapses," *Time,* August 17, 1981; "The Great Housing Collapse," *Newsweek,* March 29, 1982.

5. The CPI component has been omitted because the divergence between it and the census index is largely explained by the sample differences and by estimating procedures used in the CPI; see John S. Greenlees, "An Empirical Evaluation of the CPI Home Purchase Index, 1973-1978," *American Real Estate and Urban Economics Association Journal,* vol. 10 (Spring 1982), pp. 1-24.

6. For a more detailed discussion of this problem, see John C. Weicher, "The Affordability of New Homes," *American Real Estate and Urban Economics Association Journal,* vol. 5 (Summer 1977), pp. 209-26.

7. A review of this policy controversy is contained in John C. Weicher, *Housing: Federal Politics and Programs* (Washington, D.C.: American Enterprise Institute, 1980), chap. 6.

8. Michael S. Salkin and Dan Durning, "What Is a House Really Worth?" *Mortgage Banking,* vol. 43 (October 1982), pp. 12-20.

9. Economics Department, National Association of Home Builders, *Economic News Notes,* various issues.

10. The homeownership cost component, used in the CPI from 1953 to 1982, is widely recognized as defective, particularly in an inflationary environment, and the homeownership cost component is now being replaced with a "rental equivalent" measure of the cost of owner-occupied housing. For a discussion of the housing component of the CPI, see Phillip Cagan and Geoffrey H. Moore, *The Consumer Price Index: Issues and Alternatives* (Washington, D.C.: American Enterprise Institute, 1981), especially pp. 32-43.

11. The data on houses are published in U.S. Department of Commerce, Bureau of Economic Analysis, *Fixed Reproducible Tangible Wealth in the U.S., 1925-1979* (1980), tables A-11 and A-12. The data on land are published by the Board of Governors of the Federal Reserve System, "Balance Sheets for the U.S. Economy, 1945-1981," issued in October 1982. They appear in table 702, "Households."

12. See Cagan and Lipsey, *Financial Effects of Inflation,* table 2-11, p. 41.

13. The behavior of the Federal Reserve and the money supply is discussed in detail in Phillip Cagan, "Monetary Policy and Subduing Inflation," in this volume.

14. Weicher, *Housing,* chap. 8.

15. Richard F. Muth, "The Demand for Non-Farm Housing," in Arnold C. Harberger, ed., *The Demand for Durable Goods* (Chicago: University of Chicago Press, 1960), pp. 3-57. A recent survey of the literature is John Quigley, "What Have We Learned about Urban Housing Markets?" in Peter Mieszkowski and Mahlon Straszheim, eds., *Current Issues in Urban Economics* (Baltimore: Johns Hopkins University Press, 1979), pp. 358-87.

16. Patric H. Hendershott and Sheng Cheng Hu, "Inflation and Extraordi-

nary Returns on Owner-Occupied Housing: Some Implications for Capital Allocation and Productivity Growth," *Journal of Macroeconomics*, vol. 3 (Spring 1981), pp. 177–203; Robert M. Schwab, "Real and Nominal Interest Rates and the Demand for Housing," *Journal of Urban Economics*, vol. 13 (March 1983), pp. 181–95. The former uses a four-year period for the formation of inflationary expectations; the latter, a twelve-year period.

17. Anne Dougherty and Robert Van Order, "Inflation, Housing Costs, and the Consumer Price Index," *American Economic Review*, vol. 72 (March 1982), pp. 154–64.

18. James M. Poterba, "Tax Subsidies to Owner-Occupied Housing: An Asset Market Approach," Working Paper No. 553 (Cambridge, Mass.: National Bureau of Economic Research, March 1983).

19. Douglas B. Diamond, Jr., "The Impact of Inflation on New House Prices" (Paper presented at the annual meeting of the Western Economic Association, July 1983).

20. The "Scott U.S. Stamp Index" appears in *Scott Stamp Market Update*, issued quarterly by Scott Publishing Company since 1978.

21. Salomon Brothers, Inc., publishes an annual set of price indexes for collectibles and other assets. The latest data are for mid-1982: R. S. Salomon, Jr., "Bonds May Still Be the Only Bargains Left," June 8, 1982.

22. Cynthia Saltzman, "Your Money Matters: Once Touted as Good Investment, Art, Stamps, and Other 'Collectibles' Have Plunged in Price," *Wall Street Journal*, July 12, 1982.

23. Herman Herst, Jr., "Speaking of Stamps, Etc.," *STAMPS*, vol. 202 (February 26, 1983), p. 501.

24. This advertisement appeared in the *Saturday Review*, February 1981, pp. 43–44.

25. A careful but somewhat outdated discussion of the tax treatment of housing is George S. Tolley and Douglas B. Diamond, Jr., "Homeownership, Rental, Housing, and Tax Incentives," in U.S. Congress, House, Committee on Banking, Finance, and Urban Affairs, *Federal Tax Policy and Urban Development*, 95th Congress, 1st session, June 1977. The latest changes are described in *Capital Cost Recovery Planning under the Economic Recovery Tax Act of 1981* (Chicago: Arthur Andersen & Co. 1981).

26. For further discussion of the relationship between inflation, the tax system, and the real mortgage rate, see John Tuccillo, *Housing and Investment in an Inflationary World* (Washington, D.C.: Urban Institute, 1980).

27. For a more extensive discussion, see Robert Buckley and John Tuccillo, "An Analysis of Non-Level Payment Mortgages," in Robert M. Buckley, John A. Tuccillo, and Kevin E. Villani, eds., *Capital Markets and the Housing Sector* (Cambridge, Mass.: Ballinger, 1977), pp. 271–87.

28. Dougherty and Van Order, "Inflation, Housing Costs, and the Consumer Price Index." Revised data through mid-1983 have been provided by Van Order.

29. Salkin and Durning, "What Is a House Really Worth?"

30. William Griese, "Balloon Mortgages Coming Due: Time to Pay Up or Renegotiate," *USA Today*, July 21, 1983.

31. Larry Ozanne, "The Financial Stakes in Due-on-Sale: The Case of Cali-

fornia's State-Chartered Savings and Loans," Federal Home Loan Bank Board, Office of Policy and Economic Research, Research Working Paper No. 109, July 1982.

32. Patric H. Hendershott and James D. Shilling, "The Economics of Tenure Choice, 1955–1979," in Sirmans, ed., *Research in Real Estate*, vol. 1, pp. 105–133; data through mid-1982 have been provided by Shilling. See also Dougherty and Van Order, "Inflation, Housing Costs, and the Consumer Price Index"; and William B. Brueggeman and Richard E. Peiser, "Housing Choice and Relative Tenure Prices," in Ronald Racster, ed., *Housing Delivery System* (Columbus, Ohio: Ohio State University Center for Real Estate Education and Research, 1981), pp. 170–88.

33. Dwight M. Jaffee and Kenneth T. Rosen, "Mortgage Credit Availability and Residential Construction," *Brookings Papers on Economic Activity*, 1979, no. 2, pp. 333–76.

34. Hendershott and Shilling, "The Economics of Tenure Choice, 1955–1979"; Harvey S. Rosen and Kenneth T. Rosen, "Federal Taxes and Homeownership: Evidence from Time Series," *Journal of Political Economy*, vol. 88 (February 1980), pp. 59–75. Unfortunately, these studies do not attempt to quantify the effect of inflation, actual or expected, separately from other components of real costs.

35. For an extended discussion of homeownership trends, see Weicher, *Housing*, chap. 6.

36. Measurement of recent homeownership trends is complicated by a change in the data source, which is the Housing Vacancy Survey, conducted by the Census Bureau. The effect of the change is to lower the reported homeownership rate by 0.4 percent in 1979, the only year for which both the old and new series are reported. Thus, figures for 1979 and later are not consistent with unadjusted figures for earlier years. Fortunately, however, the entire period of disinflation is measured using the new survey.

37. *Condominium Housing in the Washington Metropolitan Area*, July 1, 1982 (Washington, D.C.: Metropolitan Washington Council of Governments, 1983), Housing Technical Report No. 1983-1.

38. Data on delinquencies and foreclosures are taken from the quarterly survey conducted by the Mortgage Bankers Association of America.

39. The most recent extensive review of the literature on mortgage delinquencies and foreclosures is contained in Maxwell Obioma Eseonu, "The Effects of Inflation on FHA Home Mortgage Default in the United States: An Empirical Analysis" (Ph.D. diss., Howard University, 1982), chap. 2.

40. The data in this table are revised and extended from Cagan and Lipsey, *Financial Effects of Inflation*, table 2-8, p. 37.

41. William Fellner, "American Household Wealth in an Inflationary Period," in William Fellner, ed., *Contemporary Economic Problems 1979* (Washington, D.C.: American Enterprise Institute, 1979), pp. 153–89, especially table 4, p. 177.

42. "Revised Deflators for New Construction, 1947–1973," *Survey of Current Business*, vol. 54 (August 1974), pp. 18–27, especially table 4.

43. Quigley, "What Have We Learned about Urban Housing Markets?" in Mieszkowski and Straszheim, eds., *Current Issues in Urban Economics*.

44. The most detailed study is Edward J. Kane, "Microeconomic Evidence on the Composition of Effective Household Savings during the 1960s and 1970s," unpublished paper, September 1983. See also Cagan and Lipsey, *Financial Effects of Inflation*, pp. 46–48. The former covers the period up to 1977, the latter to 1975. Disinflation is too recent a phenomenon to have received any systematic analysis of its redistributive effects.

45. From 1964 to 1969, the series covers only "new homes sold," meaning houses constructed by a building contractor on land he owns. From 1966 to 1971, data is available on "all homes started," which includes not only homes started but never sold, but also those built by a contractor on land owned by the eventual owner-occupant and those built by the owner-occupant himself. (Typically, "new homes sold" amount to only about 60 percent of "all homes started.") In 1971, the series became "all homes completed," again covering contractor-built homes but omitting those that were never finished. Data for years when the series overlap indicate that "new homes sold" are typically larger, with more amenities, than contractor-built and owner-built homes; therefore the earlier data in table 8 are adjusted upward in an effort to construct a consistent series.

46. U.S. Bureau of the Census, *Residential Alterations and Repairs*, Construction Reports C50, Annual 1982.

47. Ira S. Lowry, "Rental Housing in the 1970s: Searching for the Crisis," in John C. Weicher, Kevin E. Villani, and Elizabeth A. Roistacher, eds., *Rental Housing: Is There a Crisis?* (Washington, D.C.: Urban Institute Press, 1981), pp. 23–38.

48. Robert H. Litzenberger and Howard B. Sosin, "Taxation and the Incidence of Homeownership across Income Groups," *Journal of Finance*, vol. 33 (June 1978), pp. 947–61.

49. Frank deLeeuw and Larry Ozanne, "The Impact of the Federal Income Tax on Investment in Housing," *Survey of Current Business*, vol. 59 (December 1979), pp. 50–61.

50. William B. Brueggeman, Jeffrey D. Fisher, and Jerrold J. Stern, "Rental Housing and the Economic Recovery Tax Act of 1981," *Public Finance Quarterly*, vol. 10 (April 1982), pp. 222–41.

51. Lewis J. Spellman, "Inflation and Housing Prices," *American Real Estate and Urban Economics Association Journal*, vol. 9 (Fall 1981), pp. 205–22.

52. For a review of the effect of the inflation on the housing finance system, up to the mid-1970s, see Patric H. Hendershott and Kevin E. Villani, *Regulation and Reform of the Housing Finance System* (Washington, D.C.: American Enterprise Institute, 1978). A later discussion appears in the *Report of the President's Commission on Housing*, May 1982.

53. U.S. Bureau of the Census, "Projections of the Number of Households and Families: 1979 to 1995," *Current Population Reports*, Series P-25, No. 805, May 1979.

54. For a summary of these projections, see John C. Weicher, Lorene Yap, and Mary S. Jones, *Metropolitan Housing Needs for the 1980s* (Washington, D.C.: Urban Institute Press, 1982), pp. 4–13.

55. William C. Apgar, Jr., "Housing in the 1980s: A Review of Alternative Forecasts," Joint Center for Urban Studies, Working Paper, October 1982.

56. For expositions of this view, see Dwight R. Lee, "Why the Housing Industry Will Not Recover," *Journal of Contemporary Studies*, vol. 5 (Summer 1982), pp. 45–53; Philip Longman, "The Real Estate Mess," *New Jersey Monthly*, vol. 6 (July 1982), pp. 33–38, 57–64. Lee stresses disinflation, Longman the changed financial environment. A summary presentation of similar opinions appears in Paul A. Gigot, "Fading Dream: Costly Credit, Energy Viewed as Death Knell for Easy Homeowning," *Wall Street Journal*, February 17, 1981, p. 1.

57. Edward J. Kane, "S & Ls and Interest Rate Re-Regulation: The FSLIC as an In-Place Bailout Program," *Housing Finance Review*, vol. 1 (July 1982), pp. 219–44; Robert Van Order, "The Effects of Thrift Deregulation on Mortgage Markets: Some Theoretical Issues" (Paper presented at the Financial Structure Conference, Federal Reserve Bank of Chicago, May 1983).

58. Leo Grebler, "Inflation: A Blessing or a Curse?" *Annals of the American Academy of Political and Social Science*, vol. 465 (January 1983), pp. 21–34.

Corporate Liquidity under Stagflation and Disinflation

Murray F. Foss

Summary

The prolonged period of stagnation from 1979 to 1982, with two recessions in successive years that seriously eroded profits and cash positions, weakened business liquidity and led to record high bankruptcies. Instead of reducing its short-term debt in the 1980–1981 recession, business increased it and kept it high for much of 1982. As cash-conserving measures during 1982, business made severe cutbacks in its capital expenditure programs, slashed its inventories, and late in the year reduced its short-term borrowing. As a consequence liquid assets relative to short-term liabilities showed an improvement after the spring of 1982. When interest rates fell and equity prices rose last summer, corporations stepped up issuances of new securities, especially equities, to fund earlier short-term borrowing.

A feature of this study is an examination of individual firm distributions of liquidity ratios, ratios of short-term to total debt, and ratios of interest payments to cash flow through 1982. The purpose of this examination, which focuses on large, well-known companies, is to see whether the recession has left us with pockets of weakened firms that might be concealed by the overall aggregates and might hinder the recovery. The detailed examination of liquidity ratios suggests somewhat more weakness than was indicated by overall figures for all nonfinancial corporations at the end of 1982, but it was not pronounced. Ratios of short-term debt to total debt looked worse in 1982 than in 1970 but not as bad as at the end of 1974. There was evidence at the end of 1982 of a substantial increase in firms with very large interest burdens relative to cash flow.

In the first year of upturn of post–World War II expansions, average interest burdens are greatly reduced as cash flow improves. In addition, liquidity ratios typically improve, and the ratio of short-term to total debt typically decreases. These patterns are being repeated this year and should continue in 1984 as profits expand further and as business investment shows

I am indebted to Eduardo Somensatto of AEI and Jeffrey Coombs of Data Resources, Inc., for programming the computer tabulations of the Compustat data.

only moderate increases. These changes will reduce the vulnerability of firms to adverse developments, but they will obviously not eliminate the long-term adjustment problems peculiar to individual industries. The main significance of the detailed examination of firms is the conclusion not that the recovery will be hampered but that we are likely to see a relatively high rate of bankruptcies over the next few years if inflationary pressures do not come back.

This essay analyzes the changing liquidity of U.S. nonfinancial corporations, a subject that has been the focus of considerable attention and concern over the past few years. The periodic difficulties of firms in meeting their current obligations are nothing new: in fact, in the chronology of U.S. business cycles, the rise in current liabilities of failing firms is a long-established leading indicator of business downturns. But the severe inflation of recent years was accompanied by a considerable increase in indebtedness on the part of corporations for the financing of real investment. This indebtedness increased the vulnerability of firms to weakness in the economy, such as the stagnant conditions prevalent in the United States after 1979 and the severe recession of 1981–1982. Low profits reduced cash flow, many measures of liquidity were at post–World War II lows, and the interest burden, as measured by corporate interest charges relative to cash flow, remained high for an extended period. The number of bankruptcies relative to firms in business reached a postwar high in 1982 (see figure 1).

The disinflation that set in during 1982 has been accompanied by a slowdown in the growth of nonfinancial corporate indebtedness, by shifts in financing toward equities and longer debt maturities, and by a reduction in interest rates on indebtedness of given maturities. The recession forced firms to conserve cash by reducing their inventories and their outlays for plant and equipment, and by the end of 1982 common liquidity measures looked a little better than they had earlier in the year. Difficulties are not yet over, however, since the recovery is still young, and it remains to be seen how policies against inflation will be pursued during the economic expansion.

What happens to liquidity in the next year or two depends on factors such as the character of the recovery, economic policies, and inflationary expectations. Concern over liquidity persisted into early 1983 because of continued uncertainty over the business outlook. The budget for fiscal year 1984 released at the end of January 1983, as well as the Economic Report, projected a weak recovery without much improvement in the long-run outlook for inflation. If profits showed little recovery, firms would continue to feel strapped for cash, and more bankruptcies would be the fate of some corporations that experienced liquidity problems in 1982. But the vigorous economic upturn

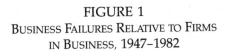

FIGURE 1
BUSINESS FAILURES RELATIVE TO FIRMS
IN BUSINESS, 1947–1982

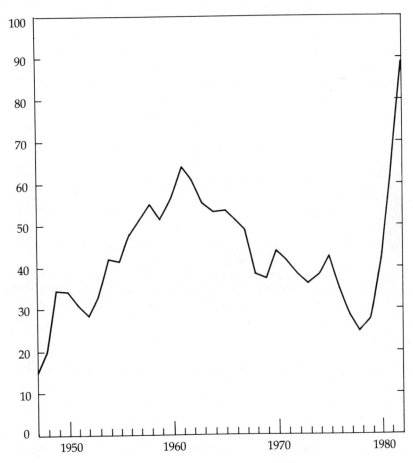

NOTE: Failures per 10,000 enterprises listed by Dun and Bradstreet.
SOURCE: Dun and Bradstreet.

of the spring and summer has changed that; indeed, in spite of the continuing disinflation, the strong increase in economic activity has given rise to new concerns that the inflation might be resumed, on the one hand, or that restraint by the Federal Reserve might abort the recovery, on the other. A major change in inflationary expectations would not only permit the monetary authorities to pursue a less restrictive policy than otherwise but would also be conducive to long-

term financing, which would relieve the pressure of the heavy overhang of short-term debt.

What we know about liquidity mainly reflects some broad aggregates that may be unduly influenced by the experience of a small
number of very large firms. What should be of interest are averages
based on individual companies and the dispersions around those
averages; examination of them alone would tell us how typical the
aggregate experience is. Disaggregation is a major feature of the
present study, which makes use of financial data for individual large,
well-known corporations from Standard and Poor's Compustat Services.

Liquidity: Recent History, Concepts, and Measures

Liquidity has been a topic of special concern to the public ever since
inflation reached double-digit levels in 1974.[1] The first important manifestation of this concern in the postwar period was the crisis over the
financial viability of New York City in the 1970s. Concern over the
ability of thrift institutions to survive was widespread in the first half
of 1982.

At present, questions are being raised about the ability of foreign
governments like Mexico and Brazil to repay debts owed to U.S. banks
and the effect of potential defaults on the financial condition of those
banks. Record numbers of mortgage foreclosures (for the post–World
War II period) have highlighted the difficulties faced by households
unable to meet mortgage payments.

In the business sector the liquidity issue became important in 1970
with the bankruptcy of Penn Central and the financial difficulties of
Lockheed Aircraft. The topic was raised for the first time as a problem
of potential seriousness for business generally after the 1974–1975
recession and came about because that recession was the most severe
to that point in the postwar period. Its prominence most recently is an
outgrowth of the inflation, the long period of stagnation culminating
in the recession that has only recently ended, and the fact that leading
roles have been played by such bulwarks of corporate business as
Chrysler and International Harvester.[2]

In many ways, the ability of governments and well-established
firms to pay their bills and meet their obligations on time is often
taken for granted in this country, so that when bankruptcy is an
actuality or threatens to become so, the impact on the public can be
deep and long lasting. The recent concern about liquidity in the corporate sector probably explains why bond ratings have been lowered
for so many firms, including some of the best known.[3] If costs of
capital are higher for the individual firm, the firm may turn to alterna-

tive means of long-term financing, such as the stock market, or it may take a more cautious attitude toward the use of its funds in order to improve its liquidity. At the micro level this situation may be nothing more than an aspect of the changing fortunes of individual companies, a phenomenon that has always been present but has not been an obstacle to growth in the economy. If it becomes common enough, however, such an attitude could have a net adverse effect on the real economy. Modern economic analysis assigns a major, if not an exclusive, role to cash flow as a determinant of spending for plant and equipment. The modern view in turn can be considered an outgrowth of earlier business cycle literature, which indeed includes a long history of business response to a cash squeeze.

Liquidity is also important because there is now more financial intermediation in the economy than in the past.[4] That is, although what we save as a nation cannot be different from what we invest as a nation, purely as a matter of definition, the routes by which saving finds its way into investment or by which investment taps the available saving can be both circuitous and multilayered. Financial intermediaries have proliferated, so that although the fraction of our output devoted to saving and investment has been roughly constant over the long run, the financial structure has become much more complex. Some analysts point to this increased interdependency as a weakness in our system.

Typically, one of the benefits of recessions has been the weeding out of inefficient firms. Being unable to pay their bills, firms either liquidated or were forced into bankruptcy. It has been said that the situation prevailing in 1982 was unique in the postwar period in that *strong* firms as well as weak ones were pulled down because customers of strong firms were unable to meet their obligations. Revere Copper and Brass, a firm with a substantial net worth, recently filed under chapter 11 because of such considerations, according to newspaper reports.

Concepts. We assume that firms have views about their liquidity that are guided by principles of rational behavior.[5] Firms may be viewed not only as profit maximizers but also as desirous of avoiding insolvency. On the assumption that the return on liquid assets is less than that on other types of assets, to maximize profitability a firm would want to keep its cash, or liquid assets, as low as possible. Maximizing profits would also lead a firm to maintain as large as possible a proportion of its liabilities in the form of short-term liabilities to the extent that short-term interest rates are less than long-term rates, and within the year short-term indebtedness can permit a firm to use debt only when it is needed. Maintaining a high proportion of short-term liabilities may be risky, however, rendering the firm vulnerable to sales disappointments or other unforeseen developments that could adversely affect cash flow. The rational firm would resolve this trade-off between risk and profit according to its risk preferences.

If firms had perfect foresight, they would be able to arrange their financing in such a fashion that they would need long-term financing only for long-term growth. A seasonal buildup in inventories, for example, would be financed by short-term borrowing synchronized with that buildup. In the presence of uncertainty, however, firms would want some kind of safety margin, the size of which would depend on management's attitudes toward risk. Long-term financing—through debt or equity—would relieve management of concern about disappointments or errors of judgment in the short run. Long-term financing also means that the firm is to some extent paying interest on debt even though the borrowed funds may not actually be employed. Thus firms can protect themselves by making use of long-term financing, for example, by lengthening the maturity of their debts or by increasing the relative importance of the liquid assets they hold.

The choices a firm makes regarding the distribution of its assets also involve a trade-off between risk and profitability that is decided by management's risk preferences. The more the firm decides to hold current assets rather than fixed assets, the safer it will be. But this safety will ordinarily also mean lower profitability. The assumption that short-term rates are always below long-term rates is not valid at times, and obviously changes in relative costs of short- and long-term financing must be quite relevant in the choice of debt maturities.

Comments about the behavior of some liquidity ratios for all nonfinancial corporations combined and the extent to which they lend support to the theoretical principles just outlined are presented below. Most of this essay, however, is concerned with an examination of conventional liquidity ratios. We may question the use of such ratios if there are plausible theories to explain the management of working capital by nonfinancial corporations. Insofar as ratios are used by economic agents active in financial markets—bankers, suppliers of credit, corporations themselves, investors generally, and financial analysts—they can have important effects on behavior in markets. It may be noted that although this paper is confined to a small number of ratios, credit-rating firms may employ dozens of ratios in actually evaluating firms and industries.[6]

A major difficulty in using ratios—an empirical approach—concerns the definition of a norm according to which any particular ratio can be judged high or low. The individual firm may be viewed in relation to industry averages and dispersions about those averages. It is more difficult to pass judgment on averages for all firms combined, not only because uncertainty about the future is inherent in economic forecasting but also because institutional arrangements may have changed. Firms may, for example, have better access to credit lines than in the past, a development that would require smaller cash holdings.

Some Common Measures. The most common liquidity ratio is the current ratio, or the ratio of current assets to current liabilities. In use since the early part of this century, it is a measure of a firm's ability to meet current obligations. We might question the validity of the distinction between current assets and, say, fixed assets, since firms have been known to sell buildings or entire subsidiaries for the purpose of raising cash. The distinction is admittedly arbitrary, but it is useful insofar as it recognizes two dimensions of liquidity: (1) the time needed to convert an asset into cash and (2) the certainty of the price to be realized by the sale of an asset.[7] But not all current assets are available for paying off the obligations represented by current liabilities, since inventories constitute a large part of current assets and a good part of these could not easily be liquidated to satisfy debtors.[8] Although many basic raw materials might find a ready market, among manufacturers work-in-process inventories (about one-third of the manufacturing stock) are goods on which some specialized fabrication has already begun. Furthermore, many goods that constitute raw materials inventories are made to order by suppliers for fabrication into highly specialized or custom goods. Many products subject to the vagaries of style or to seasonal influences will fetch only a small fraction of their cost if they are liquidated to raise cash.

The current ratio may be deficient for another reason. When we think of the impact of inflation on balance sheets, we tend to focus on fixed assets and their valuation by accountants at historical costs. The use of last in, first out (LIFO) accounting, however, which has been adopted so that current replacement costs may be reflected in cost of goods sold and in profits, also distorts the balance sheet, since LIFO inventories may be carried at prices that prevailed in the distant past. Since the proportion of inventories valued by LIFO has shifted considerably during the past decade of high inflation, it is difficult to use the current ratio to evaluate liquidity trends unless a correction is made for this bias.

Table 1 shows (first two columns) how the current ratio would be changed if inventories as carried on company books were replaced by inventories valued at prices that are truly current. The latter are estimates made by the Bureau of Economic Analysis (BEA). The main adjustment is made in the evaluation of LIFO inventories, since first

TABLE 1

LIQUIDITY RATIOS OF NONFINANCIAL CORPORATIONS, 1974–1983

End of Period	Current Ratio		Quick, or Acid-Test, Ratio	Liquid Assets Ratio
	Published	Adjusted		
1974	1.62	1.67	0.917	0.251
1975	1.68	1.75	0.981	0.301
1976	1.67	1.76	0.979	0.311
1977	1.64	1.74	0.960	0.283
1978	1.56	1.66	0.914	0.253
1979	1.51	1.61	0.879	0.236
1980	1.49	1.61	0.882	0.235
1981	1.45	1.56	0.854	0.229
1982	1.47	1.57	0.874	0.248
1983 1Q	1.47	1.56	0.882	0.258
1983 2Q	n.a.	n.a.	n.a.	0.267(prelim.)
Change to 1982 (%)				
From peak	− 13	− 11	− 11	− 24
From 1974	− 9	− 6	− 5	− 6

NOTE: n.a. = not available

SOURCES (by column):

1. *Economic Indicators*, September 1983. Current assets/current liabilities.

2. Obtained by substituting for published inventories (book value) unpublished data of the Bureau of Economic Analysis for inventories measured in current prices.

3. Current assets as published minus inventories as published, all divided by current liabilities.

4. Flow-of-funds accounts. Liquid assets divided by short-term liabilities. Liquid assets in this measure consist of demand deposits and currency, time deposits, security repurchase agreements, foreign deposits, U.S. government securities, state and local government obligations, and commercial paper. Short-term liabilities consist of loans, short-term commercial paper, bankers' acceptances, profits tax payables, and trade payables.

in, first out (FIFO) inventories are close to current costs. Note that the adjusted ratio in 1982 had fallen much less since 1974 than the published ratio. Credit analysts make use of a variant of the current ratio, namely the ratio of current assets excluding inventories to current liabilities. This statistic is referred to as the quick, or "acid-test," ratio and is shown in the third column of table 1.

Because customers may stretch out the payment of their bills when pressed for cash, credit analysts have made use of a ratio that omits accounts receivable from current assets. It is limited to *liquid* assets in relation to current liabilities. There are a number of variants

TABLE 2

DISTRIBUTION OF EXTERNAL SOURCES OF FUNDS AND DISTRIBUTION OF ALL
SOURCES OF FUNDS, NONFARM NONFINANCIAL CORPORATIONS, 1955–1982
(percent)

| | External Sources | | | | | | All Sources | |
	Net equity issues	Total market debt	Long term	Short term	All other[a]	Total	Total internal	Total external
1955–1959	12.7	57.6	39.4	18.2	29.7	100.0	66	34
1960–1964	4.8	64.0	41.9	22.0	31.2	100.0	69	31
1965–1969	3.5	61.9	32.1	29.8	34.6	100.0	61	39
1970–1974	11.0	55.6	25.4	30.1	33.4	100.0	52	48
1975–1979	3.0	61.1	24.0	37.1	35.9	100.0	56	44
1980	9.0	54.3	27.5	26.8	36.7	100.0	57	43
1981	– 8.5	76.7	25.2	51.5	31.8	100.0	63	37
1982	16.7	106.7	49.6	57.0	– 23.4	100.0	78	22

a. Profit taxes payable, trade debt, and foreign direct investment in the United States.
SOURCE: Flow-of-funds accounts.

of this measure, which consists of a cash element and a near-cash element made up of very short term marketable investments in relation to current liabilities. This ratio, based on flow-of-funds data, appears in the last column of table 1.

The Overall Picture for Nonfinancial Corporations: Trends and Cycles

It is well known that businesses have been economizing in their use of money over the postwar period, so that declines in liquidity ratios over the past several years must be taken into account. For this reason it is best to view the ratios just presented against the general background of financing by nonfinancial corporations in the postwar period. Table 2 shows a breakdown of sources of financing and of external sources from 1955 to 1982. The following points are worth noting.

1. For a period of about twenty years—from the early 1950s to the early 1970s—reliance on internal funds decreased and reliance on external funds increased. Since the early 1970s internal shares have recovered somewhat (see figure 2).

2. The great bulk of the external financing has taken the form of increased indebtedness rather than new equity issues. When equity issues were at their peak—from 1955 to 1959—they constituted only

FIGURE 2
INTERNAL FUNDS AS PERCENTAGE OF TOTAL SOURCES OF FUNDS OF NONFINANCIAL CORPORATIONS, 1946–1982

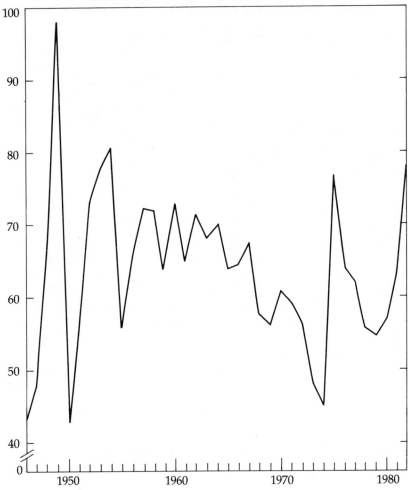

SOURCE: Flow-of-funds accounts.

12.7 percent of total external sources and only 4.3 percent of all sources. As William Fellner pointed out, business had a strong incentive to invest in real assets during the period of high inflation because it was profitable to borrow funds supplied by the household sector at negative or extremely low real interest costs.[9] The tax code has been a major factor favoring debt financing rather than equity financing, since dividends, unlike interest, are not a deductible expense.

TABLE 3

Liquidity and Debt Ratios for Nonfinancial Corporations around
Business Cycle Troughs, 1954–1982

Liquid Assets as Percentage of Short-Term Liabilities				Short-Term Debt as Percentage of Credit Market Debt			
$T - 2$	T Date	T	$T + 4$	$T - 2$	T Date	T	$T + 4$
59.7	2Q 1954	60.9	61.1	28.5	2Q 1954	27.1	26.7
46.3	2Q 1958	46.8	47.1	29.3	2Q 1958	28.3	27.9
42.0	1Q 1961	41.3	41.8	29.5	1Q 1961	29.3	28.3
22.5	4Q 1970	23.0	24.6	37.5	4Q 1970	36.3	34.9
20.8	1Q 1975	26.1	30.1	43.0	1Q 1975	42.4	39.6
22.7	3Q 1980	22.9	22.5	46.7	3Q 1980	45.4	47.6
22.7	4Q 1982	24.8	26.7[a]	49.4	4Q 1982	48.7	48.0[a]

NOTE: $T - 2$ = two quarters before trough quarter. $T + 4$ = four quarters after trough quarter.
a. End of second quarter 1983.
SOURCE: Flow-of-funds accounts.

3. Within the debt total for nonfinancial corporations, the share accounted for by short-term debt has shown an upward trend since the mid-1960s.[10]

To some extent the rise in the short-term ratio may be a reflection of federal financing, because since about 1975 the federal government has shifted its emphasis from short- to long-term financing.[11] It is of interest, however, that the more rapid rate growth in the short-term component occurred between, say, 1965 and 1975, before the change in federal debt management.

The absence of equity financing and emphasis on debt have resulted in an increasingly leveraged capital structure for American corporations. If we consider book values, equities constituted 58 percent of the sum of debt plus equity at the end of 1982—the lowest figure in the post–World War II period. To the extent that this debt has been short term, it has meant that nonfinancial corporations have been exposed to risk to a greater extent than ever. I shall discuss below some of the consequences of this exposure after first looking more closely at some liquidity and debt ratios.

Liquidity and Debt Ratios. Figures 3 and 4 show, respectively, the ratio of liquid assets to short-term liabilities and the ratio of short-term to total credit market debt by quarters from 1952 to date, as estimated in the flow-of-funds accounts. Table 3 shows the behavior of the ratio

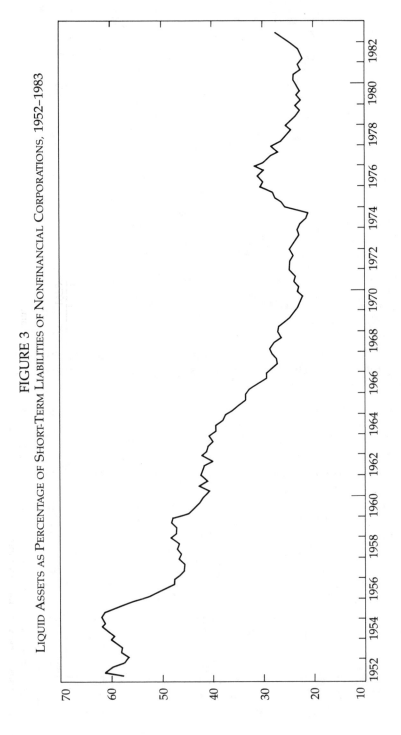

FIGURE 3

LIQUID ASSETS AS PERCENTAGE OF SHORT-TERM LIABILITIES OF NONFINANCIAL CORPORATIONS, 1952–1983

SOURCE: Flow-of-funds accounts.

FIGURE 4

SHORT-TERM DEBT AS PERCENTAGE OF TOTAL CREDIT MARKET DEBT, 1952–1983

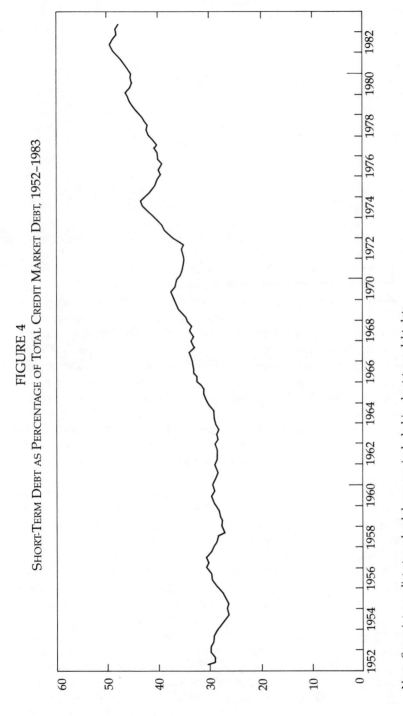

NOTE: Some intermediate-term bank loans are included in short-term debt data.
SOURCE: Flow-of-funds accounts.

of liquid assets to short-term liabilities and of short-term to total credit market debt at each business trough, just before the trough, and in the first year of recovery. The business cycle dating is that of the National Bureau of Economic Research.

Each of the figures presents a ratio that is strongly trend dominated, although figure 3 exhibits an interesting flattening out after 1970, a problem to which we shall return. The cyclical movements around troughs in each figure are brought out more clearly in table 3. Two quarters before every trough, the ratio of short-term debt to total market debt shows a decrease, a movement that has continued for at least four quarters in six of the seven upturns illustrated.[12] The exception was the rise from the third quarter of 1980 to the third quarter of 1981. The cyclical pattern of debt ratios is almost duplicated by the ratio of liquid assets to short-term liabilities: increases in the last half-year of downturn during six of seven downturns (the exception was 1960–1961) and increases in the first year of upturn during six of the seven upturns (the exception being the third quarter of 1980 to the third quarter of 1981, a period that I consider below).

Figures 3 and 4 and table 3, which are consistent with descriptions of the business cycle made by the early National Bureau investigators, show firms acting quite conservatively during the recession once the recession has been recognized. Corporations reduce their short-term debt and increase their long-term debt. During the recession they also start to build up their cash by reducing inventory investment and capital spending. During the recovery the buildup in cash continues as profits increase and as uncertainty about the outlook keeps firms from making investment commitments. At some time during the recovery, however, firms discover the need for more investment, short-term borrowing increases, and the liquid asset ratio starts to fall.

Some further perspective on the long-run decline in the ratio of liquid assets to short-term liabilities is provided in table 4, which compares real growth rates for these financial assets and liabilities with those for real inventories, real structures and equipment net of depreciation, and real output. The slow growth of real liquid assets is in striking contrast to that of tangible capital and output.

The long-run decline in the ratio of liquid assets to short-term liabilities in figure 3 reflects two main influences. First, in the early postwar period business was in a highly liquid position because fixed investment was very low during the Great Depression and because investment was restricted during World War II. The second influence seems to be the long-run improvement in the management of working capital by nonfinancial corporations.[13] The decline in liquid assets (relative to current liabilities) should be viewed as complementary to the rise in short-term debt relative to total debt, since the two ratios are

TABLE 4

GROWTH RATES OF OUTPUT, LIQUID ASSETS, SHORT-TERM LIABILITIES,
INVENTORIES, AND NET PLANT, 1953–1980

	Nonfinancial Corporations		
	3Q 1953– 1Q 1980	3Q 1953– 4Q 1969	4Q 1969– 1Q 1980
Output	4.2	4.5	3.6
Liquid assets	0.9	0	2.5
Short-term liabilities	4.5	5.5	3.0
Inventories	4.0	4.3	3.5
Net plant	3.8	4.0	3.6

NOTE: Annual rate of change compounded quarterly. Net plant figures refer to fourth quarter nearest beginning or terminal date. Financial assets and liabilities refer to non-farm only and are deflated by gross national product deflator.
SOURCES: Basic data from Bureau of Economic Analysis and Federal Reserve.

related aspects of the long-run behavior of working capital of nonfinancial corporations. This behavior of nonfinancial corporations fits in with the theory of working capital management that I have just sketched. With short-term rates generally below long-term, in the long run these companies should be viewed as profit maximizers who are not averse to taking risks, although during recessions and especially once a recession has been foreseen, their behavior tends to be conservative.

If the trend in the ratio of liquid assets to short-term liabilities reflects long-run improvements in the management of working capital by nonfinancial corporations, we may ask why the downward trend seems to have come almost to a halt after 1970, particularly in view of the acceleration in the rate of inflation in the 1970s. Possibly the data are faulty. The behavior of the liquid assets ratio could also be a response to the episodes of credit stringency in 1966 and 1969, when disintermediation dried up funds. That is, it could be viewed as a move to reduce riskiness, a condition that firms associate with the inflation. If that is so, it would be true in spite of the fact that the dangers of disintermediation have been less important as a result of changes in regulation Q that have permitted banks to offer market rates of interest on large certificates of deposit.

It is also possible that the rise in liquid asset holdings by nonfinancial corporations is related to the striking change in the composition of liquid assets, which may also be taken as a manifestation of improvement in cash management. In comparison with earlier peri-

TABLE 5

DISTRIBUTION OF LIQUID ASSET HOLDINGS BY NONFINANCIAL
CORPORATIONS AT SELECTED BUSINESS CYCLE PEAKS, 1953–1980
(percent)

	Demand Deposits and Currency	Time Deposits	Security Re-purchase Agree-ments (RPs)	Foreign Deposits	U.S. Govern-ment Securities	State and Local	Commer-cial Paper	Total
3Q 1953	55.9	1.9	—	0.2	39.3	2.2	0.4	100.0
4Q 1969	62.5	5.2	4.8	1.7	10.6	4.1	11.0	100.0
1Q 1980	37.0	21.3	10.4	8.1	2.8	2.0	18.3	100.0

SOURCE: Flow-of-funds accounts.

ods, these companies now hold much less in non-interest-bearing demand deposits and in Treasury bills and much more in certificates of deposit and commercial paper (see table 5). With the high interest rates that have accompanied the inflation, the opportunity costs of maintaining completely idle cash balances have risen sharply, and new market instruments are now available for the recent highly so-phisticated portfolio management of cash and near-cash assets. Still, although this trend would explain the decline in idle cash, it would not explain why the sum of cash plus near-cash, namely liquid assets, should increase.[14]

Finally, in this brief historical review we may ask why the ratios of liquid assets to short-term liabilities and of short-term to total debt failed to display their characteristic behavior in the upturn from the third quarter of 1980 to the third quarter of 1981. The liquid asset ratio was not greatly different from the postwar average experience; in the 1980–1981 upturn, the rise in liquid assets was somewhat below aver-age and the rise in short-term liabilities as a whole somewhat above average. What *was* quite different from past experience was the debt ratio, and this fact seems to reflect an unusually large rise in short-term debt. Apparently companies were unwilling to lock themselves into long-term debt at the extremely high long-term interest rates that prevailed, say, from the second half of 1980 to the first half of 1981.[15] It is true that short-term rates were also extremely high; in fact the yield curve became inverted. But if business expected the abnormal condi-tion on short-term rates not to persist, this attitude could explain why firms chose to use short-term financing. Although the shift to short-term debt was not consistent with the short-run risk-avoiding behavior in recessions observed in the postwar period, it was not inconsistent with the long-term debt-avoiding behavior observed in the financial patterns over the long run.[16]

Interest Burden. Last year fears were expressed that the burden of interest might become so great that bankruptcies would increase even more than they had and that the overhang of interest might stand in the way of a recovery. Interest burden is shown in table 6 as the proportion of net interest paid by nonfinancial corporations to cash flow. Cash flow, which can be defined in many different ways, is equal here to the sum of undistributed profits plus capital consumption allowances, all as defined for national income purposes.

An examination of the ratios at business cycle peaks reveals a strong upward trend through the first quarter of 1980, followed by a small decrease. The ratio, as might be expected, has usually increased from business cycle peak to trough, although the 1980–1982 experience was somewhat perverse. In the first year of upturn this particular ratio has decreased five of six times, reflecting comparative stability in net interest paid, while profits have undergone a substantial recovery. Over the year following the trough in the third quarter of 1980, however, the ratio was essentially stable as the rise in cash flow was accompanied by a pronounced increase in interest costs.

Disinflation Thus Far

Although concern over liquidity was at a peak in the spring and early summer of 1982 and profits of nonfinancial corporations fell from the first to the second half, end-of-1982 corporate balance sheets looked better than they had a year earlier. Corporations improved their cash position by making major cutbacks in investment, a policy that exacerbated the recession but permitted firms to liquidate a large volume of short-term debt late in the year. The decline in interest rates, the rise in the stock market, and the widespread view in financial markets that monetary policy had been relaxed and that a recovery was finally at hand strengthened the belief that balance sheets would show further improvement.

1982 Highlights. For all nonfinancial corporations combined, the ratio of liquid assets to short-term liabilities, after falling to 0.220 in the first quarter of 1982, rose thereafter to reach 0.248 at the end of 1982, the highest ratio since the end of 1978. The two current ratios and the quick ratio shown in table 1 did not improve, however, until the fourth quarter. The ratio of short-term to total debt peaked in the third quarter and then fell in the fourth quarter as a result of sharp reductions in bank loans, commercial paper, and finance company loans. The ratio

TABLE 6

INTEREST BURDEN: NET INTEREST PAID AS PERCENTAGE OF CASH FLOW OF NONFINANCIAL CORPORATIONS, 1953–1982
(dollars in billions)

	Business Cycle Peak				Business Cycle Trough				T + 4		
Date	Net interest	Cash flow	Ratio	Date	Net interest	Cash flow	Ratio	Net interest	Cash flow	Ratio
3Q 1953	1.2	21.9	5.6	2Q 1954	1.5	23.1	6.5	1.6	29.1	5.5
3Q 1957	2.2	30.6	7.2	2Q 1958	2.6	27.8	9.4	3.1	37.2	8.3
2Q 1960	3.4	34.1	10.0	1Q 1961	3.7	32.9	11.2	4.3	41.9	10.3
4Q 1969	14.4	59.3	24.3	4Q 1970	18.1	58.9	30.7	18.4	77.2	23.8
4Q 1973	25.2	87.2	28.9	1Q 1975	31.0	95.9	32.3	30.2	134.2	22.5
1Q 1980	56.0	169.7	33.0	3Q 1980	56.4	181.1	31.1	72.6	231.6	31.3
3Q 1981	72.6	231.6	31.3	4Q 1982	61.9	236.6	26.2	58.4[a]	266.2[a]	21.9[a]

a. Second quarter 1983.
SOURCE: Basic data, Bureau of Economic Analysis.

of short-term to total debt in the fourth quarter of 1982 was a little higher than it had been a year earlier. Declines in interest rates during 1982, especially after midyear, reduced the burden of interest in relation to cash flow.

The state of corporate liquidity partly reflects corporate profits, which were quite depressed last year. As measured by concepts of national income accounts (NIA), profits before taxes were more than one-sixth below their 1981 level. Last year's decline in profits as calculated on companies' books was even greater than the decline in NIA profits. Even so, dividends paid by nonfinancial corporations rose considerably, continuing a string of yearly increases in progress since 1971. The rise in dividends of nonfinancial corporations came about because the dividend figure is a *net* figure: dividends paid less dividends received. Dividends paid rose moderately, but dividends received declined for the second straight year, mainly because dividends received from abroad fell for the second straight year. As a consequence of the profits decline and dividend behavior, undistributed profits (book basis) fell to their lowest level in a decade.

Even in years of relatively high profits, such as 1979, profits in recent years have been less than capital consumption allowances (chiefly depreciation). The latter continued to rise last year as a result of the rising stock of fixed capital and past inflation. Cash flow—the combined sum of undistributed profits and capital consumption allowances—declined slightly on a book basis but rose a little when inflation adjustments are made to book profits and book depreciation, because deductions for inflation were greater in 1981 than in 1982. Cash flow measured by book figures appear in table 7. The inflation-adjusted figures used in the NIA version are in table 8.

External financing patterns underwent great changes during 1982, with a major shift from short- to long-term financing (see table 9). During the first half of the year, long-term rates on corporate bonds were at a virtual peak as lenders continued to demand high inflation premiums. Borrowers, however, seemed unwilling to saddle themselves with debt that might prove burdensome later, and as a result, in the first half of 1982 corporate bond issues (excluding tax-exempt bonds and mortgages) were at their lowest two-quarter rate since 1973. In fact the net volume of tax-exempt industrial revenue bond issues, which provide a relatively cheap form of financing for industrial expansion, was higher than that of ordinary corporate issues as the trend in tax-exempt bonds continued without abatement.

Although long-term borrowing was weak, short-term borrowing in the first half of 1982 remained as high as it had been in 1981, a record year for short-term debt expansion. Special influences, discussed below, seem to have played an important role in the heavy

223

TABLE 7
CASH FLOW AND ITS MAIN COMPONENTS: BOOK VERSION, NONFINANCIAL CORPORATIONS, 1976–1983
(billions of dollars)

	Profits before Taxes (book)	Taxes	Profits after Taxes	Dividends	Undistributed Profits	Capital Consumption Allowance	Cash Flow	Earnings from Abroad	Cash Flow (F/F)
1976	135.0	52.6	82.3	30.1	52.2	91.8	144.0	14.3	158.3
1977	156.5	59.6	96.8	31.9	64.9	104.9	169.8	15.1	184.9
1978	178.4	66.9	111.5	37.7	73.8	118.6	192.4	19.7	212.1
1979	191.8	69.2	122.5	39.8	82.8	135.7	218.5	30.6	249.1
1980	177.8	67.0	110.8	43.7	67.1	155.3	222.4	29.9	252.3
1981	183.0	65.5	117.5	53.5	64.0	183.1	247.1	23.7	270.8
1982	131.5	41.2	90.3	57.2	33.1	210.8	243.9	21.8	265.7
1983-2Q [a]	146.7	54.1	92.6	60.5	32.1	243.9	276.0	18.7	294.7
Percentage change,									
1981–82	−28.2	−37.1	−23.2	6.9	−48.3	15.1	−1.3	−8.0	−1.9

NOTE: See table 8 for description of column headings.
a. Seasonally adjusted annual rate.
SOURCE: Bureau of Economic Analysis.

TABLE 8

CASH FLOW AND ITS MAIN COMPONENTS: NATIONAL INCOME ACCOUNTS VERSION, NONFINANCIAL CORPORATIONS, 1976–1983
(billions of dollars)

	Profits before Taxes[a]	Taxes	Profits after Taxes	Dividends	Undistributed Profits	Capital Consumption Allowance[b]	Cash Flow[c]	Earnings from Abroad[d]	Cash Flow (F/F)[e]
1976	107.3	52.6	54.7	30.1	24.6	104.8	129.4	14.3	143.6
1977	129.5	59.6	69.9	31.9	38.0	115.7	153.7	15.1	168.8
1978	142.1	66.9	75.2	37.7	37.5	130.9	168.4	19.7	188.1
1979	134.7	69.2	65.5	39.8	25.7	149.6	175.3	30.6	205.9
1980	120.3	67.0	53.3	43.7	9.6	170.0	179.6	29.9	209.5
1981	150.2	65.5	84.7	53.5	31.2	192.2	223.4	23.7	247.1
1982	124.0	41.2	82.8	57.2	25.6	210.0	235.6	21.8	257.4
1983-2Q[f]	164.0	54.1	109.9	60.5	49.4	216.8	266.2	18.7	284.9
Percentage change, 1981–82	−17.4	−37.1	−2.2	6.9	−18.0	9.3	5.5	−8.0	4.2

a. Book profits with inventory valuation adjustment and capital consumption adjustment.

b. Includes capital consumption adjustment.

c. Undistributed profits plus capital consumption allowance.

d. Also includes earnings retained abroad. Equivalent of NIA "rest-of-world" profits after taxes (net).

e. Cash flow (NIA) plus earnings from abroad. This figure will differ slightly from flow-of-funds figures, which exclude farm businesses.

f. Seasonally adjusted annual rate.

SOURCE: Bureau of Economic Analysis.

TABLE 9
NET FUNDS RAISED IN MARKETS BY NONFINANCIAL CORPORATIONS,
1975–SECOND QUARTER 1983
(billions of dollars)

| | Net New Equity Issues | Bonds and Mortgages | | | | Short-Term Debt[b] | Total Debt Instruments |
		Total	Corporate	Tax-exempt	Mortgages[a]		
1975	9.9	28.7	27.2	2.6	−1.1	−7.9	20.8
1976	10.5	27.7	22.8	2.5	2.4	16.5	44.2
1977	2.7	33.1	22.9	6.7	3.5	36.6	69.7
1978	−0.1	32.9	21.1	7.7	4.1	47.7	80.6
1979	−7.8	28.7	17.3	10.0	1.4	67.3	96.0
1980	12.9	39.5	26.6	10.9	2.0	38.5	78.0
1981	−11.5	−34.0	22.0	13.4	−1.4	69.7	103.7
1982	11.4	33.8	18.8	15.1	−0.2	38.9	72.7
1H[c]	7.0	24.7	10.8	13.9	0.0	64.6	89.3
3Q[c]	−1.1	40.6	24.8	17.2	−1.4	49.4	90.0
4Q[c]	32.6	45.2	29.1	15.5	0.7	−23.2	22.0
1983							
1Q	35.3	32.2	18.5	9.8	3.9	5.7	37.9
2Q (prelim.)	29.2	41.9	23.3	11.5	7.1	−3.5	38.5

a. Industrial revenue bonds; issued by state and local governments and secured in interest and principal by the private user of the funds.

b. Bank loans, commercial paper, acceptances, finance company loans, and U.S. government loans.

c. Seasonally adjusted annual rate. Averages for 1982 may not agree with total for 1982.

SOURCE: Flow-of-funds accounts.

volume of short-term borrowing in the first half of last year. In any case, as interest rates receded last summer, long-term bond financing was stepped up, and the growth of short-term financing slackened somewhat. The final quarter of the year witnessed a net liquidation of short-term debt that easily eclipsed any of the quarterly debt liquidations that occurred in other periods of depressed activity.

Another feature of the year was the resumption of equity financing in the final quarter, which occurred largely under the stimulus of the rise in equity prices. Measured by the New York Stock Exchange Index, stock prices gained 30 percent from July to year end, and by one measure the cost of equity relative to debt in the final quarter of 1982 was at, or virtually at, the lowest point in twenty years.[17]

Effect of Disappointments on Borrowing. Throughout 1982 businesses intensified their efforts to conserve cash by cutting back spending on plant and equipment and inventories in the face of a deteriorating economy. The final plant and equipment results for 1982—a 1.6 percent reduction in current dollars from 1981—were a major change from expectations held early in 1982, when businesses projected an increase in their capital spending of 7 percent over the preceding year. Investment figures confined to new projects started point up these economizing measures in a very striking way. In manufacturing, spending as a whole fell by 5 percent from 1981 to 1982, but the total value of new work started decreased by 21 percent. In electric and gas utilities, the corresponding figures were 8 percent and −50 percent.

There can be little doubt that disappointments in sales and in profits played an important role in the sharp reduction in new projects started and in the gap between actual and anticipated expenditures in 1982. According to the Commerce Department, in early 1982 manufacturing firms projected a sales increase of 9.9 percent; actual sales *fell* 5.4 percent. In trade the figures were 8.2 percent expected and −1.4 percent realized, and in public utilities 16.4 percent expected and 12.3 percent realized. The Commerce Department does not collect profits anticipations corresponding to the sales anticipations, but it is safe to say that the profits disappointments must have been far greater, because prices also were below expectations, which suggests that profit margins must have been disappointingly low.[18] Thus profits would have been lower for two reasons: the physical volume of sales (and output) was below expectations, which meant higher fixed costs per unit, and profit margins were disappointing. We do have some evidence concerning profit expectations of forecasters whose forecasts are used by many large companies. According to Blue Chip Economic Indicators, the consensus forecast of the change in pretax book profits from 1981 to 1982 went from 8.5 percent in early October 1981 to 4.9 percent a month later and 0.6 percent in early December. The actual change in profits for all corporations (including financial) was −24.6 percent.

The heavy volume of short-term borrowing in 1982 may well have been a rather urgent response to disappointments in cash flow that were of record dimensions last year. The reason is the central role played by the cash forecast in cash management. The importance of the forecast seems obvious, but it is easily overlooked. It is illustrated in the following statement taken from a study of cash management practices of large companies: "The basic tools of cash management are cash forecasts. Without them a company has no way of telling how much money is needed for its operations or how much financing will be needed to support its future growth."[19] Furthermore, the fact that prices were relatively weak during 1982 and rose much less than expected may have had special significance for short-term financing decisions. Commerce Department surveys show that in early 1982 manufacturers expected prices to rise 7.7 percent. Actual prices rose 3.8 percent for 1982. As this price shortfall became evident during the course of 1982, it must have reinforced the belief among many businessmen that the high short-term interest rates of late 1981 and early 1982 would not endure.

Analysis of Individual Firm Data

The discussion so far has been based on broad aggregates for the entire nonfinancial corporate sector. Industry information is available from the *Quarterly Financial Report*,[20] which provides industry detail for two-digit manufacturing industries as well as for large mining, wholesale, and retail corporations. This information is all right as far as it goes, but in manufacturing especially the industry results may be heavily influenced by a relatively small number of very large firms. To solve this problem, I prepared a series of tabulations in which the unit of observation is the individual firm. This approach permits calculating averages in which firms have equal weight as well as various measures of dispersion. Such information can tell us how typical the long-term trends based on aggregates are and whether the past few years have left us with large pockets of firms that are very weak in terms of profitability, liquidity, and debt.

Appendix A describes the sample of large companies used for the tabulations. The tables and text that follow cover the following subjects: (1) liquidity ratios, (2) debt ratios (short-term to total debt), and (3) interest burden (interest relative to cash flow). Definitions of these ratios are given in appendix B. The data are based on annual reports through 1982.

Liquidity ratios. 1. As measured by medians, all the liquidity ratios used here have shown declines over the long run apart from cyclical fluctuations. In manufacturing, the medians of the current and quick ratios each declined at an average annual rate of approximately 2 percent from 1964 to 1979 while the liquid assets ratio fell at a rate of almost 7 percent (table 10, third row, last column).

2. Each of the ratios has shown a retardation in the rate of decrease when the fifteen-year period is split into two subperiods, 1964–1973

TABLE 10

COMPARISON OF LIQUIDITY RATIOS AND THEIR GROWTH RATES FOR
MANUFACTURING CORPORATIONS, 1964–1982

	Current Ratio		Quick Ratio		Liquid Assets Ratio	
	Aggre-gate	Compu-stat	Aggre-gate	Compu-stat	Aggre-gate	Compu-stat
Annual growth rate						
1964–73	−2.1	−2.3	−2.2	−2.2	−6.9	−8.4
1973–79	−3.0	−1.6	−2.9	−1.4	−4.9	−4.6
1964–79	−2.5	−2.0	−2.5	−1.9	−6.1	−6.9
Ratios, 1979–1982						
1979	1.712	2.224	0.948	1.186	0.212	0.186
1980	1.667	2.183	0.931	1.197	0.197	0.191
1981	1.622	2.199	0.892	1.214	0.190	0.193
1982	1.613	2.125	0.904	1.181	0.212	0.200

NOTE: Compustat figures for "Ratios" are medians of Compustat firms.
SOURCES: Compustat—American Enterprise Institute, figures based on a tabulation of Compustat data from 282 firms for the years 1964–1979 and from 368 firms for the years 1979–1982. Aggregate figures are year-end ratios from the Federal Trade Commission, *Quarterly Financial Report,* various issues.

and 1973–1979. The retardation is most pronounced for the liquid assets ratio.

3. These findings, based on medians of individual company ratios, more or less confirm the aggregate pattern for manufacturing shown in the *Quarterly Financial Report.* Aside from the fact that the *QFR* estimates are for all corporations, a strict comparison cannot be made for the entire period because the Compustat data refer to the consolidated *worldwide* corporation, whereas the *QFR* shifted from that basis to a consolidated *domestic* corporation basis in the fourth quarter of 1973.[21] It is perhaps significant that the agreement between the two series is closer for the current and quick ratios in the earlier period, but that is not true of the liquid assets ratio.

4. When the most recent years are examined, no great differences are apparent between these data and the *QFR* aggregates (table 10, bottom). The Compustat ratio of liquid assets to current liabilities, however, rises each year from 1979 to 1982, whereas the *QFR* data decline through 1981 and recover to their 1979 level by the end of 1982. But we cannot tell whether this behavior is due to the worldwide

versus domestic coverage or to a less strong cash position for the very largest firms relative to all manufacturing firms.

In addition to the medians, I also obtained the first and third quartiles of the distributions, as well as their difference, or the inter-quartile range, and the ratio of the latter to the median, which is called the coefficient of variation. In one sense the distributions did not change much from 1964 to 1979, since the first and third quartiles declined at roughly the same rate as the medians. The picture is a little different, however, when coefficients of variation are examined at business cycle peaks and especially at troughs (see table 11). Looking only at the business cycle peaks, we might conclude that the distributions looked better at the end of 1979 than at the end of 1969 or 1973, insofar as the coefficients are lower in 1979. All three of the coefficients, however, were higher at the end of 1982, the most recent trough, than at the end of 1970 and 1974.

The part of the distribution with low values is of particular interest since it includes—but is not limited to—firms strapped for cash. At the end of 1979 the ratio of the first quartile to the median of the liquid assets measure was lower than at the end of 1969 or 1973. At the end of 1982 the ratio of the first quartile to the median for all three measures was somewhat lower than at the end of either 1970 or 1974. These figures therefore suggest the possibility of a little more weakness at the end of 1982 than would be indicated by the medians alone.

To examine parts of these distributions more carefully, I calculated means of all firms that were at or below particular measures, such as the bottom tenth percentile or the first quartile, or at or above the third quartile. First I look at firms that were at or below the first quartile in 1964 to see where they stood in two other prosperous years, 1972 and 1978. We know from the basic tabulations that the median ratios for all sample firms, as well as the first and third quartiles, declined over this period. This point is illustrated again in table 12 when we read down the diagonal for any of the three ratios in the table. For all three liquidity measures, however, the firms that were in the bottom 25 percent of the distribution in 1964 had higher average ratios in 1972 and 1978 than they had in 1964 (reading across a row from left to right). Furthermore, for any given year on average (reading down a column), firms that *used* to be in the lowest quartile subsequently had higher ratios than those firms that succeeded them in the lowest ranking. This pattern suggests that a very low ranking in prosperous years is a temporary ranking probably associated with heavy investment activity.

The same pattern is evident for firms that were at or *below* the tenth percentile or at or *above* the third quartile. I also looked at firms

TABLE 11
ASPECTS OF DISTRIBUTIONS OF THREE LIQUIDITY RATIOS AT SELECTED
POINTS IN THE BUSINESS CYCLE, 1969–1982

	Current Ratio	Quick Ratio	Liquid Assets Ratio
At peaks			
1969			
A	0.452	0.524	1.390
B	0.789	0.742	0.550
1973			
A	0.437	0.473	1.600
B	0.819	0.824	0.521
1979			
A	0.386	0.420	0.789
B	0.801	0.789	0.489
At troughs			
1970			
A	0.509	0.529	1.274
B	0.810	0.784	0.563
1974			
A	0.402	0.448	1.410
B	0.830	0.811	0.584
1982			
A	0.537	0.616	1.555
B	0.774	0.745	0.489

NOTE: A = coefficient of variation, or interquartile range divided by median.
B = first quartile divided by median.

According to the National Bureau, monthly business cycle peaks were December 1969, November 1973, and January 1980. Monthly troughs were November 1970, March 1975, and November 1982. The July 1980 trough and July 1981 peak are omitted here because quarterly data were not obtained from the Compustat file.

SOURCE: American Enterprise Institute, data based on tabulation of 282 manufacturing corporations from Compustat primary file.

that ranked low (or high) in a recession year (1974) to see how they would wind up in a prosperous year (1979), and I compared them with firms similarly ranked in 1978. The pattern here is the same as that described in the preceding paragraph. Finally I looked at firms with various rankings in 1978 and followed them over the next four years. The results appear in table 13.

TABLE 12

MEAN LIQUIDITY RATIOS IN 1964, 1972, AND 1978
OF MANUFACTURING FIRMS RANKED IN THE BOTTOM QUARTILE OF RATIOS
IN 1964, 1972, AND 1978

Lowest Quartile in	1964	1972	1978
	Current ratio		
1964	1.76	2.08	1.94
1972	—	1.58	1.80
1978	—	—	1.47
	Quick ratio		
1964	0.85	1.15	1.14
1972	—	0.82	1.00
1978	—	—	0.80
	Liquid assets ratio		
1964	0.14	0.23	0.26
1972	—	0.08	0.21
1978	—	—	0.06

SOURCE: American Enterprise Institute, data based on Compustat tabulation of 379 firms in 1964, 477 firms in 1972, and 493 firms in 1978.

I also ran a test to see whether firms that ranked low with respect to liquidity in a particular year would also rank low with respect to profitability. The comparisons appear in table 14, which lists four years of average (median) after-tax returns on stockholders' equity for firms that ranked in the bottom 10 percent and the bottom 25 percent of the 1978 distribution of liquidity ratios. Median returns on equity for all companies in the sample appear in the last column. Both the profits and the stockholders' equity that underlie the return on equity are book figures and are subject to all the well-known shortcomings of such measures. But to make proper adjustments at the level of the individual firm of the sort made by BEA at the macro level—such as the inventory valuation adjustment and the capital consumption adjustment for book profits—would require much more detailed information than is easily available, and rough adjustments would be of questionable value.

Table 14 indicates that book rates of return on stockholders' equity for firms ranking low in liquidity in 1978 compare favorably with rates of return for all corporations. Of the thirty observations from 1978 through 1982, eighteen are higher and twelve lower than the respective annual averages for all the sample manufacturing corporations.

TABLE 13

MEAN LIQUIDITY RATIOS, 1978–1982, OF MANUFACTURING FIRMS
CLASSIFIED BY THE RANKING OF THEIR RATIOS IN 1978

	1978	1979	1980	1981	1982
Current ratio					
Lowest 10% in 1978	1.22	1.26	1.37	1.32	1.24
Lowest 25% in 1978	1.50	1.53	1.57	1.61	1.54
Top 25% in 1978	3.70	3.36	3.30	3.18	3.45
All firms reporting	2.47	2.36	2.36	2.36	2.41
Quick ratio					
Lowest 10% in 1978	0.67	0.72	0.80	0.79	0.72
Lowest 25% in 1978	0.83	0.87	0.93	0.95	0.90
Top 25% in 1978	2.19	1.87	1.87	1.81	2.04
All firms reporting	1.39	1.30	1.32	1.32	1.37
Liquid assets ratio					
Lowest 10% in 1978	0.04	0.08	0.14	0.13	0.12
Lowest 25% in 1978	0.07	0.12	0.14	0.15	0.14
Top 25% in 1978	0.87	0.58	0.57	0.60	0.71
All firms reporting	0.36	0.30	0.30	0.33	0.37

SOURCE: American Enterprise Institute, data based on tabulation of 377 firms in Compustat file.

TABLE 14

COMPARISON OF MEDIAN RETURNS ON EQUITY, 1978–1982

	Current Ratio[a]		Quick Ratio[a]		Liquid Assets Ratio[a]		All Sample Firms
	Lowest 10%	Lowest 25%	Lowest 10%	Lowest 25%	Lowest 10%	Lowest 25%	
1978	0.112	0.135	0.127	0.140	0.150	0.134	0.146
1979	0.194	0.179	0.164	0.160	0.161	0.152	0.159
1980	0.180	0.168	0.158	0.154	0.132	0.132	0.141
1981	0.147	0.147	0.154	0.146	0.141	0.121	0.131
1982	0.107	0.100	0.102	0.090	0.081	0.076	0.097

NOTE: Data describe all sample manufacturing firms versus the lowest 10 percent and 25 percent of firms ranked by liquidity ratios in 1978.
a. In 1978.
SOURCE: American Enterprise Institute, data based on Compustat tabulation of 375 manufacturing corporations.

233

TABLE 15
Comparison of Median Liquidity Ratios, 1978–1982

	Current Ratio		Quick Ratio		Liquid Assets Ratio	
	Lowest quartile[a]	All[b]	Lowest quartile[a]	All[b]	Lowest quartile[a]	All[b]
1978	2.171	2.329	1.250	1.266	0.159	0.240
1979	2.035	2.238	1.128	1.190	0.150	0.186
1980	2.178	2.185	1.160	1.205	0.182	0.194
1981	2.022	2.215	1.126	1.223	0.163	0.194
1982	2.014	2.133	1.121	1.189	0.157	0.201

NOTE: Data describe all sample manufacturing firms versus the lowest quartile of manufacturing firms ranked by return on equity in 1978.
a. Median of lowest quartile of firms ranked by return on equity in 1978.
b. Median of all sample firms.
SOURCE: American Enterprise Institute, data based on Compustat tabulation of 375 manufacturing firms.

Here, then, is another bit of evidence lending support to what has already been found, namely, that low ranking in liquidity in a given year is not necessarily indicative of weakness, let alone permanent weakness. The same is not true, however, when we rank the firms by profitability. Table 15 compares liquidity ratios of firms ranked in the lowest quartile according to return on equity in 1978. The ratios are below average, although some of the differences would clearly not pass significance tests. The picture is no different when we compare the bottom 10 percent in profitability with all sample corporations. In summary, tables 14 and 15 suggest that the cause-and-effect sequence runs mainly from profitability to liquidity and not the other way around.

Debt Ratios. Tables 16 and 17 provide information on debt ratios; here we use the ratio of short-term debt to total debt. The large differences in short-term debt evident in table 16 are mainly a matter of firm size, since large firms tend to have short-term debt ratios lower than the average at a point in time. The aggregate ratio for firms with assets over $1 billion, for example, was 0.172 in 1982, which is much closer to the Compustat median. Another factor is the difference in the unit—domestic versus worldwide. The 1979–1982 movements, however, are not greatly different: both rise from 1979 to 1981 and fall from 1981 to 1982, but by different amounts.

TABLE 16

COMPARISON OF RATIOS OF SHORT-TERM TO TOTAL DEBT OF MANUFACTURING
CORPORATIONS, 1979–1982, AND ANNUAL GROWTH RATES, 1964–1979

	Aggregate[a]	Compustat Medians
1979	0.231	0.144
1980	0.231	0.154
1981	0.235	0.160
1982	0.212	0.152
Annual growth rate		
1964–73	1.11	4.92
1973–79	− 0.50	− 2.82
1964–79	0.47	1.75

a. Short-term debt plus current installments on long-term debt as percentage of total debt.

SOURCES: Aggregate—Federal Trade Commission, *Quarterly Financial Report*, various issues; medians—American Enterprise Institute, data based on Compustat tabulation of 223 firms.

TABLE 17

ASPECTS OF DISTRIBUTIONS OF SHORT-TERM DEBT RATIOS AT SELECTED
POINTS IN THE BUSINESS CYCLE, 1969–1982

	Coefficient of Variation	Third Quartile/ Median
	At peaks	
1969	1.48	1.90
1973	1.48	1.90
1979	1.48	2.00
	At troughs	
1970	1.13	1.56
1974	1.59	2.16
1982	1.34	1.82

NOTE: See table 11 for definitions of peaks and troughs.

SOURCE: American Enterprise Institute, Compustat data for 223 firms.

The really striking differences appear over the long run, as may be seen in the bottom part of table 16. The pronounced decline in the short-term proportion of total debt from 1973 to 1979 must mean that the long-term proportion of total debt rose. Coinciding with the

TABLE 18

GROSS INTEREST BURDEN: RATIO OF GROSS INTEREST PAID TO CASH FLOW
OF SAMPLE MANUFACTURING FIRMS, 1969–1982

	Median	Third Quartile	Third Quartile/ Median
At business cycle peaks			
1969	0.188	0.327	1.74
1973	0.214	0.342	1.60
1979	0.243	0.390	1.60
At business cycle troughs			
1970	0.258	0.417	1.62
1974	0.243	0.439	1.81
1982	0.414	0.845	2.04

SOURCE: American Enterprise Institute, Compustat data for 234 firms.

speedup in the rate of inflation, these figures suggest that the largest firms (the Compustat sample relative to all manufacturing) recognized and could act on the advantages of taking on long-term debt during an inflationary period. It should also be noted that the behavior of the Compustat firms is quite different from that suggested in the flow-of-funds data, which show a distinct upward trend in the ratio of short-term debt to total debt over the past thirty years (see figure 4).

Table 17 provides information about the dispersion of the Compustat data at business cycle peaks and troughs.[22] The data at the peaks are remarkable for their stability. Perhaps the main thing to note about the troughs is that the 1982 ratios are below those for 1974 though above the 1970 ratios.

Finally, I ran some longitudinal analyses of firms that were in the top 10 percent or top 25 percent of the short-term debt ratios in specific years. As with the liquidity ratios, I found that firms in the extreme parts of the distribution in a particular year tended subsequently to move in the direction of the average. That is, their position, whether measured from a prosperous year, such as 1964, 1972, or 1978, or from a recession year, such as 1974, tended to be temporary and not permanent.

Interest Burden. Table 18 shows gross interest burden—interest paid divided by cash flow—at selected business cycle peaks and troughs.[23] It differs from the concept of interest burden in table 6 because the latter measures net interest—interest paid minus interest received.[24] The main point about table 18 is that although the median for 1982 is

TABLE 19

GROSS AND NET INTEREST BURDENS OF FIRMS REPORTING BOTH ITEMS,
1973–1982

	Business Cycle Peaks		Business Cycle Troughs	
	1973	1979	1974	1982
	Gross burden			
Median	0.196	0.253	0.223	0.402
Third quartile	0.359	0.402	0.428	0.713
Third quartile/median	1.83	1.59	1.92	1.77
	Net burden			
Median	0.139	0.168	0.158	0.221
Third quartile	0.301	0.373	0.367	0.613
Third quartile/median	2.16	2.22	2.32	2.77

NOTE: Gross burden = gross interest paid divided by cash flow. Net burden = gross interest paid minus interest received divided by cash flow.
SOURCE: American Enterprise Institute, Compustat data on ninety-three firms (gross) and ninety firms (net).

much higher than the median for 1974, the third quartile—reflecting firms with a heavy interest burden—rose even more over this period.

Unfortunately, far fewer companies report net interest. Table 19 shows both gross and net interest burdens for those firms reporting both types of interest. Because of interest receipts, net burdens are much less than gross, especially in recent years. Thus the change in the medians from one trough to another—1974 to 1982—is much less for the net burden than for the gross. Still, the bottom part of the table shows that the firms with heavy net burdens—the third quartile—rose in relation to the median from 1974 to 1982.

These figures on interest burden suggest that for both gross and net burdens, there has been an increase in the proportion of firms with relatively heavy burdens. These results ought, however, to be tempered by the fact that the sample with net interest figures is rather small. Furthermore, as table 6 indicated, net interest burdens have historically fallen sharply in the early stages of recovery.

Near-Term Outlook

The upturn in economic activity that began at the end of 1982 has been accompanied in the first half of 1983 by further increases in liquidity ratios, reductions in the ratio of short-term to total market debt, and reductions in interest burden.

Corporations will continue to pursue policies aimed at improving their liquidity positions for the rest of 1983 and for part of 1984. Not only will they repay bank debt and convert short-term debt to long-term debt, but they will hold back on their real investment. To a large extent 1983 should resemble the normal first year of a business recovery: plant and equipment expenditures will increase slowly at first, but inventory investment will undergo a sharp change. Combined plant equipment and inventory investment has ordinarily risen somewhat faster than the combined total of profits and depreciation in spite of typically sharp increases in corporate profits, so that some increase in external financing, which normally occurs, is also likely, but much more equity financing than usual should characterize this upturn.

Business made larger percentage reductions in its inventories in 1982 than in any other year, cutting back on purchases and slashing production. The 1982 declines were followed in the first half of 1983 by further decreases. As sales continue to improve, however, business will find it necessary to add to inventories; indeed, that seems to have occurred in the summer of 1983, and the turnaround in inventory investment from the fourth quarter of 1982 to the fourth quarter of 1983 will be the largest single component in the recovery of overall production during the year. But additions to inventories are not likely to constitute as much as a stimulus to the rise in production in 1984 as they did in 1983.

To some extent the buildup in inventory investment is a substitute for spending on plant and equipment. The Commerce Department reported in early September that, after last year's reduction, nonfarm business expects to decrease its spending on new plant and equipment by 3 percent from 1982 to 1983. The survey points, however, to a rise of 9 percent (not annualized) from the first to the second half. It is still not clear how closely business will stick to its future spending plans. Actual spending in the first half of 1983 turned out to be much less than had been anticipated earlier in 1983, although we really do not know whether this shortfall was due to lower than anticipated real volume, lower than anticipated prices of plant and equipment, or both. Cutbacks in spending planned for 1983 may turn out to be smaller than anticipated by business early in 1983 if—as seems to be occurring—the recovery in economic activity turns out to be more robust than business expected at the start of this year. It would not be difficult for businesses to resume work on projects that were canceled or postponed in 1982. Although an increasing number of firms will find existing capacity inadequate as output recovers, most industries will still be saddled with low rates of capacity utilization even at the end of 1983. Such low capacity utilization and the continuing uncertainty regarding long-term interest rates are likely to keep the rise in plant and equipment spending from 1983 to 1984 of moderate dimensions.

During the first half of 1983 most forecasters made upward revisions in their projections of real gross national product (GNP) for 1983 and downward revisions in their projections of inflation. The changes made by the administration were especially large. Its early 1983 scenario was superseded in April and again in July by new forecasts that were both more expansive and less inflationary.[25] Its July projections of real growth of 5.5 percent during 1983 and 4.5 percent during 1984, accompanied by inflation rates of 4.6 and 5.0 percent respectively, were not greatly different from the contemporaneous consensus of forecasters in the Blue Chip survey.

The administration did not make public a revision of the 2.2 percent four-quarter growth in productivity that it projected at the start of the year. A much higher figure seems likely in view of experience so far in 1983 as well as the drastic cost-cutting measures that business has been undertaking for more than a year and the more rapid path of real output now anticipated in the budget review. Business has the option of permitting larger productivity gains to appear in the form of smaller price increases (or of price decreases in some cases), in the form of higher wage rates, or in higher profit margins. Probably profits, wages, and prices will all benefit from the prospective gain in productivity. On balance, however, a widening in profit margins seems the safer and likelier business policy, given the strength and persistence of the past inflation and the desire by business to hold down the rise—and in some cases reverse the trend—in labor costs. Such a development is already under way. From the fourth quarter of 1982 to the second quarter of 1983, profits per unit of output of nonfinancial corporations rose 38 percent (not annualized) on the basis of NIA profits and 21 percent on the basis of book profits.

Given the expectations for investment and the favorable prospects for profits, we are likely to see by the end of 1983 and continuing into 1984 a considerable restoration of liquidity ratios. The very large increase in equity financing that began late in 1982 and continued into the summer of 1983 suggests that business may be reducing its emphasis on debt for long-term financing. An improved outlook for inflation and a conservative stance on financing away from debt after the difficulties of the past few years should be some of the factors favorable to more equity financing. But the main factor should be the reduced cost of equity financing relative to that of debt, reflecting the decline in interest rates and the rise in stock market prices since the summer of 1982. The cost of equity relative to that of debt can be measured in many different ways, but there can be little doubt about the cost shift favoring equity financing.[26]

Conclusions

The current liquidity position of nonfinancial corporations must be viewed in the light of the extended period of stagnation after 1979. The poor earnings performance explains why the cash position of corporations was weak for most of 1981 and why the downturn in the second half of 1981 found firms in a very vulnerable position with respect to their liquidity. During 1982 corporations made severe cutbacks in their investment, which simultaneously improved their liquidity positions but made the recession worse. Nevertheless, the economy did turn around at the end of the year, and the result can only be a further improvement in corporate liquidity, which has already been evident this year.

This essay has examined annual distributions of financial data pertaining to individual large manufacturing firms to see whether the aggregate picture for all nonfinancial corporations combined conceals areas of weakness the existence of which might alter our views about the nature of the recovery. Generally speaking, this detailed examination has not produced such a result, that is, it should not change our views about the economic expansion that is now in progress and in prospect at least through 1984. At the same time the detailed data point to some elements of weakness at the end of 1982, lending some support to the idea that the economy cannot go through as severe a recession as we have been through without some lasting effects on the solvency of some firms. Even with a good recovery, the rate of failure among business firms is likely to remain high in relation to the experience of the past several years.

I examined three measures of liquidity, or the ability of firms to meet their current obligations, paying special attention to firms with low liquidity ratios. The analysis of company liquidity ratios revealed that low rankings in a distribution of firms tend to be temporary rather than permanent and are not necessarily indicative of low profits. Still, at the end of 1982 the first quartile—embracing the firms in the bottom quarter of the distribution—was lower in relation to the median than at the end of other recessions. This pattern was apparent in all three liquidity ratios, although differences from early recessions were not great.

When short-term debt (debt due within one year) is high relative to total debt, firms may be especially vulnerable to disappointments in sales and profits. For this ratio I focused on the high end of the company distribution—the third quartile—relative to the median. By this measure 1982 occupied an intermediate position: worse than 1970 but not as bad as 1974. It may be that the heavy liquidation of short-term debt in late 1982, which is apparent in the quarterly aggregates, was accomplished with some sacrifice in liquidity. But my study of individual firms did not have quarterly data available for analysis. I also found that our sample companies increased their *long*-term debt ratios more rapidly than manufacturers in general from 1973 to 1979, suggesting a greater appreciation of long-term debt financing during inflation by large companies or greater access to capital markets than the average manufacturing firm would have.

If firms are weighed down with interest on indebtedness acquired when interest rates were high, that burden could conceivably stand in the way of a rise in fixed investment during the recovery of the economy. Interest burden is the ratio of interest paid to cash flow—the sum of retained earnings plus depreciation. Interest paid is measured two ways: gross, as interest expense, and net, or interest expense minus interest income. I focused on the high end of the distribution, which may include firms with negative cash flow. I found that between two recessions—1974 and 1982—the high end of the distribution (measured by the third quartile) had increased relative to the median for both gross and net burdens. This finding suggests a somewhat more burdensome condition than was indicated by the aggregates or by the medians of the individual firm distributions.

Appendix A. Description of Sample

The basic data presented in "Analysis of Individual Firm Data" came from Standard and Poor's Compustat primary file, which includes a group of some 850 major companies traded on the New York Stock Exchange, on the American Stock Exchange, and over the counter. The file embraces all the companies in Standard and Poor's 400 Industrials index. The information comes from annual reports to stockholders and from 10-K reports, which registered corporations must submit to the Securities and Exchange Commission. Generally speaking, the reporting unit is the consolidated worldwide corporation. This particular file contains both manufacturing and nonmanufacturing firms, but because the nonmanufacturing coverage is very limited, I decided to use only the manufacturing firms. A firm is given a single classification by Standard and Poor according to its major activity. The Compustat manufacturing file included about 550 firms in 1981.

The Compustat primary file contains 173 annual "data items," which are mainly items found on the balance sheet or on the profit-

and-loss statement. Balance sheet items refer to the end of the firm's fiscal year, whereas profit-and-loss items refer to the year as a whole. The data include firms with fiscal years ending in months other than December, but because I was interested in 1982 results and because of time constraints, my data tend to exclude most firms with fiscal years ending in the first half of 1983. My data include, however, 1982 reports of firms with fiscal years ending from July through November 1982, accounting for about one-sixth of the total.

The information that the American Enterprise Institute obtained for this study refers to annual data from 1963 to 1982, but not all companies reported all the items of concern in every year, so that the actual number of usable reports was considerably reduced. Furthermore, usable time series vary in length because Compustat did not begin to collect certain items until fairly recently. For any given table I prepared with time-series data, I usually limited myself to firms reporting the particular items of interest in each year. For some tables the number of reporting firms may differ slightly from year to year, but the number of firms analyzed varies, among different tables.

Time series for large worldwide corporations pose problems because of mergers and acquisitions, discontinued operations, and changes in accounting methods from one year to another. Registered corporations are required to "restate" their financial results by presenting back figures that are definitionally the same as those for the latest year. The Securities and Exchange Commission used to require five years of back data, but that figure has been changed to three. Compustat has a set of basic figures on a "restated" basis as well as on a reported "historical" (not restated) basis, but the detail pertaining to liquidity was so limited that I decided not to use the restated information. It is therefore hard to say what bias, if any, may exist in the data. Large firms tend, for example, to have lower ratios of cash and securities relative to current liabilities than small firms do. If the trend in mergers has been toward the absorption of small firms by big ones, then the omission of the distant historical information for the small firms would tend to understate the downward trend in this particular ratio. The relevant question is how important this distortion is. Accounting changes also pose problems. Big companies use LIFO much more frequently than small companies do. A trend toward using LIFO would bias downward a ratio of current assets to current liabilities. But I demonstrated the importance of this point in table 1, and although it obviously has some effect, it does not destroy the analysis.

Since the stock of many of these companies is listed on organized exchanges, which have profitability as well as size requirements, the Compustat sample is undoubtedly of greater than average longevity and is more profitable as well.

Appendix B. Glossary of Terms Used in Compustat Tabulations

Liquidity ratios are measures of a firm's ability to pay its current liabilities. This study refers to three such measures.

1. The *current ratio* is the ratio of *current assets* to *current liabilities*. Current assets include cash on hand and in banks, including time deposits, and government and other short-term securities, such as commercial and finance company paper; inventories; accounts receivable; and other current assets.

2. The *quick, or acid-test, ratio* is current assets, minus inventories, divided by current liabilities.

3. The *liquid assets ratio* is cash, government, and other short-term securities divided by current liabilities.

The *short-term debt ratio* is the ratio of short-term loans to the sum of short-term and long-term loans. "Short-term" includes current installments on long-term debt. A high short-term debt ratio may make a firm vulnerable to unexpected adverse events, such as sales disappointments.

Interest burden is the ability of a firm to meet its interest payments for a given year from its current cash flow. This paper uses both a gross interest measure (interest paid) and a net interest measure (interest paid minus interest received) divided by cash flow (profits after taxes, minus dividends, plus depreciation).

Notes

1. Liquidity, which deals with the ability and willingness to transform nonmoney assets into money, is intimately related to solvency. A firm is said to be "legally" insolvent when its liabilities exceed its assets and "technically" insolvent when it is unable to pay its bills on time (James C. Van Horne, *Fundamentals of Financial Management,* 3d ed. [Englewood Cliffs, N.J.: Prentice-Hall, 1977], p. 79).

2. The *Wall Street Journal* observed on March 31, 1983: "Fourteen big companies with more than $100 million in debt have lumbered into Chapter 11 proceedings in this young decade, 10 of them last year. Dozens more are involved in 'workouts'— . . . jargon for radical financial surgery—outside the bankruptcy process."

3. In the first eleven months of 1982, the rerating of bond quality of industrial and financial corporations by Standard and Poor's showed 79 percent down and 21 percent up. The annual results from 1975 to 1981 averaged 43 percent down and 57 percent up (basic data from Salomon Brothers, quoted in New York Stock Exchange, Office of Economic Research, *The Financial Health of U.S. Corporations* [New York, March 1983], p. 9).

4. Benjamin Friedman, "Financing Capital Formation in the 1980's: Issues for Public Policy," in M. L. Wachter and S. M. Wachter, eds., *Toward a New Industrial Policy* (Philadelphia: University of Pennsylvania Press, 1981), cited Gurley and Shaw, *Money in a Theory of Finance*, and Goldsmith, *Financial Intermediaries in the American Economy since 1900* and *Financial Structure and Development*, as sources that discuss this phenomenon.

5. The sketch below is based on Van Horne, *Fundamentals of Financial Management*, esp. chap. 5.

6. See the glossary of terms in appendix B.

7. Van Horne, *Fundamentals of Financial Management*, p. 79. Van Horne notes that differences in divisibility and durability are the main features distinguishing current from fixed assets.

8. At the end of 1981 the book value of inventories of nonfinancial corporations was 41 percent of total current assets.

9. William Fellner, "Corporate Asset-Liability Decisions in View of the Low Market Valuation of Equity," in Fellner, ed., *Contemporary Economic Problems 1980* (Washington, D.C.: American Enterprise Institute, 1980).

10. The flow-of-funds data include some intermediate-term bank loans (with maturities of more than one year) with short-term loans.

11. Friedman, "Financing Capital Formation in the 1980's," p. 117.

12. On average the short-term ratio has started to rise two to three quarters before the trough.

13. The theory of optimal inventory holdings at the firm level was developed by Thomas M. Whitin (see Whitin, *The Theory of Inventory Management* [Princeton, N.J.: Princeton University Press, 1953]). Baumol published a paper in 1952 that gave a theory of optimizing between cash and short-term securities: William J. Baumol, "The Transactions Demand for Cash: An Inventory Theoretic Approach," *Quarterly Journal of Economics*, vol. 46 (November 1952), pp. 545–56. Although there are other theories besides those to which I have referred, and questions have been raised regarding the usefulness of theoretical models of working capital management at the firm level, there can be little doubt that the rational approach to working capital management, which has taken the place of management by rule of thumb, has had an important effect on liquid asset holdings.

14. Some companies may have been able to earn higher returns on their short-term investments than from operations.

15. It has also been said that lenders were unwilling to make long-term loans with the price outlook so uncertain.

16. See "Effect of Disappointments on Borrowing" (p. 225, this volume) for further comments on this subject.

17. Goldman Sachs, "Financial Market Perspectives" (June 1983), p. 5.

18. Price disappointments do not necessarily mean that profit margins were disappointing, since the lower prices of some producers are the lower costs of others.

19. David I. Fisher, *Cash Management* (New York: Conference Board, 1973), p. i.

20. Formerly published by the Federal Trade Commission, now published by the Census Bureau.

21. Growth rates for the 1964–1979 period for the *QFR* series were obtained by averaging the 1964–1973 ratio (with a weight of 9) and the 1973–1979 ratio (with a weight of 6).

22. Note that the second column refers to the third quartile, or the quartile with high rather than low short-term debt ratios.

23. Retained earnings and depreciation are calculated on a book basis. Inflation has made the level of the interest burden lower on a book basis than it would be on the basis of the NIA concept of cash flow. When the rate of inflation subsides, however, as it did from 1981 to 1982, the interest burden on a book basis will appear high relative to the interest burden on the NIA basis.

24. Another difference is that the interest in table 6 includes imputations.

25. Office of Management and Budget, *Mid-Session Review of the 1984 Budget* (Washington, D.C., July 25, 1983).

26. See, for example, Goldman Sachs, "Financial Market Perspectives," pp. 5–6.

Disinflation in the Labor Market

Marvin H. Kosters

Summary

The major reduction in price inflation that was achieved during the recession of 1981–1982 was facilitated by the significant slowdown in hourly labor cost increases. This transition to smaller nominal wage increases has also created conditions that are critical for maintaining lower inflation as real economic growth is resumed and unemployed resources are more fully utilized. Because lower inflation can be maintained only if labor costs fall in line with slower nominal demand growth, the labor market adjustments that have occurred contributed to the political feasibility of pursuing policies consistent with lower inflation and enhanced the credibility of such policies.

The two recessions of the 1970s also brought about slowdowns in the rate of increase in hourly labor costs. But the extent of the adjustments that occurred was quite limited, especially in 1970–1971, and the brief contraction of 1980 produced virtually no slowdown in wage increases. The response of wages to slower inflation has not been closely comparable across business cycles, and differences have been particularly marked for union wage increases.

Differences in wage behavior across business cycles have been in part attributable to differences in the severity and duration of cycles. Still, other factors were also at work, particularly in the case of union wage settlements. Differences in union wage settlements over business cycles have been in part a result of the increased importance of cost-of-living escalator provisions since the late 1960s, but the response of union wage settlements during recessions has also been influenced by changes in relative wages that developed before the recessions. Wages of workers covered by long-term contracts, for example, had eroded in relation to wages of other workers in the economy before the 1970–1971 recession, but they had increased markedly in the last part of the 1970s. Although unions account for a relatively small fraction of the work force, the large union settlements in 1970–1971 contributed to the momentum of wage inflation at that time, but small union settlements contributed to the slowdown in wage increases in 1981–1982.

The assistance of Murray Ross in preparing this essay is gratefully acknowledged.

247

The slowdown in wage increases in 1981–1982 reflected, in addition to the recession, increased competition in product and labor markets. Two important sources of more vigorous competition were deregulation in the transportation sector and stronger competition from international sources, especially in several durable goods manufacturing industries. The combination of recession and increased competition resulted in renegotiated wage agreements and new settlements that in some cases actually reduced wages and in general provided sharply lower wage increases than had been provided by the formulas in earlier agreements.

The adjustment to smaller increases in labor costs that has occurred is consistent with inflation much lower than that experienced in the late 1970s. Changes in competitive conditions contributed to this adjustment, and the more competitive conditions will presumably contribute to keeping labor cost increases down after the recession has passed, provided that inflationary pressures from excessively rapid nominal demand growth are avoided.

Introduction

The decline in inflation since the Federal Reserve announced the shift in its policy procedures late in 1979 has been extraordinarily large. Following consumer price increases of more than 13 percent in 1979 and more than 12 percent in 1980, prices rose by less than 4 percent during 1982. The sharp decline in inflation took place in the context of a severe recession, however, that brought the unemployment rate to more than 10 percent. Although this reduction in inflation reflects, in part, transitory and cyclical elements such as the surge in oil prices in 1979 and the subsequent decline in these and other basic materials prices, the decline is mainly attributable to slower price and cost increases that were spread widely throughout the economy.

The recession of the 1970s also produced significant reductions in price inflation, but slower price inflation was not accompanied by correspondingly smaller hourly labor cost increases. The cost in unemployment and depressed production of maintaining low inflation or reducing it further depends importantly on the extent to which labor cost trends fall in line with slower nominal demand growth. With labor cost trend adjustments that were slow and incomplete during the recessions of the 1970s, turns toward expansion in nominal demand growth were followed by resurgence in inflation during cyclical recovery.

The recession of 1981–1982 has resulted in a far more pronounced decline in the rate of increase in hourly labor costs than the recessions of the 1970s did. Although this more recent recession was also somewhat more severe, the size and timing of the labor cost response seem to go beyond what might be attributed to the severity of the recession.

The more extensive, timely, and complete adjustment in labor cost trends to lower price inflation that has been achieved during this recession enhances the prospects for maintaining a lower rate of inflation during the recovery and thus lends credibility to anti-inflationary policies.

Recent labor market developments are examined in this essay in the context of developments during earlier postwar recessions. Differences in labor market behavior and conditions are discussed, and sources of increased competition that have contributed to labor market adjustments since the late 1970s are described. The adjustment in hourly labor cost trends that has already occurred, together with increased competition in the labor market and pressures for still further adjustments, points toward the prospect of maintaining a lower inflation path than has prevailed since the late 1960s if excessive nominal demand growth is avoided.

Postwar Inflation and Labor Cost Trends

The behavior of inflation and labor costs is similar over business cycles in certain important respects, but there are also major differences. These differences relate in part to differences in inflation experience in the period preceding the cycle and in part to changes in conditions and practices between business cycles. To place recent developments in perspective, it is useful to review experience in broad terms during the past thirty-five years.

Perhaps the most noteworthy development in the postwar period is that rates of inflation in the mid- and late 1970s moved to much higher levels than previously, as shown in figure 1. The peak inflation rates of 1950–1951 and 1969 fell far short of double-digit rates, even though these rates were high in comparison with rates during most of the 1950s and 1960s. A second feature is that variation in annual inflation rates has been much larger since the late 1960s than previously. The brief surge in inflation at the outbreak of the Korean War after the post–World War II inflation had subsided shows the only comparable variability. The third feature is the upward trend in unemployment during the 1970s. Annual average unemployment rates during recession years before the mid-1970s were in a range roughly comparable to the lowest rate reached in 1979 near the peak of a cyclical expansion.

As shown in figure 1, the 1981–1982 recession has brought the third major interruption in the trend toward higher inflation since the mid-1960s. It is worth noting in passing that these annual data do not show any identifiable cyclical effects of the brief recession during 1980. The two high inflation peaks of the 1970s coincided with periods

249

FIGURE 1
Wages, Prices, and Unemployment, 1948–1982

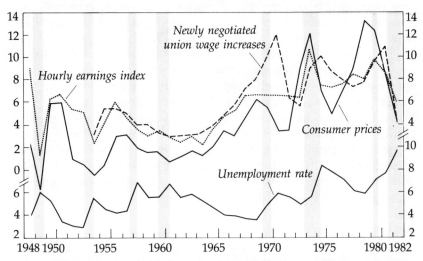

Note: Consumer prices: percentage change in consumer price index, December to December. Hourly earnings index: percentage change in adjusted hourly earnings, fourth quarter to fourth quarter; data are seasonally adjusted and are adjusted for interindustry employment shifts and for overtime (in manufacturing only); data for 1948–1963 include only manufacturing; data for 1964–1982 cover the private nonfarm economy. Newly negotiated union wage increases: median first-year wage adjustments of major collective bargaining agreements (covering 1,000 workers or more). Unemployment rate: annual average civilian unemployment rate. Shaded areas mark recessions, peak to trough, based on reference cycles established by the National Bureau of Economic Research.
Source: Bureau of Labor Statistics.

of rapid oil price increases, although this coincidence was only one element in the picture and was not present during the 1969 peak. Whether this most recent interruption in inflation will also prove to be only temporary will obviously depend on what kinds of demand expansion policies are pursued. The significant decline in labor cost increases that has occurred does provide encouragement, however, that a sharply lower rate of inflation than was experienced during most of the past decade can be maintained without incurring costs in unemployment that compare unfavorably with our experience during the 1970s.

Before examining wage trends in more detail, we should note the unusual behavior of new first-year wage increases under major collective bargaining settlements that were reached during the 1969–1970 recession.[1] Before this recession, increases in hourly earnings and new collective bargaining settlements moved roughly parallel with consumer price increases but at a rate approximately three percentage points higher, corresponding roughly to the rate of productivity growth during that part of the postwar period. In 1970 and 1971, however, newly negotiated collective bargaining settlements far outpaced consumer price increases, contributing importantly to the failure of broader measures of hourly labor cost increases to slow down very much during the recession. During the decade of the 1970s, when productivity growth slowed to negligible proportions, average wage increases slowed in relation to price increases, although this slowdown was quite uneven among industries.

In retrospect, it seems hardly surprising that analysts examining labor market performance in the early 1970s reached pessimistic conclusions about the feasibility of bringing down inflation by exercising demand restraint. The response of new wage settlements under major collective bargaining agreements to slack demand and lower inflation was initially perverse, and there was only a small and gradual decline in average wage increases. Labor cost trends, with appropriate allowance for productivity growth, cannot remain inconsistent with price trends for long. When demand growth is reduced, lower inflation can be maintained only if labor cost trends adjust downward. If wage trends prove inflexible in response to demand restraint, output and employment are depressed more severely. What happens to overall real output and utilization of resources, especially labor resources, influences the general political acceptability of a disinflation program—and therefore its prospects for being continued. The flexibility of wage trends in response to slower demand growth and declining price inflation is consequently a key factor influencing the credibility of disinflationary policies.

Trends in Unionism and Collective Bargaining

Although union members account for a relatively small and declining fraction of the work force, union wage developments are nevertheless quite important. For one thing, wages of a larger number of workers than those who are union members are affected by union agreements. Wages of some workers who are not union members are set directly by collective bargaining agreements. A larger group of workers receive wage increases closely comparable to those of workers under union agreements, either because they are employed in nonunion plants of firms that employ mainly union members or because they are nonproduction employees in union firms.[2]

The public attention that is given to union wage settlements fre-

251

quently seems disproportionate in view of the small fraction of the work force that is affected. New union wage settlements are widely reported for several reasons: visibility of union wage developments is heightened because of the large number of workers covered by a single decision; new wage decisions are reached only periodically (often at three-year intervals) and establish wage arrangements for the future; settlements occur in the context of potential or actual strikes that disrupt related economic activity; and major settlements are often the dominant influence on wages set for entire industries. In addition, several highly unionized industries are composed of a few large firms producing important products, such as steel and automobiles. In these industries both labor and management are generally well organized to exert influence on national policy to further their economic interests.

Union membership has increased only slightly during the past twenty-five years, and with a growing labor force, this small increase has produced a decline in the fraction unionized from about one-quarter to less than one-fifth, as shown in the first two columns of table 1. In addition, some 2 to 3 million workers are members of associations that engage in collective bargaining and therefore have wage-setting practices comparable to those of unions.[3] These association members are virtually all public sector employees, and including them would bring the fraction of the work force organized to about 21 percent in 1980.

The slight upward trend in overall union membership is entirely attributable to growth among government workers; private sector union membership has been extraordinarily stable. The downward trend in the fraction unionized in the private sector has consequently been more pronounced than that for the labor force as a whole. As shown in column 5 of table 1, the fraction of the private sector work force unionized declined from about 28 percent in the mid-1950s to less than 20 percent by the late 1970s. By 1982 private sector unionization declined to an estimated 15.8 percent, reflecting in part the disproportionate impact of the recession on several highly unionized industries.[4] About half of private sector union members were covered by major collective bargaining settlements at the beginning of the period, with the proportion in large bargaining situations somewhat larger after the mid-1960s.

The use of cost-of-living escalator clauses spread quite rapidly after they were initially introduced in automobile industry contracts in 1948. In the late 1950s about half the workers under major agreements were covered, but this fraction declined to 20 percent by 1966. More inflationary conditions brought escalator coverage to about 60 percent in the late 1970s, extending it to most workers under long-term agree-

TABLE 1

TRENDS IN UNIONIZATION, PRIVATE SECTOR COLLECTIVE BARGAINING, AND
COST-OF-LIVING ESCALATOR COVERAGE, 1956–1982

	Union Membership in the Economy[a]		Sectoral Union Membership[a]			Workers Covered by Major Collective Bargaining Agreements[c]	
Year	Total workers (millions)	Percentage of civilian labor force	Govern-ment workers (millions)	Private workers (millions)	Private as percentage of private labor force[b] (percent)	Total workers (millions)	Workers with escalators (percent)
1956	17.5	26.3	0.9	16.6	28.0	—	—
1957	17.4	26.0				7.8	44.9
1958	17.0	25.2	1.0	16.0	26.7	8.0	50.0
1959	17.1	25.0				8.0	50.0
1960	17.0	24.5	1.1	16.0	26.1	8.1	49.4
1961	16.3	23.1				8.1	32.8
1962	16.6	23.5	1.2	15.4	24.9	8.0	31.3
1963	16.5	23.0				7.8	23.7
1964	16.8	23.0	1.5	15.4	24.2	7.8	25.6
1965	17.3	23.2				7.9	25.3
1966	17.9	23.7	1.7	16.2	25.0	10.0	20.0
1967	18.4	23.7				10.6	20.8
1968	18.9	24.0	2.2	16.8	25.1	10.6	23.2
1969	19.0	23.6				10.8	24.6
1970	19.4	23.4	2.3	17.1	24.3	10.8	25.9
1971	19.2	22.8				10.8	27.8
1972	19.4	22.3	2.5	17.0	23.0	10.6	40.6
1973	19.9	22.2				10.4	39.4
1974	20.2	22.0	2.9	17.3	22.2	10.2	39.2
1975	19.6	20.9				10.3	51.5
1976	19.6	20.4	3.0	16.6	20.4	10.1	59.4
1977	19.7	19.9				9.8	61.2
1978	20.2	19.8	3.6	16.6	19.2	9.6	60.4
1979	20.1	19.1				9.5	58.9
1980	19.8	18.6	3.7[d]	16.1[d]	17.8[d]	9.3	58.1
1981						9.1	58.2
1982	18.6[d]	16.9[d]	3.7[d]	14.9[d]	15.8[d]	9.0	56.7

a. Includes all affiliates of the American Federation of Labor–Congress of Industrial Organizations (AFL–CIO), unaffiliated national unions, and all unaffiliated unions party to interstate collective bargaining agreements; excludes employee associations and single-firm and local unaffiliated unions.

ments. By the end of the 1970s workers covered by major collective bargaining agreements accounted for less than 10 percent of the work force, and only about 5 percent of the work force was accounted for by the class of agreements that have generally received the most public attention—major long-term agreements in the private sector with cost-of-living escalator provisions.

Much of the discussion in this essay is devoted to wage developments under long-term major collective bargaining agreements in the private sector. These wage developments have been more significant for national labor market and stabilization policies than might be suggested by the number of workers and the fraction of the work force directly affected. These overall magnitudes and trends should nevertheless be kept in mind in order to place in perspective the influence of major union wage developments on labor costs in the economy.

Collective Bargaining and Overall Wage Changes

Although data are available in less detail before the mid-1960s, they indicate that average wage increases and collective bargaining settlements responded quite promptly to cyclical changes during the 1950s and that both inflation and wage trends were extraordinarily stable during the first half of the 1960s. By the middle of the 1960s, more

---

(Notes to table 1 continued)

b. Private labor force = civilian labor force less government employees.

c. Major collective bargaining agreements are those covering 1,000 or more workers. Escalators refers to clauses in bargaining agreements that link wage increases to changes in some price index; "guaranteed" cost-of-living adjustments are excluded.

d. The surveys of union membership by the Bureau of Labor Statistics were discontinued in 1980, and sectoral breakdowns of union membership were not published after 1978. These estimates extending the series through 1982 were constructed by relying primarily on data reported by the AFL-CIO, which accounts for about 80 percent of union membership. Estimates of total union membership were made by adjusting the AFL-CIO figures for reaffiliation by the United Automobile Workers in 1980 and differences in membership reporting between the Bureau of Labor Statistics and the unions and checking the resulting estimates against reported membership changes in other unions. Public sector union membership estimates assume a stable rate of growth of the fraction of union members in the public sector. The resulting public sector estimates are consistent with data reported by the largest public sector unions accounting for three-fifths of public sector membership, which show virtually no growth between 1980 and 1982.

SOURCES: Data on union membership are from Bureau of Labor Statistics, *Directory of National Unions and Employee Associations*, various years, and *Directory of U.S. Labor Organizations, 1982–1983* (Washington, D.C.: BNA Books, 1982). Data on major collective bargaining agreements are from Bureau of Labor Statistics, *Current Wage Developments*, February 1974, and *Monthly Labor Review*, January 1983.

detailed data on wage increases under major collective bargaining agreements were available, a pattern of three-year contracts had evolved in many industries, and new contracts were negotiated in cycles that remained quite stable through the 1970s. Other important changes that occurred, however, contributed to differences in wage behavior over business cycles. The main changes influencing relationships between the different measures of wage increases were the acceleration of inflation during the late 1960s and the subsequent spread of cost-of-living escalator provisions to compensate for the erosion in real wages that could otherwise result from inflation over the duration of long-term contracts.

In each of the major slowdowns in inflation since the beginning of the 1970s, wage increases under newly negotiated bargaining settlements responded with a lag to smaller price increases and higher unemployment. Not only was the lag in 1970 and 1971 particularly long, but the level of new wage settlements was extremely high compared with that of either consumer price increases or overall increases in labor costs. This pattern, unusual by comparison with later business cycles, can be traced, at least in part, to wage developments in the last part of the 1960s.

As shown in figure 2, increases in the broadly based hourly earnings index were larger than median wage increases that went into effect for workers covered by major collective bargaining agreements in each year from 1965 through 1969. Consumer price inflation rose from 1.9 percent during 1965 to 6.1 percent during 1969. This was also a period in which the fraction of workers who were covered by escalator provisions in long-term contracts was quite low (as shown in table 1) and escalator formulas had relatively low limits (or "caps") on the payoffs they provided in response to price increases. Newly negotiated wage increases, on the other hand, were consistently larger than increases in average wages, with a gap that widened from 1969 through 1971. The three-year wage contracts expiring in 1970 and 1971 had been negotiated on the basis of experience with inflation rates near 3 percent, which contrast with peak inflation rates of about 6 percent in 1969 and 1970. The very large newly negotiated wage increases in 1971, and the rise of union wage increases above the average for other workers in the economy in 1969 and 1970, can in large part be attributed to pressures for union wages to "catch up"—in relation both to other wages and to prices—after falling behind during the earlier period of rising inflation.

These large newly negotiated wage increases, particularly from 1969 through 1971, were not exclusively the result of new settlements following the expiration of three-year agreements. Wage settlements

FIGURE 2
WAGE INCREASES FOR MAJOR UNIONS AND IN THE PRIVATE ECONOMY, 1965–1982

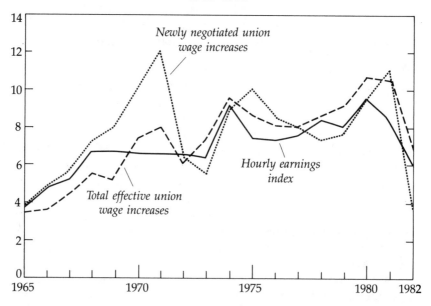

NOTE: Newly negotiated union wage increases: median wage adjustments effective in the first year of major collective bargaining agreements. Total effective union wage increases: median wage adjustments for all workers under major collective bargaining agreements; these data include adjustments during the year that result from deferred wage increases and cost-of-living escalator provisions in addition to wage increases under new settlements. Hourly earnings index: percentage change in private nonfarm hourly earnings index, fourth quarter to fourth quarter.
SOURCE: Bureau of Labor Statistics.

in the construction industry were also extraordinarily large at this time, and one- or two-year contracts were common in construction.[5] Although these large construction settlements pushed up the average for workers covered by major collective bargaining agreements, the pattern of rising newly negotiated wage settlements was essentially the same in manufacturing, where the peak increase was 10 percent in 1971, as compared with the 12.2 percent peak for all industries shown in figure 2.

After 1971 disparities between the two measures of union wage increases and average wage increases in the economy were quite small and less persistent than previously. It is noteworthy that, in contrast to the period before 1970, median wage increases for all the union workers covered by major collective bargaining were larger than increases in the hourly earnings index in every year after 1972. Newly negotiated first-year wage increases, on the other hand, were generally smaller than wage increases that went into effect for union workers as a whole. The increased use of cost-of-living escalator provisions, with generally higher limits on the increases they provided, and more generous payoff formulas made annual union wage increases much more responsive to changes in inflation. At the same time, however, the combination of fixed annual wage increases (based on productivity trends estimated in the 1960s that were higher than those realized in the 1970s) and cost-of-living escalator provisions produced union wage increases larger than those for the average worker. As a consequence, union wage increases were persistently larger than increases in the hourly earnings index after 1972, a reversal of the pattern that prevailed before the 1970s.

Changes in the effects of cost-of-living escalator provisions for workers under major collective bargaining agreements are shown in table 2. The percentage of these workers under agreements that included cost-of-living escalator provisions rose from about 20 percent in the mid-1960s to about 60 percent in the last part of the 1970s. During this latter period the fraction of workers under major agreements with escalator provisions was approximately equal to the fraction of workers covered by three-year wage contracts.[6] The construction industry, in which agreements usually extend for only one or two years, apparently accounted for about half the workers not covered by three-year agreements.

The contributions to average wage increases that resulted from escalator provisions reflect both changes in coverage and changes in inflation. Only some 5 percent of average wage adjustments in 1968 and 1969, for example, was attributable to payments under escalator provisions, but escalator provisions accounted for about 25 percent in 1975 and almost 35 percent in 1979. During 1976, the low point of inflation in the mid-1970s, escalator payments accounted for about 20 percent of overall wage adjustments for workers covered by major collective bargaining agreements. In 1982, when inflation dropped dramatically, the contribution of escalators dropped to less than half its average for the preceding three years of high inflation, and it accounted for about 20 percent of the overall wage increase. Escalator formulas, of course, provide their payoffs only after a lag, and consequently changes in escalator payments during any given year do not fully reflect the effects of the inflation rate that prevailed during the same year.

TABLE 2

EFFECTIVE WAGE RATE ADJUSTMENTS UNDER MAJOR
COLLECTIVE BARGAINING AGREEMENTS, 1968–1982

	Total Wage Adjustment, All Industries	Source of Adjustment		
Year		Current settlement	Prior settlement	Escalation provisions
1968	6.0	3.2	2.4	0.3
1969	6.5	2.4	3.8	0.3
1970	8.8	5.1	3.1	0.6
1971	9.2	4.3	4.2	0.7
1972	6.6	1.7	4.2	0.7
1973	7.0	3.0	2.7	1.3
1974	9.4	4.8	2.6	1.9
1975	8.7	2.8	3.7	2.2
1976	8.1	3.2	3.2	1.6
1977	8.0	3.0	3.2	1.7
1978	8.2	2.0	3.7	2.4
1979	9.1	3.0	3.0	3.1
1980	9.9	3.6	3.5	2.8
1981	9.5	2.5	3.8	3.2
1982	6.7	1.7	3.6	1.4

NOTE: Total wage adjustments measure the increase in wages (as a percentage of straight-time hourly earnings) effective during the year. Adjustments resulting from current settlements reflect wage increases in newly negotiated agreements; adjustments resulting from prior settlements include both deferred increases and "guaranteed" components of payments under cost-of-living escalator provisions; and adjustments resulting from escalator provisions include wage increases explicitly contingent on changes in the revelant price index.

SOURCE: Bureau of Labor Statistics, *Current Wage Developments*, various issues.

Wage Changes for Union and Nonunion Workers

Comparisons of union and nonunion wage increases are available for the manufacturing sector for the twenty-year period from 1959 through 1978. For the first half of the period, only medians are available. Beginning in 1976 measures of union and nonunion wage increases are available from the employment cost index. This index covers all private industry workers, but it includes data for manufacturing workers only.

These data for manufacturing (table 3, part A) show first-year union wage increases and effective wage increases for union and nonunion workers that were roughly comparable during the early 1960s. Median wage increases that went into effect were somewhat larger for

TABLE 3
UNION AND NONUNION WAGE INCREASES, 1959–1982

A. Manufacturing Wage Changes

Year	First-Year Union[a]	Total Effective Change[a]		First-Year Union[b]	Total Effective Change[b]	
		Union	Nonunion		Union	Nonunion
1959	3.4	3.4	3.3	—	—	—
1960	3.4	3.4	2.5	—	—	—
1961	2.5	2.7	1.0	—	—	—
1962	2.5	2.6	1.6	—	—	—
1963	2.6	2.6	2.8	—	—	—
1964	2.3	2.2	2.0	—	—	—
1965	3.4	2.9	3.2	—	—	—
1966	4.0	3.2	3.9	—	—	—
1967	5.5	4.0	4.6	—	—	—
1968	6.4	5.0	5.0	—	—	—
1969	6.9	5.0	5.1	7.3	5.3	4.6
1970	7.3	5.7	5.1	7.6	6.4	4.7
1971	8.2	6.1	4.7	9.2	7.1	4.0
1972	5.5	5.2	5.0	5.7	5.4	4.4
1973	5.7	6.2	5.6	6.0	6.4	6.0
1974	7.5	8.0	8.0	8.1	8.7	7.7
1975	8.6	8.2	6.3	8.7	8.1	5.9
1976	8.3	7.7	6.5	8.4	7.8	6.1
1977	8.3	8.0	6.5	7.9	7.7	6.0
1978	8.0	8.3	7.2	7.9	8.0	6.8

B. Employment Cost Index

Year	Manufacturing Wages and Salaries		Private Industry Wages and Salaries		Private Industry Compensation	
	Union	Nonunion	Union	Nonunion	Union	Nonunion
1976	—	—	8.1	6.8	—	—
1977	8.3	7.4	7.6	6.6	—	—
1978	8.7	7.9	8.0	7.6	—	—
1979	9.4	7.9	9.0	7.6	—	—
1980	11.0	7.9	10.9	8.0	—	—
1981	8.9	8.3	9.6	8.5	10.7	9.4
1982	5.8	5.6	6.5	6.1	7.2	6.0

NOTES: The upper panel of table 3, "Manufacturing Wage Changes," reports data on wage changes in the manufacturing sector for union workers covered by collective bargaining agreements and for nonunion workers employed by firms that normally grant general wage increases. (Firms that adjust wages on the basis of merit or seniority, nonunion than for union workers from 1965 through 1967. Beginning in 1965, however, new wage increases for union workers began to exceed wage increases placed in effect for both union and nonunion workers, and this pattern continued through 1972. By 1970 effective wage increases for union workers exceeded those for nonunion workers. Although effective union wage increases were consistently larger than for nonunion workers throughout the 1970s, a large fraction of these increases was produced by cost-of-living escalator provisions in long-term wage contracts. After 1972 first-year union wage increases were again roughly comparable to wage increases going into effect for union workers as a whole.

These data on union and nonunion wage increases in manufacturing are broadly consistent with those in the comparison made earlier (figure 2) between wage increases under major collective bargaining agreements and the hourly earnings index. Both show somewhat larger average wage increases for nonunion than for union workers in the late 1960s, large first-year union wage increases from the last part of the 1960s through 1971, and union wage increases somewhat larger than for nonunion workers for the next decade. In manufacturing, as for the economy as a whole, this pattern was in large part the result of change from weak cost-of-living escalator protection in the late 1960s, when inflation was accelerating, to extensive use of escalators by the mid-1970s. In manufacturing, for example, the fraction of manufacturing workers under union agreements with escalators doubled from

---

(Notes to table 3 continued)

for example, are excluded.) Effective wage adjustments for union workers are percentage increases in straight-time average hourly earnings resulting from previously negotiated agreements, deferred increases from previously negotiated agreements, and COLA provisions. For nonunion workers, adjustments reflect wage changes that went into effect during the period. First-year measures for union workers include all changes negotiated during the year and scheduled to go into effect during the first twelve months of the contract.

The lower panel of the table, "Employment Cost Index," reports changes in wages and salaries and in compensation for manufacturing and for the private nonfarm economy. The wages and salaries index is based on straight-time average hourly earnings. Compensation includes, in addition, the cost of employer-supplied benefits (such as pensions and social security). The employment cost index is not limited to production and nonsupervisory workers (in contrast to the manufacturing data in the upper panel of the table) but instead includes wages of all employees. Since this index is based on wage scales for specific occupations and industries, it is in principle not affected by employment shifts within and among industries.

Dashes indicate data not available.

a. Median adjustment (percent).

b. Mean adjustment (percent).

SOURCE: Bureau of Labor Statistics, *Current Wage Developments*, various issues.

the mid-1960s to the mid-1970s, rising from about 15 percent to more than 30 percent. One effect of widespread cost-of-living escalator provisions for workers under long-term contracts was to reduce the tendency for cumulative disparities in relative wages during a period with wide swings in the inflation rate. The temporary, cyclical changes in wage alignment that took place in the late 1960s were experienced to only a limited extent during the 1970s.

The combination of escalator provisions and fixed annual wage increases under many long-term agreements, however, gradually raised wages in several highly unionized industries relative to wages in the rest of the economy. During the last part of the 1970s, when inflation was unusually high and productivity growth had virtually disappeared, union wage increases were consistently larger than non-union increases. This disparity is evident both within manufacturing and for the private sector as a whole, as shown by union and nonunion wage comparisons from the employment cost index. To the extent that a pattern-setting influence of major union wage agreements was significant, it seems to have been confined largely to relationships among wages in highly unionized sectors rather than extending to wages elsewhere in the economy.[7]

Sectoral Collective Bargaining Cycles

Long-term collective bargaining agreements became quite prevalent as wage-setting arrangements in the union sector during the postwar years. Most workers covered by long-term major collective bargaining agreements and most workers in very large bargaining situations were covered by three-year contracts. Despite occasional strikes and delays in reaching settlements, the expiration dates of these contracts assumed considerable stability after the mid-1960s.

This relatively stable pattern of contract expirations and schedules for new negotiations created a system of overlapping long-term contracts. To the extent that pressures for maintaining relationships among wages set by these contracts were significant, this system tended to set wage trends that were not quickly diverted by changes in economic conditions that lasted for only a year or two. Increased use of cost-of-living escalator provisions during the late 1960s and the 1970s did, however, make wages set under these long-term contracts more responsive to changes in inflation than previously. But wage increases under escalator provisions were only one component of the bargaining agreement, and other components of the wage-setting formulas were usually modified only upon expiration of contracts. A three-year cycle evolved for these long-term agreements that by the late 1960s comprised two years of heavy bargaining followed by a light bargaining year (1969 and 1972, for example), this three-year cycle remaining substantially unchanged until the early 1980s.

The typical pattern of wage increases under these long-term agreements brought the largest increases when agreements were negotiated, with smaller increases scheduled for the two subsequent years. With expanding cost-of-living escalator coverage and higher inflation during the 1970s, however, wage increases actually realized during the second and third years of agreements became more closely comparable in size to first-year wage increases negotiated in the same year.

To review the pattern of major collective bargaining settlements and their effects on wage trends, this section examines changes in average hourly earnings in seven industry sectors from 1965 through 1982. As shown in table 4, the timing of contract expirations and new negotiations affecting these sectors remained quite stable over the period. The reported annual increases in average hourly earnings, of course, reflect factors in addition to collective bargaining. These data are not adjusted for overtime, changes in employment mix, or effects of strikes. In addition, for some manufacturing industries, such as electrical equipment, only a relatively small fraction of workers is covered by collective bargaining in the two largest firms that were used to establish the timing of contract expirations. Even in the automobile industry, as another example, wage developments are affected mainly by the three dominant firms, but different timing is applicable to the fourth.

These seven industry sectors were chosen on the basis of their regularity of contract timing and the feasibility of identifying particular bargaining situations with an industry sector affected. Three-year bargaining cycles that were quite stable were also present in other industries, but in several of these other industries, such as aerospace and agricultural machinery, industry wage increases were affected by other wage decisions with different timing. In still other industries, such as airlines, wage increases were affected by agreements with several unions, but these unions were not on the same three-year cycle. Nevertheless, the seven industries included in table 4 account for about half the workers outside the construction industry who were covered by major collective bargaining agreements.

The data reported in table 4 make the tendency for larger wage increases to be realized during the first year of new agreements especially noticeable before 1973, although there is a great deal of variation in the size of increases. In order to examine the systematic differences between wage increases under newly negotiated agreements and wage increases under existing contracts for these seven industries,

TABLE 4

SECTORAL CHANGES IN AVERAGE HOURLY EARNINGS FOR SEVEN INDUSTRY
SECTORS AFFECTED BY MAJOR COLLECTIVE BARGAINING AGREEMENTS,
1965–1982
(percent)

Year	Coal	Steel	Electrical Equipment	Auto-mobiles	Meat Packing	Trucking	Telephone Communica-tions
1965	4.5	1.5 [a]	3.6	5.0 [a]	2.7	3.6	3.0
1966	7.1 [a]	2.9	3.1 [a]	3.4	4.6	2.2	3.3
1967	0.3	2.8	5.2	1.4	3.5 [a]	3.1 [a]	2.1
1968	7.2	5.8 [a]	6.4	11.9 [a]	8.2	6.6	9.3 [a]
1969	9.6 [a]	6.8	4.3	4.1	6.5	5.3	3.5
1970	8.1	3.2	6.7 [a]	1.9	8.7 [a]	9.8 [a]	4.6
1971	0.4	13.2 [a]	6.0	12.9 [a]	3.2	14.0	11.7 [a]
1972	13.5 [a]	9.0	6.8	10.7	8.5	8.7	11.5
1973	8.6	10.0	5.8 [a]	6.0	6.3 [a]	8.6 [a]	9.1
1974	9.6	15.3 [a]	10.2	12.3 [a]	10.2	7.6	13.5 [a]
1975	14.8 [a]	9.8	7.9	9.2	8.0	5.3	13.0
1976	6.0	8.0	8.0 [a]	7.8	7.6 [a]	8.1 [a]	11.2
1977	5.7	13.2 [a]	7.5	10.9 [a]	8.0	9.7	10.5 [a]
1978	17.8 [a]	11.6	7.9	10.3	8.0	9.0	6.3
1979	5.6	10.2	8.8 [a]	4.9	8.9 [a]	9.3 [a]	8.8
1980	7.4	10.4 [a]	11.3	17.7 [a]	9.8	9.8	10.0 [a]
1981	5.9 [a]	9.0	8.2	9.3	5.0	6.6	11.8
1982	6.1	5.4	6.6 [a]	2.4 [a]	−3.3 [a]	2.7 [a]	6.7

NOTE: All figures are changes from fourth quarter to fourth quarter. The specific industry categories that were used for this analysis are from the following standard industrial classifications (SIC codes are in parentheses): Bituminous Coal and Lignite Mining (12); Blast Furnace and Basic Steel Products (331); Electric and Electronic Equipment (36); Motor Vehicles and Car Bodies (3711); Meatpacking Plants (2011); Trucking and Trucking Terminals (4213); Telephone Communications (481). These industrial categories were chosen to reflect, insofar as feasible, the effects of major collective bargaining agreements covering workers in these industries. In some industries, such as electric equipment and meat packing, only a small fraction of the workers are covered by the collective bargaining agreements with timing of expiration noted in the table.

a. Newly negotiated wage increases went into effect during the year.

SOURCES: *Employment and Earnings, United States, 1909–1978*, 1979; *Employment and Earnings, Supplement*, July 1983.

compare average wage increases in these industries with increases in the consumer price index, and trace the behavior of wages over the business cycle, annual data computed from table 4 are displayed in figure 3. The spread shown in the figure is the difference in each year

FIGURE 3

PRICES AND WAGE BEHAVIOR IN SEVEN INDUSTRY SECTORS, 1965–1982

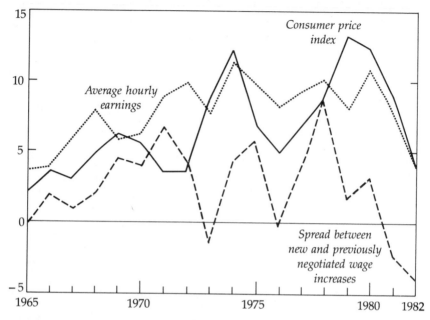

NOTE: Consumer price index: percentage change, December to December. Average hourly earnings: percentage increase for seven industry sectors (unweighted), fourth quarter to fourth quarter. Spread between new and previously negotiated wage increases: percentage increase in average hourly earnings for industries in which new settlements occurred (unweighted average) less percentage increase in average hourly earnings in industries in which wages are adjusted under existing contracts (unweighted), fourth quarter to fourth quarter. (See table 4 and notes for identification of industry sectors and of industry and year in which new settlements occurred.)

SOURCES: Table 4 and Bureau of Labor Statistics.

between wage increases affected by new negotiations and increases that took place in the absence of new negotiations. As shown in the figure, wage increases under newly negotiated contracts were consistently larger than those that occurred during the term of existing contracts from 1966 through 1972. Indeed, the spread continued to widen during the recession through 1971, contributing importantly to rising wage increases in these industries and to the resistance to a slowdown in average wage increases in the economy.

In contrast to this pattern at the beginning of the 1970s, average wage increases for these industries later in this period were influenced only to a small extent by the spread between the size of wage increases that resulted from newly negotiated agreements and those resulting from the wage-setting formulas in existing agreements.[8] Moreover, both average wage increases in these industries and the spread associated with new negotiations responded much more quickly at the end of the decade to the recession and the slowdown in consumer price inflation than in the two previous cycles. Again, the most important factor contributing to this change in behavior was the operation of escalator provisions. Wage behavior was affected in two important ways by escalator provisions at the end of the 1970s and at the beginning of the 1980s. Rising inflation was translated by cost-of-living escalators into larger wage increases during the term of contracts, reducing the tendency for wages under existing contracts to fall behind those covered by new negotiations at three-year intervals. But escalator provisions also translated a decline in inflation, such as that from 1980 to 1982, into smaller wage increases under existing contracts.

Another factor that contributed to slower wage increases in several industries after 1980 was the dramatic increase in wage premiums that has occurred since the early 1970s in all but two of the seven industries (see table 5). In some of these industry sectors, the increase in relative wages during the decade before 1982 was quite pronounced. In the coal and automobile industries, for example, where wages averaged 40 percent higher than wages in the private nonfarm economy in the late 1960s, relative wages rose further by about 20 percent. In the steel and telephone communications industries, relative wages rose by about 30 percent from wage premiums of 35 and 8 percent, respectively, in the late 1960s. Only in meat packing did the wage premium decline by a few percentage points in 1982 from a 22 percent premium in the late 1960s. The renegotiation of agreements in the automobile industry in 1982 and in the steel industry in 1983 apparently occurred in response to job losses produced by the combination of recession and increased competition from abroad affecting these industries; wage premiums had become unsustainably high, although there has not yet been a significant reduction in relative wage ratios in these industries. The average hourly earnings ratios reported in table 5 include only wages; hourly labor cost differences are also influenced significantly by benefits costs. Data available for the automobile and steel industries indicate that labor cost measures that include benefits are considerably higher in relation to average labor costs in the economy and that labor cost premiums that include benefits have increased even more sharply than those for wages alone during the decade before 1983.[9]

TABLE 5

RATIOS OF INDUSTRY AVERAGE HOURLY EARNINGS TO PRIVATE
NONFARM AVERAGE HOURLY EARNINGS

Year	Coal	Steel	Electrical Equipment	Auto-mobiles	Meat Packing	Trucking	Telephone Communica-tions
Average 1964–69	1.40	1.35	1.03	1.40	1.22	1.24	1.08
Annual							
1964	1.00	1.04	1.02	1.00	1.01	1.03	1.03
1965	1.00	1.01	1.01	1.01	1.00	1.02	1.02
1966	1.03	1.00	1.00	1.00	1.00	1.01	1.01
1967	0.99	0.99	1.01	0.97	0.99	0.99	0.98
1968	0.99	0.99	1.00	1.01	1.00	0.98	1.01
1969	1.01	0.97	0.98	0.99	0.99	0.98	0.97
1970	1.10	0.95	0.99	0.95	1.02	1.01	0.96
1971	0.97	1.01	0.98	1.01	0.98	1.07	1.00
1972	1.03	1.02	0.97	1.04	1.00	1.09	1.05
1973	1.04	1.05	0.96	1.03	0.99	1.10	1.06
1974	1.06	1.12	0.98	1.06	1.01	1.10	1.11
1975	1.14	1.15	1.00	1.10	1.02	1.09	1.19
1976	1.13	1.14	1.00	1.10	1.02	1.10	1.23
1977	1.08	1.20	1.00	1.13	1.02	1.11	1.26
1978	1.22	1.23	0.99	1.14	1.02	1.11	1.23
1979	1.17	1.26	1.00	1.11	1.03	1.13	1.24
1980	1.16	1.27	1.03	1.21	1.04	1.15	1.26
1981	1.19	1.29	1.03	1.22	1.01	1.13	1.30
1982	1.20	1.30	1.05	1.19	0.93	1.10	1.32

NOTE: All figures are fourth-quarter averages; annual data are ratios that are indexed based on the average for 1964–1969 = 1.00. The average ratios reported for 1964–1969 are measures of wage levels in each industry relative to private nonfarm average hourly earnings. To obtain a measure of wages in a given industry relative to the private nonfarm average for a particular year, the "normalized" ratios must be multiplied by the five-year average at the top of the table.

SOURCES: *Employment and Earnings, United States, 1909–1978,* 1979; *Employment and Earnings, Supplement,* July 1983.

Wage and Benefit Concessions

Although wage concessions are not an unprecedented phenomenon, most observers agree that since 1979 they have been more widespread and significant than at any time since the 1930s. There is less agreement, however, on their significance for labor cost trends.[10] Observers

266

who view them as temporary and likely to be reversed with the advent of recovery emphasize that many concessions have occurred in plants threatened with closure, in sick industries, or in situations subject to temporary economic distress. Those who view them as having more lasting significance emphasize the departure from past bargaining formulas and practices that they represent and changes in competitive conditions that they reflect. An examination of some of the main features of wage decisions that include concessions, with attention to the areas in which these concessions occurred, can provide some insight into conditions that produced the concessions and into future wage prospects.

To analyze the prevalence of wage decisions involving concessions, it is necessary to review information that is available on individual wage decisions. Although comprehensive data are not available, perhaps the most systematic sources of data on individual wage decisions are reports published by the U.S. Department of Labor.[11] The decisions reported regularly in these reports—intended to monitor union wage developments—include most of the largest and most noteworthy union wage decisions. The implications for labor cost trends in industries that are affected by major union decisions are generally more significant than is suggested by the numbers of workers directly affected. Wage decisions for nonunion employees are in general not independent of decisions affecting union employees of the same firm, and firms not directly affected by particular wage decisions generally need to take into account wage decisions of competing firms in the same industry. These kinds of secondary effects, however, are not easily identified, and neither small situations nor nonunion decisions are usually covered in these Department of Labor reports.

In reviewing individual wage decisions to identify concessions, it is necessary to adopt a definition of "concession." Several dimensions of wage and benefit decisions were reviewed to identify and classify wage decisions that involved concessions. Decisions involving actual reductions in either wages or benefits should obviously be regarded as concessions. In addition, however, wage and benefit decisions that did not include an actual reduction in some component of the compensation package were categorized as concessions under the following circumstances. First, situations with no wage increase or with deferral of an increase were included. Second, changes that resulted in smaller increases than were provided under the formulas built into earlier agreements were included. Identification of situations of this latter type is facilitated by the tendency that developed during the postwar period toward formula-based settlements in several industries. In general, decisions were regarded as concessions whenever they operated to reduce labor cost trends, either directly or as com-

267

TABLE 6
CHARACTERISTICS OF CONCESSIONS IN MAJOR WAGE AND BENEFIT DECISIONS, 1979–1982

	Workers Affected and Situations (in parentheses)			
	1979	1980	1981	1982
Wage or benefit concessions	106,350 (8)	212,940 (14)	487,628 (33)	1,726,513 (84)
Contracts renegotiated before expiration	134,350 (7)	103,590 (4)	132,435 (19)	854,716 (21)
Concessions in wages				
Deferral of wage increase	76,000 (1)	53,840 (2)	1,793 (3)	495,000 (3)
Wage freeze or cutback in increase	4,000 (2)	6,150 (2)	221,460 (9)	1,063,606 (40)
Wage cut	3,550 (2)	46,840 (4)	78,285 (13)	111,200 (24)
Wage cut of 5 percent or more	1,550 (1)	44,200 (2)	77,235 (11)	78,600 (20)
Other concessions affecting labor costs				
Work rule changes that reduce labor costs	2,000 (1)	120,000 (3)	58,900 (6)	274,997 (8)
COLA reduction, deferral, or limit	2,000 (1)	12,000 (1)	228,800 (7)	602,506 (11)
COLA frozen or discontinued	4,800 (3)	112,850 (6)	86,500 (5)	96,730 (16)
COLA diversion	2,000 (1)	4,100 (1)	1,600 (1)	880,266 (10)
Offsets to wage or benefit concessions	76,000 (1)	90,150 (3)	12,400 (3)	51,850 (7)
Plant closing or business failure threat	81,550 (4)	108,040 (4)	91,900 (11)	24,320 (6)

SOURCE: Bureau of Labor Statistics, *Current Wage Developments* and *Monthly Labor Review,* monthly issues, 1979–1982.

pared with arrangements and formulas that were included in existing or expiring agreements.[12]

Several characteristics of concession decisions during the past four years for some 140 situations covering 2.5 million workers are

TABLE 7

UNION STATUS AND INDUSTRY CHARACTERISTICS FOR MAJOR WAGE AND
BENEFIT CONCESSION DECISIONS, 1979–1982

	Workers Affected and Situations (in parentheses)			
	1979	1980	1981	1982
Union status				
Union	93,350 (8)	187,140 (11)	256,453 (30)	1,637,916 (74)
Nonunion	13,000 (1)	25,800 (3)	231,175 (4)	88,597 (10)
Applicability of decision				
Single firm	104,350 (8)	212,940 (14)	424,910 (28)	1,299,063 (64)
More than one firm	2,000 (1)	—	62,718 (5)	427,450 (20)
Single plant	5,200 (3)	6,350 (3)	16,610 (13)	6,417 (12)
More than one plant	101,150 (6)	206,590 (11)	471,018 (20)	1,720,096 (72)
Duration				
Current: less than one year or indefinite	2,000 (1)	37,850 (6)	241,515 (11)	147,387 (27)
Long-term: more than one year	104,350 (8)	175,090 (8)	246,113 (22)	1,579,126 (57)

NOTE: Numbers of situations reported by union status for 1979 and 1981 exceed total situations because concessions for some nonunion workers accompanied concessions negotiated by unions in what can be regarded as the same situation.

SOURCE: Bureau of Labor Statistics, *Current Wage Developments* and *Monthly Labor Review*, monthly issues, 1979–1982.

summarized in tables 6 through 8. These data, together with the concessions in the steel industry in 1983, indicate that about one-third of the 9 million workers reported as covered by major collective bargaining agreements have been affected by wage or benefit concessions. The concessions have taken several different forms, a considerable range of industries was affected, and many cases involved renegotiation of existing agreements before these agreements expired.[13] Concessions that involved renegotiation of existing agreements to provide smaller wage increases or to reduce labor costs in other ways have often been called "give-backs," although this term

269

TABLE 8

INDUSTRY WAGE AND BENEFIT CONCESSION DECISIONS, 1979–1982

Industry	Workers Affected and Situations (in parentheses)				
	1979	1980	1981	1982	Total
Total for all industries	106,350 (8)	212,940 (14)	487,628 (33)	1,726,513 (84)	2,533,431 (139)
Construction	—	—	1,000 (1)	23,750 (14)	24,750 (15)
Steel	—	13,840 (1)	—	47,700 (5)	61,540 (6)
Metal fabrication	2,000 (1)	—	2,190 (3)	14,550 (5)	18,740 (9)
Automobiles	76,000 (1)	57,000 (2)	252,000 (4)	564,816 (5)	949,816 (12)
Rubber	2,000 (1)	57,750 (3)	735 (2)	27,100 (4)	87,585 (10)
Equipment manufacturing	3,200 (2)	43,350 (5)	37,700 (5)	72,277 (18)	156,527 (30)
Meat packing	—	—	40,700 (2)	15,850 (5)	56,550 (7)
Airlines	1,600 (1)	800 (1)	43,800 (5)	28,300 (6)	74,500 (13)
Trucking	—	—	2,500 (2)	249,200 (4)	251,700 (6)
Other transportation	20,000 (1)	7,200 (1)	70,000 (1)	112,500 (5)	209,700 (8)
State and local employees	—	33,000 (1)	24,200 (2)	415,200 (8)	472,400 (11)
Other	1,550 (1)	—	12,803 (6)	155,270 (5)	169,623 (12)

SOURCE: Bureau of Labor Statistics, *Current Wage Developments* and *Monthly Labor Review,* monthly issues, 1979–1982.

has also sometimes been used to refer to changes from expiring agreements with similar effects.

The data in table 6 show a growing number of workers reported as affected by wage concessions during the four-year period from 1979 through 1982. Although concessions that occur in connection with renegotiation of existing contracts are most easily identified, concessions also involved many workers affected by regularly scheduled negotiations. In 1982 workers affected by renegotiated contracts accounted for about half the workers affected by concessions, and contract negotiations in the automobile industry accounted for a large share of these workers (see table 8).

In 1979 and 1980 wage concessions mainly took the form of deferral of wage increases, often with arrangements for recouping these forgone wage increases later. By 1981 and 1982, however, a wage freeze or a cutback in the size of scheduled wage increases was more common. Actual wage cuts were experienced by only a small fraction of the workers affected, but when cuts occurred, they were generally larger than 5 percent though usually less than 10 percent. The wage cut of 9 percent for workers in the steel industry that occurred in early 1983 was quite a dramatic concession compared with those reported in table 6, but it came considerably later than the concessions in several other industries.

Changes in work rules were frequently an element in concessions affecting labor costs, but changes in cost-of-living escalator formulas and arrangements were most common. Reductions in payoff formulas and deferral of escalator-related payments became increasingly common during the period. Diversion of at least part of the funds previously paid in increased wages to help meet the increased costs of benefits, such as health care plans, became an important type of concession in 1982. Other benefit cutbacks included such items as fewer holidays or less time off and less generous overtime arrangements.[14]

Agreement to accede to concessions is a somewhat bitter pill for union leadership to swallow. To sweeten the medicine, it is sometimes reported that other offsetting changes were negotiated. Such offsets to concessions in other parts of an agreement appear to have played a relatively minor role in the overall picture, with the exception of the first year in which the president of the United Automobile Workers was placed on the Chrysler board of directors. In addition to specific offsets, the threat of plant closure or of business failure was frequently a factor in stimulating concessions, although it was not very important in 1982. More generally, preservation of jobs was an important consideration in negotiations leading to concessions, but unless the viability of a particular plant or firm was at issue, such situations were not included in the plant closing or business failure category in table 6.

Most of the concession decisions reviewed involved union situations (table 7), as would be expected from reports devoted primarily to covering union situations. Concessions on the part of nonunion workers reported in table 7 were generally applicable to nonunion employees of firms in which production workers were covered by major collective bargaining agreements, and union concessions were typically preceded by concessions by nonunion employees. Concession agreements were most commonly applicable to single firms with more than one plant, although the concessions in the steel industry in 1983 involved the major multiplant steel-making firms. Since many of the concessions involved modifications of long-term bargaining agreements, most of the workers were affected by new agreements extending for more than one year into the future.

The industry breakdown of concessions shown in table 8 indicates a heavy concentration in the automobile industry, beginning with concessions negotiated by Chrysler as a condition for the federal loan guarantee and ending in 1982 with those negotiated by Ford and General Motors. Data for 1983 would show a heavy concentration in the steel industry, in view of the fact that some 250,000 workers were affected by concessions negotiated in that industry. Despite this concentration in the automobile and steel industries, concession decisions were also spread over a considerable range of other industries. Perhaps more important than the specific numbers of workers affected by the concessions reported is the influence on wages in the industries involved. Thus, for example, these concessions include the key wage decisions influencing wages throughout industries such as trucking, airlines, automobiles, rubber, and steel (in 1983).[15]

Perspectives on Concessions

The common feature in these wage concession decisions is a recognition on the part of management, and an acceptance on the part of labor (perhaps grudgingly), of a decline in demand for labor at existing wage levels. To examine the sources of the decline in demand, it is useful to begin with the simplest model of demand for union labor. Abstracting from international trade and assuming complete unionization of an industry, we see that the short-term demand for labor depends primarily on possibilities for substitution between the industry's product and all other goods and services. In addition, of course, short-term derived demand for labor would be affected by cyclical conditions, and long-term demand by technological change and substitution of capital for labor. The cyclical slump that began in 1980, and persisted for some industries through 1982, obviously had an important influence on the timing and extent of wage concessions.

But other developments resulting in increased competition were also at work, and these changes in competitive conditions can be expected to continue to exert an influence during recovery.

One source of increased competition in the late 1970s was deregulation. Removal of entry and rate regulation introduced more competition among existing firms in the airline and trucking industries. It also stimulated new entrants, providing new and frequently nonunion competition. In addition to the effects of deregulation on airfares and trucking rates, more competition was introduced into factor markets for labor services.[16] The introduction of more flexibility in railroad regulation led to more competition in that sector of the transportation industry. Federal budget pressures also meant smaller subsidies for railroads and urban transportation systems, producing effects similar to those of a sectoral reduction in demand.

In the automobile, steel, rubber, and equipment manufacturing industries, international markets were the main source of increased competition. Product characteristics and quality contributed along with costs to stronger import competition in domestic markets. The high value of the dollar also contributed to increased competition from international sources at the beginning of the 1980s. Moreover, as discussed in the preceding section, the large rise in wage premiums in several of these industries relative to wages of the average worker in the economy placed these industries at a serious labor cost disadvantage compared with their situation a decade earlier and with wage relationships in competing countries abroad.

Many of the competitive forces affecting industry sectors in which concessions were negotiated came from sources other than cyclical slack in demand, and competition from these sources can be expected to remain significant as the economy recovers. Competition has increased among existing firms, and additional competition has come from new entrants, from new production locations, and often from nonunion labor. Increased competition in domestic markets from international sources has been highly visible and widely reported, especially for automobiles and steel, but increased competition faced by domestic producers in international markets has also been important in industries such as equipment manufacturing. To the extent that policies are avoided that would inhibit competition from these sources, pressures to control labor costs will continue as an element of maintaining competitive positions in product markets.

Wage and benefit concessions can be discussed in terms of how collective bargaining arrangements and practices have been affected as well as from the viewpoint of competitive pressures that fostered them. The two main features of postwar bargaining practices that were affected by wage concessions are pattern bargaining and formula-based wage increases under long-term agreements. The concessions that were negotiated represent some erosion in pattern-bargaining arrangements that established industrywide wage levels, and they constitute a significant departure from the formulas that became entrenched during the 1960s and 1970s.

The main elements in the formulas that evolved for long-term agreements were a fixed annual increment to wages, cost-of-living escalators to compensate for inflation, and maintenance or enrichment of benefits. The appropriate size of the fixed annual wage increase came to be viewed as in the 3 percent range during the 1960s, and escalator provisions became prevalent in the 1970s. The costs of providing a defined package of benefits tended to rise more rapidly than the average price level, primarily because of health costs, which have typically been the largest component of the benefit package. This formula was spelled out most explicitly in the Experimental Negotiating Agreement in the steel industry, where it was applicable during the decade from 1973 to 1983. Although long-term agreements that incorporated all these elements of the formula were not always fully achieved in practice even by the major unions with the largest wage gains, the basic formula provided a benchmark for claims to which union workers came to feel entitled. In the case of steel, of course, the formula provided an explicit basis for such a claim.[17]

The goal of pattern bargaining was to "take wages out of competition" insofar as it was feasible to do so. In some instances pattern-setting agreements with individual firms were the mechanism employed, and in other instances bargaining took place between unions and employers' associations. Just as in the case of formulas for long-term agreements, pattern-bargaining goals were not always fully realized, of course. These arrangements were always vulnerable to the threat of nonunion competition, a threat that began to materialize in trucking and airlines under deregulation. Even industries in which competition from nonunion sources was not a factor, such as automobiles and steel, were vulnerable to competition from international sources. Erosion in the market share of domestic producers occurred in both these industries despite protectionist measures that began for steel in 1969 and for automobiles in 1981. The recent concessions from industrywide wage levels that began with Chrysler in 1979 have had precursors, such as the longstanding wage differential for American Motors. Nevertheless, recent concessions seem to have produced more fragmentation in industry wages than was experienced previously, when intraindustry wage differences were, with some important exceptions, kept under stable control.

This discussion of the sources and general characteristics of concession wage decisions provides a basis for considering the fragility of wage trends embodied in the new agreements that they produced. Wage developments in the future in several industries can be expected to depend importantly on federal policies. In industries such as steel and automobiles, management and labor can be expected to press jointly for protection against imports to prevent further erosion in domestic market shares and to fend off reduction in wage premiums relative to wages in other industries. Moreover, as economic recovery proceeds and restores profitability in the industries concerned, workers and their unions can be expected to press claims for wages "forgone" through concessions.[18] If prices begin rising more rapidly and inflation prospects deteriorate, pressures for larger wage increases will mount further.

With regard to collective bargaining practices, increased industry wage fragmentation and erosion in pattern bargaining produced by concession decisions can be expected to be followed by efforts to "patch up," or at least to stabilize, intraindustry wage patterns. Although the concessions constitute an important break in the earlier established long-term wage formulas, no new formulas have yet become established or widely accepted as a basis for long-term agreements, and competitive forces will exert continued pressure on wage premiums in industries in which premiums expanded markedly during the 1970s. If we take this perspective, the relevant question concerning future wage developments under major collective bargaining situations is not whether or not concessions constitute an important change in the course of collective bargaining. In some important respects, they do. The relevant question is instead whether policies will be pursued, at both the microeconomic and the macroeconomic level, that will sustain and build upon the changes they constitute.

Incomes Policies

Since there have been several periods during the past thirty-five years in which wages and prices were subject to mandatory controls or to "voluntary" restraints, it hardly seems appropriate to review inflation experience without reference to intermittent incomes policy programs. Since the kinds of incomes policies employed were quite varied, it is useful to begin by describing them briefly.

The first period of controls came during the Korean War in 1951 and 1952. The program involved mandatory controls on wages and prices during this two-year period.[19] During the rest of the decade, no systematic incomes policies were employed, although modest exhortations surfaced occasionally in the mid-1950s. The next incomes policy episode was voluntary and was known as the "guideposts" during the 1960s. Although the guidepost period can be viewed as extending from 1962 through 1968, it began for all practical purposes with discussions with the steel industry during 1962, and the already eroding credibility of the policy was further diminished after the airline machinists balked in mid-1966. The policy was formally ended at the beginning of 1969.[20]

The third incomes policy program began with a wage and price freeze in August 1971 and ended in the spring of 1974. This general program was preceded by an essentially voluntary program for construction wages that was introduced in March 1971. The comprehensive, mandatory program of controls on wages and prices that began in August 1971 lasted until January 1973. Wage controls during 1973 can perhaps best be regarded as voluntary in that neither a numerical standard nor formal administrative procedures were employed, and the entire program ended in April 1974.[21] The fourth period of incomes policy was again voluntary. It began in January 1978, was made more explicit in October 1978, and was abandoned at the end of 1980.[22]

In all, some form of incomes policy has been applied during about fourteen of the past thirty-five years. With the exception of the Korean War wage and price controls, inflation rose dramatically by the time each episode was abandoned. Particularly after the Korean War controls, restraining labor cost increases has been an important rationale for incomes policy programs. Since in practice this rationale meant that newly negotiated wage increases under collective bargaining agreements were subject to the closest scrutiny, wage increases under collective bargaining agreements during these incomes policy programs are of particular interest.

During the guidepost years, hourly labor cost increases remained quite stable through 1965, as did consumer price increases. From 1966 through 1968, however, average wage increases rose, paralleling inflation, and then stabilized at a rate in the 6 to 7 percent range through 1973. Newly negotiated wage increases rose gradually beginning in 1962, rose more rapidly after 1965, and reached their peak in 1971.

Newly negotiated wage increases under major collective bargaining agreements were sharply lower in 1972 than in 1971 and the preceding three years, although measures of average wage increases showed only relatively little variation from 1968 through 1973. The moderation in new union wage settlements in both 1972 and 1973 supports the view that incomes policy may have had a very significant influence, but the similarity of wage settlements in both years despite the abandonment of a numerical wage standard, the removal of administrative procedures applied to wage decisions, and the surge in inflation in 1973 raises questions about this interpretation. In 1974 inflation rose further, and all measures of wage change also jumped sharply.

When the voluntary incomes policy program was introduced in 1978, inflation had already risen substantially from its low point in 1976. New wage increases under collective bargaining agreements reached their low point in 1978, when the standards were expressed only in general terms for most of the year, but new wage increases and average wage increases under collective bargaining agreements moved up more rapidly—along with inflation—in 1979 and 1980 when the standards were stated more explicitly.

The slowdown in average wage increases beginning in 1981, and in wage increases under collective bargaining agreements in 1982, was much more pronounced and occurred with a much shorter lag in relation to inflation than was the case during the two earlier major cycles of the 1970s. Wage behavior since 1981 cannot be attributed to any informal or explicit incomes policy. Even the wage and price monitoring agency that was established in late 1974 was abolished in early 1981, and it is difficult to find any official government statements that could be interpreted as mild persuasion addressed to those involved in wage or price decisions. In addition, protectionist policies—to the extent that they were pursued—had the effect of blunting the full force of competition (for example, the agreement to limit automobile imports).

Although this review of incomes policies is admittedly brief and informal, it demonstrates the wide variation in price and wage performance and changes in performance that occurred when such policies were pursued. It seems difficult to avoid the conclusion that incomes policies were not the main forces at work influencing inflation. Instead, their effects seem to have been peripheral at best and probably largely irrelevant except for possible delays that they introduced in adjustments in the labor market to higher inflation.[23]

Recent Developments

The recession of 1981–1982 did not initially produce major reductions in the rate of increase in labor costs and prices even though this recession followed close on the heels of the brief contraction during 1980. Significantly lower inflation for most measures of labor costs and prices began to emerge only in 1982. By this time real growth in the economy, though uneven, had been quite weak for more than two years. The decline in inflation that took place in 1982, however, was quite general. Price increases were sharply lower than in the preceding year. Measures of hourly labor costs showed much smaller increases in 1982, as table 9 indicates, including especially first-year wage increases under major collective bargaining agreements. Moreover, both prices and labor costs decelerated during the year, with

TABLE 9

QUARTERLY WAGE, PRODUCTIVITY, AND PRICE CHANGES, 1981–1983

Wages and Labor Costs

Period	Hourly earnings index	Average hourly earnings	Average hourly compensation	Total compensation	Employment cost index			
					Total wages and salaries	Union wages and salaries	Nonunion wages and salaries	First-year union wage increases
1981	8.4	7.9	9.8	9.8	8.8	9.6	8.5	8.8
1982	5.9	4.9	7.8	6.4	6.3	6.5	6.1	3.8
1981								
1st quarter	9.3	9.6	11.5	15.2	11.2	7.0	13.9	7.1
2d quarter	8.5	8.0	7.3	7.8	8.2	10.8	7.4	11.8
3d quarter	8.5	8.0	9.6	8.2	8.2	11.2	6.6	10.8
4th quarter	7.3	6.1	7.6	8.2	7.4	9.1	6.6	9.0
1982								
1st quarter	6.5	5.1	10.0	7.0	8.2	5.7	9.5	3.0
2d quarter	6.4	5.8	5.8	5.3	4.5	6.1	3.6	3.4
3d quarter	6.2	4.6	7.2	8.2	7.4	8.2	7.0	5.4
4th quarter	4.8	3.7	5.8	5.3	4.9	5.7	4.5	3.8
1983								
1st quarter	4.8	4.5	6.8	7.0	4.9	4.1	5.3	-1.2
2d quarter	3.3	3.3	4.3	4.9	4.9	4.9	4.9	2.9

Period	Productivity		Prices			Unemployment
	Output per hour	Unit labor costs	Implicit price deflator	Personal consumption expenditures	Consumer price index	Civilian unemployment rate
1981 annual	1.9	7.7	9.6	8.1	8.9	7.6
1982 annual	-0.1	7.9	5.8	5.1	3.9	9.7
1981						
1st quarter	5.2	6.0	11.6	8.0	10.9	7.4
2d quarter	0.4	6.9	6.6	6.5	9.6	7.4
3d quarter	3.8	5.6	10.0	9.1	11.9	7.4
4th quarter	-4.4	12.6	9.5	8.6	5.9	8.4
1982						
1st quarter	0.1	9.9	3.7	4.9	3.3	8.8
2d quarter	-0.4	6.2	5.4	3.6	6.2	9.4
3d quarter	2.3	4.7	2.2	7.5	7.9	10.0
4th quarter	1.3	4.4	3.7	4.5	0.8	10.7
1983						
1st quarter	3.7	3.0	5.3	2.3	-0.2	10.4
2d quarter	6.1	-1.6	3.3	4.9	5.1	10.1

NOTES: Annual data, in general, are measures of the percentage change from the preceding quarter, and quarterly figures measure the percentage change from the previous fourth quarter expressed at an annual rate. The hourly earnings index and average hourly earnings series cover the private nonfarm sector and are seasonally adjusted. The employment cost index covers the same sector and is not seasonally adjusted. The average hourly compensation, output per hour, unit labor costs, and implicit price deflator are based on data for the nonfarm business sector and are seasonally adjusted. Annual data for the consumer price index are from December to December. Figures for first-year union wage increases and unemployment are averages over the period indicated.

SOURCES: Bureau of Labor Statistics, *Current Wage Developments*, various issues; Department of Commerce, *Survey of Current Business*, various issues.

rates of increase at the end of 1982 and the beginning of 1983 generally smaller than increases during the year as a whole.

The lower inflation of 1982 reduced hourly labor cost increases directly for workers affected by cost-of-living escalator provisions and also reduced pressures for wage increases from other workers in the economy. In addition, general market weakness sharply limited the ability of firms to absorb labor cost increases or to pass them along in higher prices. The recovery of productivity growth during 1982 relieved the pressure of unit labor costs on prices and reduced pressures for wage increases by permitting real wage gains, despite smaller nominal wage increases, for the first time since 1976 and, before that, 1972.

By the end of 1982 and the beginning of 1983, hourly labor cost increases were in the range of 5 to 6 percent. Price increases during the year were in the 4 to 5 percent range. Productivity growth in the 1 to 2 percent range during the next couple of years as the recovery proceeds would not be out of line with the relatively low productivity growth experience of the last part of the 1970s. These conditions provide a basis for stability, or even modest improvement, in inflation even if labor cost trends remain roughly unchanged. Under these conditions further real wage gains and a significant recovery in profit margins could take place. The possibility that the recovery might proceed too rapidly is perhaps the main threat to this relatively benign scenario, although major price shocks could also impair the outlook.

Conclusions

Adjustments in the labor market have a critical role to play as the economy adjusts to sustainably lower inflation. The high unemployment associated with a transition to lower inflation focuses attention on the need for redeployment and possible retraining of workers, particularly when shifts in international trade and foreign competition are also significant forces, as in the 1981–1982 recession. Yet the primary adjustment that must take place to maintain lower inflation is the adjustment to smaller increases in wages and in hourly compensation costs.

In analyses of wage developments, union wage increases are frequently given particular emphasis, as they are in this essay. The outcome of union wage bargains provides highly visible information on adjustments that are taking place, and bargaining positions and occasional strikes during settlement negotiation bring them to public attention. In addition, wages set by collective bargaining are critical for labor costs in several basic industries.

It is important, however, to keep union wage developments in perspective. Only a relatively small fraction of the work force is unionized, and the direct effect on wages as a whole of all unions taken together is consequently quite limited. Although wages of many closely related workers may be affected by union settlements, their general pattern-setting significance is exaggerated in most popular discussion. The most significant pattern-setting influence of unions seems to have been limited mainly to relationships among several of the major unions rather than to their influence on wage trends elsewhere in the economy.

Relationships among wages negotiated by certain major unions, such as those in the automobile and steel industries during the late 1970s, resulted from common wage-setting formulas in long-term agreements that evolved in the early 1970s. The growing wage premiums produced by these formulas were probably not mainly a result of deliberate efforts on the part of the unions to expand these wage premiums and to accept the implied loss of jobs that might be entailed. The growing premiums may instead have resulted from a gradual and belated recognition on the part of both management and labor that these formulas had become outdated. That these formulas produced overall labor cost increases that brought relative wages to unrealistically high levels may have been partly obscured by the fact that some parts of the formulas, notably cost-of-living escalators, were well adapted to the environment of highly variable inflation rates of the late 1970s.

Developments since 1979 have gradually brought about contract revisions to reflect the slower productivity gains and the smaller real wage increases that could be paid to the average worker in the late 1970s. The increased competition introduced by deregulation of transportation industries was one important factor stimulating adjustment. Growing inroads of foreign competition were another. These contract revisions made important contributions to a realignment of wages in the economy that will be essential if some of these industries are to regain viable, competitive positions in world markets.

Although new wage settlements under major collective bargaining agreements have recently been extraordinarily small, newly negotiated wage settlements have not been a reliable indicator of overall wage trends. Changes in inflation and in other economic trends have frequently produced cumulative changes in wages under long-term agreements that required very large shifts in the size of new settlements to restore relationships that prevailed earlier or to adapt to changing circumstances, such as slower productivity growth or a new competitive environment. The effects of short-term cyclical conditions, for example, have sometimes been swamped by adjustments to other conditions that built up in the past. Consequently, incomes policies that were designed to influence the size of new wage settlements have frequently been inappropriate from the viewpoint of adjustments required for realignment of wages as well as generally ineffective in restraining their size.

Changes in the economic environment during the postwar period led to changes in wage-setting arrangements to accommodate higher and more variable rates of inflation. In particular, cost-of-living escalator provisions in long-term contracts became an important factor in union wage trends and changed the behavior of union wages over business cycles. In addition, lagging overall productivity growth and changes in competitive conditions in a number of highly unionized industries, in combination with the recession of 1981–1982, introduced still further adjustments in the form of concessions from the wage-setting formulas that had evolved.

Broadly based measures of hourly labor costs have responded more quickly and completely to the reduction in inflation that resulted from the recession of 1981–1982 than they did to the recessions of the 1970s. The reason in part relates to the fact that in this most recent recession, union wage developments contributed to the slowdown in overall wage costs rather than to delaying a slowdown by partially offsetting slower wage increases in much of the rest of the economy. Just as in earlier business cycles, however, this moderating contribution of union wage increases can be expected to be temporary, even though still further adjustments to realign domestic wage relationships are essential to restoring competitiveness in some industries. Further realignment of wages may be more difficult to achieve in view of growing resistance to concessions and in view of the recovery that is under way, but the increased competition that has been applicable to many of the highly unionized industries, together with the pronounced reduction in overall labor cost increases that has taken place, establishes the basis for sharply lower inflation than that experienced during much of the 1970s.

Notes

1. Major collective bargaining situations are those covering 1,000 workers or more.

2. The fraction of employed wage and salary workers *represented* by labor organizations, for example, is apparently two or three percentage points higher than the fraction who are *members* of labor organizations. In addition, broader linkages in wage behavior have been termed "wage contours" (John T. Dunlop, "The Task of Contemporary Wage Theory" in John T. Dunlop, ed., *The Theory of Wage Determination* ([New York: St. Martin's Press, 1957]). On the

other hand, data from the *Current Population Survey* indicate that the fraction of employed wage and salary workers who are organized has been two to five percentage points lower than union membership as a percentage of employed nonagricultural workers (C. D. Gifford, ed., *Directory of U.S. Labor Organizations, 1982–83* [Washington, D.C.: BNA Books, 1982]).

3. The largest of these associations is the National Education Association, which has some 1.7 million members.

4. In an article reporting on major cutbacks in union staff by the United Steelworkers and on negotiations for wage cuts of more than 10 percent for remaining staff employees, the dues-paying membership of the United Steelworkers is reported to have declined from 1.4 million in 1979 to 700,000 in 1983 (*Wall Street Journal*, July 1, 1983). The secular decline in private sector union membership has apparently not been mainly attributable to attrition as a result of declining employment in highly unionized industries, however. Data on the outcome of union representation elections show a steady decline since the early 1940s in the percentage of elections won by unions. The number of workers voting in such elections has been quite stable since the mid-1950s, but the fraction of elections won by unions declined from about 65 percent at that time to about 43 percent in 1981 (compiled from National Labor Relations Board, *Annual Reports*).

5. See, for example, Marvin Kosters, "Wages, Inflation, and the Labor Market," in William Fellner, ed., *Contemporary Economic Problems 1976* (Washington, D.C.: American Enterprise Institute, 1976) p. 138 (table 5).

6. Although data on the number of workers covered by long-term contracts are not available directly in statistics reported regularly by the Bureau of Labor Statistics, estimates can be made by accumulating numbers of workers covered by newly negotiated three-year agreements over contract cycles. Estimates constructed in this way indicate that approximately 60 percent of workers under major collective bargaining agreements were covered by three-year contracts in the 1970s.

7. Although union wage increases are commonly supposed to exert a pattern-setting influence on other wages in the economy, evidence from several studies contradicts this view. See, for example, Robert J. Flanagan, "Wage Interdependence in Unionized Labor Markets," in *Brookings Papers on Economic Activity*, no. 3 (Washington, D.C.: Brookings Institution, 1976), pp. 635–73; Daniel J. B. Mitchell, "Union Wage Determination: Policy Implications and Outlook," in *Brookings Papers on Economic Activity*, no. 3 (Washington, D.C.: Brookings Institution, 1978), pp. 537–82; George E. Johnson, "The Determination of Wages in Union and Nonunion Sectors," *British Journal of Industrial Relations*, vol. 15, no. 2 (July 1977), pp. 211–25; and Marvin H. Kosters, "Wage Standards and Interdependence of Wages in the Labor Market," in William Fellner, ed., *Contemporary Economic Problems 1979* (Washington, D.C.: American Enterprise Institute, 1979), pp. 233–60. For evidence supporting the traditional view, see Susan Vroman, "The Direction of Wage Spillovers in Manufacturing," *Industrial and Labor Relations Review*, vol. 36, no. 1 (October 1982), pp. 102–13.

8. It should be noted that the high peaks in the spread between new and previously negotiated wage increases in 1975 and in 1978 (as well as in several

of the other years separated by three-year intervals) reflect the effects of a single new wage settlement in the bituminous coal industry.

9. In 1982 hourly earnings in the private nonfarm economy averaged $7.67. Average hourly earnings in the automobile and steel industries used for construction of table 5, however, were $13.01 and $13.36, respectively. Average hourly compensation in the nonfarm business sector of the economy was $11.12 in 1982, as compared with more than $23 in the steel industry and more than $20 in the two largest automobile companies, General Motors and Ford, and slightly below $20 per hour for Chrysler.

Trends in ratios of hourly wages and total compensation costs during the ten years from 1973 to 1982 are shown in the following table for data available from the automobile and steel industries.

Year	Automobiles		Steel	
	Wages	Compensation	Wages	Compensation
1973	1.45	1.62	1.40	1.48
1974	1.47	1.67	1.48	1.60
1975	1.51	1.76	1.53	1.70
1976	1.53	1.78	1.56	1.74
1977	1.57	1.77	1.59	1.80
1978	1.58	1.79	1.65	1.82
1979	1.58	1.86	1.69	1.85
1980	1.62	2.11	1.71	1.95
1981	1.69	2.09	1.74	1.94
1982	1.67	2.10	1.76	2.14

SOURCE: Automobile (Ford Motor Company) data are taken from annual reports. Steel industry data were obtained from the American Iron and Steel Institute.

10. Some of the major differences in views on the significance of union wage and bargaining developments after 1979 are presented in Audrey Freeman, "A Fundamental Change in Wage Bargaining," and Daniel J. B. Mitchell, "Gain Sharing: An Anti-Inflation Reform," both in *Challenge*, July/August 1982, pp. 14–17 and 18–25, respectively. Additional commentary and useful distinctions are presented in John T. Dunlop, "Working toward Consensus," in an interview in the same issue of *Challenge*, pp. 26–34.

11. Specifically, *Current Wage Developments* and *Monthly Labor Review*.

12. A degree of subjectivity is almost inevitable in classifying wage decisions as concessions and in categorizing the kinds of concessions involved. The most significant concession situations are quite readily identified, however, using informal guidelines.

13. Some of the more noteworthy instances of new concessionary contracts negotiated before expiration of existing contracts are Chrysler (late 1979 and again at the beginning of 1980 and 1981), trucking master freight (in January 1982, with expiration of the new contract scheduled for March 31, 1984), Ford and General Motors (February and March 1982, with new contracts expiring in September 1984 replacing contracts scheduled to expire in September

1982), and basic steel (February 1983, with a new contract scheduled to expire in July 1986 replacing a contract scheduled to expire in July 1983).

14. The significance of changes in work rules and cutbacks in benefits of various kinds is difficult to judge in the absence of detailed information on the situations and practices involved. Changes in work rules were tabulated when they were mentioned in reports on wage decisions, but cutbacks in a diverse range of benefits were not tabulated separately in table 6. One interesting form of concession, with presumably very small immediate consequences for current labor costs, was the establishment of differentially lower wages for newly hired workers, which was an element in several concession decisions.

15. State and local employees account for a large number of the workers reported in table 8. Partly because the reports reviewed cover only large situations, the workers were mainly New York City employees and employees in a few other northeastern and midwestern cities. State and local budgets in these regions, however, were disproportionately affected by the recession.

16. See, for example, David R. Graham and Daniel P. Kaplan, "Airline Deregulation Is Working," *Regulation*, May/June 1982, pp. 26–32; Robert E. Mabley and Walter D. Strack, "Deregulation: A Green Light for Trucking Efficiency," *Regulation*, July/August 1982, pp. 36–42 and p. 56; and Herbert R. Northrup, "The New Labor Relations Climate in Airlines," *Industrial and Labor Relations Review*, vol. 36, no. 2 (January 1983), pp. 167–81.

17. The Experimental Negotiating Agreement was initially negotiated in March 1973 for implementation in contract talks before the expiration of the existing agreement on August 1, 1974. The negotiating agreement basically provided for (1) annual wage increases of 3 percent, (2) cost-of-living escalator protection, (3) maintenance of benefits as defined in the existing contract, and (4) a no-strike bonus of $150 for each employee. These elements of the formula for a new long-term agreement were the starting point for bargaining, and both parties agreed to arbitration procedures in the event of unresolved issues in return for agreement to forgo strikes or lockouts to support bargaining positions.

The essential elements in this Experimental Negotiating Agreement were renewed in 1974 and in 1977 for implementation in connection with negotiating in 1977 and 1980. The agreement was not extended in 1980, however, for negotiations before expiration of the contract extending to August 1983.

18. Although long-term collective bargaining agreements embodying concessions provide for lower wage levels during their remaining terms than would have been realized in the absence of concessions, many of the agreements have a somewhat tentative and provisional character. The series of concessions by Chrysler employees, for example, was followed by a new agreement providing an immediate wage increase of seventy-five cents per hour in December 1982, and union demands for additional wage increases have been stimulated by the company's return to profitability in 1983. Union contracts with Ford and General Motors scheduled to expire in September 1984 include reopener provisions contingent on production volume and profitability. The steel agreement scheduled to expire in July 1986 provides for restoration of wage cuts over the life of the contract in addition to possible cost-of-living increases.

Acceptance of concessions on a broad scale during the recession was probably conditioned by the psychological impact of widespread layoffs in several industries, the visibility of large plant closures, and real threats to the viability of a number of large firms. The fact that concessions became quite common and included industries such as trucking, automobiles, and steel also made individual concession decisions easier to obtain. As these conditions fade into the past, workers' attitudes may shift toward those expressed in the slogan of the 1983 United Automobile Workers' convention, "Restore plus more in '84." These circumstances suggest the possibility that strikes might increase significantly from their extraordinarily low levels since 1980 and particularly in 1982.

19. Harry P. Yoshpe, ed., *Emergency Economic Stabilization* (Washington, D.C.: Industrial College of the Armed Forces, 1964).

20. See Craufurd D. Goodwin, ed., *Exhortations and Controls* (Washington, D.C.: Brookings Institution, 1975).

21. Marvin H. Kosters, *Controls and Inflation* (Washington, D.C.: American Enterprise Institute, 1975).

22. Jack A. Meyer, *Wage-Price Standards and Economic Policy* (Washington, D.C.: American Enterprise Institute, 1982).

23. In assessing the impact of incomes policy programs, it is extremely important to analyze the overall effects on inflation by examining the course of inflation after programs were terminated as well as during the periods when such programs were under way. Such analyses have in general produced smaller estimates of the effects of incomes policies on inflation than the estimates made while such programs were in progress and estimates that show little effect on overall price levels of the program as a whole. That is, effects on inflation have been small and only temporary. See, for example, Alan S. Blinder, *Economic Policy and the Great Stagflation* (New York: Academic Press, 1979); Robert J. Gordon, "The Impact of Aggregate Demand on Prices," *Brookings Papers on Economic Activity*, no. 3 (Washington, D.C.: Brookings Institution, 1979); and Meyer, *Wage-Price Standards and Economic Policy.*

Collective Bargaining and Industrial Relations: The Past, the Present, and the Future

Mark Perlman

Summary

This essay focuses on some of the institutional underpinnings of the material taken up in Marvin Koster's essay, which immediately precedes it. Specifically it concerns three questions: (1) What has generally happened to collective bargaining institutions, particularly in the manufacturing sector, during the past third of a century? (2) What went "wrong" in the past two decades, so that we seem to be at a new watershed in our labor relations practices? and (3) What are the likely options?

The essay is in four parts. There is an introductory section describing the relative decline of the manufacturing sector from the standpoints of domestic American employment and its contributions to American world trade, two popular reactions to the causes and to what can now be done, and my own reading of the situation. These two reactions argue that nothing constructive can really be done (decline is an inevitable part of the development process) or that we can pursue policies designed to retain that part of the manufacturing sector that is essential either to maintaining some form of full employment or to our capacity for national defense. The watershed event that brought about

I am indebted to several individuals for help in the preparation of this essay. These include all of my fellow authors in this volume, Marina v. N. Whitman for help in locating some data, and my former colleagues (Naomi Perlman, Drucilla Ekwurzel, Lyndis Rankin, and June Cox) of the *Journal of Economic Literature* for help in the preparation of the manuscript. I would also like to acknowledge that I spent a small but not trivial fraction of my time while resident scholar at the Rockefeller Foundation's Bellagio Study and Conference Center working on the final draft of this paper; thus I wish to take the opportunity to thank the foundation for its support.

the current situation is identified as the insinuation of the federal government as a major party into the setting of the patterns of industrial relations contractual terms. The current situation is such that foreign competition has erased much American leadership both in our historical export markets and now in our domestic markets.

Part two goes back to events during World War II, when insinuation of federal authority into the formulation of labor relations contracts really began. The prewar institutional inheritance is identified, and the immediate and ultimate effects of two critical War Labor Board decisions are examined. This legacy of the War Labor Board serves as the key to understanding what happened to our labor unit cost competitiveness.

Part three deals with the further development of the insinuation of federal authority since 1945. It reviews the effects of the Taft-Hartley Act, particularly the use of its emergency provisions, and the impact of the Landrum-Griffin Act and what it did to the power of national union leaders and their capacity to confine union wage and benefit demands. It also shows how the War Labor Board legacy resulted in an apparent widespread conviction that labor unit costs had a capacity to rise without adversely affecting sales, because we were blessed with an almost God-given or inevitable 3 percent annual productivity growth or because the effective elasticity of domestic demand for American manufactures was very low (inelastic) or both.

The final section deals with "the questions of the hour." After reviewing the changed economic setting (1950 to 1980), it goes on to identify the conflict between our more or less free trade policy and the loss of much of our national competitiveness in the manufacturing sector. This loss, which seems to have originated in changes in unit labor costs, has other causes as well, including the costs of such social reform programs as environmental improvement, workers' safety protection, and affirmative action. What has happened to the way unions operate is considered next, and the decline of employment and loss of union membership in the manufacturing sector are once again stressed. The paper concludes with a discussion of the emerging policy options. One, designed to maintain high employment and high real wages, is to rely on some form of effective protection (tariffs are only the most obvious form). Another is to look at just which specific sectors of the manufacturing economy are essential to our defense needs and to confine our legislative intervention to them, an approach that pays less attention to full employment as a priority objective for the manufacturing sector. This last choice suggests that much of what we once thought essential may no longer be technologically so. I conclude by asserting what I think will emerge. It consists of more bipartite bargaining, a situation with a lot of abrasiveness and conflict, but one that has a good likelihood of restoring our previous leadership in the world market for manufactures.

Introduction

This essay discusses the institutional underpinnings of the current wage patterns analyzed in Marvin Koster's immediately preceding essay. It accepts and draws on three of his basic conclusions; it goes further and quite possibly suggests some views that either are not implicit in his analysis or go well beyond what he is prepared to consider likely in the foreseeable future.

The three following points are his conclusions that are important to my position:

- Union wage agreements have a disproportionate quantitative impact on the quality or specific contents of most other wage and labor relations policies.

- Such policies, particularly in the steel and automobile industries, were affected by the general slowdown in productivity growth and by inflationary trends in such a way as to cause unexpectedly large increases in unit labor cost. Among the results were very high wages, very high prices, a major reduction in unit sales, a consequent large reduction in production, and high industrial unemployment.

- Since 1979 labor relations negotiations—in the two industries specifically and in manufacturing and several service industries generally—have reflected a new situation. As a result new contracts not only have contained fewer gains for workers but have in many instances actually reduced elements of the previous wage packages (actions popularly termed "give-backs"). These reactions have been greater and were accomplished more efficaciously than in any of the previous post–World War II recessions.

My study and its consequent views go somewhat beyond Koster's framework. It is concerned with three questions:

- How did the collective bargaining process and wage determination policies that proved so inadequate in the late 1970s and early 1980s come to be? When and why were they seemingly so successful?

- What happened in the 1960s and the 1970s to make them increasingly less successful so that we seem to have passed a watershed in our labor relations institutions, particularly in the manufacturing sector, which will operate differently in the future from the way they operated from 1940 to the mid-1970s?

- How will unions (which I believe will still have a quantitatively disproportionate influence on all labor relations patterns) cope with the impact on unit labor costs and wages of the unit-cost-increasing demands of other organized "reform" groups (such as environmentalists and the proponents of affirmative action), which also have discovered effective industrial power by uniting?

Unlike a goodly part of Koster's discussion, this essay focuses mostly on the manufacturing sector, a sector that has in recent decades undergone a relative retrenchment in its importance to the national economy. In 1954, 31 percent of national income originated in manufacturing; by 1981 this portion had fallen significantly, to 24.1 percent.[1] These changes, though clearly reflected in our international trade balances, are even more important from the standpoint of the changes in the industrial (and occupational) composition of our labor force. In 1951 more than a third (35 percent) of the employed labor force was engaged in manufacturing; by 1981 the figure was down to about one-fifth (21.7 percent). This shift reflects more than anything else America's almost continuously changing role in the international division of labor and manufacturing output.

This essay perforce deals with only one limited element of the basic problem, namely, what has been happening to the style as well as to the consequences of labor relations in our manufacturing sector, a sector clearly vital to our remaining a military superpower. Less than a quarter of a century ago this sector seemed domestically and internationally the picture of health, but now it presents in some critical industries (basic steel, automobile, and machine tools) many of the stigmas of an advanced stage of debilitation.

Three decades ago our manufacturing industry not only was producing the overwhelming majority of the products for our home market but also was heavily involved as an exporter in world trade. Today's picture is different, and tomorrow's seems likely to be even more so. While changes in managerial attitudes toward overseas procurement (to say nothing of overseas investment) have played direct roles, most of this change is due to adverse developments in unit labor costs in our domestic manufacturing. My emphasis is that study of these adverse developments must start with an understanding of labor contracts and particularly with the bargaining institutions that shaped them, because it is retrospectively obvious that the labor relations institutions in our manufacturing sector during the past two decades have proved incapable of coping successfully with the economic pressures put on them.

Some take the position that the decline of the broad American manufacturing sector is an example of some Brooks Adams[2] or Oswald Spengler[3] law of historical evolution. They argue that the decline of some economies and the emergence of others are the inevitable experience of economic change. Institutions are not only the cause of economic realities but also a response to them. And as these economic realities evolve, economies rise, mature, and retreat, and so also do their implementing institutions. To interfere either with the process of economic maturation or with institutional obsolescence by tinkering with national trade policies is adjudged to be as empirically futile as it is theoretically shortsighted.

Others argue differently. Their position is that if America is not to be merely a pawn in other countries' labor relations contests (for example, American workers become subject to short-term layoffs because the international flow of intermediate goods is interrupted[4] or to long-term discharges because the prices of American manufactured goods are not market competitive[5]) and if America is truly to remain a political superpower, it must have a hard-core, largely market-competitive manufacturing base such that it can produce the materiel necessary for prolonged international strife (with or without overt military confrontation). Those taking this second position have an explicit interest in coming to grips with what "has gone wrong" with our unit labor cost patterns and, more particularly, with the institutional mechanisms that have evolved. Underlying their view is a compelling conviction that an examination of our experience will lead to necessary reforms and that the future course of economic events need not be what destiny now seems to have prescribed. In other words, if manufacturing competitiveness is a function of technology and labor costs, new technologies must be introduced, and new labor relations bargains must (and can) be struck. In practice these bargains are products of the interaction of management, labor institutions (like unions), and whoever else tries to get into the negotiations. What is likely to be changing in labor negotiations is the essence of this paper.

But whether one takes the first or the second position, the record of what has been happening to our labor relations, besides being an interesting story, is one that admits of a variety of explanations. Labor relations constitute a topic so likely to be considered an exercise in ideology that I start with a plea that my analysis not be considered simply an evaluation of the working principles of today's unionism or even an estimate of the past or present choices of its leadership.[6] Both emerged under an evolving institutional system. And our concern is with the system, not with them. Nor should what I have to say be seen as any sort of denunciation of the science of personnel management as it, too, has emerged in practice. Indeed, my intended starting premise is that we Americans have learned much about what has made our unionism politically and ideologically so stable and that, in our need to come to grips with a new set of economic crises, we should not discard most of our previous findings. Rather, my point is that the outcome of our present international industrial manufacturing competition, along with a good deal of its consequent structural unemployment, has been, if not contrary to our post–World War II expectations, certainly destructive of our recent national sociopolitical hopes. The current problem, as I see it, is how to get managements and unions to adjust to a set of recent and probably long-run world economic changes in manufacturing. In my judgment we have passed a watershed, and we have to redesign some of our institutional practices.

My initial thesis is that starting in the 1940s and continuing well into the 1960s a national labor relations outlook developed that stressed the key role of the "outsider," usually a governmental representative, and the importance of "industrial peace at almost any unit cost." The outsiders were not part of the traditional industrial government process (namely, the process of determining how factories work on a day-to-day basis). Not immediately and continuously concerned with the conventional factory-by-factory industrial government process, they were generally intelligent men of good will brought in to resolve specific conflicts, and in so doing they often interposed their own values or priorities, irrespective of what the technical manufacturing facts were. Underlying this procedural change and frequently found in the awards was the introduction of a complex set of social convictions, which contained some profound economic implications. Among these was a formerly correct belief that the demand for American manufactured products was so inelastic that repeated increases in labor costs could easily be absorbed either by raising prices or by some combination of raising prices and introducing certain labor-cost-saving technologies as substitutes for dangerous jobs.[7] The short-haul "validity" of this point appears to have gone generally unchallenged for all of the 1940s and the 1950s. Its limitations started to become apparent in the mid-1960s. And its eventual erroneousness started to become clear by the early and mid-1970s.

A second of my theses is that even before the war a nationwide conviction had clearly begun to develop that many union demands were psychologically unreasonable, in the sense that before the New Deal much of the resistance by employers to unionism had been unreasonable. The solution was to expand the powers of federal agencies (which had been created in the 1930s to police unfair labor practices by employers) to cope with similar unfair practices by unions. This shift put the federal government, specifically the National Labor Relations Board, even more in the center of the usual labor relations process than it had been.

A third of my theses is that if unions' behavior was judged to be excessively aggressive, the principal reason was an erroneous conviction that the fault lay with the established union leaders, who had become too powerful because they had been too long in office and were consequently megalomaniacs. It was Michels's Iron Law of Oligarchy,[8] writ American. The proposed (and then legislated) solution was to reduce these leaders' powers of control over their unions' policies; congressional leaders suggested that this change could be accomplished by reducing the national union leaders' hold over the policies of the various union locals and by expanding certain voting rights of the rank and file. The articulated promise was that the rank and file, not suffering from the leaders' megalomania and conscious of the technical details of the factory-floor production processes, would be more reasonable and would understand the employers' economic realities. The promise was that if unions were made more democratic, they would be more aware of the real economics of their industries, and union policies would be designed accordingly. In fact, the reverse seems to have been the more general rule. Local unions, generally aware only of local working conditions, had little or no reason to understand the nature of product competition in their industries. It was the national union leaders, if anyone in the union movement had such a holistic view, who might be expected to have a perception of the broad, worldwide economic picture. In sum, the assumption about who were the real "nasties" was generally wrong; and the proposed and legislated solution, by misdiagnosing the real origins of economic aggressiveness, greatly exacerbated what was already a difficult situation.

My fourth thesis is that there has long been a conflict between those who have faith in the method of collective bargaining and those who prefer the method of legal enactment. Underlying much of the labor history of the past century have been repeated efforts to use legislative or quasi-judicial processes to resolve industrial relations disagreements.[9] One way of looking at the situation was to assert that the method of collective bargaining ought to involve three, not two, parties because the public sooner or later suffered (or enjoyed) the consequences of what the agreements contained. Just who was to be that third party is an interesting, if unexamined, segment of current as well as recent American history.[10] There have been in the past and there remain no shortages of "committees of concerned citizens," increasingly represented by *pro bono publico* lawyers, who have offered to be and in fact have become part of the resolution of all sorts of labor relations questions.[11] These questions now include not only traditional matters such as fair wages and working conditions but also new items like the provision of fair employment opportunities for minorities once discriminated against. Other items similarly came to be considered; these include improvement of industrial impact on the environment, mandated consumer safety protections, mandated workers' health and safety engineering, and so on. Each of these clearly and profoundly affected unit manufacturing costs as well as managerial prerogatives and capital substitution (at home and abroad). Given the facts of comparative unit output costs and our American international trade policies, there was eventually a tremendous impact upon American employment levels. And that is where we are.

Having identified my theses, I can now turn to examining institutional history. I start by concentrating on union-management relations, particularly the nexus between employers and their employees. From the time of the New Deal until the late 1950s, the percentage of union membership in the manufacturing sector grew.[12] Its growth appeared to give some measure of industrial peace and certainly a large measure of civil order. In my judgment the growth of unionism in the manufacturing sector was not simply the result of New Deal legislation; it was in large measure due to several other kinds of governmental intervention. The most critical of these from the economic standpoint occurred during World War II, when the public members of the War Labor Board intervened and not only established unionism in the strongest of the traditional anti-union bastions, the steel industry, but also entirely reshaped the wage compensation process by introducing a distinction between wage rates and fringe benefits in order to preserve the semblance of fixed wage rates.

For several subsequent decades practices devised during the war became standard or almost so. Generally involving resort to "public representatives," who put their primary emphasis on social equity and minimum interruption of production, they paid less attention to considerations of production costs. Insofar as industrial peace was the goal, their approach seemed to work. And whenever strikes or similar discord seemed to threaten peace in critical industries, industrial agreements would be hammered out by tripartite boards through mediation and occasionally arbitration.[13]

This was an era of substantial productivity growth, high demand for American products at home and abroad, and (in the main) full employment, as well as a low rate of price inflation. All these reflected considerable past investment in physical and human capital as well as some intense interest in continuing improvements in what we now call high technology.

It would be intellectually wrong to suggest that these policies of "peace at any price" were without some clear and unchallengeable merits. Industrial peace achieved only after bitter and grudge-creating strikes and then entailing very high increments in unit labor costs has often been conducive to subsequent poor productivity; the same seemingly overgenerous awards given willingly before a strike (or after only a short or "symbolic" one) have by way of contrast been likely to enhance productivity. Thus there seems at the time to have been a genuine logic to quick and generous settlements.

But over time the general expectations of third-party generosity and the era of good will it generated lost much of their seeming ex post glow. Thus it was that during the mid-1960s the magic quality of this formula began to disappear. Its loss was not simply a matter of the manifestations of Hegelian inner contradictions. Other external considerations appeared. It was a time when "disinterested outsiders," not usually part of the labor relations process, were having a new and important economic effect on the cost side of the manufacturing production process. Appeals for all sorts of historically needed reforms were regularly being made to the government, usually by disinterested *pro bono publico* lawyers. Thus what happened during the late 1960s was that blacks, Hispanics, and feminists moved to "get their just shares" of the industrial relations pie through federal governmental intervention.[14] And so did those who felt that industries' pollution policies were imposing unwarranted social costs on the physical and aesthetic health of the general citizenry. Their successes, particularly in retrospect, greatly added to unit production costs in manufacturing.

Nor in the same years did the labor unions themselves remain inactive; they too put in newer and stronger claims, not only for additional real wage increases but also for governmentally enforced, cost-increasing, improved occupational safety and health protection.

And domestically at least two other critical changes occurred during these years. The first was an unprecedented swelling of our labor force as the post–World War II baby boom came of labor force age; more jobs "had to be found," and more jobs were created. And perhaps for that and other reasons during the 1960s and particularly in the 1970s, the rate of productivity growth in the manufacturing sector first began to shrink and then actually turned negative.

During this period of the 1950s and 1960s, substantial economic changes had also occurred in the rest of the Western industrialized world. The once humbled manufacturing economies of Western Europe and Japan had regained (often with American help) and exceeded their previous vitality. They became domestically and internationally competitive. The establishment of the European Economic Community with its opportunities for large markets encouraged economies of scale. At the same time it encouraged American multinational firms to locate manufacturing plants in EEC countries and elsewhere, either as subsidiaries or as joint ventures. These moves transferred technology and jobs and reshaped managerial outlooks. Thus domestically established industries began to face the growth of manufacturing competition not only in what had been their overseas markets but also in what had been their home markets. The changes also seem to have come with an unanticipated speed.

Why was this foreign penetration not halted? I offer a number of reasons, but of course there are more. First, we were *legally* committed to free trade. We were consequently unable within our law to raise those trade barriers that we had used so freely during the nineteenth and the first third of the twentieth centuries. Second, third, and fourth, for all of the reasons connected with all of the previously mentioned domestic policies, our national productivity growth seriously slackened. And finally, there were many who believed then (as now) that any form of foreign trade protection was undesirable, and they were willing to see the American economy come to specialize in what it "did best," namely, produce food and services.

For those who have come to think otherwise (the second position earlier described), there is an emerging effort "to turn the clock back." These advocates can be sorted into three groups: (1) those who believe that larger domestic employment at what are now conventional real wage rates is more important than the economic benefits of less costly imports (the protectionists); (2) those who believe that we can regain or retain domestic and international trade competitiveness by recasting our unit cost structures in manufacturing through tying wages to productivity gains, substituting high-technology capital for some labor, and expanding employment in some manufacturing and mostly in the service industries (the bargainers or unit labor cost revisionists); and (3) those who claim that all can be made well by reducing, even erasing, the legislation that has increased unit costs in manufacturing through tax, environmental, or affirmative action laws (the recidivists).

Given the recent high unemployment, particularly in such basic industries as ferrous and nonferrous metals, machine tools, and automobiles, what is emerging is a reluctant yet obvious reconsideration of unit labor costs. Recent union wage and fringe benefit bargains have apparently contained all sorts of obvious (as well as hidden) give-backs. The negotiations have been frequent and generally direct. And what seems to me most noteworthy is that labor relations are returning to direct bipartite negotiation, a bipartitism of management and union leaders.

Labor Relations Trends during World War II

The 1940 Institutional Inheritance. To understand what happened during the war years, it is useful to summarize the previous sociohistorical climate:

• Congress had effectively outlawed the union-busting, "yellow-dog" contract.[15]

• The workers' right to collective bargaining had been strengthened by changes in the Supreme Court's interpretation of the interstate commerce clause and the "freedom of contract" provisions in the Fifth and Fourteenth amendments to the Constitution.[16]

• At the federal level and in some states, quasi-administrative institutionalization of the workers' right to form unions and to force employers to bargain collectively had occurred, intentionally but initially with only partial success. A federal agency, the National Labor Relations Board, had been created to supervise (and in that sense to define and impose) its perceptions of union "job territories," fair labor relations practices, and related matters.

• A civil war had broken out within the labor union movement, and there had been widespread development of industrial unionism on both sides, such that parts of both sides of the dichotomized movement were losing their skilled labor domination.[17]

• Congress had passed the Fair Labor Standards Act (1938), establishing minimum hourly wages and the normal maximum hourly workweek (without penalty payments for overtime).[18]

• An entente, if not an alliance, had been created between the labor union movement and the New Deal (northern, urban) wing of the Democratic party.[19]

What follows is a discussion of what occurred to the patterns of labor relations during the war, of decisions that were forged in the name of securing military materiel quickly without significantly inflating the national retail price structure. If this recital seems excessively detailed, its comprehension is necessary because its very success came to justify, if not to create, the institutions that some two or three decades later were so adversely to affect our patterns of unit labor cost and productivity growth, the international market competitiveness of our manufacturing products, and even the preservation of our domestic markets for manufactured goods.

The Basic Wartime Shifts: Enter the War Production Board, the War Labor Board, and Effective Tripartitism. In 1940 the United States found itself in the process of rearming by becoming increasingly involved in providing war materiel for the British.[20] The Roosevelt administration, clearly aware of the residual bitterness in the American industrial relations community, delegated the organizing of its rearmament program to a new unit, the Office of Production Management (OPM). This move enjoyed less than full national, to say nothing of congressional, support.[21] So to give it a face of further national unity, its nominal leadership consisted of a management "giant," William Knudson of General Motors, and an influential CIO union leader, Sidney Hillman, president of the Amalgamated Clothing Workers. This arrangement seemed particularly appropriate because it implied an equal responsibility between industry and labor for conversion to a wartime footing. Its senior staff was drawn largely from academia and the executive bureaucracy.

After the Pearl Harbor attack, the OPM was replaced by the War Production Board (WPB). It was immediately apparent that handling a labor force that was so full of accumulated grievances relating to wages and working conditions and that was also in some need of industrial and geographical reallocation to serve the nation's production requirements was too big an assignment to delegate to a mere subcommittee of the WPB. For that reason, a separate War Labor Board (WLB) was created; it was in tripartite form to obtain or perhaps to stress national unity, with management, labor, and certain public (meaning administration) authorities working together to achieve labor peace and uninterrupted production.[22]

Many of the issues that had previously divided the industrial community (union recognition, wage raises, improved working conditions, and a greater voice in job administration) continued to exist. There were, in addition, obviously important changes in the labor market. With the demand for industrial labor growing as production expanded and the military draft absorbing increasing numbers of young men, the legacy of the Great Depression, the unemployment reserve, disappeared. Many women entered the labor force. By the end of 1941, when the Japanese attack made us de jure as well as de facto a warring party, the conversion of the production side of the economy was well under way. And a completely justified fear of wartime shortages of consumer goods and of consequent price inflation led to the realization that the conventional market mechanisms, imperfect as they may have been, had become thoroughly inadequate. Price controls were established.

The War Labor Board's principal task was to ensure that the vital war industries had ample supplies of the necessary labor. This end it achieved by minimizing labor relations conflicts (slowdowns and strikes) and by constraining changes in the wage structure. These tasks were accomplished by establishing (1) wage controls, more precisely a nominal wage freeze, and (2) judicial-like procedures to allow for making a minimum number of necessary exceptions. These procedures included, *inter alia*, hearings, findings, and rulings. The rulings involved wage scales, job definitions, recognition of bargaining units, and (hardest to handle) the invention of effective, even novel, principles to aid in the reallocation of labor to those war industries and firms where the military procurement authorities thought it was most needed.[23] The plan was to preserve local labor market wage scales when and where possible but if necessary to make adjustments so that some labor would be encouraged to remain where it was and some to move to the sites of new wartime factories.

Two critical decisions. In my view, two of the most important rulings promulgated by the WLB dealt with the steel industry. One, the 1942 "little steel formula," dealt with the equity question and permitted a catch-up increase for workers in all those firms and industries where the pay scales seemed to have been prematurely frozen by the timing of the freeze. For about two years that decision served to stabilize the allocation of labor reasonably successfully.

But as the war progressed, an increasingly large number of firms, particularly those in the critical steel industry, found that their comparatively low wage scales (based on well-established historical job definitions) were making it more and more difficult for them to hold on to their labor force. Firms in the rapidly expanding aircraft industry, for example, were creating numerous new job classifications and training procedures that permitted them to promote workers rapidly and thereby get around the nominal wage freeze. So a new formula had to be devised; it emerged from a 1943–1944 case brought before the WLB by an Illinois steel firm.[24] In its presentation the steelworkers' union proposed using remuneration formulas previously reserved for managerial personnel. What was *essentially new* was that the formulas provided that these benefits were to be considered something other than conventional wages.

The previous WLB principle, the "wage freeze," was nominally to be preserved. But a new principle was to be introduced. After lengthy hearings the WLB issued what came to be its all-important order.[25] This decision, in spite of some assurances to the contrary, was "not a rose by another name"; it was clearly a real wage increase and, as time was to show, it became *the* significant break with the past in how American workers' remuneration was to be calculated. The decision suggested a host of new "nonwage" benefits; employers could now offer their employees (provided the union accepted) certain health and supplementary unemployment insurance schemes.[26] That ruling also referred to possible future negotiation of supplemental retirement benefits as well as certain kinds of long-service vacation payments. Thus, without apparently violating the wage freeze, old and established firms (where promotion could not easily occur "overnight") were enabled to hold on to their old labor as well as to attract necessary recruits. The ruling also gave the steelworkers' union the dues checkoff, which was the basis of a disciplinary hold on its members.

From the standpoint of what later happened, it seems to me that the most important changes first introduced by the WLB and effectively institutionalized by repeated practice were the new method of achieving difficult agreements and the creation of a new concept of remuneration, fringe benefits. It became routine to expect that difficult disputes would "go to the White House," the president would intervene, and in that way a third-party role would be present in what had until then been strictly bipartite labor contract negotiations. The "new voice," the governmental "outsiders," plus the union representatives could usually be expected to outvote the employer two to one.

It would be a major error to assume that the public members, that is, the representatives of the administration or the public at large, were mere pawns in the hands of the union representatives; they were men of independence and integrity. But the public members' overwhelming concern was *perforce* the preservation of the harmony essential to war materiel output, and what they agreed to was in virtually every case clearly the least-cost choice.[27] Thus the principle of tripartitism as well as the fringe benefits contents of the awards had in the process become legitimate and, as such, were to have important consequences in later labor-management institutional relationships.

The legacy of the War Labor Board. In retrospect the WLB was successful in holding down out-and-out wage increases. In practice, nonetheless, it helped certain unions, particularly (but not always) those in the CIO, to get and expand their footholds in once union-free industries. And, as already stressed, it established the principle, later concurred in by the Internal Revenue Service, that fringe benefits were to be considered legitimate production costs and as such not technically part of the employee's pay envelope. They were thus not subject to the employee's personal income taxation. This principle has now (some thirty to forty years later) come to haunt the cost structures of most American industries; upon it hangs the subsequent mushrooming of health insurance plans, of the number of paid holidays and vacations, of supplemental unemployment and retirement benefits and numerous other schemes affecting unit labor costs.[28]

These changes, apparent in principle in the early 1950s, became bold-faced realities by the late 1970s.[29]

The Postwar Era

Taft-Hartley: Changes in the National Labor Relations Act. In retrospect it seems clear that by the end of 1938 there had developed a strong, if not almost predominant, political sentiment in the country that unions either had become too strong or were abusing their power.[30] The elections of that year seemingly reversed the earlier pro-union national sentiment. Although the wartime tightness of the labor market made it easier for unions to organize, their organizational drives often antagonized not only the public (as seen in newspaper opinion) but also many new union members, who saw little reason to pay for representational services that the job surplus seemed to make unnecessary.[31] The exigencies of wartime materiel procurement made anti-union legislation untimely. But the anti-union sentiment was there.

Nineteen forty-six was a year of explosive reaction to wartime controls. The wartime lid on price controls was blown off by a national cattle farmers' "strike," and retail prices virtually doubled. The postwar adjustment period was also characterized by a tremendous increase in strikes, strikes occasioned by a fear that prewar wages and unemployment patterns would reappear, by frustration at having had to work so continuously during the lengthy war years (the basic workweek had been lengthened to five and a half days), and by a general social malaise (perhaps the inevitable outcome of a major geographic shift of population and the passing from the scene of the great unifying bond, the desire for and the dream of military victory). Added to these were the feelings of veterans who had returned home persuaded that their sacrifices had not been matched by persons of similar military age who were not in the services but had remained at home and had prospered.

Whatever the combination of causes, Congress, after overriding a presidential veto, amended the 1935 Wagner Act to add to its rather short list of possible unfair labor practices by employers a somewhat longer list of similar union failings. The new Labor Management Relations Act of 1947,[32] more popularly called the Taft-Hartley Act, caused the NLRB to reverse its previous pro-union (really pro-CIO) tilt. One factor that seemed to dominate much public discussion was the impact of strikes in key industries, particularly coal mining, steelmaking, and railroads (handled under their own previous legislation), where work stoppages appeared to bring the economy virtually to a halt. The act contained specific provisions for handling these strikes; it provided for the establishment of tripartite "fact-finding" boards, the duty of which was to find facts and report their findings to the president, who was then to make whatever legislative proposals he thought appropriate.[33] In practice, these boards went well beyond the fact-finding stage and usually mediated the ultimate settlement.[34]

Although the Taft-Hartley act became an essential rallying point in the presidential election campaign of 1948, a contest that Truman, much to most people's surprise, won, Truman was unsuccessful in his efforts to repeal the act. Congress seemed no longer particularly sympathetic to the unionists' cause. More to the point, public interest focused on (and often seemed enraged by) those strikes that paralyzed the national economy. It tended to accept the mediated findings of the "fact finders," and tripartitism became a normal part of the settlement of key negotiations.

It was an era of full employment, or at least of very little unemployment, and employers wishing to hold on to the workers they had were inclined to give them pretty much what they (or their union leaders) said they wanted, particularly if the demands were blessed by the fact finders. It was also a time when the Keynesian policy of demand management was working.[35] Incomes rose faster than prices; annual productivity gains not only seemed to be substantial but also were assumed to be permanent. Those wage increments not absorbed by productivity gains were readily passed on in the form of higher prices to consumers. The United States, the only major industrial nation that had not been devastated by the destruction of World War II, was enjoying a prosperity never before experienced; it was "manufacturer and lender to the world." These were, indeed, our halcyon years.

The Impact of the War Labor Board Legacy. The prevalence of so general a sense of economic well-being inevitably led all parties to ask for increased benefits ("more, more, and more," to apply Gompers's rule), whether in the form of high prices or of higher wages. Fortunately, industrial productivity was similarly growing. When sober minds sought to restrain wage increases, strikes invariably followed and, particularly when fact-finding boards were used (in the coal-mining, steel, and automobile industries), in the end wages rose. The White House became a regular stop in the journey of working out key labor relations contracts.

Thus the wartime pattern was continued and institutionalized; it was in fact the new established national labor policy. Whenever a national strike crisis, signifying a serious breakdown in bipartite discussions, occurred, the White House called for the now established tripartite arrangement, which inevitably came up with a "solution," but in the process the roles of the management and the union representatives changed. The latter often seemed to become government-oriented administrators at the expense of concentrating on their internal union-political ties. Management negotiators similarly became more conscious of maintaining industrial relations peace and less anxious about changes in the costs of production. These shifts did not occur all at once; the changes were subtle and cumulative and were hardly perceived.

John R. Commons, one of the original analysts of the American industrial relations system, had much earlier drawn a useful distinction between "industrial government" (by which he meant the institution that shaped life on the factory floor as well as the labor cost and capital substitution elements in industry) and "government in industry" (where he was referring to a common propensity of civil servants or academic experts to substitute their own value priorities and judgments for the more direct face-to-face approaches used by the directly affected parties).[36] Commons also believed, probably following Charles Merriam, that if an expert was to be used, such an expert must be "on tap, not on top."

The public members of these emergency boards all too easily became in effect "experts on top," if only because the national political mood was adjudged to be so hostile to the inconveniences of a protracted strike as to be unable to tolerate a head-on collision between the industrial parties. Moreover, as invariably happens, many of the leaders of the labor unions and management anticipated the so-called national mood and more frequently than not eschewed any appearance of intransigence or of being "tough guys" and let the public fact finders take the credit or blame for what was decided. Looking back from the vantage point of three decades, it is apparent that emergency boards' recommendations/awards (whatever they may have done to the critical bipartite relationships) contributed to the rapid growth of a high national labor cost structure, not only by permitting high hourly wages, fringe benefits, and indexation but also by allowing rigidity in work rules and certain other shop practices. But, as long as each year saw higher profits and our national productivity growth rate remained high, these critical changes in our labor relations institutions and our competitive cost structures went unopposed, indeed often unnoticed.

Collective bargaining had developed into extraordinarily detailed contracts, which spelled out a wide variety of matters, such as seniority rights depending on job, shop, plant, or even firm considerations. Job descriptions themselves became more and more complex and were put into the labor contracts. Labor contracts mushroomed in detail as well as in length. Their complexity quickly affected the role of national union leaders and their relations with the union locals and their individual members. Any member with a minor grievance could demand as much attention as the bigger issues like basic pay rates had once required. To stay in office, national union leaders had to cater to avalanches of such grievances. What had earlier been perceived as basically a recognition of status, the union-management agreement, became an ever-growing list of situational specifications, which more and more came to be interpreted through legal processes.

Lawyers representing unions met lawyers representing employers, and not infrequently these two groups of lawyers plied their craft before other lawyers, often defined as representing the public's interest, sitting as arbitrators. These arbitrators were even less constrained by traditions of judicial restraint (particularly judicial notice) than the nation's courts. The results in the labor relations field included more and more reliance on legal process in the resolution of day-to-day differences. In time an understanding of detailed legal processes became the essence of labor–management negotiations; it influenced what labor and management wanted and how they went about getting it. Labor leaders, who had once been selected because as skilled workers they were knowledgeable about their industry's production processes (as seen on the shop floor), tended increasingly to become "union ex–civil servants," specialists in dealing with governmental bureaucrats or legislators, or men who had pretensions to being "legal eagles." Managements, perhaps for other reasons as well, underwent similar transformations.

The Landrum-Griffin Reforms. By their very nature labor relations involve a great deal of persuasion, and they have often involved various forms of obvious or subtle coercion. Stories about the viciousness of managements' practice of the art of persuasion make up no small part of the literature, including detailed scholarly histories as well as lyrical ballads of American labor history. By the 1950s, the beginnings of a comparable literature about the viciousness of coercive union leadership was developing. Congressional hearings about labor racketeering succeeded similar hearings about radicalism in the public service. In 1959 Congress passed the Landrum-Griffin Act,[37] the avowed purpose of which was to open union practices to review through some system of public due process; one practical consequence was to reduce union leaders' discretionary powers, particularly as they were exercised over the activities of recalcitrant locals. What union national presidents had often done was to put the offending locals under "receivership," which meant that their affairs were handled by an official sent out by the national office, whose activities were judged by the national office rather than the local's rank and file. These receiverships often lasted for months and years and were the source of deserved and undeserved censure. It is not hard to justify the reforms that were sought: the record was all too full of evidence of injustices perpetrated on rank-and-file members. But the nature of the reforms was in truth far more complicated than the legislation suggested. Labor relations had become very "big business," and the temptations for employers to bribe local (and on occasion national) union leaders were immense because so much time and money could be involved. But the simple corrective device envisioned in the federal legislation was to make unions more democratic, that is, to give the rank and file more opportunity to express their views about what was going on. And that did not in any real sense come to grips with the complex implications of the wage and fringe benefit aspects of the locally voted contracts. Furthermore, an additional bureaucracy was created in the federal Department of Labor to oversee developments and process complaints, thus further pushing in the wedge of tripartitism.

No one who has ever raised children or participated in a free-for-all meeting should have had many illusions about what happens in an open one-man/one-vote union electoral process. Union procedures may have become somewhat more democratic, but in the process union demands and policies surely became far more covetous. If an established leader thought that a future contract in long-run perspective ought to yield a real increase of a mere x percent, every aspiring competitor for his leadership role said, "Why not $2x$ or even $3x$ percent?"

The attempt to democratize unions and at the same time keep their policies economically reasonable was not one of the great successes of the 1960s. The traditional questions of social ideology, of cooperation between various grades of skilled workers, of protection against victimization, of how to cope wih jurisdictional rivalries, of how to use strike funds efficiently if not always judiciously, did not disappear, but they seemed to play a less important role than they had in the past. Issues of legal rights, when and how to appeal to quasi-judicial boards about matters such as "unfair labor practices," or complaints about safety, environmental, and discrimination issues occupied more and more of the time of the union administrative leadership. And in the process of these changes, explaining what an industry could afford to pay, what its productivity growth needs were, and what the effects of the foregoing were on prices and the quantities demanded in the market got shorter shrift than it required.

The Questions of the Hour

The Economic Setting. In real terms the American economy grew by 1980 to be 4.5 times its 1940 size. Since the population multiplied by 1.7 times during that same period, the real per capita improvement was somewhat less but still a spectacular 2.6 times.

In the period since 1940 the greatest growth of per capita income in the history of this and many other nations has occurred. In 1967 dollars, per capita personal income in 1940 was $1,417; in 1978 it had grown to $3,999, or at an annualized growth rate of 2.8 percent. This growth rate was, of course, not uniform from year to year. Nonetheless, from 1940 until 1980 there were no years of acute depression and very few years of recession; according to the data, it was the best of times. Doubtless, the data hid some realities, insofar as the composition of the typical American household changed markedly and many of the nonpecuniary services once regularly performed by the housewife by the late 1970s had to be purchased with cash.

Three shifts seem to me to lie at the root of these changes. One was the great increase in the size, earnings, and productivity growth of our labor force. A second pertains to the apparent success through the mid-1960s of one version of the Keynesian demand management mandate—put purchasing power in the hands of those who will spend it quickly; this view made ours a consumption-oriented economy. The third pertains to the nature of the basic wage-bargaining process.

In some significant ways the most profound shifts during the period were associated with changes in the labor force. The great unsung American industrial miracle of the 1960s and the early 1970s was the absorption of so many new workers, particularly at a time when employment in agriculture and manufacturing was decreasing. There were about 105 million workers in 1980 in comparison with about 53 million forty years earlier. This increase, a mighty 98 percent, reflected a truly massive growth in the proportion of women in the regular labor force. In 1940 only 28.8 percent of the women sixteen to sixty-four years of age were in the labor force—this at a time when few women went beyond twelve years of schooling. By 1980, 54.2 percent of women in this age group were in the labor force, and a much greater proportion of the younger women went on to university training. How profound a shift in mores or life style this number reflects is only now being fully comprehended. Insofar as working women do not tie themselves to the conventional tasks of housekeeping and child raising, it has surely meant a major revolution in the structure of households and the future of the traditional West European cultural patterns.

The labor force, of course, is only one component of the labor supply; the other is the average hours worked. What is as remarkable as the growth of numbers in the labor force is the relative stability of the average number of hours worked. The forty-hour week became the national legal standard in 1940; previously there were no pecuniary penalty rates for overtime employment.

Certain critical changes like the decline of productivity growth and the advent of high rates of price inflation will be mentioned later.

Trade Policy. An important element in American economic policy has been our trade program. During the 1930s the United States rapidly eliminated its historical trade protectionist policies. After the war, when American industry was undoubtedly the world's leader and seemed likely to continue to be so (our productivity in the agricultural and manufacturing sectors of American industry was then the understandable envy of the world), the arguments for free trade seemed particularly appealing. During the 1950s and the early 1960s our manufacturing competitiveness continued to seem equal to the task of preserving our domestic markets from foreign imports, even though during those same years we were steadily, if not perceptibly, losing some of our historical and postwar export markets. The usual view was that we gained much from free trade and that industrial shifts were natural and inevitable as some of our industries lost out to foreign firms and others grew. Such was the nature of the thinking of the time that these compositional changes in our industrial structure were not assessed as critically important, certainly not in the long run. All of this may have been no error. Nonetheless, in retrospect the assessment may have been *simplice*. Too many things happened, most of them too fast. Insufficient thought was given to what domestic and international policies could and did do to establish an honestly appropriate exchange rate for the dollar or to its consequences for the size and direction of trade flows. What internationalization of the purchase of intermediate products, including the purchase of items produced by American firms' foreign subsidiaries, was doing to our domestic industrial structure and to our national defense capacities went all but unnoticed. And the possible need to preserve cadres of skilled American craftsmen (to say nothing of avoiding wide-scale general unemployment) was overlooked. Instead, what we focused on was that Japanese automobiles seemed both cheaper and better.

Awareness and Blindness. Lest anyone conclude that the early 1960s was a period when no novel thinking was being done, the contrary is surely the case. Demand management, or what was called "Keynesian economics," was approaching the zenith of its theoretical and policy popularity. The economic recession, which had characterized the last years of the second Eisenhower administration and most of the Kennedy administration, was coming (or being brought) to its end. It was generally accepted that the active policy contribution was a wise reduction in the federal tax rates. It was the era of "fine tuning," when it was believed that knowledge of the secrets of macroeconomic policy, if fully understood and resolutely applied, was sufficient for designing and maintaining economic growth.

What was studied less, and not particularly carefully at that, was what was going on at the microeconomic level. And what was going on there has now proved to be disastrously important. Had we only been aware of the ominous lack of investment capital, the frightening ballooning of wage and fringe benefit costs, the full costs of any number of highly desirable social welfare and environmental improvement programs, and the ossification of many areas of industrial management, we might have behaved more wisely than we did. Our faith in research and development was too broad. Historically our strengths had been in taking others' ideas (the locomotive, automobiles, radios, radar, and so on) and producing them better (through attention to quality control) and more cheaply (through mass assembly of standardized parts). Now we focused almost exclusively on the rapidity of new inventions, such as nuclear fission, transistors, microchips, and bubble controls; and others, notably the French and Japanese, concentrated on our previous areas of comparative production excellence. They improved the new products and sold them more cheaply.

The Impact of Widespread Environmental and Other Reforms. Lest it be concluded that the problem was simply a question of wages and labor costs, the point should be made that the 1960s was no less an era of many reforms, all of which caused the employer to bear previously unanticipated costs. Among these were requirements to eliminate air and water pollution. The cost of these in 1978 has been estimated at $16.3 billion.[38] Another costly reform was the establishment of the Occupational Safety and Health Administration, which was designed to reduce, if not to eliminate, industrial illnesses. The costs, as in the previous case, were supposedly passed on to consumers in the form of higher prices. Of course, it is possible that these costs were not passed on; lower-priced imports could be and perhaps were substituted for the previously purchased American products.

Our affirmative action activities, designed to establish equity in the marketplace, also added costs to the production process insofar as less-experienced personnel were given employment opportunities, which equity but not industrial efficiency clearly suggested that they deserved.

The Decline of the Old and the Questionable Future of the New Unionism. Unionism had traditionally been strongest in the manufacturing sector. By 1953 employment in that sector as a percentage of employed workers had peaked. Unionism, always an underachiever in the services sector, was not able to bring new entrants in that sector into its ranks as rapidly as the sector grew. By the end of the 1970s unionism was generally no longer clearly as dominant in establishing wages and working conditions as it had traditionally been. More and more reliance was being placed on passage of legislation (the method of legal enactment),[39] a process that made the political activities of workers and their organizations more important and their economic activities less so. The acceptance of the role of the third party (tripartitism) was the original thin edge of this wedge. Environmental and civil rights reforms were the forces that drove the wedge solidly in. What was left for collective bargaining between management and labor was considerably narrowed, and the original two-way negotiating powers of both parties were particularly clipped. Legislatively mandated investment and employee safeguards became a pecuniary incubus for management; impotence in national union relations with rebellious locals and the like became a nightmare for economically responsible union leaders. It was a far cry from the conditions that had prevailed in our labor relations system half a century earlier.

During the past two decades the situation changed just as it changed almost a century ago. Gompers's discovery of the importance of craft workers' particularism (what Selig Perlman called "job-consciousness")[40] had given America essentially a non-Socialist labor movement, one that had few illusions about changing the entrepreneurial function. The revised unionism of the 1970s and probably the 1980s is a unionism not so much built on the particularism of the trade or craft worker as relying increasingly on what it takes to get effective national or state political action, a unionism that, consequently, looks increasingly to legislation to "protect" it from foreign competition.[41]

The Development of the Current Crisis. In some senses what proved afterward to be the most important strike of the post–World War II period was the long steel strike of 1959. By the time it ended, many problems, if not lessons, had begun to be perceived. For one, the union leadership realized that the threat of imported foreign steel had made attrition strike policies too frightening and costly a technique. The major American steel customers (particularly the automobile manufacturers) were never again going to get caught by an absence of foreign reserve suppliers.

It is doubtless probable that these same automobile manufacturers, to whom access to foreign steel had seemed such a powerful weapon, totally overlooked the likelihood that foreign manufacturers, who at the time seemed potentially so "helpful" to them, could and would so quickly mature into a monster, which has in less than two decades driven the American automobile producers almost to the wall. Obviously factors like the OPEC cartel also intervened to create the present situation; American manufacturers concentrated on heavy, gas-guzzling cars longer than they should have. But, from the standpoint of our interest, what was remarkable and remains so, even yet, is the absence of any well-articulated realization by employers that the steelworkers' embarrassing 1959 lesson, something the union perceived all too well in 1959–1960, was a matter of equal potential disaster for American employers. Safe in their conviction of durability of an American capacity for annual productivity growth, both total factor and labor, neither side (nor anyone in the government, for that matter) seemed to have been seriously aware of the emerging foreign competitive capacities.

Awareness of the decline in international price competitiveness of American goods began to develop in the late 1960s but became an obsession only in the late 1970s, when it became increasingly clear that, in addition to soft industries like textiles, clothing, and shoes,[42] three of the bedrock American manufacturing industries—automobiles, machine tools, and steel—were likewise in deep trouble. In retrospect the awareness should have become apparent at the time of the original OPEC oil price increase, but for some inexplicable reason the 1973–1974 gasoline shortage did not make an appropriate impression. It was the Iran oil crisis of 1979 that did. And it is with the outgrowth of that crisis that much of our current thinking seems to be involved.[43]

The Johnson and Nixon administrations were the periods when the "new" industrial relations practices flowered most. President Johnson was *the intervener par excellence*, but even he came to grief when he tried to persuade the machinists' union to accept his "voluntary" wage guidelines in 1967.[44] And although President Nixon asserted that he wanted less government, by 1971 he had installed wage and price controls. The breaking point in the continued acceptance of the new industrial relations system was the "forced" resignation of

Secretary of Labor John Dunlop during the Ford administration.[45] By then it was becoming clear that the magic of White House or Labor Department intervention, which had blossomed most during the heyday of the Kennedy presidency and Secretary of Labor Arthur Goldberg's tenure, was mostly over. The Carter administration was not as successful in arm twisting (or other forms of persuasion) as its predecessors had been. Times and conditions had changed. And in my view the basis of a watershed had developed.

One of our three major automobile manufacturers has had to be bailed out by the federal government; a second was and still may be shaky; and the third, though working on a clearly profitable margin, does so in good part because it relies on overseas manufacturing and purchasing. Our steel industry, if it is to survive largely because of its critical national military defense role, will do so only as a fraction of what it was before World War II. And we who were once a major exporter of machine tools are now increasingly a large net importer. From a trade standpoint, these changes may make sense; from a national defense or a domestic employment standpoint, they do not.

These three industries serve well to point up the current labor relations problem. Their unit labor costs are high, high by American average standards and even higher by the standards of their principal overseas competitors. What this picture does not show is the degree of subsidization that these industries enjoy in other countries because of the importance of their role in providing employment.

Deployment of the Labor Force. The restructuring of the American economy at first glance suggests changes in products.[46] Currently we import more than a quarter of our automobiles, almost 20 percent of our steel, half of our consumer electrical products, and almost a third of our machine tools. And although there is basis for hoping that, as America pulls out of its economic recession, increased sales will lead to the purchase of more of our home-produced products, there is every reason to anticipate that the previous levels of employment in manufacturing will not be fully regained.

Our losses in sales in the past were no doubt in great measure due to our failure to keep up with the productivity growth of other competitive economies, both in the developed and in the developing nations. As for the former, the U.S. productivity growth in manufacturing from 1960 to 1973 was at a 3.0 percent annual rate; in 1973–1981 it fell to a 1.7 percent annual rate. In the ten countries of the Organization for Economic Cooperation and Development that are competitors, the comparable figures were 6.4 percent and 4.7 percent respectively. And the recent strength of the dollar exacerbates the strength of

311

the price competitiveness of non-American goods and the weakness of the price competitiveness of American goods.[47]

Another, more encouraging factor for the future is the anticipated slower growth of the American labor force. It increased at about a 2.7 percent annual rate in the 1970s; we have every reason to believe that the rate of increase will just about halve (to 1.5 percent) in the 1980s.[48] Thus we will be taking in fewer untrained or inexperienced workers and enjoying a more and more experienced labor force. Besides this point, the recession has caused considerable trimming of excessive managerial, certain kinds of technical, and other white-collar workers. We ought to have a trimmer, more efficient labor force in the middle and later 1980s. American productivity growth in manufacturing did improve—if not substantially, certainly significantly—in 1981 and 1982.

But the deployment of the labor force, irrespective of all of the foregoing, remains a great problem. A recreated automobile or steel or machine tools industry is not going to depend as much on labor or as little on robotics as it did in the 1960s and 1970s. Annual real wage increases are not going to come as easily in the face of more difficulty in getting jobs. More prosperous we may well be, but the truly halcyon years are not going to return immediately.

The Options. The key points are that the American manufacturing sector has lost much and seems likely to lose most of its international competitiveness and that by the end of 1982 this underlying fact was beginning to be perceived as even more structural than cyclical.

Our preferred international trade policy, with its record of imported cars, steel, machine tools, electronics, textiles, and leather products, was coming under attack. Part of the response has been to consider relying more on legal enactment; part of it has been to get back to bipartite collective bargaining, which is perforce a denial of the advantages of third-party intervention (and in practice the method of legal enactment).

The recommended methods have been twofold: trade protection (through governmental intervention) and cost reductions (generally but not completely relying on changes in wage rates, employment levels, and negotiated productivity increases). Getting the government off the scene is far from an easy process; the Supreme Court has recently decided that it is not enough to change the administrative regulations. Much new legislation is likely to be written, and the congressional process has usually been time consuming and cumbersome. But what has been most illuminating has been the eventual willingness of both union leaders and union members to return to lower wage and benefit packages, albeit reluctantly and usually after more than one vote. What is no less a change has been the newly strengthened posture of managements to press harder for even greater concessions, concessions large enough to restore American dominance in its own, to say nothing of some external, markets. In sum, the give-backs we have seen are likely to be only the forerunners of what is to come. This toughened bargaining is the new national labor relations policy; it is likely to leave us with a more competitive manufacturing sector, but also one with significantly fewer workers. And it may well offer lower guaranteed wage rates, with more of the workers' income in the form of annual or semiannual bonuses, depending on profits and continued productivity growth.

In the meantime a lobby is developing for a return to some form of guarantee for American products in domestic and even in some foreign markets. Protection need not mean tariffs or quotas; it can rely on administrative procedures (techniques improved if not perfected by the Japanese and the French). Thus within the now conventional (since 1945) free trade network, it is possible to see the government playing its accustomed role of apparently modifying most pressures by intervening on the price side. This scenario is an alternative to the one mentioned directly above. And as with Strauss's *Ariadne auf Naxos*, an opera where two plots are played simultaneously, we may be witness to a similar playing of the two options at the same time.

One other consideration is that, for better or worse, there have been recent technological shifts that would in themselves have very much reshaped our industrial relations patterns, because of both the mixture of products and the levels of employment that go along with such changes. Let me mention five, although a far longer list could be offered:

• The existence of immense amounts of steel scrap (convertible by arc furnace to basic slabs) has made us significantly less dependent on the presence of domestic American blast furnaces, the traditional sources of slabs. And this is to say nothing of new ways to process ore; specifically, I refer to some Swedish research on a plasma approach.

• The development of a large set of ferrous metal substitutes will, if the relevant scales of production can be achieved, create new industries—polymers, ceramics, and carbon composites have already been introduced in defense and defense-related industries. What was once clearly in the jurisdiction of the steelworkers' union may become part of the chemical workers' job province.

• Increased robotization of production for reasons of improved quality control seems inevitable. Given the almost seven years of drought in automobile production, the pent-up demand for automobile replacement, even with robots doing much of the work formerly done by men and women workers, may offer several years of transitional prosperity to that depressed industry. This was what happened when automatic typesetting was introduced into the printing trades, as described years ago by George Barnett.[49]

• The issue of jobs versus other costly social reforms (that is, environmental improvement) is seen more clearly than it was in the late 1960s and 1970s as a trade-off. The economic costs of many worthy social programs, including affirmative action and even some aspects of consumer protection, are likely to come under closer scrutiny by unions and other public groups. The *modus vivendi* for handling these new trade-offs is likely to be a bipartite (labor-management) assertion that the legislation be amended to minimize the government's present role. That the administration or the courts will willingly concur should not be taken as a given, but, as Mr. Dooley put the matter almost a century ago, repeated election returns do influence even the most stalwart of judicial (and legislative) minds.

• The era of accommodative business and union leadership is on the wane. Republican administrations have not solved businesses' crises. Democratic administrations, particularly viewed retrospectively, have not in recent decades been able to show much positive achievement in the way of raising real incomes, providing job security, or expanding union power. Threats from union leaders no longer cause the political mighty to tremble; it is time for labor's voice to be addressed to management decision makers directly rather than through some congressional or administrative network.

At the outset of this paper I identified a conflict between (1) those who wanted a return to pre-1945 American protectionism, at least long enough for our internal market scale to introduce unit price economies of a size to make us domestically and ultimately internationally competitive, and (2) those who saw the abandonment of our more or less free trade policies as an irrevocable step to national economic decline. My analysis suggests that the choice is not so clear. What will change are the roles the actors will play. True, we may backtrack somewhat on our commitment to more or less free trade, but because of the multinational aspect of our corporate ownership, we are not likely to move to accommodate the basic principles of autarky, in Henry Clay's day called the "American system."

What will emerge? I see it as a new kind of management—fewer conciliators and more cost reducers—and a modification of union behavior, not one returning to the pure job-consciousness of the pre-

New Deal era but one that very cautiously considers the uses of the method of legal enactment. This "new" unionism will not espouse abandonment of legal enactment; to do so would be to antagonize unnecessarily the beneficiaries of the minority groups who also must be attracted to union membership. But the implications of legal enactment, with its consequent roles for the courts and the officials of executive branch agencies, will be examined cautiously. We may yet see the day when some union officials will repeat Matthew Woll's trip to a congressional committee hearing to testify *against* minimum wages as an unwelcome legislative interference by the federal government. The key question then will become, How will this modified or even "new" unionism handle the traditional claims to job territories when it also has to cope with well-organized pressure groups trying to overcome historical job barriers? John R. Commons would have said that this is the stuff of dynamic industrial government and the growth process is never that predictable.

In sum, as I see it, just as the demand-management economy had its period of fashion, circa 1933 to 1980, so the era of labor relations tripartitism has had its era. If our economy is groping toward a new economic phase emphasizing accumulation of savings and industrial reinvestment, so our labor relations are groping toward a new phase of down-to-earth job-conscious negotiations. One era is ending; the institutions of the new era will have to make the adjustments; they will in most senses look much as they have, but in their finer aspects, they will be a bit different.

Notes

1. My fellow author Murray Foss points out that had I used two "high-employment" years, 1948 and 1979, this downward movement would not have been so evident (24.9 percent for 1948 and 24.8 percent for 1979). Nonetheless, I will let the generalization, as phrased, stand; it seems to me the one appropriate to the situation in which we find ourselves.

2. Brooks Adams, *The Law of Civilization and Decay* (New York: A.A. Knopf, 1943); and idem, *America's Economic Supremacy* (New York: Macmillan Company, 1900).

3. Oswald Spengler, *The Decline of the West*, 2 vols. (London: George Allen and Unwin, 1932 [1918]); trans. (New York: A. A. Knopf, 1926–1928).

4. For example, in late 1982 a strike of the Canadian workers of the Chrysler Corporation stopped the flow of components to its U.S. plants, thereby causing the corporation to furlough many of its U.S. workers.

5. This change was evident even during the years of the Carter adminis-

tration, when the dollar was internationally very weak. Obviously, the renewed strength of the dollar since the advent of the Reagan administration has exacerbated the situation.

6. For a discussion of the determination of governmental practices in one of the more efficient and democratic American unions, see Mark Perlman, *Democracy in the IAM* (New York: Wiley, 1962); and idem, *The Machinists: A New Study in American Trade Unionism* (Cambridge, Mass.: Harvard University Press, 1961). The general conclusion is that specific "job-conscious" administrative and economic conditions play a greater role than more purely ideological principles when "push comes to shove."

7. The United Mine Workers union, particularly as led by John L. Lewis from 1940 to some time late in the 1950s, is the example par excellence of this point.

8. Robert Michels, a German-born sociologist, theorized that in every democratic organization there is a basic tendency for the elected officers to try to take over control from their electors in order to preserve (and usually to expand) their powers and tenure.

9. Much of the terminology of West European and American labor relations comes from the seminal study *Industrial Democracy* published by Sidney and Beatrice Webb in 1897 and 1920. In it they identify three methods used by workers to accommodate their collective economic needs while trying to protect themselves from the vicissitudes of the modern industrial system: (1) mutual insurance, (2) collective bargaining, and (3) legal enactment. The first centers on the capacity of the group to use its individual resources collectively (for example, pooling the earnings of uninjured workers to help the family of the injured). The second envisions a conscious and institutionalized nexus between stable groups of workers (that is, trade unions) and their employers; this nexus is purely bipartite, and its ambit can cover all the various matters involved in modern industrial life—"can" suggests some differences of opinion and allows for considerable bitter conflict. The third, the method seemingly preferred by the Webbs themselves, made the administration of minimum rates and maximum hours and the specification of the great majority of matters affecting employment the subject either of direct parliamentary legislation (as in factory acts, including maximum hours/minimum wages laws) or of indirect control through governmentally established administrative/quasi-judicial agencies. The Webbs had doubts about the efficacy of the second method, that is, bipartite collective bargaining, both because it could be and often was disorderly and because it was best at helping those who were in a position to help themselves; the third method, legal enactment, was "more civilized" and could be made to apply to those too weak to help themselves. The Webbs were great believers in the wisdom and efficiency of the British civil service; that faith explains in no little degree their preference for the third of the three methods.

10. An early example of legislative delegation of the administration of industrial relations regulations was the Australian Arbitration Court, founded in 1904. The hopeful promises it offered are described by its founder, Mr.

Justice [Henry Bournes] Higgins, in his *A New Province for Law and Order* (Sydney, Australia: Workers' Education Association, 1922). The ensuing record is discussed in Mark Perlman, *Judges in Industry: A Study of Labour Arbitration in Australia* (Melbourne, Australia: Melbourne University Press, 1954). Higgins's court system was declared unconstitutional in 1954 and has been replaced by a conventional court and an administrative tribunal, the two meeting the 1954 constitutional test imposed by the Australian High Court. The American National Labor Relations Board, originally authorized in 1935 and substantially reorganized in 1947, was a less ambitious attempt to regulate industrial relations matters through the delegation of legislative power.

11. The clergy and academics are the "concerned groups" with the most regular records of self-selection.

12. U.S. labor union membership as a percentage of nonagricultural employment seems to have peaked in 1956; the qualification relates to the method of collecting the data. The important thing is not the precise year of greatest unionization but that only a fraction of those eligible to join unions do so; others benefit from what unions gain (the so-called free rider phenomenon), and there seem to be many more who do not see any advantages in membership.

13. Labor histories of this period are few, but Charles O. Gregory and Harold A. Katz, *Labor and the Law*, 3d ed. (New York: Norton, 1979), offers a good summary of many of the issues.

14. Although trade unionists may have been among the first to institutionalize the method of collective bargaining, they certainly have no monopoly on its use. Compare the introduction to Mark Perlman, *Labor Union Theories in America: Background and Development*, 2d rev. ed. (Westport, Conn.: Greenwood Press, 1976). In recent years many self-described underdog groups (women, the Nisei, blacks, Hispanics, the elderly, and homosexuals) have also used the method, sometimes with greater success in the courts and the executive branch than in the legislatures. But we live in a time when law is effectively made in all three.

15. These were agreements made by individual workers and their employers that the former were not to join any union during the period of their employment. The 1931 Norris-LaGuardia Act nullified these contracts, that is, made them unenforceable in the federal courts. Many states then passed legislation making them unenforceable in their jurisdictions. Two classic treatments of this period and the issues involved are Felix Frankfurter and Nathan Greene, *The Labor Injunction* (New York: Macmillan, 1930); and Edwin E. Witte, *The Government in Labor Disputes* (New York: McGraw-Hill, 1932).

16. Until 1937 the Supreme Court usually held that legislative efforts to set maximum hours and minimum wages, indeed to interfere with most details of employment agreements, were infringements of the due process clauses of the Fifth and Fourteenth amendments. In 1937 the Supreme Court reversed itself and, in the Jones and Laughlin case, involving the National Labor Relations Act of 1935 (the Wagner-Connery Act), allowed the federal government to intervene directly in the establishment of unionism in most American

industry. Its logic was that because labor relations practices affected interstate trade, the federal government had a right to interfere. From a layman's standpoint, what the Court did was to change its focus from the two amendments to the interstate commerce clause (which it had previously seemed to overlook).

17. Compare Philip Taft, *The A. F. of L.* (New York: Harper & Brothers, 1959); Walter Galenson, *The CIO Challenge to the AFL* (Cambridge, Mass.: Harvard University Press, 1960); and Arthur J. Goldberg, *AFL-CIO, Labor United* (New York: McGraw-Hill, 1956).

18. It may come as a surprise to many that Matthew Woll, the official spokesman for the AFL, testified against the 1938 Fair Labor Standards Act. His logic was that it did not help the unionized workers who had already won the forty-hour week and were earning wages far in excess of the pittance the law then set as the minimum. And as one who had lived through the pro-union Wilson administration of World War I and the subsequent anti-union government during the 1920s, he was aware that the method of legal enactment was a two-edged sword, which could be used in both directions.

19. In the presidential campaign of 1944 the phrase "Clear it with Sidney [Hillman]" seemed to have become the Democratic party's shibboleth. Hillman was president of the Amalgamated Clothing Workers (CIO) and co-leader of the Office of Production Management.

20. Memories are short. The Roosevelt administration faced a very hostile Congress in its efforts to aid the British and even to develop an effective rearmament program. It seems unnecessary to go into detail, but the historical facts show that the administration's bill to continue the draft—certainly a step essential to our rearming—in the summer of 1941 (even after France had fallen, the hostility of the Japanese was apparent, and the Soviet Union seemed on the verge of surrender) passed in the House of Representatives by a single vote.

21. While it is true that Franklin Roosevelt managed to get reelected to the presidency in 1940, it is also true that all the contemporary observers (to say nothing of the polls) suggested not only that the country was bitterly divided about American participation in sending arms to Britain and Russia but that the division was growing more and more intense. The mine workers' union was particularly bellicose in its economic demands, and the railroad unions, too, were talking strike at the time the Japanese attacked. Fortunately from the standpoint of what happened later, the Japanese attack served to crush the isolationist opposition to Roosevelt's war program; the congressional vote to declare war was a single vote short of unanimous, and the internal division disappeared within a few hours.

22. Compare United States National War Labor Board (1942–1945), *The Termination Report of the National War Labor Board: Industrial Disputes and Wage Stabilization in War Time*, 3 vols. (Washington, D.C., 1947–1949), for an analysis and a history of its activities. A useful comparative assessment of the lessons "learned" can be found in Thomas Holland, "The [1950] Labor Management Conference, Washington, D.C." (mimeographed), 1950, which was prepared as a working paper for those interested during the early days of the Korean

War in resolving the kinds of problems handled by the World War II board. Holland's assessment, unlike the board's earlier assessment of its successes in its official termination report, was one of disillusionment.

23.   There is much more to this story than has been popularly realized. It deals with a set of memorandums prepared by Simon Kuznets during the year before and about two years after the declaration of war. Kuznets, using his knowledge of national income and product accounts, argued (ultimately but not initially persuasively) that the army was underordering materiel. After the army wildly increased its orders, he pointed out that there was, nonetheless, a limit to the amount that could be ordered for direct military use without adversely affecting the capacity of the civilian economy to produce that amount. He was less persuasive in his efforts to get the military authorities to understand that the sectors of the industrial economy the army was using were among its least imaginative or innovative sectors and that the selection of materiel design was, to paraphrase Clemenceau, "too important to be left to the generals." The history of this fascinating episode of academic economist/ Army General Staff interaction is described in John E. Brigante, *The Feasibility Dispute: Determination of War Production Objectives for 1942 and 1943* (Washington, D.C.: Public Administration Cases, 1950). Strangely enough, Brigante's study, originally prepared as a Princeton University doctoral dissertation in political science, led to Kuznets's getting his first doctorate *honoris causa* (Princeton); only later did the economics profession apparently come to realize that aspect of what "the economics profession had indeed wrought."

24.   Directive, Order, and Opinions in Case No. 364, August 26, 1942G: "In the Matter of Carnegie-Illinois Steel Corporation; Columbia Steel Company; the American Steel & Wire Corporation of New Jersey; National Tube Company; Tennessee Coal, Iron, & Railroad Company, and the United Steelworkers of America CIO." This is Appendix SS-1 of NWLB, *Termination Report*, pp. 1044–67. The lengthy (but not unanimous) opinion was largely but not completely written by Wayne L. Morse, later U.S. senator from Oregon but at the time on leave from the deanship of the University of Oregon law faculty. He took particular pains to incorporate in his opinion a thorough factual review of the nature of competition in that industry's labor market.

25.   Case No. 111-6230-D (14-1 etc.): "In the Matter of Carnegie-Illinois Steel Corporation, et al. and United Steelworkers of America–CIO," November 25, 1944. This too can be found in NWLB, *Termination Report*, pp. 1068–78.

26.   The decision flatly refused a wage increase, and it also denied the establishment of a fund for steelworkers in the armed forces. Although it refused to order a guaranteed annual wage for each worker for the life of the contract, it appeared to accept the principle that such a demand was legitimate and should be studied for postwar application. It accepted the principle of severance and dismissal pay and ordered the litigants to enter into negotiations on the matter. It admitted the principle of employers' paying for "reasonable sick leave plans [as] agreed to by the Company and the Union." It set shift differentials in specific pecuniary amounts. It defined which holidays were to be with pay at penalty rates. It denied geographic wage differentials, but it did set up an elaborate system for joint determination of wage scales for

newly defined jobs. There were other provisions as well, but the most significant was the last (XIV. Group Insurance Plans): "The Board will approve, under the wage stabilization program, reasonable group insurance plans agreed to by the Company and the Union but it declines to order such a plan on the [present set of] facts." It is from this award that most of the current fringe benefit systems derive.

27. Of course this is a subjective generalization. Many employer members of the WLB dissented regularly, and their reasons for doing so not infrequently touched explicitly on the issue of least-cost choice. At one time Wayne Morse, never a "tender blossom," dissented so vigorously that he actually urged his colleagues to review the oaths they had sworn as WLB members. But, with all these exceptions, the *Termination Report* stresses the harmonies rather than the occasional disharmonies.

28. Two unions, in particular, are credited with pioneering the postwar development of fringe benefit plans: the autoworkers and the steelworkers. But this generalization does less than justice to some of the older unions in the garment trades, where the establishment of union health clinics had occurred years, even decades, before. The difference was that the garment workers' clinics were not explicitly financed as tax-free nonpecuniary wage benefits.

29. The following data illustrate the changes:

General Motors—U.S. Hourly Workers

Year	Average Total Labor Cost (dollars)	Average Hourly Wage[a] (dollars)	Average Hours Worked
1947	1.55	1.51	38.3
1950	1.93	1.82	41.5
1955	2.62	2.41	42.5
1960	3.39	3.06	40.1
1965	4.30	3.73	42.7
1970	6.29[b]	5.05	37.7
1975	10.59	7.96	38.2
1976	11.23	8.72	42.1
1977	12.56	9.64	42.3
1978	13.76	10.56	40.1
1979	15.25	11.54	39.0
1980	18.45	13.34	37.2
1981	19.80	14.76	37.6
1982	21.50	15.12	37.3

a. Includes night shift premium, overtime premiums, and holiday and vacation pay.
b. End-of-year figure.
SOURCE: Office of the Chief Economist, General Motors Corporation; data as of March 24, 1983.

30. Compare Charles Clinton Killingsworth, *State Labor Relations Acts* (Chicago: University of Chicago Press, 1948).

31. Unemployment rates were, at least by today's standards, very low. In 1949 the rate rose to 5.9 percent, a level it did not reach again until 1958, when it was a "shocking 6.8 percent," the highest rate recorded until after 1970.

32. Much of the labor relations litigation in the period 1945–1952 was handled under the War Labor Disputes Act, which seemed to give the president far more power to force settlements than anything in the Taft-Hartley Act. But when in 1952 (during the Korean War) President Truman, to get the steel industry back into production during a strike, seized the American steel industry, he found to his dismay that the Supreme Court held his action unconstitutional. Reliance since then has been either on the emergency provisions of the 1926 Railway Labor Act or on the comparable provisions of the Taft-Hartley Act.

33. Compare Title II of the Taft-Hartley Act.

34. I do not find this practice illogical. If the members of the Emergency Fact Finding Board could find a way out, was not that too a "fact"? In practice, it was only if they could not find that "magic" formula that it was necessary for the president and the Congress to go through the time-consuming and technically difficult process of defining what had seemed until then the "undefinable." The Australian experience during the same period seems to confirm what I conclude.

35. I know better than to try to define the "Keynesian policy of demand management," but I aver that at the time people, including such stalwarts as Presidents Kennedy, Johnson, and Nixon, thought they knew what it implied, and each concluded at one time or another that it worked.

36. John R. Commons, *Industrial Goodwill* (New York: McGraw-Hill, 1919).

37. Officially the Labor-Management Reporting and Disclosure Act.

38. Edward F. Denison, "Pollution Abatement Programs: Estimates of Their Effect upon Output per Unit of Input, 1975–78, "*Survey of Business*, vol. 59, no. 8, pt. 1 (August 1979), pp. 58–59.

39. See note 9.

40. Selig Perlman, *A Theory of the Labor Movement* (New York: Kelley, 1949 [1928]).

41. Compare Sol C. Chaikin, "Trade, Investment, and Deindustrialization: Myth and Reality," *Foreign Affairs*, vol. 60 (Spring 1983), pp. 836–51. This article ought to be assigned reading for anyone who is trying to grasp the dilemmas faced by contemporary union leaders.

42. The "loss" of these industries occurred during a period when there was concurrent American industrial expansion in other sectors; those affected adversely got precious little sympathy.

43. I do not intend to suggest that everyone was blind to what was occurring, but I do suggest that those who spoke out were generally ignored. For an after-the-fact analysis, see Robert E. Reich, "Making Industrial Policy," *Foreign Affairs*, vol. 60 (Spring 1983), pp. 852–81.

44. It is interesting that the machinists' union, the International Association of Machinists, in my judgment probably the most efficiently and democratically run of the large American unions, is often the most recalcitrant about accepting external guidance. Perhaps it is just because it is democrati-

cally run that the leadership plays such a circumscribed role. This union resisted for over half a century numerous leadership-inspired efforts at racial integration (always voted down by the full rank and file) until the leadership resorted to accepting a National Labor Relations Board order as the formal reason for a much-needed change in the basic union constitutional system. President Johnson, for all of his arm-twisting charm, more than met his match when he tried to get the machinists to abide by voluntary guidelines. At the time it seemed to me that the IAM leadership was fully informed of the social desirability of continuing the anti-inflation policy as represented by the guidelines, but it too could not budge a rank and file that was convinced of industry's ability to pay and that had a long-term commitment to rising living standards. My years of studying the IAM reaffirm my conviction that even unions committed to only the most consensual, limited social reform (as the IAM has usually been) are fundamentally job-conscious and are terribly particularistic when it comes to protecting the independence of their own procedures.

45. John T. Dunlop, secretary of labor during part of the Ford administration and surely the most experienced labor relations practitioner of our times, staked his political career on a bill to permit on-site picketing by the building trades. His reasons for doing so involved a web of union commitments to him as well as his own view that prohibition of such picketing was "not worth its cost." In the end President Ford, probably reacting to longtime personal pressures and contrary to commitments presumably given to his secretary of labor, vetoed the bill. Dunlop then resigned. As an academic Dunlop can only be compared to John R. Commons in his impact on American labor relations. His theoretical work, mostly done early in his career, remains basic to the formal academic analysis of industrial relations practices. He has been at the forefront of the study of these practices since the beginning of World War II. As an academic and as a labor relations practitioner, his firsthand knowledge of the details of factory life and the nitty-gritty of American industrial government is probably unmatched, now or in the past. He is among the first to be called in any labor relations emergency. Nonetheless, it may well be that his very virtues—his ability to call the shots as they will eventually fall—have worked to diminish the capacities of the actual negotiators. It is the teacher's traditional dilemma: should he tell the students the answer or let them find it out for themselves, and that *at considerable personal and social cost*?

46. See note 42.

47. Patricia Capdevielle, Donato Alvarez, and Brian Cooper, "International Trends in Productivity and Labor Costs," *Monthly Labor Review* (December 1982), pp. 3–18.

48. This change is the result of an inevitable slowing of the rate of growth of female labor force participation (which is presumably approaching an asymptote) and of the entry into the labor force of the smaller "baby bust" cohorts.

49. George Barnett, *Chapters on Machinery and Labor* (Cambridge, Mass.: Harvard University Press, 1926).

CONTRIBUTORS

William Fellner—*Project Director*
Sterling professor of economics emeritus at Yale University, former member of the Council of Economic Advisers, and past president of the American Economic Association. Resident scholar with the American Enterprise Institute.

Sven W. Arndt
Resident scholar in International Economics and Director, International Trade Project, American Enterprise Institute. Previously, Director of International Monetary Research, U.S. Treasury Department and Professor of Economics, University of California, Santa Cruz.

Phillip Cagan
Professor and chairman of the Department of Economics at Columbia University and former senior staff economist for the Council of Economic Advisers. Visiting scholar with the American Enterprise Institute.

Murray F. Foss
Visiting scholar with the American Enterprise Institute. Formerly senior staff economist for the Council of Economic Advisers.

Gottfried Haberler
Galen L. Stone professor of international trade emeritus at Harvard University and past president of the American Economic Association and of the International Economic Association. Resident scholar with the American Enterprise Institute.

Marvin Kosters

Former associate director for economic policy at the Cost of Living Council. Director of research of the Center for the Study of Government Regulation and resident scholar with the American Enterprise Institute.

Mark Perlman

University professor of economics at the University of Pittsburgh and adjunct scholar with the American Enterprise Institute.

John C. Weicher

Resident fellow in economics with the American Enterprise Institute, former deputy assistant secretary at the U.S. Department of Housing and Urban Development, and past president of the American Real Estate and Urban Economics Association.

SELECTED AEI PUBLICATIONS

The AEI Economist, Herbert Stein, ed., published monthly (one year, $18; single copy, $1.50)

Taxing the Family, Rudolph G. Penner, ed. (174 pp., cloth $15.95, paper $7.95)

A Conversation with Jacques de Larosiere (26 pp., $2.95)

Interindustry Differences in Productivity Growth, John W. Kendrick (68 pp., $2.95)

Agenda for the Study of Macroeconomic Policy, Herbert Stein (37 pp., $2.95)

The High-Employment Budget and the Potential Output: A Critique Focusing on Two Recent Contributions, William Fellner (24 pp., $2.95)

The First Year of Socialist Government in France, Bela Balassa (22 pp., $1.95)

Science Policy from Ford to Reagan: Change and Continuity, Claude E. Barfield (142 pp., cloth $13.95, paper $5.95)

Progress of Economic Reform in the People's Republic of China, D. Gale Johnson (43 pp., $2.95)

Patterns of Regional Economic Decline and Growth: The Past and What Has Been Happening Lately, Mark Perlman (56 pp., $2.95)

Politics vs. Markets: International Differences in Macroeconomic Policies, Stanley R. Black (38 pp., $2.95)

The Employment of Immigrants in the United States, Barry R. Chiswick (37 pp., $2.95)

Current Problems of Monetary Policy: Would the Gold Standard Help? Phillip Cagan (26 pp., $2.95)

The Political Economy of Austria, Sven W. Arndt, ed. (224 pp., cloth $16.95, paper $8.95)

Policies for Coping with Oil-Supply Disruptions, George Horwich and Edward J. Mitchell, eds. (188 pp., cloth $15.95, paper $7.95)

The International Monetary System: A Time of Turbulence, Jacob S. Dreyer, Gottfried Haberler, and Thomas D. Willett, eds. (523 pp., cloth $25.95, paper $14.95)

Meeting Human Needs: Toward a New Public Philosophy, Jack A. Meyer, ed. (469 pp., cloth $34.95, paper $13.95)

• *Mail orders for publications to:* AMERICAN ENTERPRISE INSTITUTE, 1150 Seventeenth Street, N.W., Washington, D.C. 20036 • *For postage and handling, add 10 percent of total; minimum charge $2, maximum $10* • *For information on orders, or to expedite service, call toll free 800-424-2873* • *When ordering by International Standard Book Number, please use the AEI prefix—0-8447* • *Prices subject to change without notice* • *Payable in U.S. currency only*